Asher Kat

Reforming the Russian legal system is a comprehe
that are shaping legal reform in the republics of the former USSR. Looking
beneath the flow of day-to-day developments, the book examines how traditional indigenous Russian legal values, and the seventy-four-year experience with communism and "socialist legality" are being combined with Western concepts of justice and due process to forge a new legal consciousness in
Russia today.

Drawing on extensive research and personal experience in Russia, the
author begins with a broad historical survey of pre-revolutionary and Soviet-
era legal developments, which provide a backdrop to the reforms initiated
by Gorbachev and Yeltsin. Chapters analyzing reforms of constitutional law,
criminal law and procedure, the Procuracy and the laws governing the transition to a market economy illustrate the recurring themes of the book: the
interaction of crosscurrents in Russian legal culture, and variations in the pace
of legal reform from republic to republic and region to region.

This book is addressed to students, lawyers, and business people interested
in the former USSR, as well as to scholars of Russian politics and law.

REFORMING THE RUSSIAN LEGAL SYSTEM

Cambridge Russian Paperbacks: 11

Editorial Board

Reforming the Russian legal system

GORDON B. SMITH
University of South Carolina

CAMBRIDGE
UNIVERSITY PRESS

CAMBRIDGE UNIVERSITY PRESS
Cambridge, New York, Melbourne, Madrid, Cape Town, Singapore, São Paulo

Cambridge University Press
The Edinburgh Building, Cambridge CB2 2RU, UK

Published in the United States of America by Cambridge University Press, New York

www.cambridge.org
Information on this title: www.cambridge.org/9780521450522

© Cambridge University Press 1996

First published 1996

A catalogue record for this publication is available from the British Library

ISBN-13 978-0-521-45052-2 hardback
ISBN-10 0-521-45052-7 hardback

ISBN-13 978-0-521-45669-2 paperback
ISBN-10 0-521-45669-X paperback

Transferred to digital printing 2006

TO DOAK

What we attest to today is that any undertaking should begin and end not with a resolution but with man. Law is only a necessary means of maintaining order in society, an instrument not of the State's manipulation of man, as of a cog in the state machine, but a means of appealing to man, and to his earthly needs and grievances. A law-governed society begins with the recognition of these simple truths. Of course, the establishment of whatever replaces the Soviet system, in which man is not a little cog and not even an abstract "human factor" but an intransient eternal asset, will require the labor of many generations.

Anatoly Sobchak
Mayor, St. Petersburg
For a New Russia (New York: The Free Press, 1992), p. x

Contents

Preface

A political joke making the rounds of Moscow and St. Petersburg recently goes as follows: "Gorbachev led us to the edge of an abyss; but under Yeltsin we have taken a big step forward!" To many Russians today the cataclysmic events of the past several years do indeed resemble an abyss – an abyss of crime and corruption, ethnic chaos and violence, inflation, unemployment, and the collapse of the social, medical, scientific, artistic, and educational infrastructure. The initial euphoria that greeted glasnost, perestroika, and democratization has been replaced by an overwhelming sense of frustration, fear, and fatigue with politics and politicians. Under these circumstances, it is easy to be pessimistic about the chances for a successful transition to democracy and a market economy in Russia. Yet progress is being made. In late 1993 a new constitution was enacted. The gridlock between the presidency and parliament that erupted into violence in October 1993 has ended and the two centers of power are working together to draft budgets, stem inflation, enact badly needed legislation, and fight crime.

Law and lawyers are on the forefront of these reform efforts, just as they were in the 1950s and 1960s under Khrushchev. However, those reforms were cut short by Khrushchev's ouster and a return to stolid and authoritarian rule under Leonid Brezhnev. The collapse of the Soviet Union in late 1991 created an imperative of replacing its former discredited legal and political institutions with new, more legitimate ones. Russian jurists have played a key role in introducing a new constitution, drafting news laws of criminal law and procedure, enacting laws governing commercial relations and privatization, and seeking to ensure greater impartiality and fairness in court proceedings. To a considerable extent, the success or failure of Russian jurists in reforming the legal system will determine the prospects for the emergence of a viable democracy in Russia.

Reforming the Russian Legal System examines the process of transforming the Russian legal system. The Russian legal system is still very much in a state of flux, consequently, I have endeavoured to focus on recurring themes and explore the dynamics of legal reform rather than dwell on day-to-day developments in the law. The book is addressed to a diverse general audience – students, lawyers, people interested in pursuing business opportunities in the former USSR, as well as scholars of Russian politics and law.

The process of reforming Russian law today is seen as the product of several crosscurrents. Fundamental to the reforms is an effort to reconcile and combine three strands of legal culture. First, the reform must address indigenous Russian legal traditions that stress the prerogatives of the state, *proizvol'* (arbitrariness), and afford only weak recognition of property rights and civil liberties. Second, Russian legal reform today also reflects elements of the country's seventy-four-year experience with communism and "socialist legality" that emphasized social protection of workers, women, and children, stressed the collective rather than the individual, insured law and order, and manifested greater concern with achieving desired results than with the desirability of the process by which they were achieved. Other elements of the Bolshevik past – police surveillance, terror, human rights violations, "telephone justice," a *de facto* presumption of guilt, and forced psychiatric "treatment" of political prisoners – have been renounced. As Russians reject their communist past and its systematic violations of human rights and civil liberties, Russian legal reformers are struggling with incorporating elements of Western European and Anglo-American concepts of justice and due process into the Russian legal system. The question is not whether they can reconcile these competing strands of legal culture to form the basis of a new legal system – that is being done today. Rather the question this book attempts to answer is, "What will the emerging new Russian legal system look like?"

Democracies seldom enjoy peaceful births, rather they more frequently emerge from revolutions, wars, and turmoil. Neither do legal systems spring up spontaneously in former communist societies. Notions of laws, rights, due process, and constitutional governance develop gradually in the native soil of a society only as they come to be accepted by the people. The process of legal reform in Russia has been and will likely remain disjointed, marked by periods of progress and backlash. Similarly, the pace of legal reforms varies substantially from one region to another, reflecting differing regional and ethnic traditions and values, and the differing attitudes of local politicians. But regardless of these fluctuations, in every corner of the former USSR a new legal system is being built and a new legal culture is being formed. This book endeavours to examine this process and analyze what it means for the future course of Russia.

This book was written with the assistance of many individuals and institutions and it is a pleasure to record my gratitude and indebtedness to them. I wish to thank the University of South Carolina, especially the Department of Government and International Studies for supporting my work over the years. I am grateful to my colleagues for their encouragement, criticism, and friendship. I also wish to acknowledge support from the National Council for Soviet and East European Research, which enabled me to undertake a substantial portion of this project.

One of the pleasures of the academic community is being able to share ideas with colleagues. I am indebted to Professors Jane Henderson, Eugene Huskey, Peter Maggs, Robert Sharlet and Peter Solomon for their comments and criticisms of various portions of this work. I am indebted to four of my graduate students, Jane Gottlick, David Hurt, Aleksandr Loshilov, and Roger Moore, who assisted me in the research and preparation of the manuscript. I also wish to thank John Haslam and Michael Holdsworth, my editors at Cambridge University Press, who helped in the conception of this book and have consistently encouraged me throughout the process of writing it.

Finally, I want to thank Brooke, Hillarie and Doak for their steadfast love, encouragement, and patience while I was working on this project.

1 Pre-revolutionary Russian law

> The trouble with us Russians is that the Tartar is so close behind
> us. We are a semi-barbarous people still. We put Parisian kid
> gloves on our hands instead of washing them. At one moment we
> bow and utter polite phrases, and then go home and flog our
> servants.
>
> Ivan S. Turgenev[1]
(1818–1883)

During his travels to London in 1698 Peter the Great encountered
some English barristers wearing their wigs and gowns. "Who are
those men?" Peter inquired of his escort. "Lawyers," was the reply.
"Lawyers!" exclaimed Peter, "What is the use of so many? I have only
two in my whole empire, and I mean to hang one of them as soon as
I return."

The law and lawyers have not traditionally been accorded much
power or status in Russia. Yet, like Peter, a current generation of Russian leaders wishes to reform and modernize Russian society and, in
so doing, is eagerly adopting Western practices, concepts, and mores.
At the heart of these reforms is the need to create a society based on
the rule of law (*Rechtsstaat*). However, in order to establish such a legal
system, Russia must overcome not only three-quarters of a century of
communist rule, but also several hundred years of legal backwardness
under the tsars. It will be virtually impossible for Boris Yeltsin or any
other leader to make a clean break with the past, because the past has
helped to shape and define Russian legal culture – the values, attitudes and orientations that people in Russia have toward the law. In
this chapter we explore Russian legal culture, as a backdrop to the
current debate on legal reform. We argue that traditional Russian
values and notions about law, compounded by Russian nationalism,
are likely to slow the development of a Western-style legal system in
Russia. In analyzing the developments that shaped Russian law in the

pre-revolutionary period, we have chosen to highlight several enduring characteristics and themes in Russian legal culture. We begin with non-Western influences on Russian law.

Non-Western origins of Russian law

The Russian legal tradition, like Russian society generally, is neither Western European, nor wholly Eastern. Russian legal culture is a curious mix of numerous traditions and influences, some indigenous, some dating back to the Byzantine Empire, some to the 250-year Mongol–Tatar occupation, and still others introduced from Western Europe beginning in the eighteenth century.

As in the West, early Russian law was based on custom. The earliest known remnants of Russian law were embodied in Oleg's Treaty with Byzantium in 911. This document proclaimed that striking someone with a sword requires compensation to be paid in silver and set other punishments for specified actions. Other treaties between the Kievan prince and Byzantium defined the status of foreigners, the process for ratifying treaties, and the law of shipwreck.

The adoption of Christianity by Grand Prince Vladimir of Kiev in 988 opened Russia to a wealth of canon law from Byzantium. Not the least of the innovations introduced by the Orthodox Church was the notion of written law. The very process of codifying existing customs in writing changed people's conceptions about the law, giving it an impersonal character, independent of the whims of clan or family leaders. Canon law was also important since it claimed sole authority over family matters such as marriage and divorce.

The first attempt to codify customary laws was the *Russkaya Pravda*, thought to have been compiled under Yaroslav the Wise in approximately 1016 in Novgorod. Subsequent redactions of the *Russkaya Pravda* were adopted by the prince and dated 1036 and 1072.[2] Among the provisions of the *Russkaya Pravda* were revenge for murder and monetary payment for damages. The *Russkaya Pravda* began with the rule for blood feuds: "If a man kills a man the following relatives of the murdered man may avenge him: the brother is to avenge his brother; the son, his father, or the father, his son; and the son of the brother of the murdered man or the son of his sister, his respective uncle. If there is no avenger, the murderer pays 40 *grivna* wergeld."[3] Like the ancient *leges barbarorum* of the Germanic tribes, the first written codes of law in Russia concentrated on criminal rather than civil matters and focused on regulating the interactions between families.

In later versions of the *Russkaya Pravda*, Byzantine influences were evident, such as the provision that masters should be liable for crimes committed by their slaves.

The *Russkaya Pravda* did not recognize property or contract law and incorporated few general principles or legal theories. What contemporary lawyers refer to as the law of torts was considered largely a criminal matter. Litigation was voluntary; there were no permanent judges, no system of courts and no legal profession. Judgments were decided by oath (kissing the cross) or by ordeal of fire or water. In later redactions of the *Russkaya Pravda* testimony of witnesses was introduced. It was up to the injured party to collect for damages or exact punishment, as the concept of the state as an interested party had not yet developed. There was no right to appeal. None of the versions of the *Russkaya Pravda* in existence today distinguish judicial authority from familial, political, or religious authority of clan leaders, princes, local officials, landowners, or church officials. It is also unclear just how widely the authority of the *Russkaya Pravda* extended. Some scholars argue that it extended to all of the Slavs in the central and western regions, while others argue that the *Russkaya Pravda* applied only to a few principalities.

As in the West, Russian society in the eleventh century was evolving into a feudal state, in which feudal relations were only weakly defined by customary law. However, between 1050 and 1150 feudalism in Western Europe became rationalized through the drafting of feudal and manorial laws. Russia, however, remained remote and isolated from these developments. In the words of the late Russian historian Georgi Vernadsky, Russia was characterized by "feudalism without feudal law."[4]

Richard Pipes notes that throughout Western Europe, vassalage became a contractual relationship entered into by both parties and that this notion of contract later expanded to form the basis of social contract between the state and society. In Russia, however, serfdom was not a contractual arrangement entered into freely. Pipes observes, "The endemic lawlessness of Russia, especially in the relations between those in authority and those subject to it, undoubtedly has one of its principal sources in the absence of the whole tradition of contract, implanted in western Europe by vassalage."[5]

Russia's geographic isolation from the Frankish West and the Crusades was compounded by the Mongol–Tatar occupation of Russia from 1240 to 1480. The Mongol invaders swept across the steppes, subjugating everyone in their path and imposing on them a strict administrative system designed to facilitate the extraction of tribute. The occupation under the Mongols further isolated Russia from cultural and legal developments in Western Europe, and retarded the natural development of law. By the end of the Mongol occupation, Russian civil law had not advanced markedly beyond the primitive state of the *Russkaya Pravda* of four centuries earlier.

In the area of public law, however, the Mongol–Tatar invaders left an indelible imprint. By establishing an administrative structure for extracting tribute, the invaders unified the diverse principalities of medieval Rus' and laid the foundations for the notion of the state and state autocracy. The *Yasa* of Genghis Khan set forth the autocratic power of the khan and the duty of each subject to him. According to Vernadsky, "this principle was later incorporated into the practice of the Tsardom of Moscow, which, in a sense, might be considered an offspring of the Mongol Empire."[6]

The Mongol occupation of Russia was broken largely due to internal disputes and factional rivalries. During the last years of Mongol occupation, the Grand Duchy of Muscovy ascended to primacy among the principalities, due in large part to its role as tax collector and administrative center. With the consolidation of the diverse principalities of western and central Russia under Moscow, the demands on the Grand Prince to redress wrongs and to hear petitions became unwieldy. A hierarchy of courts emerged, with the Boyars' Duma, a council composed of representatives of the landed nobility and gentry classes, at the top. It heard cases in which no law was known to exist or in which there was ambiguity in the existing laws. Subordinate to the Boyars' Duma were approximately forty special boards, *prikazy*, which had jurisdiction over specific areas: military, land, foreigners, serfs, etc. Proceedings in civil cases tended to be adversarial. The two parties had primary responsibility for initiating cases and presenting evidence. Witnesses were allowed to present testimony. Judicial procedures remained rudimentary and primitive, however. A legal profession had yet to emerge. Divine justice was routinely invoked, through oaths (kissing the cross), judicial duels, or casting of lots. Corruption appears to have been common, leading to the institution of appeals on the grounds of deliberate miscarriages of justice, procedural violations, bribery, or unjust decisions. In criminal cases, judicially sanctioned torture leading to confessions was routine.

Drawing on the autocratic heritage of the Mongols, Tsar Ivan the Terrible consolidated power, subjugating the hereditary nobility of Russia and forcing them into service to him. Similarly, the peasants were bound to their landlords and, through their landlords, to the tsar. The institution of tsarist autocracy extended even beyond that of the Mongol overlords, however, by incorporating the Byzantine concept of the unity of church and state. With the fall of Constantinople to the Turks in 1453, Russia came to view itself as the true repository of Christianity. Tsars referred to themselves as "Tsar-Autocrat chosen by God" and the doctrine of the "Third Rome" not only transformed the state into a political and administrative entity, but also imbued it with messianic zeal.

Thus, the early influences on the development of Russian law came from the south and the east, rather than from Western Europe. It was only with the emergence of the Russian Empire in the early eighteenth century and the Westward-looking leadership of Peter the Great that European influences began to reshape traditional Russian law.

It is often claimed that Russia inherited its legal traditions from Roman law. This claim is only partly true. Russia did not share in the reception of Roman law after the eleventh century as did Western Europe, for reasons stated above. Roman law only began to influence Russian law in the eighteenth century and the conduit was Western Europe, not Byzantium, as commonly believed. Justinian concepts of law did not reach Russia directly through the *Corpus iuris civilis*, but third-hand through three legal codes: the *Zakon sudnyi lyudem*, a tenth-century Bulgarian code written under Tsar Constantine; the *Kormchaya Kniga*, a code of canon law of the Orthodox Church of 1274; and the *Knigu zakonnaya*, a twelfth or early thirteenth century code. In fact, the *Corpus iuris civilis* was unknown in Russia until the end of the seventeenth century.

Russia emerged into the seventeenth century with a complex and cumbersome array of customs, legal traditions, tsarist decrees, clerical rulings, and administrative decisions. The judicial system was rudimentary, the legal profession non-existent, and the powers of the tsar and the state unconstrained by law, the church, or the landed nobility, not to mention the masses.

By the mid-1600s the morass of legislation required a new compilation, which was ordered by Tsar Alexei, Peter the Great's father, and undertaken by the Zemsky Sobor (Land Assembly). The *Sobornoe ulozhenie* of 1649 consolidated existing laws, decrees, statutes, and regulations covering a wide range of matters including religious, political, economic, and criminal affairs, customs and duties, and judicial procedure. The criminal punishments incorporated in the *sobornoe ulozhenie* were especially severe, as noted by numerous European statesmen and travelers. The collection, however, did not amount to a systematization or rationalization of Russian law designed to modernize and fundamentally reform legal practice. The impetus for Westernizing influence on the Russian legal system had to come from the top, from the tsar himself. Throughout much of the seventeenth century, the tsars, the church, and the state all had vested interests in maintaining the cumbersome, indigenous system.

When Peter the Great assumed the throne in 1692 he immediately began a series of wrenching reforms designed to modernize and strengthen the Russian state. As a young man, Peter studied carpentry, shipbuilding, and navigation, because he recognized that Russia needed to have a modern navy to compete with its adversaries. From 1697 to 1698, he led a delegation of his advisors and craftsmen on an extensive tour of Europe to acquire greater knowledge of European societies.

Much of Peter's rule can be interpreted as a reaction to the traditional Muscovite past. He envisioned a modern Russian state, freed from the superstitions and corruption of the church and from the conservatism of the Muscovite establishment and all that it represented. He adopted a military uniform, shedding the priestly robes of the Muscovite tsars. He changed his title from tsar to emperor. He strove to raise the Russian people from their ignorance and backwardness, but in so doing, he was quite willing to resort to ruthless tactics. Thousands of his adversaries were jailed, exiled to Siberia, or executed. Peter forced his first wife, Eudoxia, to become a nun for resisting his reforms. His son, Alexis, also resisted his father's innovations and was condemned to death, but died in prison before his execution could be carried out.

Peter promulgated a revolution from above. At great human expense, he built a new capital, St. Petersburg, which was intended to be Russia's "window on the West." He abolished the patriarchate and established the synod, dominated by the laity, to govern the church. He ordered all military officers to shave their beards "for the glory and comeliness of the State and the military profession," and levied a tax on those citizens who persisted in growing beards.[7] He established the Academy of Sciences, including a section for legal studies, and encouraged members of the nobility to study abroad.

Peter reorganized the haphazard, unwieldy governmental bureaucracy into nine *collegia*, patterned after the Swedish model of administration. In addition, he is credited with establishing the first treasury and a universal system of coinage to replace the previous system of barter. This facilitated the collection of taxes to support his military campaigns. Peter's reforms strengthened the Russian state and forced Western enlightenment on a segment of the population, the intelligentsia, that was to become an important conduit for the transmission of Western ideas to Russia.

In the field of law, Peter's reforms were largely concerned with strengthening the power of the state, and thereby enhancing his own power over the regional nobility. The use of law and the legal system to reinforce the power of the autocrat is a second enduring feature of Russian legal culture.

Autocracy and the law

Until the middle of the seventeenth century, Russians had no concept of the state as Westerners know it. The state, insofar as they thought of it at all, meant the sovereign (*gosudar'*) – that is, the tsar – his private staff, and his family. Like the father of an extended family, the prince or tsar emerged as the sole proprietor in public right of all the subjects and all the territory in his principality. The concept of the state, when it did develop, reflected both this autocratic, arbitrary, and personalistic conception of power of the sovereign and the despotic powers accorded the head of the extended family in early peasant society. The father was sovereign of the household, an autocrat in the broadest sense of the word. He literally owned all the property of the clan and its members as well; they could be sold as one might sell a cow. He alone was responsible for punishing members of the family; whipping a son to death was not uncommon. In parts of Siberia, as late as the mid-nineteenth century, a father who killed a family member was liable only to a penance issued by the church.

In the eighteenth century, the Russian autocracy transformed itself beyond previous traditional roles into the predominant political and economic force in the country. Russian rulers of the eighteenth century emulated Western monarchs, beginning what has been called "the absolutist" phase of Russian autocracy. The tsars, like monarchs in Sweden and Prussia or the emperors of Napoleonic France, sought to extend their authority to regulate state and society. As such, a new image of authority was needed to legitimate the monarch's exercise of power: the responsibility of the tsar to guarantee the general welfare of the society. Thus, the law became an instrument of the autocracy, rather than a check on the tsar's power over the society.

Peter the Great is credited with introducing the notion of legality (*zakonnost'*) into state affairs in Russia. He appointed three separate commissions during the period 1700–1720 to systematize the thousands of legislative acts, decrees and regulations that had been promulgated since the *Sobornoe ulozhenie* of 1649. Chief among the goals of the state set forth in Peter's General Regulation of 1717 was the protection of justice. While justice was a primary goal of the Petrine autocracy, Peter remained suspicious of judges and lawyers and did not accede to legal restrictions on his power. Judges were instructed merely to apply statutes and refrain from legal interpretation.

Peter's distrust of lawyers and the courts prompted him to erect an elaborate infrastructure to supervise the functioning of judicial organs. The Senate, a judicial and advisory body composed of members of the nobility appointed by the tsar, was charged with supervising the courts and punishing "unrighteous judges." In 1722 a new office, the procurator-general, was created to oversee the activities of the Senate to ensure that all edicts and decrees were promptly and fully implemented. The procurator-general functioned as a military-style commanding officer over the Senate and all branches of state administration and, indeed, the first appointees to the post were former military officers and close associates of the tsar.

To curb the discretion of judges, Peter adopted an inquisitorial procedure and a system of legal codes. The rules setting forth the operations of the courts were set forth in the Military Statute of 1716, which incorporated several provisions borrowed from the Swedish, Danish, and German military codes. The statute made no distinction between civil and criminal cases, trials were conducted behind closed doors and secrecy prevailed. The best proof was voluntary confession and torture was an acceptable vehicle for obtaining confessions. However, the code specified that the judge could only order the torture of a defendant in cases where he felt "complete suspicion." In civil cases the judge could order torture "if in great and important civil cases a witness becomes difficult, or confused, or changes the expression on his face."[8]

The tsar's personal power was at all times superior to any rule, law or statute. Thus, Article 1 of the *Svod Zakonov* of 1832 proclaimed "The All-Russian Emperor is an autocratic and unlimited monarch. Obedience to his supreme power not only from fear but also from conscience is ordained by God Himself."[9] Furthermore, this same pre-eminence over the law extended to the tsar's numerous officials, advisors and ministers when they could claim that they were acting on the tsar's behalf. Thus, in practice there was no way to distinguish the monarch's decrees or imperial commands from administrative rulings.

The autocratic power of the tsar was not only absolute and unrestrained by law, it was often arbitrary. The Russian concept of *proizvol'* is difficult to translate and even more difficult for Westerners to understand. *Proizvol'* can be variously defined as arbitrariness, despotism, tyranny, and mercy. Thus, the beneficence or wrath of the tsar could come at any moment, without warning or just cause, and citizens were absolutely subject to his mercy. Unlike most Western societies that consider arbitrariness and despotism to be failings of legal systems, in Russia *proizvol'* was accepted as a natural part of life, and sometimes even considered a virtue.

The Russian nobility supported this system of personal authority vested in the tsar because it was through this system that they were awarded ranks and estates. A strong judiciary would only serve to constrain their ruthless actions and disrupt their personal ties to the sovereign by forcing them to submit to the regularized standards of law. The provincial nobility grew in power and numbers during the eighteenth century to the point that they could act as a counterweight to the tsar. But rather than rise up against the monarchy, as happened in several West European states, the provincial nobility in Russia elected to use their power to direct and manipulate the tsar behind the scenes rather than confront him directly. They preferred to keep their influence personalistic and informal, rather than protect their interests through adopting regular judicial procedure and rule of law.

The legal profession was not highly regarded during much of the pre-revolutionary period. Judicial careers were associated with low social status. The chancelleries were dominated by a class of clerks, recruited from non-noble families at an early age, who were trained to read, write, and fill out forms. According to Wortman, "they pursued the same tack through their lives, learning to avoid the appearance of thought or interpretation."[10] The low status attached to the chancellery prevented lawyers from developing a sense of being revered defenders of the law.

Both Peter and his daughter, Empress Elizabeth (1741–1762), attempted to elevate the status of lawyers by encouraging the nobility to pursue legal training, but to little avail. The quickest route to noble status, wealth, and power remained a military career. Empress Elizabeth brought to Russia such noted European jurists as Frederich Strube de Piermont and Phillippe Henrich Dilthei to elevate the training of Russian lawyers. Dilthei, an Austrian, became the first professor of law at Moscow University when it was founded in 1755. Despite these efforts, Western European influences on Russian law were destined to remain limited as long as they were perceived as impinging on the power of the monarch.

Catherine II (1762–1796) wished to bring Russia up to the standard of the other European empires. Like her predecessors, she imported noted West European legal scholars, changing the intellectual climate and laying the groundwork for legal reforms. In 1775 a new hierarchy of local, district, and appellate courts was established. The following year she ordered an ambitious plan of legal codification, which was, however, thwarted by her unwillingness to accept legal restrictions on her power as sovereign. Again in 1767 she convened a legislative commission to explore the possibilities of reforming the legal system. However, in charging the commission she took pains to deprecate the Roman law systems of Western Europe, which she felt had vested too much legislative power in the hands of judges.

Alexander I (1801–1825), a progressive and reform-minded tsar who admired the logical consistency of the Germanic and French codes, was also determined to modernize the state apparatus and bring order to the chaotic state of Russian laws and legislation. Alexander was much influenced by the ideas of the Enlightenment and the French Revolution which entered Russia largely as a result of the Napoleonic Wars. Prior to the Russian victory over Napoleon's army, Western ideas and influences touched only a tiny elite class of intellectuals who traveled and studied abroad. Russian soldiers returning from France after the war, however, brought back ideas and concepts that filtered down to the grassroots of Russian society.

Alexander commissioned yet another codification effort, which looked to European states for advice on how to proceed, only to fall victim to arguments concerning the uniqueness of Russia and the non-applicability of the Napoleonic Code to Russia. The influx of Western ideas during the first half of the nineteenth century sparked a renewed debate among the intellectuals as to whether Russia should chart its own course or follow the lead of Western Europe. Alexander himself was torn over this issue. While he favored several modernizing reforms, including legal reform, he was loathe to undertake a restructuring of the political power structure of the state, lest it result in the overthrow of the monarchy, as occurred in France. Ultimately, Alexander settled for reforms designed to reconfigure state administration, while preserving the unquestioned power and status of the tsar. He replaced Peter's colleges with ministries, patterned on the French system, and created a civil service recruited by examination rather than by heredity and patronage. The civil service examination included topics such as natural law. Roman law, private law, and criminal law. Law faculties expanded in the universities and noted foreign scholars were invited to lecture.

Alexander's successor, Nicholas I (1825–1855), made little pretense of supporting democratic political or legal reforms. Nicholas came to power following the Decembrist uprising, an abortive attempt by a group of military officers from aristocratic families who called for the establishment of a constitutional regime and the abolition of serfdom. Confronting the first organized challenge to the authority of the tsar, Nicholas was determined to reinforce law and order in Russian society. His efforts to codify Russian laws were undertaken with the aim of clarifying and strengthening the powers of the state, rather than introducing reforms that would move Russia in the direction of developing a European-style democracy with rule of law. Nicholas promulgated the doctrine of the preeminent role of the state known as "official nationality." First proclaimed in 1833 by Count Serge Uvarov, the tsar's minister of education, the decree contained three principles: Orthodoxy, autocracy, and nationality. Orthodoxy referred to the official church and its role as the ultimate source of ethics and ideals that gave meaning to human life and society. Autocracy meant the absolute power of the sovereign, which was considered the indispensable foundation of the Russian state. Nationality referred to Russian nationality, which was preeminent over all other peoples within the rapidly expanding empire.

Under Nicholas I, codification efforts were renewed. The tsar appointed a group of St. Petersburg legal scholars, under the direction of Count Mikhail Speransky, to undertake an ambitious project of compiling a comprehensive systematic collection of Russian laws, the most ambitious project yet attempted in Europe. The result was the *Polnoe sobranie zakonnov Rossiiskoi imperii* (Complete Collection of Laws of the Russian Empire), which was completed in 1830 and filled forty-eight massive volumes. Two years later the *Svod zakonov* (Digest of Russian Laws), a fifteen-volume digest, attempted to organize the laws into a workable form. Commenting on the work of the commission, Speransky noted: "Another fate [than that of Western Europe] was intended for Russia by Providence. None of the inheritance of Rome fell to us. Our legislation had entirely to be drawn from sources of its own."[11] An unintended result of these codification efforts was that the status of lawyers was raised and their professional role in government was enhanced.

Thus, until the legal reforms of 1864, there was a fundamental ambivalence concerning Russian law: on the one hand there was a desire to protect justice and order in the state; on the other hand there was a resistance by the tsars to anything that would constrain the exercise of their personal whim or will. This ambivalence about the rule of law and the power of the state remains today an enduring feature of Russian and Soviet legal culture.

Westernizing influences, the intelligentsia, and legal reform

By the nineteenth century, the pressures to reform the tradition-laden, cumbersome, and antiquated legal system in Russian had grown. The legal system reflected the gross inequities of Russian society. There were separate courts specifying different punishments for members of the nobility, the clergy, the urban intelligentsia, and the peasants, while the tsar, his family, and his highest advisors remained above the law entirely. The courts were supervised by notoriously corrupt provincial governors. The nineteenth-century satirist Mikhail Saltykov-Shchedrin noted that it was more prudent to invest in bribes to provincial governors than to invest in bank deposits, because bribes spared one harassment by the authorities, which could be even more costly. Saltykov-Shchedrin, who had himself served as a deputy governor of Tver and Ryazan provinces under Alexander II, wrote a collection of stories entitled *Provincial Sketches* in which he lampooned provincial governors. One of his characters is portrayed as having a soup bowl in place of a head. Inevitably, the governor stumbles in a rutted street, shatters his "head," and is thereafter condemned to go through life headless – with no perceptible impairment of his mental faculties. Another of Saltykov-Shchedrin's fictional provincial governors, widely held as a progressive forward-thinking man, is found dead one morning, devoured by his own fleas.

By far the greatest social ill in Russian society, however, and one that demanded immediate change, was serfdom. Throughout the sixteenth and seventeenth centuries serfdom spread, not by contractual agreements between peasants and landlords, but by decree. As the tsar granted lands to his military officers and members of the aristocracy as rewards for loyal service, the peasants occupying those lands became bound to the land as well as to the landlord and the tsar.

Serfs had no legal rights, nor could they expect or demand humane treatment from their landlords. They could not pursue careers other than farming nor assume financial obligations without their masters' consent and it was not uncommon for masters to arrange marriages for their serfs. Serfs were not free to travel. They were obliged to farm the landlord's fields, leaving little time for working their own meager land plots. Landlords could sell their serfs much as they sold property. In fact, the criminal code of 1754 listed serfs only under the heading of property of the gentry.

Whereas the gentry gained independence from service obligations to the tsar in the mid eighteenth century, the peasants remained bound to the land and to the landlord for another century, compounding the injustice against them. For the peasants, the concept of absentee landowner was difficult to accept. In their view, the soil was given by God and all who toiled and labored on it should be able to enjoy its use. The concept of private ownership of land was not recognized in Russian law until 1782 and such ownership was restricted to the nobility. The peasants' land was held in a primitive agrarian communal institution, the *mir*, but was subject to provincial regulation and high rates of taxation.

The plight of the serfs deteriorated throughout the first half of the nineteenth century. By 1840 there were more than 1 million serfs serving full-time as household servants for landowners.[12] Scattered uprisings and peasant rebellions, sparked by mandatory grain collections and compulsory military service, were brutally suppressed. Official records of the tsarist government report more than 500 peasant uprisings in the nineteenth century prior to the emancipation of the serfs in 1861.[13]

Alexander II (1855–1881) came to power following the reactionary rule of Nicholas I, determined to bring about progressive social and political reforms. The tsar concluded the manifesto announcing the end of the Crimean War with a promise of reform. Inexorable pressures – both economic and moral – were building for the abolition of serfdom. As agriculture grew more competitive, many landlords could no longer afford to care for their serfs. The intelligentsia of all philosophical orientations opposed the institution of serfdom as morally wrong.

Emancipation of the serfs finally came on March 3, 1861. At the time, serfs constituted some 45 percent of the population.[14] Except in the Ukraine, land was sold not to individual peasants but to the peasant commune, which divided the land among its members and was responsible for taxes and the provision of recruits for the army. Because few peasants could afford to buy land from the gentry, the government acquired the land for them and was reimbursed through heavy redemption payments, which rapidly created a class of impoverished peasants. Thus, for many serfs, the so-called emancipation altered only slightly their everyday existence.

Alexander II's reforms were not limited to the emancipation of the serfs. He was also responsible for implementing the most significant legal reforms of any modern tsar. The second half of the nineteenth century is often referred to as "the Golden Age of Russian law." During a span of some fifty years, major reforms were introduced to bring the Russian judicial system into accord with those of Western Europe. A professional bar was established with high standards and lawyers gained new status and prominence in society. What led to these remarkable innovations? The impetus for legal reform came largely from two sources: the necessity for new laws to facilitate expanding contacts with other European empires, and lobbying by a Western-educated intelligentsia that viewed adherence to rule of law as an essential characteristic of civilized European states.

The need for legal reform was first manifested in commercial law. Russian trading statutes were wholly inadequate for modern trading practices. New trade laws were adopted from Western Europe, including concepts such as negotiable instruments, bankruptcy, maritime law, and the establishment of a commercial court.

Legal reforms were also mandated by dramatic changes on the domestic scene. Russia was alive with new ideas and social movements throughout the nineteenth century. The members of the nobility who participated in the 1825 Decembrist uprising, demanding the establishment of a constitutional monarchy, expanded rights to political participation, and rule of law, helped to set the agenda for Alexander II's reforms a full generation later. So too, the intellectuals of the 1840s influenced Alexander's views of social contract between citizens and the state. The writings of John Locke and Jean-Jacques Rousseau; the utopian socialists, Claude-Henri Saint-Simon, Charles Fourier, and Pierre-Joseph Proudhon; and the German Romanticists, Georg Hegel and Friedrich Schelling, were widely read and discussed by the intelligentsia of Moscow and St. Petersburg in the 1840s and 1850s.

Western European influence on Russian law did not come without opposition. The influx of Western culture generated a reactionary backlash among those who rejected its new ideas and chose instead to preserve the uniqueness of Russian society. By the nineteenth century, the conflict between the Western ideas introduced since the time of Peter and the indigenous Slavic mores was manifested in two opposing schools of thought – the Westernizers and the Slavophiles. The Westernizers held that Russia must follow the Western model of development. The Slavophiles, on the other hand, glorified the superior achievements and historic mission of Orthodoxy and of

Russia. While the Westernizers promoted industrialization, secularization, rule of law, and the rise of a middle class, the Slavophiles stressed the simple idealistic virtues of the Russian peasant, the peasant commune, Orthodoxy, rural life, and autocratic rule of the tsar.

Many of the intellectuals who advocated legal reforms in the mid-nineteenth century were graduates of the Imperial School of Jurisprudence, a secondary boarding school providing legal training to boys beginning at 11 to 15 years of age. The program of study spanned seven years – three years devoted to language, history, mathematics, and other general subjects, followed by four years of legal study including courses on Roman law, civil and criminal law and process, financial law, police investigatory procedure, forensic medicine, and comparative legal practices. Students in the school tended to come from the ranks of middle and lesser nobles, classes that had traditionally risen through military service. Thus, the students in the School of Jurisprudence (*pravovedy*) could identify neither with the aristocratic elite, nor with their fathers who served the elite through bonds of military service. Wortman notes: "they would seek their guiding ethos in their education and the ideas imparted by their teachers and their reading. Many of them would find their self-definition in a new conception of the importance of law."[15] The School of Jurisprudence left an indelible impression on several generations of influential Russian lawyers and judicial officials, imbuing in them a respect for the law and an appreciation of legal theories and political thinking popular in Germany, France, and England. Among the noted graduates of the School of Jurisprudence were Konstantin Pobedonostsev, who became a professor of civil law at Moscow University and later a tutor to Alexander III and Nicholas II; Prince Dmitri Obolensky, who later would be the chief architect of the 1864 legal reforms; Dmitri Rovinsky, who would go on to serve as provincial procurator in Moscow and was widely admired for cleaning up a corrupt and inhumane criminal system in the city; and Nikolai Stoyanovsky, who became chief procurator in the Moscow and later the St. Petersburg Senate. The School of Jurisprudence provided a rarefied atmosphere conducive to literary, and artistic, as well as philosophical exploration. It is not accidental that several of the graduates of the School of Jurisprudence, such as Peter Tchaikovsky and the composer and music critic Aleksandr Serov, achieved fame outside the field of law.

By the early 1840s, the graduates of the School of Jurisprudence were filling low-level posts in the Ministry of Justice and other influential institutions and beginning their career ascent. They encountered tradition-bound and often corrupt bureaucratic administrations and, encouraged by the reform atmosphere during the first years of Alexander II's reign, began to push for changes in the Russian legal system.

Many of the *pravovedy*, including Obolensky, emphasized the need for an independent judiciary. The judiciary, Obolensky insisted, is the vital foundation of the state. "Judicial authority preserving the personal and proprietary rights of citizens is the basis upon which the entire edifice of state administration rests ... The judge as *judge* should belong to no estate. He is the servant of *truth*, and therefore should be its independent representative."[16]

Law and legal studies gained in status and popularity as Russian intellectuals became familiar with Western legal philosophy. Students at the leading universities became energized by the legal debates over the role of the state, the ability of citizens to protect their rights and interests in court, the establishment of a constitutional democracy, and expanded rights of political participation. By the end of the 1860s law students constituted more than one-half of all students enrolled in universities in Russia.[17]

Alexander turned to the *pravovedy*, commissioning them to work on drafting proposals for a total restructuring of the Russian legal system. Not surprising, many of the proposals were heavily influenced by West European legal thinking and experience. Obolensky, who led a group of reform-minded jurists in the Naval Ministry, advocated the establishment of public courts with adversarial procedure based on the Polish model. Obolensky's suggestion that Russia adopt a foreign legal system was the first such recommendation and generated sharp criticism from conservative, nationalistic members of the tsarist administration. The fact that Obolensky drafted the proposals while in Rome reinforced the suspicions of many of his critics. Other jurists suggested additional judicial revisions, including the establishment of a system of justices of the peace patterned on the British system, the creation of a professional bar, and the need to distinguish questions of law from those of fact in civil cases. The proposed revisions were largely influenced by jurists monitoring developments in Germany, Italy, Hungary, England, France, and other European states.

In 1861 Alexander II charged the state Chancellery with drafting the judicial reform. The next year the commission completed *The Basic Principles for the Reform of the Courts*, which provided the outlines for a new legal system in Russia, one that would bring Russia into line with legal systems in Germany, France, Italy, and Great Britain. *The Basic Principles* called for the establishment of an independent court system, open to the public, incorporating oral, adversarial procedure, and in which judges would have discretion in determining verdicts. *The Principles* also necessitated the creation of a professional bar and the introduction of a jury system. In its deliberations, the commission was influenced substantially by the Civil Statute introduced in Hanover, Germany in the late 1840s. The Hanoverian statute had, in turn, been heavily influenced by French law.

The introduction of the jury system was one of the most controversial elements of the *Basic Principles*, but supporters of the innovation argued that it would help educate the citizenry in the law and develop in them a greater respect for the law. They argued that the existing inquisitorial system, by dividing authority between judges and prosecutors, tended to diminish judicial authority and often resulted in administrative authorities intervening in or totally disregarding judicial proceedings.

Most of the provisions of the *Basic Principles* were incorporated in the Court Statutes of 1864 and approved by Alexander. The legal reform of 1864 created a modern judicial system, one that, at least on paper, was among the most progressive in Europe at the time. In civil matters, the courts were given complete discretion, ending the practice of administrative interventions. In criminal matters, provisions were introduced to protect against arbitrary arrest and provided for the right to defense, although the police continued to enjoy the rights of preliminary detention and immunity from responsibility.

With the reform, the newly established courts were led by judges who, for the first time, manifested a sense of competence and integrity in the judicial system. A professional Russian bar was founded with high professional standards and set for itself the goal of extending the rights of the individual relative to the state.

Despite the progressiveness of the 1864 judicial reforms, the contradiction between the development of a system of rule of law and preservation of unbridled power of the autocracy remained and was the subject of high-level disputes. The reforms stopped well short of instituting constitutional government or legalizing political parties. Particular resistance to extension of the rule of law was encountered in numerous government ministries and agencies where officials wished to perpetuate their administrative latitude in making policy and resolving conflicts through administrative bargaining. Resistance to the legal reforms of 1864 was also strong in the provinces where the gentry opposed any encroachment on their authority. Meanwhile, in Moscow and St. Petersburg, political developments unfolded that would result in the tsar's retreating from the provisions of the 1864 reforms soon after they were enacted. We turn now to the rise of anarchistic and terrorist movements, the reaction they generated, and their impact on the evolution of the Russian legal system.

From reform to reaction

Alexander II and his advisors had hoped that the legal reforms of 1864 would engender a new respect for law in the population. However, instead of placating those calling for change, the reforms invited increasingly strident political demands and sharpened the reactionary policies of the conservative aristocracy. Unrest swept the universities in 1861 and 1862. At St. Petersburg University, students occupied the administrative offices and closed the university with strikes. In 1866 a deranged student attempted to assassinate the tsar. In order to restore discipline and control over the universities, the tsar named the conservative Count Dmitri Tolstoy as minister of education. Press censorship was tightened and criminal cases involving political activities were exempted from regular judicial proceedings.

A new, younger generation of intellectuals took their philosophies to the streets, following the examples of such radicals as Nikolai Chernyshevsky, Mikhail Bakunin, Dmitri Pisarev, Sergei Nechaev, and Felix Dzerzhinsky. Many of the younger generation advocated nihilism as the spiritual liberation and, ultimately, the political liberation of Russia. The nihilists rejected all conventions, norms, and institutions in Russian society.

Many of the instances of violence in the early 1870s were spontaneous countermeasures against increasingly brutal tactics by the police. By the late 1870s, a well-organized conspiratorial anarchist society, the People's Will, had emerged. Members of the People's Will hoped that a few well-chosen terrorist acts would seriously disrupt the excessively centralized tsarist regime and inspire the peasants to rebellion. The People's Will called for Alexander II's death and made numerous bold attempts on his life. In one incident, the tsar's dining room in the Winter Palace was totally destroyed by explosives, but the tsar escaped unharmed.

Alexander turned to the courts and to his newly appointed minister of justice, Count Konstantin Pahlen, to neutralize the revolutionary movement. Pahlen, the first minister of justice to hold a law degree, had risen rapidly within the Ministry of the Interior. In the on-going debate over judicial independence he took a compromised position between the governors and the police, on the one hand, and the courts on the other hand.

Pahlen attempted to stigmatize and isolate the revolutionaries from the general public by prosecuting them in open court. However, the prosecution was overconfident and underprepared, having never before confronted the rigors of an open and fair trial of political offenders. In the most notorious case, the 1877 trial of 193 political dissidents, the defense attorneys mounted a vigorous defense of their clients and attacked the government's flimsy case against them, as well as deplorable breaches of procedure by governmental investigators and prosecutors. The accused had languished in prison for three years during the preliminary investigation, seventy-five of them died or lost their sanity while in prison.[18] Of the 193, ninety were acquitted, sixty-four were found guilty and sentenced, but the court recommended mercy in twenty-seven of these cases. Angered by the lenient verdict, the government immediately arrested many of the acquitted revolutionaries and imposed administrative penalties on them.

The following year, Vera Zasulich, a member of the People's Will, shot and wounded the military governor of St. Petersburg, who had ordered the flogging of a political prisoner. Since Zasulich had admitted the crime and there was no question of her guilt, Pahlen decided to request a jury trial. He hoped that a guilty verdict by a jury of citizens would show lack of public support for the revolutionary movement. Behind the scenes, however, Pahlen attempted to obtain assurances of a guilty verdict from Anatoly Koni, the presiding judge in the St. Petersburg Circuit Court. Koni, a distinguished lawyer and legal scholar dedicated to judicial independence, refused. The prosecution handled the evidence badly. Zasulich's attorneys, on the other hand, turned the proceedings into a trial of the legitimacy of the tsarist regime. The courtroom was packed with Zasulich's supporters, who saw the case as a triumph of public opinion over the oppression of the autocracy. When the jury found Zasulich not guilty, the courtroom erupted with cries of "Bravo!" and "Vera, Verochka!"

The acquittal of Zasulich confirmed the suspicions of the tsar and his advisors that the new courts, rather than functioning as impartial tribunals, were becoming vehicles for expressing anti-regime sentiments. After the Zasulich trial, the government gave up all pretense of legality in its struggle against the revolutionaries. Administrative punishments and military justice prevailed, sparking even bolder attacks by the anarchists.

By 1881, the increased use of police repression had not succeeded in quelling popular unrest. Alexander decided again to try a more moderate policy that he hoped would lead to a rapprochement. He appointed Count Mikhail Loris-Melikov as minister of the interior and instructed him to develop a plan to counteract terrorism. Melikov's proposal called for sweeping reforms to broaden public participation in policy-making. Alexander approved the proposals and was to have signed them into law on the afternoon of March 1, 1881, but he was assassinated on his way to a ceremonial review of the troops that morning. The People's Will had carefully plotted the murder, placing members along all the routes from the Winter Palace to the parade ground. Each terrorist carried a nitroglycerin bomb. The two anarchists who lobbed their bombs at Alexander's carriage died instantly in the explosion. The tsar's legs were blown off by the force of the blast; he died in the arms of his son and heir, Alexander III, who swore to avenge his father's death by initiating a reign of terror against the anarchists.

Alexander III, a dedicated reactionary, was determined to suppress revolution and maintain autocracy at all costs. He instituted counter-reforms giving the authorities sweeping powers to deal with the press and political critics of the regime. "Temporary Regulations" were instituted to protect state security and public order. Summary search, arrest, imprisonment, exile, and secret trials by courts-martial became common. The number of persons exiled to Siberia or imprisoned for political crimes shot up almost four-fold.[19] Alexander II's former liberal advisors and ministers resigned in protest and were replaced by well-known conservatives and reactionaries, such as Konstantin Pobedonostsev and Dmitri Tolstoy. Pobedonostsev, who had grown more conservative throughout his career, expressed fears that Westernization, urbanization, and industrialization would bring unhealthy changes to Russia.

In order to strengthen its hold on the increasingly restive peasants, the regime established the office of *zemsky nachal'nik* (land captain), whose responsibilities included exercising direct control over the peasants throughout the empire. The land captains, who were appointed by the minister of the interior, had the power to approve or disapprove of peasants elected to local offices, to override the decisions of the communes, and to fine, arrest, and imprison peasants.

The counterreforms of Alexander III engendered even harsher responses from the radicals. Despite the stepped-up measures of the secret police, remnants of the People's Will continued their underground activities. In 1887, a group that included Alexander Ulyanov, Lenin's older brother, was arrested and executed for plotting to assassinate the tsar. By failing to respond to earlier demands for more moderate reforms, the tsarist regime now confronted groups that would only be content with the total, violent destruction of the tsarist system.

The "Temporary Regulations," imposed in 1881 following Alexander II's assassination, were renewed and remained in force until 1917. Russians lived under a system of virtual martial law for the last thirty-six years of the Romanov dynasty. By turning from its earlier commitment to honor the rule of law and by elevating itself above the law, the autocracy during the last half of Alexander II's reign and throughout the reigns of Alexander III and Nicholas II undermined the regime's claims to legitimacy. The last of the Romanov tsars chose to hold on to power through the use of military and police force and the autocracy was eventually overthrown when even those instruments proved incapable of propping up an increasingly illegitimate system.

Judicial administration in the provinces

Russia has always been a country marked by dramatic regional variations. The Russian Empire by the end of the nineteenth century had expanded to incorporate roughly one-sixth of the earth's land surface. From its Pacific shores to the western frontiers with Poland, the empire stretched over 6,800 miles. From the northernmost reaches above the Arctic Circle to the desert borders with Turkey and Persia it covered more than 3,500 miles.

While the immensity of Russia afforded it some degree of isolation throughout history, it also has raised problems. Transportation and communications, necessary ingredients to any modern state, were virtually non-existent before the 1860s when railway and telegraph communications were established in European Russia. The trans-Siberian railway was not completed until 1903. Coordination of administration over such a massive area has always resulted in dual pressures – on the one hand, a tendency to instill uniformity through a hypercentralized administrative structure in which most power rests at the center, and, on the other hand, a competing tendency to decentralize administration by granting a limited degree of local and regional autonomy.

Russia's isolation also meant that, until the early nineteenth century Russian society was largely isolated from the events and ideas that influenced the course of Western European development. In Russia, there was no Renaissance or Reformation. The separation of church and state, each with its own independent realm of authority, was totally foreign to Russian thinking. The Industrial Revolution came late to Russia; when industry developed, it was not due to the rise of a middle class of entrepreneurs but to state decree and foreign investment encouraged by the state.

The expansion of the Russian Empire continued unevenly from the sixteenth through the nineteenth century, beginning with the consolidation of the empire in the territories west of the Urals, including the Baltics, the Don region, and the North Caucasus, and then expanding into contiguous territories to the east and south. The causes of Russian territorial expansion were many. First, the empire was surrounded by sparsely settled territories that invited incorporation. Second, lacking any natural borders, the empire tended to expand in search of security. Third, empires of the nineteenth century often measured their power and influence in terms of the extent of territory they controlled and the size of their populations. Fourth, because much of the arable land in Russia was of poor quality and traditional farming techniques tended to deplete the soil quickly, the peasants were constantly seeking more fertile farming areas. Finally, because England, France, and other European powers could no longer expand their territories on the European continent without precipitating war, they turned toward the acquisition of extensive colonial holdings that would provide sources of raw materials for their industry and markets for their industrial goods. The Russian Empire, anxious to compete and be recognized as a major European power, was afforded the opportunity to expand into contiguous territories that presented many of the advantages of a colonial empire.

The expansion of Russia, especially in Asia, the Caucasus, and the Baltics, inevitably introduced non-Slavic peoples into the empire. By the time of the Revolution in 1917, Russia was a multiethnic state consisting of peoples speaking more than 150 distinct dialects or languages. They ranged from Catholics and Protestants in the western regions of the Ukraine, Belorussia, and the Baltics, to Orthodox believers in European Russia, to Shiite Moslems in Central Asia, Buddhists in the Far East, and shamanists in isolated villages throughout eastern Siberia.

The immensity of the Russian landmass and the diversity of its population presented a challenge to the tsarist government – how does one make and administer policy over such an extensive area with such diverse populations? V. O. Klyuchevsky, the distinguished historian of the nineteenth century, remarked, "the state expands, the people grow sickly."[20] From the time of Ivan the Terrible, the rulers of Russia sought to compensate for the diversity and expansiveness of the empire by relying on a heavily centralized and hierarchical system of state administration. A major reason Peter the Great instituted the Procuracy was to extend more effective control over various state administrative agencies. The problem of controlling provincial institutions had been particularly vexing to Peter. Local authorities drew on a long tradition of local administration and justice that disregarded changes emanating from Peter's newly established capital in St. Petersburg. The vastness of Russia combined with a rich legacy in provincial potentates undermined Peter's attempts to instill a uniform judicial system and universal norms of administration throughout the empire.

Under Catherine II, procuratorial supervision was extended to the provincial and local levels. In the wake of the Pugachev Rebellion in 1773 Catherine sought to strengthen government in the provinces by decentralizing power. The empire was divided into fifty provinces (*gubernii*), each with an appointed governor. Under Catherine the rights and powers of the provincial nobility were expanded, giving them greater discretion in making and implementing policies at the local level.

The reign of Nicholas I represented the opposite trend toward greater centralization of authority. He promulgated the doctrine of "official nationality" that proclaimed the three values of orthodoxy, autocracy, and nationality. As part of Nicholas's reaction to the Decembrist uprising, he expanded the Third Department – political police – into a nation-wide network to report on local conditions and stamp out all opposition.

The emancipation of the serfs in 1861 forced the provincial nobility to turn their attention to the courts as a means of protecting their economic interests. Whereas they previously existed as regional administrative agents of the tsar and could rely on protection through the administrative/command structure, after emancipation the gentry could no longer rely on administrative interventions to preserve their interests, and so instead turned to the courts. Minister of Justice Konstantin Pobedonostsev recognized the need for legal protection of the property rights of the gentry: "The first concern of the law should be the protection of the *creditor*, for his legal interests are the interests of *property*, and the interests of property are inseparably tied to the internal security and internal prosperity of the State itself.''[21]

Alexander II, recognizing the need for greater local authority in the aftermath of the emancipation of the serfs, created district and city assemblies (*zemstva*). The assemblies were granted limited self-rule and provided representation for the peasants, although seats in the assemblies were awarded on the basis of the amount of land owned, insuring the predominance of the provincial nobility. The assemblies did not replace the centralized institutions of power – the police, governors, and procurators – rather, they coexisted with them. On most legal matters, the centralized institutions were clearly predominant.

The *zemstvo* system was instituted only in Russian areas, not in the borderlands. In the newly acquired Baltics, Caucasus, and Central Asia, Russian occupation and conquest remained primarily military in character. The establishment of Russian rule interfered little with the native economy, religion, law, or customs.

The judicial reforms of 1864 were implemented gradually throughout the European portion of Russia. By the time of Alexander II's death in 1881 the reforms had been implemented in only thirty-three provinces. In some border areas, such as the Baltics, Siberia, and the Caucasus, the judicial reforms were not implemented until the end of the nineteenth or beginning of the twentieth century. Finland, Poland, Courland, Livonia, the Central Asian protectorates of Khiva and Bukhara, and Jews living in the Pale of Settlement were initially permitted a significant degree of autonomy, both legal and political. However, this would change under Alexander III and Nicholas II. The Polish constitution was abrogated in 1831, the Finnish constitution was suspended in 1899, the charters of Courland and Livonia were thoroughly subverted and the indigenous peoples of Siberia and Asia, as well as the Jews were fully subordinated to Russian governors by the turn of the century. Only Khiva and Bukhara managed to retain some degree of autonomy, only to fall to the Bolsheviks in the 1920s.

The trends and tendencies we have noted in this survey of the development of the Russian legal system prior to the Bolshevik seizure of power in 1917 have demonstrated an enduring quality and have direct relevance to the current attempts to reform the Russian legal system. The Russian legal system today is still struggling with its origins and late development. There exists in the former Soviet Union a relative low level of legal culture and this is due, in part, to the fact that the Russian legal system had not developed strong support nor a high degree of institutionalization prior to the Revolution.

Second, the history of Russian jurisprudence displays a fundamental ambivalence toward whether the law and legal institutions should restrict the power of the state. Count Benckendorff, Nicholas I's Minister of the Interior, asserted: "Laws are written for subordinates, not for the authorities!"[22] His remark illustrates the strongly held view that laws are designed to protect and implement the interests of the state. The state, whether in the form of the tsar or the Communist Party leadership, rules absolutely and arbitrarily. Since the state represents the collective interests of the entire society, its interests take precedence over those of the individual. The competing view holds that the state and the sovereign are also bound by the law. The latter principle, which is fundamental in Western legal systems, and in England dates back to the Magna Carta of 1215, remains contested in Russian legal culture even today.

A third tendency evident in the history of Russian law is that reform, when it has been introduced, has been the result of the activities of a Westernizing intelligentsia. Jurists and other members of the intelligentsia, having read major works of Western writers and having traveled abroad, came to reflect norms and values at odds with those of the tsarist administration. Their ideas, which initially were considered dangerous, gradually earned wider acceptance and ultimately defined the reform agenda.

Reform in Russia, however, has not been a continual, incremental process, rather it has been cyclical and dialectical in nature. Reform initiatives have generated periodic backlashes. Conservative forces, finding reforms unsettling and threatening, have tended to seek refuge in the traditional values of orthodoxy, centralized power in the autocracy, and Russian domination over other ethnic minorities. For their part, the reformers have often proven to be uncompromising zealots, making a conservative backlash more likely.

Finally, Russian legal history demonstrates a marked center/periphery dichotomy. We have noted a tendency for the regime to seek uniformity through centralization of power. On the other hand, there has been a tendency to grant a limited degree of local and regional autonomy, especially in non-Russian areas. In some regions, remoteness from the center has enabled local leaders to pursue reforms more aggressively. In other regions local authorities have actively resisted reforms with virtual impunity.

As we have noted, the turbulent years following the introduction of the judicial reforms of 1864 never really permitted the development of a broad, public acceptance for the notions of judicial independence and rule of law. The downward spiral of terrorist activities of the anarchists answered by increasing repression by the tsarist regime eroded what little support existed for a modern, functioning system of rule of law. Hopes for restoring the momentum for legal reforms rose briefly during the 1905 Revolution and the tsar's reluctant submission to a constitution, but the onset of World War I, the collapse of the monarchy, and the Bolshevik seizure of power, would intervene to isolate Russia from the West and further retard its legal development.

2 The Bolshevik experience

> The formal law is subordinate to the law of the Revolution. There
> might be collisions and discrepancies between the formal
> commands of laws and those of the proletarian revolution ... This
> collision must be solved only by the subordination of the formal
> commands of law to those of party policy.
>
> Andrei Ya. Vyshinsky,
> Stalin's procurator-general (1935)[1]

The development in Russia of a modern European legal system
incorporating concepts of rule of law, protection of citizens' rights
vis-à-vis the state, and judicial independence was, as we have seen,
hampered by a sclerotic and reactionary monarchy overwhelmed by
social and political forces beyond its control. The collapse of the monarchy and the successful Bolshevik *coup d'état* against the Provisional
Government, rather than destroying the Russian Empire, essentially
enabled it to endure, albeit in a new form. For almost three-quarters
of a century, power remained centralized in the hands of a few; most
citizens were relegated to the status of subjects rather than real partici-
pants in political decision-making; Russians enjoyed considerable
advantages not shared by other ethnic groups; and law primarily
served the interests of the state rather than the individual.

As we have seen, the Russian Empire lagged behind the rest of
Europe in developing a capitalist economy, a democratic political
system, and a modern legal system, in part due to its physical isolation
during much of the seventeenth, eighteenth and early nineteenth centuries. The brief period of reforms and modernization leading up to
1864 had a profound influence on the thin stratum of Westernized
urban intelligentsia, but it was cut short by anarchist terrorist provo-
cations eliciting increasingly repressive measures by the police. After
the Revolution of 1917, Russia found itself again cut off from the West
and Western legal culture for largely ideological reasons.

Given the relative shallowness of the roots of Western legal traditions in Russia and the USSR's long isolation from the West after
the Revolution, it is not surprising that the legal system evolved substantially differently than those in Western Europe. In this chapter we
examine the seventy-five-year experiment with socialism and the
extent to which Marxist–Leninist concepts of law have become
ingrained in Russian legal practice and legal culture. We begin by
analyzing the ideological roots of the Soviet legal system.

The Marxist concept of law

Law plays a subsidiary role to the economy in Marx's analysis of capitalist society. "The mode of production in material life determines the
general character of the social, political and spiritual process of life,"
Marx wrote.[2] Thus, law is part of the superstructure built on the economic infrastructure or foundation of society. According to Friedrich
Engels: "The economic structure of society always forms the real basis
from which, in the last analysis, is to be explained the whole superstructure of legal and political institutions, as well as of the religious,
philosophical, and other conceptions of each historical period."[3]

Marx viewed such abstract concepts of justice, rule of law, and
equality before the law as fictions, veiling the true class character of
the law. Bourgeois justice, with its emphasis on contract and private
property, excluded the masses. In the area of public law in capitalist
society, Marx held that law merely reinforces the interests of the
owners of the means of production, whose interests are represented
through political, legislative, executive, and judicial institutions of the
state.

With the abolition of classes under communism, Marx reasoned,
there would be no further need of law, since there would no longer
be a ruling class needing the law to suppress or coerce other classes.
In time, law and the state would wither away altogether. So too, the
Marxist interpretation argued that all crime is, at its root, a manifestation of class antagonisms. With the abolition of classes under communism, all crime would vanish. The Marxian conception of law
manifested a pronounced degree of utopianism that influenced Russian radicals during the last two decades of the tsarist regime and
Bolshevik jurists during the first two decades of Soviet power.

Like many political activists and radicals of his time, Lenin was
attracted to the study of law, completing his degree at St. Petersburg
University in 1891 as a correspondence student, having been expelled
for revolutionary activities. Since the 1860s, the law schools had been

in the forefront of political and social reform, often attracting students dedicated to revolutionary change. Lenin's older brother, Aleksandr Ulyanov, also had been a law student at St. Petersburg University. However, in 1887 he was arrested for his part in an attempt to assassinate Alexander III and was executed. The execution had a profound effect on the young Vladimir Il'ich Ulyanov, who thereafter devoted himself to revolutionary activity under the pseudonym Lenin.

The writings of Marx and Engels provided only scant guidelines for Lenin to follow in constructing a socialist state. Marx was first and foremost a social critic, not an architect of the new economic and political order. In the area of legal administration, Marx offered even fewer prescriptions. He merely stated that all crime is the result of social and economic contradictions; when those differences are eliminated under socialism, crime will vanish. Like Marx, Lenin envisaged the eventual transition to a communist society in which coercive instruments of the state and law would no longer be necessary and would, indeed, wither away. However, Lenin argued that during the transition from capitalism to communism it would be necessary to establish a "proletarian dictatorship" under which law and the state would continue to exist. In this phase, the coercive power of the state and legal institutions would be utilized to defend the interests of the masses, rather than those of a small ruling elite. The only concrete precedents for the administration of justice available to Lenin were the informal, popularly elected revolutionary tribunals established during the Paris Commune (March 28–May 28, 1871) and the 1905 Revolution in Russia.[4]

Decree No. 1 on the courts of the Bolshevik government, published on December 7, 1917, abolished the tsarist judicial system, the Procuracy, and the bar. A new system of people's courts and revolutionary tribunals was established. The people's courts had limited jurisdiction: criminal cases involving sentences up to two years and civil cases of disputes over 3,000 rubles. In order to reflect greater citizen participation, the people's courts included two lay judges who sat with the full-time professional judge. The revolutionary tribunals became a primary vehicle for political repression in defense of the revolutionary order. To promote participation of the masses in the judicial process, one judge and six lay assessors (lay judges) were elected to each tribunal.

The procedures governing the functioning of the newly established people's courts and revolutionary tribunals were kept intentionally simple. The Bolsheviks, reacting to the elaborate and often arcane system of judicial due process under the tsars, wished to construct a system in which citizens would settle their disputes "with simplicity, without elaborately organized tribunals, without legal representation, without complicated laws, and without a labyrinth of rules of procedure and evidence."[5] In some instances, accused persons were brought before public gatherings at which comrades would serve as social accusers or defenders. Guided by a revolutionary sense of justice, the tribunals cracked down on economic crimes. Members of the aristocratic and middle classes were often convicted on flimsy evidence. The collapse of pre-revolutionary legal institutions resulted in a dramatic increase in crime. One account states that the numbers of robberies and murders in Moscow in 1918 were ten to fifteen times higher than in 1913.[6]

The situation Lenin confronted in the lawless and chaotic days following the overthrow of the Provisional Government in November 1917 called for a legal system to provide law and order. He wrote:

There is no doubt that we live in a sea of illegality and that local influences are one of the greatest, if not the greatest obstacle to the establishment of legality and culture . . . It is clear that in light of these conditions we have the firmest guarantee . . . that the Party create a small, centralized collegium capable of countering local influences, local and any bureaucratism and establishing an actual, uniform conception of legality in the entire republic and the entire federation.[7]

In the face of the deteriorating situation, Bolshevik jurists grappled with the problem of coercion and law. Some favored an end to state coercion. For instance, one tribunal official proclaimed, "The socialist criminal code must not know punishment as a means of influence on the criminal."[8] Others were reluctant to abandon punishment altogether. Lenin opted for strict state coercion to stamp out vestiges of bourgeois society. In the political pamphlet *State and Revolution*, he had outlined the fundamental principles of revolutionary justice: smash the old state machine and set up new revolutionary tribunals; make these tribunals simple, informal, and open to mass participation; subordinate law to revolutionary goals and the party (for all law has a class character; if it does not serve the Bolsheviks' purposes, it will be serving the purposes of counterrevolutionary elements); and use merciless force toward the eventual goal of reaching a society in which there will be no need for coercion. He concluded, "to curb increases in time, hooliganism, bribery, speculation, and outrages of all kinds . . . we need time and we need an iron hand."[9]

Thus, in the early days of the Soviet regime, there coexisted two countervailing trends in Soviet law: the Marxist, utopian trend, which stressed both the withering away of the state and the creation of popular, informal tribunals to administer revolutionary justice, and the dictatorial trend, which advocated the use of law and legal institutions to suppress all opposition.[10]

Two of the leading proponents of the utopian trend in law were Piotr Stuchka and Evgeny Pashukanis. Stuchka was one of the founders of the Communist Party in Latvia. He graduated from St. Petersburg University faculty of law in 1888. After the revolution he became the first commissar of justice and chief of the Section of Law and State and the Institute of Soviet Construction, both part of the Communist Academy. Later he was named the first president of the USSR Supreme Court. Stuchka's legal philosophy was very much in line with that of Lenin; he advocated the creation of a distinctive, revolutionary "Soviet law" to govern the transitional period from capitalism to communism. Stuchka also argued, like Lenin, for a class-based conception of law. Only after all classes were abolished under communism would law and the state wither away.

The withering away of law figured much more prominently in the work of E. B. Pashukanis. Pashukanis, the son of a Lithuanian peasant, also studied law at St. Petersburg University prior to World War I, but due to his revolutionary activity he was forced to leave Russia and finished his legal education at the University of Munich. Pashukanis argued that contract relations in capitalist society extended to virtually all branches of the law. Thus, labor relations were seen as a series of worker/employer contracts; family law as a series of contracts among family members; and public law a series of contracts between the citizen and the state.

For Pashukanis, law mirrors the capitalist notion of commodity exchange relations and reaches its highest point of development under capitalism. The "commodity exchange theory of law" came to dominate Soviet juridical thinking in the late 1920s. Pashukanis argued that "Soviet jurists and legislators were not creating a proletarian or socialist system of law, but were merely putting to their own use the bourgeois law that they had inherited."[11] The task confronting Soviet jurists, he argued, was not the creation of a distinctive body of Soviet law, rather the transformation of pre-existing laws to meet the needs of the Revolution during the transitional period to communism, at which time law and the state would no longer be necessary. Pashukanis' major work, *The General Theory of Law and Marxism*, was written during the midst of the New Economic Policy (NEP) that marked a tactical retreat from the gains of the Revolution.[12] Just as private ownership was permitted under the guise of "proletarian state capitalism," Pashukanis argued that the Bolsheviks could use legal norms to seek tactical revolutionary aims of destroying the old order, yet he never lost sight of the central Marxist tenet: "the withering away of law is the yardstick by which we measure the degree of proximity of a jurist to Marxism."[13]

Pashukanis and other utopian jurists envisioned the day when economic planning and technical regulation supplant the need for legal coercion: "the role of the purely legal superstructure, the role of law – declines, and from this can be derived the general rule that as [technical] regulation becomes more effective, the weaker and less significant the role of law and the legal superstructure in its pure form."[14]

By 1930, the Communist Academy had brought all Soviet legal scholarship and education under its control and Pashukanis' theories were the accepted dogma. Rival schools of thought were discouraged; the Institute of Soviet Law was absorbed into the Communist Academy, its scholarly journal was abolished and the institute's director, A. A. Piontkovsky, a noted expert on criminal law, was dismissed. Piontkovsky had been one of Pashukanis' harshest critics, charging that Pashukanis had confused the ideal-type concept of commodity exchange relations with a theory of law. Other critics disagreed with Pashukanis' position that all law is the product of capitalist society, thus ignoring the importance of Roman law and feudal law, or the possibility of a distinctive Soviet law. In the early 1930s, the tone of Pashukanis' critics became increasingly strident; some accused him of "bourgeois legal individualism," "legal nihilism," and even his former associate, Stuchka, openly criticized his approach.[15]

With the end of NEP and Stalin's initiation of rapid industrialization and collectivization of agriculture, official support for the withering away of the state and law rapidly diminished. Stalin's program for the rapid, forced reconfiguration of Soviet society called for a strong and stable state apparatus and effective mechanisms to enforce its policies and laws. In his address to the April 1929 Central Committee Plenum, Stalin warned against promoting hostile and antagonistic attitudes toward law and the state among the masses.[16] Renewing his campaign against the wealthy peasants (kulaks), he argued for an intensification of the dictatorship of the proletariat, rather than the withering away of the state. Stalin awkwardly tried to reconcile the

Marxist notion of withering away of the state with his own need for a stable and powerful legal regime:

We are for the withering away of the state, while at the same time we stand for strengthening the dictatorship of the proletariat which represents the most potent and mighty authority of all state authorities that have existed to this time. The highest development of state authority to the end of making ready the conditions for the withering away of state authority: there you have the Marxist formula. Is this "contradictory"? Yes, it is "contradictory". But it is a living, vital contradiction and it completely reflects Marxist dialectics.[17]

In an effort to preserve his status as the leading legal theoretician, Pashukanis revised his theories, by stressing the role of the state and state coercion in guaranteeing the functioning of the legal superstructure. Writing in 1932, Pashukanis notes:

Law in the conditions of the proletarian dictatorship has always had the goal of protecting the interests of the working majority, the suppression of class elements hostile to the proletariat, and the defense of socialist construction . . . As such, it is radically different from bourgeois law despite the formal resemblance of individual statutes.[18]

By justifying the political role of the state and state coercion, on the one hand, and the withering away of criminal law and judicial due process, on the other hand, Pashukanis inevitably contributed to Stalin's reign of terror. Pashukanis and his associate, Nikolai Krylenko, drafted new codes of "criminal policy" to replace the existing codes of criminal law and process. These draft codes subordinated judicial process to political expediency, thus legitimizing the use of terror. Arguing for "political elasticity" of laws and against the notion of stability of law, Pashukanis declared: "For us revolutionary legality is a problem which is 99 percent political."[19]

By the time of the 17th Party Congress in 1934, Stalin's position had definitely shifted to emphasize legal formality and stability of laws. Andrei Vyshinsky, Stalin's newly appointed procurator-general, criticized Pashukanis and Krylenko for "legal nihilism."[20] Contract law was resurrected in order to rationalize economic relations among emerging state enterprises. In 1936, during the drafting of a new constitution, family law was revived and strengthened. Divorces were harder to obtain and abortions were outlawed. The new constitution inserted the right of ownership of personal property and calls for new codes of civil and criminal law implied an end of Pashukanis' emphasis on "criminal policy" and "elasticity." Stalin proclaimed, "stability of the laws is necessary for us now more than ever."[21] Pashukanis was arrested in January 1937 and disappeared into the labor camp system (Gulag). The experiment with the Marxist concept of withering away of the state and law had ended. Law and the state had become the handmaidens of Stalin's dictatorial power.

The dual state

One of the enduring paradoxes of Soviet legal history is that after years of neglect due to the influence of the Marxist notion of withering away of the state and law, important strides were made under Stalin in reinstituting Romanist concepts of law, a professional bar, and formal courts deciding cases based on sophisticated, written codes of criminal and civil law and procedure. At the same time, however, the power of the state was used to stamp out all opposition to Stalin and his regime. This included the widespread use of legally sanctioned terror against Soviet citizens.

In his hallmark study of the Nazi legal order, Ernst Frankel developed the concept of the "dual state," consisting of the "prerogative state" in which the political leadership enjoys virtually unchallenged power and the law merely reinforces its rule by force and political expediency, and the "normative state" in which sanctioned legal norms prescribe the permissible boundaries of citizen–state relations.[22] The legal system in the USSR under Stalin clearly resembled Frankel's "dual state."

Stalin's policies of forced industrialization and collectivization of agriculture called for stable laws to enforce his directives. At his insistence, the Procuracy's jurisdiction was expanded in 1932 and again in 1935, professional legal education resumed in 1937, and new drafts of criminal and civil law and procedure appeared in 1938.

The single biggest contribution of Stalin to the enlargement of the normative state, however, was the enactment of a new constitution in 1936. The constitution clearly set out the powers of the state and the rights and duties of Soviet citizens. The areas of state and administrative law, which had been banished from law school curricula under Pashukanis' influence, were revived. Article 14 of the constitution called for the drafting of new all-union civil and criminal codes. Those codes, which appeared in draft form in 1937, reestablished the individual as a "juridical person" with the capacity to enter into legal relationships. Similarly, the civil code defined and classified various types of property: state property, collective property, and personal property. In their influential texts on civil and criminal procedure, Kleinman and Strogovich criticized the atmosphere of "procedural nihilism" that had characterized Pashukanis' approach. They argued that the simplicity and "elasticity" favored by the utopian Marxist jurists resulted in the weakening of the role of civil and criminal proceedings and undermined the authority of the courts.[23]

While the renewed respect for law and the normative state under Stalin can be seen as a progressive step, law was used to reinforce Stalin's dictatorship and much of the terror was carried on outside of established judicial institutions. The authoritarian tone of legal policy was voiced by Andrei Vyshinsky, Stalin's procurator-general and chief prosecutor in the great purge trials of the 1930s. Vyshinsky defined law as a set of rules laid down by the state and guaranteed by the state's monopoly of force.[24] In the wake of Stalin's dictatorial legal policies, utopianism all but vanished. Vyshinsky, speaking before a group of public prosecutors in 1936, stated: "the old twaddle about the mobilization of socially active workers . . . must be set aside; something new is needed at the present time."[25]

Inevitably, the lines dividing the "prerogative state" and the "normative state" were fuzzy. In many instances, laws were vaguely defined intentionally in order to permit state prosecutors maximum flexibility in apprehending and convicting "enemies of the people." Perhaps the clearest example of the carryover of Pashukanis' ideas of "elasticity" in the law was the infamous doctrine of analogy. Analogy was introduced into Soviet criminal law during NEP and reflected the emphasis of that time on revolutionary justice. According to the doctrine of analogy, a person could be punished for committing an act that, although not expressly prohibited in the criminal code, is analogous to a prohibited act. The effect of the doctrine of analogy was to widen the already wide definition of political crimes afforded in Article 58 of the Russian criminal code of 1926. Article 58 included fourteen sections, concerning crimes ranging from "anti-Soviet agitation" to "sabotage" and "terrorism."

Much of the legal administration of the Stalin years was carried on outside of established judicial institutions. Special boards of the Ministry of Internal Affairs were set up to facilitate campaigns against anti-Soviet elements and to silence potential opponents. The boards were given extraordinary powers and were not required to follow established judicial procedure. They had the authority to imprison or exile for a term of up to five years anyone considered to be "socially dangerous." In the late thirties and again in the 1940s the maximum sentence was extended to ten and then twenty-five years. Proceedings of the boards were not public, the accused had no right to counsel, and there was no appeal of verdicts. The laws enforced by the boards were often changed abruptly and without publication, so that numerous persons were convicted for acts that they did not know to be illegal. The boards consigned millions of Soviet citizens to "corrective labor camps." Some Western analysts estimate the prison labor force by 1941 at 3.5 million.[26] Thus, the security police apparatus was the single largest employer in the Soviet Union and wielded not only political but tremendous economic power.

Although the dictatorial trend in Soviet law reached its peak in the mid-1930s, the intrusion of the prerogative state in Soviet law was already apparent as of the end of NEP in 1928 and 1929. By June 1930, the RSFSR procurator complained to the 16th Party Congress that political authorities were not only commandeering and preempting legal institutions in the rural areas, but were actually interfering with them in their campaign against the kulakhs.[27] Laws enacted in November 1929 provided compensation to victims of "kulakh violence" and established severe criminal sanctions for the "rapacious slaughter of livestock."[28]

With the introduction of Stalin's "revolution from above," the whole society began to work on a command basis. Internal passports were issued in 1932 to cut down on workers moving from one job to another, and labor books were introduced to record an individual's work record. Collective farmers were not issued internal passports and, consequently, were unable to leave their farms. Criminal penalties were imposed for labor violations. The death penalty was extended to various economic offenses such as hoarding of silver coins, "wrecking" (sabotage), negligence resulting in damage to state property, and theft of public property. Absenteeism or chronic tardiness in appearing for work was interpreted as an act against the state and punished by up to five years in prison. In line with Stalin's conservative family policies, abortions were outlawed except in cases of medical necessity, and laws on divorce were made much more restrictive.

The secret police combed the streets at night in their infamous "black marias" (black sedans), stopping at apartments to pick up people whom "informers" had reported. Rumors or a careless comment by a child at school were sufficient to result in imprisonment or death for a parent. Many Soviet citizens recall the years when they had suitcases packed with warm clothing waiting by the door in case they should be awakened by the secret police in the night and taken away.

Under Stalin's lead, the secret police were authorized to shoot their victims without trial, most frequently for supposedly sabotaging Stalin's economic campaigns. Among those secretly tried and executed and those executed without trial were bacteriologists charged with causing an epidemic among horses; officials of the food industry charged with sabotaging food supplies; and several agricultural experts, state farm officials, and academics accused of mismanagement and "wrecking." Higher-level officials charged with sabotage were treated to elaborate show trials at which most confessed after long periods of interrogation and torture by the secret police.

In April 1935, not long after the assassination of Leningrad party boss Sergei Kirov, a new provision was introduced into the law that extended criminal penalties including execution, to children as young as twelve. The purpose of the law was to allow police interrogators to threaten those under investigation with the prosecution and execution of their children.

The terror culminated in three major show trials of Stalin's political rivals during the period from 1936 to 1938. The first trial began on August 19, 1936. Sixteen persons, including Stalin's former associates on the Politburo, Zinoviev, and Kamenev; were charged with being members of a Trotskyite terrorist circle. The trial was held in the October Hall of the House of Trade Unions and heard by the Military Collegium of the Supreme Court. The audience consisted of a group of carefully selected, well-rehearsed employees of the security police (NKVD) and approximately thirty foreign journalists and diplomats.[29] With only two exceptions, the accused pleaded guilty to a long list of charges, including organizing the murder of Kirov and plotting the murder of Stalin and several other members of the Presidium of the Communist Party. No evidence was offered in the trials other than the confessions wrested from the accused while they were held by the secret police. All were convicted and executed within twenty-four hours of the verdict. No appeals were permitted.

With Zinoviev eliminated, Stalin turned his attention to two remaining adversaries, Bukharin and Rykov. Before plotting their elaborate show trials, however, he first dismissed Henry Yagoda as head of the NKVD and replaced him with Nikolai Yezhov. Six months after his dismissal, Yagoda was arrested and later he was tried and executed. Yagoda carried to his grave extensive knowledge of Stalin's involvement in Kirov's murder and countless other atrocities.

The second major show trial took place in Moscow in January 1937. Among the seventeen persons arraigned were Grigori Pyatakov, deputy commissar for heavy industry, and the publicist Karl Radek. In a new twist, many of the defendants were accused of economic sabotage (wrecking trains, introducing gas into coal mines, and so on). All were found guilty, and most were shot.

Throughout 1937, Yezhov rounded up and liquidated Yagoda's former senior subordinates in the NKVD. More than 3,000 NKVD officers were executed in 1937 alone.[30] Many others committed suicide, some by leaping from the windows of their Lubianka offices in full view of the Moscow populace. The purge, known as the *Yezhovshchina* after the newly appointed secret police chief, reached a climax in May through September 1937. Arrests, exile, imprisonment, and execution affected all sections of the population, but focused especially on the elite. Stalin's terror machine continued unabated until the German invasion of the Soviet Union in 1941 and resumed not long after the victory was secured in 1945.

Both the war and the reconstruction after the war required the imposition of strict controls on Soviet society. In 1946 Stalin launched a campaign against the intelligentsia and the arts. A new decree on collective farms eliminated virtually all forms of private economic activity. In 1948 purges resumed in Leningrad. The party officials who led the city through the 900-day siege were arrested and shot.

On January 13, 1953 an ominous item appeared in *Pravda*, announcing the arrest of a group of Kremlin physicians who had supposedly confessed to the murder and attempted murder of various leading Soviet figures. Stalin was apparently planning to use the alleged "Doctors' Plot" as an excuse to launch a new wage of purges. However, on March 4, before the purge could begin, it was announced that Stalin had suffered a stroke two days earlier. He died on the evening of March 5, 1953. The circumstances surrounding Stalin's death remain obscure.

Stalin dominated the Soviet political and legal system for more than a quarter of a century, and his influence was felt long after his death. Stalin created and perfected the use of mass terror to insure his primacy in the system and the blind obedience of his advisors and the citizens. While state-sponsored coercion had been very much in evidence under Lenin during the revolution and the civil war, Stalin carried the use of police terror to new levels. Western estimates, now corroborated by Soviet authorities, indicate that more than 40 million

Soviet citizens may have perished as a direct consequence of Stalin's brutal policies.[31]

While use of terror and arbitrary pseudo-judicial procedures under Stalin greatly expanded the "prerogative state," they also generated a consensus after his death that extra-judicial means should be brought under control. The excesses of the Stalin period created an atmosphere that afforded Soviet jurists their first opportunity in more than thirty years to introduce meaningful legal reforms. Not surprisingly, the most important area of needed reform was in protecting citizens' rights *vis-à-vis* the state.

Perhaps the greatest legacy of Stalin was the defeat of the utopian, Marxist school of jurisprudence that favored revolutionary, informal justice, and the creation of a coherent and powerful system of state judicial administration. Subsequent efforts to reform it notwithstanding, Stalin's organizational edifice for the Soviet legal system survived more or less in its original form until the demise of the USSR in December 1991. We turn now to a brief survey of the Soviet legal system that Stalin created.

Sources of Soviet law

Drawing on its Romanist roots, the Soviet legal system was a civil law system, in which comprehensive codes of law play a central role. In contrast to the Anglo-American tradition of common law with its emphasis on judicially created laws through precedent, the Soviet legal system emphasized statutory laws – primarily codes and statutes – that were legislative enactments. According to Soviet constitutional theory, all power rested in the people, who in turn, elected representative bodies (soviets), which had sole power to pass legislation.[32] The 1936 Constitution envisaged the drafting of centralized uniform codes of law for all the constituent republics, however the only one to be adopted was the 1938 Law on Court Organization. In 1957 the constitution was amended giving the union-republics the power to draft codes of law. The Supreme Soviets of the fifteen union-republics enacted a number of codes of law spanning a broad array of legal issues: civil law and procedure, criminal law and procedure, family law, land law, labor law, corrective labor law, water law, health care law, public education law, mineral resources law, and forestry law. All-union codes existed for air transport, merchant shipping, and customs law, while all-union charters (*ustavy*) were enacted for communications, rail transport, and inland water transport. In addition to these codes, legislative bodies enacted more specific laws, decrees, and edicts. For example, all-union laws were enacted on universal military service, on the protection and use of historical and cultural monuments, and on the Procuracy.[33]

Subordinate to these legislative acts were a wide array of "normative acts": decrees (*postanovlenie*), regulations (*rasporyazhenie*), edicts (*ukazy*), orders (*prikazy*), instructions (*instruktsiie*), and rules (*pravila*). Decrees and regulations were normally issued by the USSR Council of Ministers and occasionally by individual ministries and state committees in directing the economy and executive apparatus. Edicts, orders, instructions, and rules were enacted by ministries, state committees, and other administrative agencies. Normative acts of executive bodies were issued on the authority delegated from superior executive and legislative bodies and could be annulled by them. In addition, the Procuracy had the right to supervise the conformity of such normative acts to the law; however, the Procuracy's power was advisory; it did not have the right to suspend or annul normative acts of Soviet state administration.

Due to its unusual nature, the socialist economy resulted in the need for legally binding acts managing employment relations and property and contract disputes within state enterprises, collective farms, trade unions, and social organizations. Disputes *within* such organizations were resolved by internal administrative procedures and, to a limited extent, by judicial proceedings. Disputes arising *between* state, cooperative, and other institutions and organizations were resolved through a system of state arbitration tribunals (*arbitrazh*).

The system of *arbitrazh* was created in 1931 primarily to reconcile disputes between state enterprises; however, by the mid-1930s it evolved into a system of economic courts. The tribunals had the power to summon parties and witnesses, require submission of documents, and consult experts. According to the 1960 Statute on State *Arbitrazh*, the tribunals could force compliance with contracts, settle tort claims between enterprises, and impose fines. *Arbitrazh* decisions were binding, there was no judicial appeal process, and awards were enforced by warrant.

Another peculiarity of the Soviet legal system was the special status and quasi-governmental role of the Communist Party. Article 6 of the 1977 Constitution proclaimed the CPSU "the leading and guiding force of Soviet society, the nucleus of its political system and of [all] state and public organizations."[34] Party organs issued numerous resolutions, decisions, decrees, programs, directives, rules, statutes and instructions. While most of these were limited to internal party matters and, therefore, not officially considered normative acts, they were binding on all party members and set the programmatic agenda for official state enactments. In many cases, important pieces of new legislation were initiated with joint decrees by party and government bodies. Such joint decrees, however, were largely symbolic and not considered by Soviet legal scholars to be superior to legally binding normative acts of official state bodies.

Technically judicial determinations in the Russian legal system do not establish precedents and are not a source of law. Nevertheless, judicial practice and appellate court judgments inevitably influence court decisions at subordinate levels. Although codes of law are quite comprehensive, they nevertheless contain gaps which the courts attempt to fill. For example, the noted scholar of Soviet law, William Butler, has demonstrated that the doctrine of necessary defense owes much to judicial decisions.[35] The USSR Supreme Court and the supreme courts of the union-republics also issued guiding explanations which were binding on lower-level courts and other agencies and were often cited along with references to legislative acts when courts decided cases.[36]

Because the Soviet legal system did not recognize precedents, most judicial decisions were not published. Even many Supreme Court decisions remained unpublished. During the Stalin era, judicial proceedings were often conducted in closed chambers and court decisions were considered state secrets.

Since law does not evolve by judicial precedents, it falls to legislative bodies to undertake periodic revisions of the law codes, bringing them up to date and responsive to new developments. Codification is, however, a laborious process. For example, work on the revision of the 1926 criminal code began in 1939 and was completed only in 1960. As we have seen, major codification efforts were undertaken during Stalin's reign (although few came to completion) and even more active codification followed his death in 1953.

Court structure and procedure

Although there were several revisions in the supervision and competence of Soviet courts between the late 1920s and the collapse of the USSR in 1991, the general court structure remained essentially the same. At the lowest level were district or city people's courts which heard approximately 95 percent of all civil and criminal cases of first instance.[37] Local courts were divided into "chambers" or divisions for civil and criminal cases. Usually several judges served in each chamber and they often specialized in particular types of cases (family law, criminal law, labor law). In some cities and regions, judges divided the region into zones with a judge hearing all the cases arising from that particular zone. At this lowest level, cases were heard by one professional judge and two people's assessors. Until the reforms of 1989 professional judges were elected in general elections in their respective districts for a term of five years. No prior legal experience or education was required. In the 1930s the majority of judges had no legal training, but by the early 1960s more than 95 percent of all judges had a higher legal education.[38]

Given the crucial role of the judge in the Soviet legal system, it is not surprising that the party carefully screened all candidates for election to the bench. Virtually all Soviet judges above the local level were party members, and all judges fell under the party's power of appointment, or nomenklatura.[39]

As in other civil law systems employing inquisitorial rather than adversarial procedure, judges in the USSR played an active part in judicial proceedings. They were the first to call for evidence and question witnesses – before either the prosecution or the defense. Their function was not only to determine innocence or guilt, but also to educate the accused and all present in the courtroom about Soviet morality. Soviet judges were an important instrument of socialization. When pronouncing sentence, judges often berated the accused for failing to uphold socialist values, for being drunk in public, or for setting a bad example to children.

People's assessors were citizens, elected at general meetings of factories, offices, collective farms, or residential blocs and screened by local party officials, who served for a term of two and one-half years. Their function resembled that of a jury in a common-law system, however they not only decided guilt or innocence, but also were full, participating members of the bench with the right to call and question witnesses, examine evidence, and set punishment. All judicial decisions were voted on in closed chambers, so it is not known what impact people's assessors had on the courts' decisions. It is assumed that the judges' prestige and legal education were deciding factors in the resolution of cases. At the appellate level and above, where the questions under review were procedural or involved technical points of law, cases were decided by panels of three professional judges.

Above the local courts were regional courts and the supreme courts of the union-republics and autonomous republics of the former USSR. These courts acted as the courts of first instance in cases designated by law or in cases deemed too complex for local courts. They also heard cases on appeal or protest. Protests generally were made by the prosecutor or the president of the people's court in a criminal case when the lower court acquitted, or in a civil case where the prosecutor felt a mistake or error in judgment had been made.[40] Appeals or protests had to be filed within seven days for criminal cases and within ten days for civil cases. Such actions suspended execution of the court's judgment. Protests against a verdict that had entered into force could be brought within one year.

At the pinnacle of the Soviet judicial system stood the USSR Supreme Court. The Supreme Court played a substantially different role than the Supreme Court in the United States. It was not a constitutional court, ruling on the constitutionality of acts of executive or legislative bodies. Its primary functions were to hear appeals of cases arising from the republic supreme courts and from military tribunals and to issue instructions and guidance to lower-level courts. The USSR Supreme Court consisted of twenty judges appointed by the USSR Supreme Soviet for a term of five years with the possibility of reappointment.[41]

The party and legal policy-making

The Communist Party, as Lenin stated, was the self-proclaimed "mind, honor, and conscience of the Soviet people." Political decision-making authority lay in its highest ranks. The 1986 Party Program called for the "further enhancement of the role and importance of the Communist Party as the leading and guiding force of Soviet society." In the realm of judicial policy, the program stated: "the strengthening of the legal basis of state and social life, the unswerving observance of socialist legality and law and order and the improvement of the work of the judicial organs, organs of supervision of the prosecutor's office, and justice and internal affairs organs have been and remain a matter of constant concern for the Party."[42]

The party's hegemony in the administration of justice derived from several sources. Party approval was required before a person could be appointed to any influential position in the legal apparatus: judge, procurator, advocate, or police official. This power to fill personnel positions – nomenklatura – was a significant control device that the party used to maintain its strict hold on administration. Party organs also directly nominated persons for election, including judges and even people's assessors. The personnel screening process extended to the lowest levels of the party organization. The result was that all those who investigated, prosecuted, defended, presided, and even studied the administration of justice in the Soviet union had to pass through a system of political filters before they could take office or assume their responsibilities.

The party also played a central role in coordinating the work of all judicial bodies. Party officials met with local law-enforcement officials on a frequent and regular basis to plan anti-crime campaigns. A single campaign against a specific type of crime in a region might require the participation of the Procuracy, police, courts, the republic's Ministry of Trade, factory managers, comrades' courts, trade unions, councils on crime prevention, and primary party organizations. Commissions on juvenile affairs, Komsomol organizations, fire, public safety, and pollution inspection agencies, and the State Standards Committee might also be involved. The party played the central role of overseeing the general coordination of these agencies.

Despite the inclusion of a judicial independence clause in both the 1936 and 1977 Constitutions, Soviet jurists never fully adopted the notion of an independent judiciary in the Western sense. Party organs were instructed to play an active role in supervising the judicial process. A 1971 editorial in the USSR Ministry of Justice's journal, *Sovetskaya yustitsiya*, stated: "Guidance by the Communist Party surpasses all political and judicial means of assuring that the courts observe socialist legality in their actions . . . The task of local Party organizations is, while not interfering in the judicial process, actively to influence courts to improve their work, to instill in officers of the court a high sense of discipline, and fulfill party and government decisions."[43]

In 1956, a study group of the prestigious Institute of State and Law of the Academy of Sciences was impaneled to address the issue of the legal abuses of the Stalin years and to suggest measures to avoid repetitions. While establishing the principle of non-interference in legal cases, the authors concluded that "the court does not stand and cannot stand outside of politics . . . beyond the guidance of the Party."[44]

There is a fine line, however, between party supervision and direction, on the one hand, and party interference, on the other. Impermissible party interference in the administration of justice occurred not infrequently when a party organ or official directly intervened in the disposition of an individual case by bringing political pressure to bear on the arresting officer, investigator, prosecutor, judge, or defense attorney. Former Soviet defense lawyers who emigrated to the West reported that judges rarely received instructions in individual non-political cases. They noted, however, a more subtle influence. "Judges got the word from the way the wind was blowing."[45] This was especially the case during organized campaigns against various crimes. During an anti-bribery campaign, one Soviet defense attorney privately exclaimed, "If you have a bribery case these days, you might as well give up."[46] Thus, anti-crime campaigns tended to blur the line between administration and adjudication. During campaigns, there was the risk that party and police organs would usurp the proper role of judicial institutions.

Party interference was not restricted to anti-crime campaigns, however. Advocates, judges, procurators, police, and investigators were required to make monthly, quarterly, and annual reports to the party apparatus on the cases in which they had been involved. A former advocate from Leningrad observed that too many acquittals were frowned on by party officials.[47] Rapid increases of the crime rate also reflected badly on police officials, procurators, and local party secretaries.

Even more damaging to professional careers than underfulfilling quotas for arrests, convictions, or a reduction of the crime rate was the discovery of a major scandal involving official corruption or organized crime. Regional party secretaries were held ultimately responsible for coordinating all services of the central ministries in their respective regions.[48] This included supervision of the orderly fulfillment of economic development programs, provision of social services, and maintenance of law and order. Should top-ranking personnel in a principal industrial enterprise be arrested for embezzlement or theft of property from the factory, should a scandal surface concerning graft and corruption in the allocation of housing or other social services, or should it come to light that the police and the Procuracy in the region have conspired to falsify reports understating the extent of crime, the regional secretary was likely to be held personally accountable. For example, a well-publicized case of high-level corruption in the Azerbaijan Republic in 1975 resulted in five executions and prison sentences for fifty-nine other officials, including several local party secretaries.[49] If the secretary managed to save his own position, it was because he had successfully disassociated himself from his subordinates – the factory manager, the heads of regional social service department, or the chief of police and the procurator.

Party members were subject to a certain amount of double jeopardy, being accountable both to regular courts and to disciplinary action by the CPSU. Article 12 of the Party Rules states: "A Party member shall bear dual responsibility to the state and the Party for the violation of Soviet laws. Persons who have committed indictable offenses are expelled from the CPSU."[50] In fact, it was not unusual for judges to ask whether accused party members had been disciplined by their party organizations for alleged offenses.[51] Such information could be highly prejudicial since party scrutiny of accused members did not afford the same procedural guarantees granted to criminal defendants in court and the standards for assessing "guilt" were quite different.

Crime in the USSR

According to Marx, crime is the manifestation of class antagonisms. With the abolition of classes under socialism, all crime should vanish. Although crime did not vanish in the USSR, certain types of criminal activity were much less prevalent than in Western societies. Comparing crime rates is, however, difficult because crime statistics in the Soviet Union were considered classified "state secrets." Nevertheless, there appeared to be far fewer robberies, murders, and other violent crimes by Soviet citizens than in the United States. Strict gun control, the threat of harsh punishment, the omnipresent police, and the low incidence of drug abuse largely accounted for this. There was also less monetary incentive for violent crime in the USSR than in the West. Most Soviet citizens had ample amounts of money; consequently, there was less motivation to commit robbery. The theft of desirable consumer goods was quite common, however, because they were in great demand and difficult to obtain legally.

Soviet sources indicated that between 80 and 85 percent of all violent crimes were committed under the influence of alcohol and usually involved family members, close friends, or neighbors.[52] Committing a crime under the influence of alcohol is not a mitigating factor, according to Soviet law, but an aggravating factor. Alcohol abuse, which was widespread in the former USSR, is the primary cause of almost three-fourths of all divorces.[53] Overcrowded housing conditions combined with alcohol abuse often result in domestic violence.

Anonymous street crime, until recently, was much less frequent in the Soviet Union than in other societies, although there were reports in the press of youth gangs attacking total strangers on the street "simply for something to do."[54] Juveniles accounted for approximately 12 percent of all murders, 22 percent of all robberies, 59 percent of burglaries, and 49 percent of all rapes in the mid-1970s.[55] The portrait of the juvenile offender in the USSR does not differ greatly from that in other societies: the offender was usually male, lived in a city, came from a broken home, and undertook delinquent acts while under the influence of alcohol and as a member of a group. School dropouts were twenty-four times more likely to engage in criminal activity than were juveniles who remained in school. Similarly, youths who came from homes in which violence was common were nine to ten times more likely to become juvenile offenders.[56] A Soviet sociological study of juvenile offenders found that three-quarters were introduced to alcohol in the home – almost half before the age of thirteen.[57] As a rite of passage around the age of twelve or thirteen, a boy was expected to split a bottle of vodka with his father to celebrate becoming a man.

Punishment and rehabilitation of offenders

Marxist–Leninist ideology was perhaps more evident in sentencing and corrections than anywhere else in the Soviet legal system. Soviet ideology stressed state property over private property, and this was reflected in criminal law. The maximum sentence for the theft of personal property was two years; the maximum sentence for the theft of state property was three years.[58] Negligent destruction of private property could be punished by deprivation of freedom for a term of up to one year, while the term extended to three years for the negligent destruction of state property.[59]

Some activities that are normal in other societies were illegal and strictly punished in the USSR for ideological reasons. According to Marxist–Leninist doctrine, charging interest, speculation, and profiteering are all means of obtaining "unearned income" and are, therefore, exploitative. Speculation was defined as "buying up and reselling goods for the purpose of making a profit" and could result in a prison term of two years, confiscation of property, and a fine of 30 rubles.[60] The penalty for speculation on a grand scale was two to seven years.

Article 154-1 of the Criminal Code of the RSFSR illustrated one of the more Kafkaesque aspects of the Soviet planned economy. In the USSR, the price of bread was artificially kept low in order to make it affordable for the average citizen. The price of feed for chickens and livestock, by contrast, was quite high. Consequently, many Soviet citizens bought bread to feed to their animals on their private land plots.

Article 154-1 was introduced in 1963 specifically to stop this practice. A fine was levied for the first offense, but for subsequent offenses the penalty could include up to one year of deprivation of freedom.

The maximum sentence for a first-time offender in the former USSR after the 1958 reform of criminal law was fifteen years, but for most crimes the sentence was no more than seven years.[61] Soviet jurists were highly critical of Western legal systems that routinely mete out life sentences. One prominent jurist exclaimed, "How can you say that you have a system of corrections in the United States when you lock up prisoners for life?" By Soviet logic fifteen years should be adequate time to rehabilitate a criminal.

Soviet law allowed the parole or conditional release of prisoners who had served as little as one-half of their sentences. Parole with compulsory work assignment could also be awarded after serving just one-third of the sentence. In addition, periodic amnesties were granted, usually commemorating a political holiday. In 1970, for instance, the sentences for most inmates were reduced in honor of the hundredth anniversary of Lenin's birth. In 1979, a selective amnesty was announced for many categories of women and juvenile inmates in honor of the International Year of the Child. Presumably, amnesties were intended to underscore socialist values. By releasing a prisoner early in honor of Lenin's birth or some other patriotic event, it was hoped that the former inmate would be more supportive of the party and the values it sought to uphold.

The death penalty, by shooting, was applied in the former USSR in cases of treason, espionage, terrorist acts, sabotage, banditry, disrupting the work of prison camps, hijacking, and intentional homicide committed under aggravating circumstances (e.g. murder for profit, murder to cover up a previous crime, murder of a pregnant woman, rape-murder, or especially brutal murder). Capital punishment was also occasionally employed to punish state or party officials among others in extreme cases of theft of state property, counterfeiting, speculation on a large scale, and bribe-taking under certain circumstances.[62] Party and state officials were expected to be model Soviet citizens. If they abused their positions of public trust for their own profit, they were severely punished. For instance, in 1985, the head bookkeeper of a construction firm in the Ukraine was accused of forming a criminal conspiracy with a number of stores in Kiev to steal state property. Over a period of years, the group systematically embezzled more than 327,000 rubles (almost $225,000). The Kiev oblast criminal court sentenced the bookkeeper to death. His accomplices were sentenced to long terms in labor colonies.[63]

The ideological stress in the USSR on the value of labor was reflected in corrections and the punishment of criminals. Few prisons exist in the former Soviet Union, and they are only for hardened criminals who are too dangerous to be supervised at the normal labor colonies. The majority of inmates serve their sentences in labor camps that are stratified in terms of degree of security, difficulty of work, quality and quantity of food, and privileges. For example, one source indicates that in a strict-regime camp (maximum security), inmates are expected to work in difficult jobs (frequently involving outdoor work such as construction, lumbering, mining, and so on). At a medium-security facility, the work is usually indoors, and the ration consists of bread, salt, and water with one hot meal every other day.[64] Inmates may be transferred from one regime facility to another as a reward for good behavior. Infringement of the rules of the labor colony can also prolong the sentence of an inmate or even result in a transfer to a stricter regime facility. Thus, there is every incentive for the inmate to cooperate with the camp authorities. The Soviet correctional system had an astonishingly high success rate. In the early 1970s it was estimated that only 9 to 23 percent of all inmates repeated offenses, compared to more than 60 percent in the United States.[65]

The educational role of Soviet law

As in other societies, law in the USSR both guided and punished. Whether it emphasized the rehabilitation of offenders or communicated a "moral lesson" by executing officials guilty of stealing state property, the Soviet legal system was designed to play an educational role. Law is a teacher; it conveys and enforces societal values and channels behavior into acceptable norms and patterns. Harold Berman notes a paternalistic strain marked Soviet law and practice:

The subject of law, legal man, is treated less as an independent possessor of rights and duties, who knows what he wants, than as a dependent member of the collective group, a youth, whom the law must not only protect against the consequences of his own ignorance, but also must guide and train and discipline ... It is apparent that the Soviet emphasis on the educational role of law presupposes a new conception of man. The Soviet citizen is considered to be a member of a growing, unfinished, still immature society, which is moving toward a new and higher phase of development. As a subject of law, or a litigant in court, he is like a child or youth to be trained, guided, disciplined, protected. The judge plays the part of a parent or guardian; indeed, the whole legal system is parental.[66]

Paternalism is not a recent development in Soviet law. In 1917, D. I. Kursky, Lenin's commissar of justice, remarked, " It does not matter that many points in our decrees will never be carried out; their task is to teach the masses how to take practical steps."[67] Soviet law, apart from governing the interactions of citizens and the relation of their rights and duties, was concerned with the development of citizens' moral well-being and their "law-consciousness." Article 20 of the RSFSR Criminal Code stated that the goal of punishment was not only retribution for undertaking a crime, but it also strove to achieve the "correction and reeducation of the criminal in a spirit of honest orientation to labor, exact observance of laws and respect for the rules of the socialist community."[68]

The dual purpose of Soviet law – to punish and to educate – surfaced in various concrete legal policies. In 1957, for example, Khrushchev initiated "anti-parasite" laws aimed at those profiting from the fringe economy: prostitution, begging, vagrancy, private speculation, and other sources of "unearned income." Any able-bodied adult who was found leading an "antisocial, parasitic way of life" could be brought before a general meeting of townspeople and banished. Proceedings were neither trials nor the actions of a court; as such, they were condemned by many jurists as inconsistent with the concepts of "rule of law" and socialist legality. Proponents argued, however, that the parasite laws and their method of enforcement pointed toward realization of the utopian Marxist notion of the withering away of the institutions of the state.

Anti-parasite legislation was introduced in nine republics. With the exception of Latvia, parasite laws were not enacted in any of the European republics of the USSR where Western traditions of law were more ingrained. While jurists appear to have been unable to alter the draft parasite laws, their objections were heeded in the major republics.

The legal establishment in general, and the Procuracy in particular, chafed under Khrushchev's policies of informal judicial proceedings and public participation in the administration of justice. Not only did these anti-parasite tribunals circumvent established judicial institutions, thus lowering their credibility, they often were guilty of gross violations of citizens' rights. Furthermore, no appeals were permitted.

Gradually, legal populism became eclipsed by another significant legal development in the late 1950s – the codification of fundamental principles of criminal law and criminal procedure. A trend toward the "juridization" of law swept Soviet jurisprudence after Stalin, enhancing the role of established legal institutions and the legal profession. Jurists associated with this orientation argued that measures pertaining to fringe elements in Soviet society should be relegated to the general area of criminal law. A benchmark of this trend toward "juridization" was the May 4, 1961 RSFSR decree on parasitism that subsequently served as a model for similar legislation in most of the other republics. The decree gave jurisdiction over parasite cases to the criminal courts, bypassing the comrades' courts, which could give only light sentences. Also spurned in the legislation were the public meetings of residential units. For cases of parasitism, the new legislation specified punishments of two to five years of exile with compulsory labor.

In the first six months after the enactment of the decree, there were at least 600 convictions.[69] Of those convicted in 1961, more than half received sentences of four or five years.[70] Despite this harsh policy, there apparently was considerable selectivity in enforcement and prosecution, even during a time of increasingly strident public campaigns against parasites. In the first half of 1961, approximately 96 percent of all parasites were given warnings, not prosecuted, because they heeded the warnings and found proper work.[71]

The case of the anti-parasite legislation illustrates several aspects of the Soviet legal system. The anti-parasite laws were originally initiated to punish anti-social behavior and to socialize Soviet citizens by enlisting their assistance in combating parasitism and hooliganism. In time, however, the professional legal establishment exerted its influence and incorporated the anti-parasite laws into regular judicial procedure. Since Khrushchev, such "juridization" has been a hallmark of socialist legality.

The case of the anti-parasite laws also illustrates the use of law in the USSR as a means of social engineering, that is, as a means of ordering human relations to further the values of Soviet society. This practice is not unique to the Khrushchev era. Gorbachev's much publicized anti-alcohol campaign mobilized the legal establishment in order to discourage alcohol consumption. Prosecutions for public intoxication increased dramatically, and those convicted received harsher penalties.

The USSR's seventy-five-year experiment with socialist law has left an indelible imprint on the Russian legal system and the way in which Russians view the law. As we have seen, law in the USSR emphasized the role of the state over the rights of the individual. Although the utopian, Marxist influences on law declined during the Stalin era, overshadowed by the dictatorial trend, they were not eliminated entirely. It was also during the Stalin years that a third trend, most often referred to as "socialist legality" began to emerge. "Socialist legality" was associated with stability of laws, codification, due process and judicial independence, concepts valued and promoted by an increasingly active legal profession. In chapter 3 we will explore the process of legal reforms from the mid-1950s to the present.

3 The history of legal reform

A law-governed state not only required observance of justice and
human rights, it represented a knife in the very heart of the
system.

Anatoly Sobchak[1]
Mayor, St. Petersburg (1992)

Change was imminent after Stalin's death in 1953. Having endured
constant and pervasive fear for more than two decades, the Soviet
people were ready for a respite from dictatorial coercion. Stalin's
successors moved quickly to destroy the most coercive aspects of
Stalin's "prerogative state" and to rebuild party and state organs,
including legal institutions. Even before the leadership succession
was resolved following Stalin's death, the outlines of the legal
reform began to emerge. Over the next decade, legal reform would
emphasize four main themes: reducing the repressiveness of Soviet
law, restoring judicial due process, redefining the relationship of
citizens and the state, and popularizing the administration of justice.
The first three directions of legal reform soon came to be identified
with the concept of "socialist legality," while the latter represented
a return to the Marxian notion of the withering away of formal
legal institutions.

While the elimination of the worst abuses of the prerogative state
was achieved rather swiftly after Stalin's death, the process of
expanding the "normative state" – the concepts of rule of law, citizens' rights *vis-à-vis* the state, judicial independence, and equality
before the law – has taken much longer. In this chapter we analyze
first the legal reforms of the late 1950s and early 1960s, noting in particular the factors that enabled the reforms to succeed and the issues
on which they focused. We then explore the process of legal reform
introduced by Mikhail Gorbachev in the late 1980s before concluding

with some generalizations about the nature of legal reform in the last years of the Soviet Union.

Eliminating Stalin's repression

Following the long and brutal reign of Stalin, it is not surprising that jurists, politicians, and the citizens favored a less draconian legal system. The first steps of the post-Stalin leadership were to abolish his system of extra-judicial terror. The special boards of the Ministry of Internal Affairs were abolished. All criminal cases, including political crimes, had to be prosecuted in the people's courts with regular judicial procedure, and the secret police could no longer make arrests without the authorization of a judge or procurator. The NKVD, the secret police, was reorganized and brought under state and party control. Lavrenty Beria, Stalin's head of the NKVD, was arrested for crimes against the state and executed.[2]

Stalin's successors also moved quickly to reduce the level of repressiveness of Soviet law. For years under Stalin the unchallenged dogma had been that extremely harsh penalties were an effective deterrent to crime. This notion soon was questioned by Soviet jurists and criminologists, including A. A. Piontkovsky, A. A. Gertsenzon, and V. M. Chikhvadze.[3] On March 23, 1953, just three weeks after Stalin's death, an amnesty was announced for many of the victims of the dictator's oppression. Among those released were not only political criminals, but also persons convicted of minor offenses, who nonetheless received long and harsh sentences. The amnesty also took into account special circumstances – pregnancy, old age, sickness, and youth. In 1954 parole was reintroduced, permitting adult criminals to be released after serving two-thirds of their sentences and minors after serving only one-third of their sentences.

Legal specialists proposed decriminalizing many common economic offenses and less dangerous acts, favoring instead administrative and disciplinary sanctions.[4] In 1954 the penalty for petty theft from state-owned factories was reduced from seven to ten years in a corrective labor colony, to a range of only three months confinement to six months corrective labor without confinement.

The momentum for legal reform increased substantially following Khrushchev's denunciation of Stalin and his crimes at the 20th Party Congress in 1956. Khrushchev's "secret speech" criticized Stalin for abusing his power, breaching the Leninist principle of collective leadership, establishing a personality cult, and orchestrating a twenty-year reign of terror against innocent citizens. Furthermore, Khrushchev denounced Stalin for purging the military command and disregarding intelligence reports of the impending German attack, which had left the country woefully unprepared for war. Finally, Khrushchev attacked Stalin for undermining the role of the party and for the purging of rank-and-file party members. The assembled delegates sat in stunned disbelief during Khrushchev's four-hour tirade. Khrushchev's principal motive in denouncing Stalin appears to have been chiefly to rally popular support in the on-going struggle for power. But by denouncing the legal abuses and extra-judicial coercion of the Stalin era, the effect was to enhance the role of law in Soviet society and elevate the status of jurists. In his speech, Khrushchev advocated strengthening "socialist legality" and lawyers took advantage of this window of opportunity to push through major revisions in criminal and civil law.

In December 1958 the Supreme Soviet enacted new Fundamental Principles of Criminal Law and of Criminal Procedure that substantially reduced the level of repressiveness of the former Stalinist system. On the bases of these, each union-republic passed its own new criminal code and code of criminal procedure. The legislation abolished the doctrine of analogy that had led to much abuse under Stalin. The maximum sentence was reduced from twenty-five to fifteen years and the maximum term of exile was shortened from ten to five years. The maximum age for juvenile offenders was raised from 12 to 14. (It had been 16 from 1929 to 1935.) There was also greater differentiation in the treatment of juvenile and adult offenders, especially in corrective labor facilities.

Restoring due process

In the area of judicial process, the 1958 Fundamental Principles of Criminal Law gave judges greater latitude to consider both mitigating and aggravating circumstances in sentencing. In the Fundamental Principles of Criminal Procedure there were new rules of evidence that repudiated Procurator-General Vyshinsky's tenet that confession was all-sufficient to prove guilt, especially for cases of counterrevolutionary crimes. The new evidentiary guidelines gave little weight to confessions and required that guilt be established by other substantive evidence. Also, Vyshinsky's standard that *probability* of guilt was sufficient to warrant conviction was abolished. The Fundamental Principles of Criminal Procedure clearly established the burden of proof on the state and required proof to be "objective, full and all-round." A "full" investigation referred to the obligation of state prosecutors and agencies of inquiry to investigate criminal acts, collecting and verifying all information, including evidence that might exonerate the accused. "All-round" proof approximated the Western standard of "beyond a reasonable doubt."

This evidentiary requirement notwithstanding, the new Fundamental Principles of Criminal Procedure fell short of formally recognizing the presumption of innocence. The presumption was included in the legislative commission's initial draft fundamental principles, but it encountered opposition from conservative prosecutors and party officials who were afraid of increasing the rights of the accused. They succeeded in blocking inclusion of the presumption of innocence in the final document approved by the Legislative Proposals Commission of the USSR Supreme Soviet.[5]

The revised Fundamental Principles of Criminal Procedure also failed to resolve the oft-criticized restriction on the right to legal counsel during the preliminary investigation. The preliminary investigation has no direct counterpart in common law systems. A criminal investigation normally begins by request of the police and is carried out by professional investigators subordinate either to the Procuracy, the Military Procuracy, the KGB, or the Ministry of Internal Affairs. A suspect could be detained for up to seventy-two hours without contact with an attorney and might then be held an additional seven days while charges are prepared or dropped. Once a charge is formalized, the suspect becomes the accused and the formal preliminary investigation begins.

During the preliminary investigation, evidence is gathered, witnesses questioned, and suspects interrogated. A dossier is compiled, often amounting to several hundred pages. When the investigators are reasonably certain that a crime has been committed and that they know the identity of the guilty party, they seek an indictment. The Procuracy must confirm the decision to indict and oversees the entire investigatory process. If the investigators determine that no crime has been committed or that the accused is not the guilty party, they may drop the charges and/or continue the investigation. Preliminary investigations were supposed to be completed within two months, however two-month extensions were routinely granted. Further extensions could be obtained from the republic procurator, the chief military procurator, or the procurator-general. In some cases, suspects were held for up to nine months during the preliminary investigation without benefit of a lawyer; it was not uncommon for even this limit to be exceeded illegally.

The absence of the right to counsel during the critical phase of the preliminary investigation had long troubled Soviet jurists. By the time the investigators have gathered sufficient evidence to indict the accused, the person's guilt has already been established. In fact, more than 99 percent of all persons indicted are ultimately convicted and less than 1 percent acquitted.[6] There is also a potential conflict of interest in that in most cases the investigatory bodies that decide whether to indict someone of a criminal offense report to the Procuracy, which will be charged with prosecuting the case. Soviet jurists seriously questioned whether exculpatory evidence is given due regard under such a system.

While the accused does not have the right to counsel during the preliminary investigation, he or she may secure the assistance of an attorney who may undertake an independent investigation. Soviet criminal procedure law states that neither the accused, the defense counsel, nor the victim shall be denied the right to gather evidence and interrogate witnesses in a criminal case. Despite calls by advocates and legal scholars for extending the right of counsel to the preliminary investigation, the 1958 reform was swayed by the arguments of the procurators and investigators that defense attorneys would hamper expeditious handling of criminal investigations and were unnecessary as the investigator was obliged to be "objective." The new legislation only extended the right to counsel to two categories of individuals, who were judged to be unable to protect their own interests – juveniles and the mentally or physically incapacitated.

Citizens' rights and the state

Progress in the third area of proposed legal reform – the elevation of the rights of the individual *vis-à-vis* the state – has taken substantially longer to be realized. A 1956 editorial in the party's theoretical journal, *Kommunist*, attacked the traditional Stalinist interpretation of legality and stressed the need for a concept of legality designed to protect the rights and interests of citizens.[7] A study published by the USSR Academy of Sciences argued that citizens' rights are even binding on state authorities. It concluded:

That the organs of state power be bound by law is an indispensable condition for the existence of legality and the subjective rights of citizens in relations with state authorities. For an organ of power to be bound by law means that it must fully observe the requirements contained in legal standards and unswervingly fulfill all obligations imposed on it by the law in the citizens' interests.[8]

Other Soviet jurists argued that cases involving citizens' personal and property rights should be examined by the courts, rather than by administrative agencies. They further demanded that state officials bear material and criminal responsibility for such violations.[9] Unlike either the utopian or dictatorial concepts of law, socialist legality began to resemble the Western concept of "rule of law." Notable exceptions remained, however. In sentencing, crimes against socialist property were considered more serious and were more severely punished than crimes against personal property.

One of the most significant developments in the Soviet legal system after Stalin's death was the revival of procuratorial supervision of citizens' grievances against state administration. The Statute on Procuratorial Supervision in the USSR of May 24, 1955 expanded the Procuracy's terms of reference relative to general supervision. The statute for the first time spelled out procuratorial powers of protest, representation and proposal. In addition, it established the right of procurators to demand from officials information and documents concerning violations of laws.

Until the revision of civil law and procedure by the new USSR Fundamental Principles in 1961 (and their incorporation in the RSFSR codes of civil law and civil procedure in 1964), Soviet citizens had very restricted ability to initiate civil cases against state agencies; they had to rely on procurators to investigate their grievances. The 1961 Fundamental Principles of Civil Law and Fundamental Principles of Civil Procedure permitted judicial review in a few areas of interest to average citizens: imposition of administrative fines, disputes arising from the assignment of state-owned housing, and work-related grievances. While these changes broadened the range of cases in which citizens could directly petition the court to protect their rights and interests, other important areas were excluded from judicial review, such as grievances arising from various social programs provided for Soviet citizens including health care, pensions, and education.

In 1965 the All-Union Scientific Research Institute on Soviet Legislation of the Ministry of Justice sponsored a conference to discuss drafting a Fundamental Principles of Administrative Responsibility that could have substantially expanded citizens' right to judicial review of their grievances arising out of the actions of state agencies and officials. On October 31, 1967 the USSR Supreme Soviet created a commission to codify legislation on administrative responsibility. Their proposal was to create a separate system of administrative courts governed by a code of administrative law procedure.[10] Other jurists favored transferring all administrative cases to the regular people's courts.[11] Both variants were aggressively resisted by the Procuracy, which saw the expansion of judicial review as an infringement on the Procuracy's power of general supervision of administrative agencies.[12]

Before progress could be made in expanding citizens' ability to utilize the courts to protect their interests, however, the conservative Brezhnev leadership began to curtail consideration of legal reforms. The window of opportunity afforded by Khrushchev's de-Stalinization campaign was closing. It is significant that the new leaders were only willing to entertain proposals for legal reforms up to the point where they began to impinge on the powers and prerogatives of the state.

Popular participation in the administration of justice

Although "socialist legality" was the predominant trend in Soviet law after Stalin, in the early 1960s there was a resurgence of legal utopianism fostered by Khrushchev. In order to stem crime, he urged housing units, factories, and shops to resuscitate comrades' courts and other informal tribunals. These informal "courts" made up of ordinary citizens in places of employment and housing districts were charged with resolving minor disputes and infractions ranging from petty theft from factories to improper rearing of children. Speaking to the 21st Party Congress in 1959 Khrushchev declared: "The time has come when more attention should be paid to the comrades' courts, which should seek chiefly to prevent assorted kinds of law violations. They should hear not only cases concerning behavior on the job, but also cases of everyday deportment and morality, cases of improper conduct by members of the group."[13]

The comrades' courts had a dual function: (1) to educate the public about the rules of socialist society, thereby preventing acts which would be detrimental to society, and (2) to punish and re-educate violators of established laws and prescribed behavior patterns. Khrushchev urged the populace: "to uncover the violator, not only when he has committed a misdeed or an offense, but also when he demonstrates variations in acceptable norms of behavior which may lead to anti-social deeds. People can, by timely measures, suppress their bad indications."[14]

The USSR Supreme Court and the procurator-general transferred appropriate cases to the comrades' courts for disposition.[15] A new Model Statute on the Comrades' Courts was enacted in 1959, expanding their jurisdiction to include disposition of minor criminal cases which, in the court's opinion, could be successfully handled informally by social pressure.[16] The comrades' courts were empowered to levy fines up to 50 rubles, to compel guilty parties to pay for damages they caused, and to require mandatory labor for the welfare of the collective. By the end of 1963, approximately 197,000 comrades' courts were disposing of more than 4 million cases per year.[17]

The renewed interest in the comrades' courts after 1959 was indicative of a resurgence of the utopian trend in Soviet law. An article in *Sovetskoe gosudarstvo i pravo* restated the Marxian vision of a society free of state coercion:

Communism is a society that will have neither state nor law, but compulsion is not something that must necessarily be a function of the state, nor must normative regulation be a matter of law . . . In a communist society there will be no law, as there will be no state compulsion. The difference between legal measures and the measures to be applied to persons violating the norms of social behavior under communism consists in the fact that they will rest not upon state compulsion but solely upon public opinion, the strength of the group, social influence.[18]

The traditional utopian themes of the withering away of the state and law and the need for informality and popular participation in the administration of justice were echoed in numerous press commentaries and in the statements of party officials.

The utopian trend in Soviet law was also evident in the revival of the *druzhina* (voluntary people's militia) and the anti-parasite tribunals. Reports of comrades' courts and anti-parasite tribunals meting out prejudicial, arbitrary justice and meddling in non-judicial matters were common. Under considerable pressure from Khrushchev to curtail anti-social behavior, the legal profession pushed to incorporate anti-parasite laws and the comrades' courts into established judicial procedures.

From 1965 through 1968 an ongoing debate was aired in the Soviet press on the role of public participation in the administration of justice. The lines were clearly drawn between investigators and officials of the Ministry for Safeguarding Public Order in favor of public participation, and jurists, defense attorneys, and legal consultants

opposed. An influential article in *Sovetskoe gosudarstvo i pravo* by
G. Z. Anashkin, chairman of the Criminal Cases Collegium of the
USSR Supreme Court decried the practice of sending criminal cases
to comrades' courts.[19] He also declared that public opinion represents
an illegal interference in the courts' consideration of criminal matters.
In September 1965, *Pravda* published an article "for purposes of discussion" reviewing the history of popular justice and calling for
greater emphasis on the government's (not the public's) role in maintaining law and order.[20]

The decline of the comrades' courts was signaled in a 1967 case
involving increased liability for repeated instances of a crime.[21] The
comrades' court of the Moscow Wool-Spinning Mill fined a worker
30 rubles for petty theft of wool. A few months later she committed
the same act. The May Day District People's Court in Moscow convicted her under Paragraph 2 of Article 96 of the RSFSR Criminal
Code requiring increased liability for repeated instances of the same
crime. Although the Moscow City Court upheld the decision, the
Judicial Collegium of the RSFSR Supreme Court, acting in accordance
with its supervisory procedure, ruled that the defendant had been
charged incorrectly. In the Collegium's opinion, the second larceny
would have been recognized as a repeated instance only if the first
instance had been tried in a people's court. The decision was given
wide publicity in the journal of the Russian Republic's Supreme Court.
The case had two far-reaching implications for the comrades' courts:
(1) the comrades' courts were recognized by the Soviet legal establishment as extra-legal bodies, and (2) in the future, fewer cases involving
petty crimes would be brought before the comrades' courts.

By the end of the 1960s, popular justice was in full retreat. A lengthy
article in *Izvestiya* called for stricter supervision of the comrades'
courts and questioned the utility of public involvement in the administration of justice:

A form that is democratic in nature does not in and of itself determine content
as well. This is a wide door, and, along with advanced views, backward and
philistine attitudes gravitate toward it . . . It is precisely in this sphere [every-
day life] that it can do great harm by generating old and nasty characteristics –
unsociability and hostility among people. A public hearing that cannot rise
above the level of bickering teaches bad lessons.[22]

The decline of the anti-parasite legislation and the comrades' courts
can be directly attributed to an increasingly assertive professional
legal establishment which sought to abolish these institutions or, at a
minimum, incorporate them into regular judicial procedure. Juridiz-

ation became a hallmark of the Brezhnev era, in large part because of the greater stress on professionalism and the greater tendency for Brezhnev to consult with jurists in the making of legal policy.

Brezhnev and the quest for stability

As we have observed, after Khrushchev's ouster in 1964 the legal profession took steps to bring "popular justice" under control.[23] Jurists attacked the utopian notion of public participation in the administration of justice. A campaign was undertaken to professionalize legal administration and increase the legal competence of judicial personnel. "Socialist legality" again became the principal slogan of the legal apparatus. The return to socialist legality was consonant with the general trend under Brezhnev and his successors of allowing more input from specialists in formulating policy.

Due to increasing economic pressures and the generally more conservative bureaucratic leadership style of the Brezhnev regime, however, the emphasis of socialist legality shifted from protecting the interests of individual citizens to protecting the economic interests of the state and insuring law and order. The 25th Party Congress in 1976 stressed the need for legal regulation of economic activity to increase production, to strengthen the economic system, and to counter fraud, theft of socialist property, and the padding of accounts and plan-fulfillment reports. R. A. Rudenko, the late procurator-general, noted that the Procuracy had been ordered to strengthen its supervision of legality in economic organizations.[24]

The long awaited new Constitution of 1977 reaffirmed the central role of the party and reinforced the interests of the state, but did little to expand the rights of citizens.[25] For example, the constitutional provision on the right of free speech, press, association, assembly, and public meeting included the caveat "in accordance with the people's interests and for the purpose of strengthening and developing the socialist system."[26] Article 59 made explicit the connection between citizens' rights and duties to the state: "The exercise of rights and liberties is inseparable from the performance by citizens of their duties. USSR citizens are obliged to observe the USSR Constitution and Soviet laws, to respect the rules of the socialist community, and to bear with dignity the lofty title of USSR citizen."[27]

Article 60 required every able-bodied citizen to work, noting that "the evasion of socially useful labor is incompatible with the principles of a socialist society."[28] Article 61 required citizens to protect and enhance socialist property. "It is the duty of the USSR citizen to combat the theft and waste of state and public property and to take good care of the people's property."[29]

The 1979 Statute on the Procuracy also incorporated several new provisions relating to economic violations. For example, Article 3 stated that "the fight against violations concerning the protection of socialist property" is one of the fundamental responsibilities of procurators.[30] Furthermore, the laws protecting socialist property and the punishments for economic crimes were substantially strengthened in the December 1982 amendments to the Criminal Code of the RSFSR.

For those who failed to conform to the Brezhnev leadership's view of advanced socialism the state responded with ruthless coercion. The Brezhnev regime had begun on a conciliatory note. For almost a year after coming to power, no leaders of dissident nationality or religious groups were arrested. Some 200 Baptists who were in prison at the time of Khrushchev's ouster were released early. The Brezhnev regime also indicated a willingness to listen to (if not act upon) the grievances of the Crimean Tatars and other disgruntled ethnic groups.

This period of relative tolerance toward divergent political views was short lived, however. In June 1965, the leadership permitted the KGB to resume arresting dissidents. The process began in Leningrad and continued in the Ukraine with more than thirty arrests. The crackdown culminated in September 1965 with the arrest of authors Andrei Sinyavsky and Yuli Daniel in Moscow. The authors, whose books had been smuggled out of the USSR and published in the West, were charged under Article 70 of the RSFSR Criminal Code with "anti-Soviet agitation and propaganda." The arrest and trial of Sinyavsky and Daniel were a watershed in the dissident movement in the Soviet Union as hundreds flocked to sign petitions for their release.[31] Despite the popular support, Sinyavsky and Daniel were convicted and sentenced to long terms in a labor colony. Aleksandr Ginzburg, who compiled a transcript of the trial and had it smuggled to the West, was arrested in January 1967. Vladimir Bukovsky was arrested one week later for demonstrating against Ginzburg's arrest, while Pavel Litvinov, grandson of Maksim Litvinov, Stalin's foreign minister, was threatened by the KGB for circulating a samizdat transcript of Bukovsky's trial. By this time, more than a thousand Soviet citizens had signed petitions against the mounting repression.[32]

The Soviet invasion of Czechoslovakia in August 1968 sparked a new wave of demonstrations and arrests. The "Prague Spring" with its slogan "Communism with a human face" had been closely watched by political dissidents and reform-minded jurists in the USSR, who hoped that liberalization in Eastern Europe would lead to greater tolerance at home. When the Czech experiment was brutally crushed by Soviet tanks, Russian intellectuals reacted in anger and disillusionment.

In the politically charged atmosphere of the late 1960s, two figures rose to prominence in the dissent movement: Aleksandr Solzhenitsyn and Andrei Sakharov. In 1945, Solzhenitsyn was arrested in East Prussia when authorities intercepted some of his letters that contained unfavorable references to Stalin. He was tried *in absentia* and sentenced to eight years in a labor colony. Solzhenitsyn's first novel, *One Day in the Life of Ivan Denisovich* was published during the literary thaw of the early 1960s, but his subsequent works were rejected for publication. In May 1967, Solzhenitsyn penned an open letter to the writers' union, denouncing literary censorship and criticizing the union for its acquiescence to literary controls. He was expelled from the writers' union and, in February 1974, Solzhenitsyn's citizenship was revoked and he and his family were forcibly expelled from the USSR.

Sakharov, the father of the Soviet hydrogen bomb, joined the dissent movement following the Soviet invasion of Czechoslovakia. The addition of such a highly respected voice as Sakharov's to the growing chorus of dissidents apparently alarmed the authorities sufficiently to step up reprisals. The KGB focused particularly on those in the human rights movement, like Sakharov, who were trying to forge links between various dissident elements, including ethnic and religious groups with grievances against the Brezhnev regime. Sakharov was stripped of his security clearance, which was tantamount to dismissal from his research institute. He would later be placed under house arrest in Gorky on dubious legal grounds and denied access to Western journalists.[33]

In the late 1960s, the embryonic dissent movement began to employ Soviet law as an instrument for promoting democratization and securing civil rights. This practice, which was advocated initially by the distinguished Soviet mathematician Aleksandr Yesenin-Volpin, in effect put pressure on the regime to abide by its own laws. The dissent journal, *The Chronicle of Current Events* was founded in 1968, in large measure, to document violations of socialist legality. Nonetheless, the authorities were undeterred. While administering a psychiatric examination to dissident Bukovsky, one psychiatrist declared: "You keep talking about the Constitution and the laws, but what normal person takes Soviet law seriously? You are living in an unreal world of your own invention; you react inadequately to the world around you."[34] Like hundreds of other dissidents, Bukovsky was held in a hospital for the criminally insane and subjected to cruel and debilitating "treatments."

In 1970 the Fifth Main Directorate was created in the KGB to counteract dissent. The following year, the KGB was instructed to close down the *Chronicle of Current Events* and through arrests and harassment managed to suspend its publication for eighteen months. A series of changes in Soviet laws in the 1970s also signaled the tougher stance on dissent. These measures increased penalties for illegal use of telephones and printing presses;[35] strengthened residency restrictions for released prisoners, making it more difficult for them to live in major cities;[36] and altered the law on citizenship to make it easier to deny citizenship to "those who defame the lofty title of citizen of the USSR."[37]

The 1980 Moscow Olympics provided another pretext for rounding up dissidents. In the spring of 1980, the KGB was averaging five to ten arrests per week.[38] Among those arrested on the eve of the Olympics was Anatoly Koryagin, a psychiatrist who had documented the torture of dissidents in psychiatric hospitals. He was sentenced to twelve years of imprisonment and exile. Koryagin was released in February 1987, having served seven years of his sentence.[39]

Brezhnev had come to power following the unsettling reforms and turmoil of Khrushchev's rule promising stability and consultation with the large bureaucratic interests that dominated policy-making in the USSR. By the late 1970s and early 1980s, however, stability had turned to stagnation. Brezhnev's penchant for consultation resulted in the more conservative, law-and-order agencies – Procuracy, the KGB, and the Ministry of Internal Affairs – having a disproportionate influence on legal policy, while defense attorneys, judges, and legal scholars, who were not as highly organized, had much less ability to influence policy. Special privileges and virtual immunity from prosecution shielded the nomenklatura, which took advantage of their positions to accept bribes, organize racketeering schemes, and embezzle state resources. The entire system, including judicial institutions, was riddled with corruption.

Brezhnev died in November 1982 and was quickly succeeded by Yuri Andropov, his former hard-line KGB chief. Not surprisingly, Andropov's policies continued the Brezhnev line of stressing the interests of the state over those of the individual and clamping down on manifestations of dissent. During Andropov's fifteen-month rule, legal measures were especially used to enhance work discipline. Police rounded up idle workers in movie theaters, bathhouses, and stores and demanded to see their work documents. They sometimes called employers to verify that the apprehended workers were not supposed to be on the job. Under Andropov's leadership, new laws were enacted that raised the penalties for absenteeism, tardiness, drunkenness on the job, managerial incompetence, and theft of state property by workers. The campaign for improving labor discipline culminated in the enactment of the Law on Labor Collectives. The new legislation enlisted the support of the labor collectives in the fight for better work discipline by awarding bonuses on the basis of collective, rather than individual, performance. The work discipline and anti-corruption campaigns begun by Andropov faltered under his successor, Konstantin Chernenko, but were renewed in increasing vigor by Mikhail Gorbachev during his first three years in office.

Another ominous sign of the resurgence of the dictatorial trend in Soviet law was the revision of the law on criminal liability for state crimes, which dealt with subversion. In January 1985, the law was amended to add "passing official secrets to foreigners" to the list of anti-state crimes. Violation of this provision of the law was punishable by the deprivation of freedom for a term of up to three years.[40] Given the fact that "official secrets" in the USSR, prior to the introduction of glasnost, included crime statistics, information on fires, plane crashes, and other disasters, and health statistics, as well as scientific and technical information, the new law had a chilling effect on scientific publication and international scientific cooperation. It also discouraged contact between Soviet citizens and foreigners in the USSR, especially foreign correspondents.

At the same time, there was a tendency toward decriminalization of some petty offenses, handing them over to administrative agencies, the comrades' courts, and labor collectives. Fewer offenses, especially those of minors, were being punished by incarceration. There was a growing awareness in the USSR among social workers, juvenile affairs officers, the courts, police and prosecutors that incarceration in a correctional institution may further corrupt, rather than rehabilitate, young offenders.[41]

Brezhnev and his successors reinforced the stability of the state and law, but long overdue legal reforms languished. Perhaps most debilitating of all, public respect for the law and legal institutions fell precipitously. By 1985 corruption had become so commonplace that it was necessary to pay bribes to secure virtually any service. *Emigré* jurists noted that advocates routinely demanded under-the-table payments, "gifts," and other favors in exchange for timely and competent legal advice. Such "gifts" could more than double the income of an advocate.[42] Corruption fed the public's cynicism regarding the Soviet legal system, further eroding its legitimacy. The greatest task confronting Gorbachev when he came to power in March 1985 was to restore public trust in the institutions of the state, most notably the courts.

Gorbachev and legal reform

Gorbachev was uniquely suited to the task of restoring public confidence in the legal system. The son of a collective farmer from the Stavropol' district, Gorbachev distinguished himself at an early age as an energetic and pragmatic student and Komsomol leader. His political loyalty and resourcefulness were rewarded in 1950 when he was admitted to the Faculty of Law of Moscow University. The law schools were in the forefront of reforms following Stalin's death in 1953. De-Stalinization and the debates surrounding the need for legal reforms undoubtedly had a marked influence on Gorbachev's thinking.

The process of reforming the Soviet legal system evolved in a manner markedly similar to the course of Gorbachev's general reform program. That is, legal reform proceeded through a number of stages. The first stage (glasnost) reflected the new openness of Soviet society; it was followed by the enactment of legislation on economic reform policies and expanded citizens' participation in political life; finally, reform began to address the core issues of the development of a legitimate, law-governed society. We examine each phase of legal reform in turn.

Legal glasnost

As with glasnost generally, glasnost in the realm of law moved unevenly through various stages, and dealt with issues ranging from attacking the privileged status of the former political elite, to re-examining Soviet legal history, criticizing the performance of judicial and law enforcement agencies, and addressing crime and other social problems in a candid fashion.

A common theme of Gorbachev's anti-corruption campaign of 1985 and 1986 was the need for all officials to abide by the law, and the need to punish those who abuse their positions for private gain or to obtain privileged treatment. Charges of official corruption were published in national and local newspapers throughout the USSR, and resulted in the firing, or forced resignations, of as many as half the regional and local party first secretaries.[43]

Legal glasnost also entailed the reexamination of Soviet legal history, in particular the abuses of the Stalin and Brezhnev regimes. In his speech on the eve of the seventieth anniversary of the revolution, Gorbachev acknowledged that legal abuses during the Stalin era resulted in "many thousands of victims." He added: "The guilt of Stalin and his immediate entourage before the party and the people for the wholesale repressive measures and acts is enormous and unforgivable."[44] In May 1988, a televised documentary film showed scenes from the purge trials and included personal testimony from some of the survivors of Stalin's infamous Gulag.

Criticism of the Brezhnev era concentrated on the abuse of power for personal gain by Brezhnev, his family, and other members of the political elite. The most notorious case to come to light involved Yuri Churbanov, the son-in-law of the late Leonid Brezhnev, who pleaded guilty to abusing his office as USSR deputy minister of internal affairs. Churbanov and eight of his colleagues were convicted in December 1988 of accepting bribes worth 415,000 rubles. He was sentenced to twelve years' imprisonment.[45]

The attack on official corruption, begun in 1985, was soon expanded to official meddling in the activities of the courts, the police, and other judicial agencies. In his address to the 27th Party Congress in 1986, Gorbachev stressed the need to safeguard the principles of judicial independence and equality of citizens before the law.[46]

Exposés of "telephone justice" were published, illustrating the degree to which party and government officials intruded into the activities of the courts. In a 1988 survey of 120 judges, 60 reported that within the past year they had been approached by a party or government official with a suggestion as to how to decide a particular case.[47] Another study estimated that party officials intervened in 10 to 12 percent of all cases.[48]

In an interview with the Austrian communist newspaper Volksstimme soon after the 27th Party Congress, RSFSR Minister of Justice Aleksandr Sukharev called for insuring the equality before the criminal courts of members of the CPSU and citizens who are not members of the party.[49] This was just the first salvo in a campaign by jurists to lessen party influence in the determination of cases, and to prevent preferential treatment of party members in criminal cases.

In 1986, the procurator-general charged that certain party officials consider themselves "above the law."[50] He urged local prosecutors to "stay within the strict framework of the law" in their efforts to combat crime.[51] He added: "Law guarantees inviolability of the individual and of citizens' homes, and a comprehensive, full, and objective investigation" of crime.[52]

In a widely read article in *Literaturnaya gazeta* in May 1986, Arkady Vaksberg criticized judicial irregularities and the failure of many judicial officers to observe proper legal procedures.[53] Citing numerous accounts of judicial misconduct, Vaksberg concluded that there are too many Soviet lawyers making "legal mistakes" for the irregularities to be regarded as "atypical."[54]

During Gorbachev's first two years in office, numerous exposés appeared in nationally circulated newspapers and magazines concerning interference in criminal investigations by local party and government officials, fabrication of evidence, erroneous application of the death penalty, and other miscarriages of justice and due process violations.[55] The most notorious case was the Vitebsk Affair, in which a man was wrongly accused, and sentenced to death, for the rape and murder of several dozen women over a fifteen-year period. Fortunately, another man being held on other charges confessed to the murders before the death sentence was carried out. A follow-up investigation found that prosecutors and investigators had been under considerable pressure from local party officials to solve the case, and had used "illegal methods" to obtain evidence and testimony. According to an editorial commentary in *Literaturnaya gazeta*, the case was not unusual.[56]

In mid-1986, local and regional party officials mounted a counteroffensive against glasnost, especially as it related to criticism of their performance. Scattered attempts were made to intimidate the press or suppress critical reports.[57]

One of the most significant areas in which glasnost influenced Soviet legal policy was in the reporting of crime and crime statistics. Criminal activity that had been routinely hushed up by the authorities began to be reported openly. Exposés of organized crime were particularly prominent in the press.[58] Numerous cases of racketeering, embezzling, and protection schemes, frequently involving party and Komsomol members, were also uncovered.[59]

In his first year or two in office, Gorbachev did not set out to reform the Soviet legal system in a systematic way. Rather, his policy of glasnost was employed principally to increase the accountability of party, state, and economic officials, to root out the corruption that had become so pervasive during "the period of stagnation," and to force the retirement or dismissal of many Brezhnev-era officials and replace them with his own more reform-minded clients.

Legal perestroika

Having created an atmosphere in which legal violations could be openly discussed and criticized, Gorbachev proceeded to utilize legal measures to realize his economic reform objectives. The thrust of Gorbachev's reform initiatives from 1985 until the 19th Party Conference in 1988 centered on restructuring the Soviet economy in order to stimulate economic performance, improve the technological level of production, increase efficiency in utilization of resources, and reinstitute work discipline. Not surprisingly, then, the largest portion of new legislation introduced during this period came in the area of economic law.

On February 8, 1987, *Pravda* published a new draft Law on the State Enterprise.[60] The law called for the election of enterprise directors, and also made enterprises self-financed. Prices remained centrally set, however. The law also provided for unprofitable enterprises to be declared insolvent and closed. The Law on the State Enterprise, thus, incorporated many of Gorbachev's early economic reform goals, giving them formal legal structure.

One of the most persistent problems in the Soviet economy had been under-utilization of labor reserves. With projections for a serious decline in the growth rate of the Soviet labor force by the year 2000, the Gorbachev administration moved quickly to attempt to rationalize the assignment of workers within the economy. On September 12, 1985, *Pravda* published a joint decree of the USSR Council of Ministers and the Central Council of Trade Unions on "work place attestation."[61] The aim of the decree was to curb labor hoarding by Soviet enterprises. The decree also encouraged enterprises to scrap obsolete equipment.

New legislation was also introduced in 1985 and 1986 to step up supervision and punishment of economic crimes, including poor work discipline, substandard production, theft of state property, and intoxication in the workplace. On July 1, 1986, a decree of the Presidium of the USSR Supreme Soviet went into force that increased the financial liability of workers for damages caused by them to the enterprise in which they worked.[62]

In 1986 the Gorbachev leadership also launched a vigorous campaign against black market activities and organized crime. On May 23, 1986, the Presidium of the Supreme Soviet adopted a decree "On Intensifying the Struggle against Derivation of Non-Labor Incomes."[63] The decree increased penalties for the unauthorized use of state-owned vehicles, machinery, or equipment. The maximum fine was raised from 30 rubles to 100 rubles, and to 200 rubles for officials. Article 156 of the RSFSR Code of Administrative Violations was stiffened with regard to the illegal use or expropriation of state property, tools, and equipment, and failure to report income derived from handicrafts or "after-hours labor."[64] A new clause was added to Article 157 of the Code, applicable to persons engaged in a prohibited trade (e.g. blackmarketeers). The decree also increased criminal liability for taking bribes.

In 1987 and 1988 several other new enactments redefined ownership and property rights in the USSR. The Law on Joint Ventures, for the first time since the revolution, enabled foreign corporations to have an equity interest in Soviet enterprises. In June 1988, the Supreme Soviet passed the Law on Cooperatives with the intent of stimulating private economic activity.

Two decrees relating to agriculture were published in the Soviet press on September 25, 1987.[65] The first decree related to the *podryad* (contract) system of assignment and remuneration, and called for placing all farms and food enterprises on full self-financing by 1988–1989. The second decree sought to stimulate production on private plots and to incorporate this production into the general economy. Both decrees were consistent with Gorbachev's stated desire to expand the realm of private initiative in the food and consumer goods sectors.

The most significant piece of new legislation to appear in the field of agriculture was the new draft Model Kolkhoz Statute, which was announced on January 10, 1988.[66] The draft statute called for greater farm autonomy, transition to self-financing by 1988–1989, and self-management. Under the provisions of the statute, members of kolkhozes were granted a greater degree of participation in the affairs of the collective, including the right to select chairmen and set their salaries. Individual plots of kolkhoz members were no longer limited in size, nor was the number of livestock that members could keep. The new statute was clearly an attempt to bring collective farm law into conformance with the Law on the State Enterprise by granting farm workers the same participatory rights enjoyed by industrial workers.[67]

Legal democratization

From mid-1988 until 1991, the pace of economic reforms slowed, and emphasis in Gorbachev's activities shifted to the political arena. While Gorbachev championed competitive elections, and succeeded in establishing a more powerful presidency, economic problems continued to fester. In large part, the economic crisis confronting the Soviet Union by 1990 was a product of the reform policies themselves. Gorbachev's economic reforms succeeded in dismantling the centrally planned economy, yet the reforms were sufficiently limited and compromised that a market system was unable to develop to fill the void.

The 19th Party Conference

While the period 1985 to mid-1988 witnessed a flurry of new legislation to implement Gorbachev's ambitious economic perestroika, changes in the legal system itself were much more modest. However, a new direction in "legal democratization" was signaled by Gorbachev at the 19th Party Conference in June 1988. Speaking to the conference, Gorbachev called for the development of a legal system in which "the supremacy of law is ensured in fact" and advocated a radical overhauling of the Soviet legal system, with a goal of creating a socialist *Rechtsstaat*.[68] According to Soviet jurists, in order for the rule of law to exist in the USSR, the following principles had to be observed:

- The rights of individuals must be paramount. Laws should guarantee the rights and liberties of Soviet citizens, including restricting the ability of the state to infringe those rights. The 19th Party Conference's resolution "On Legal Reform" called for "the legal protection of the individual and secure guarantees of the Soviet people's political, economic and social rights and freedoms."[69]

- The role of law in Soviet society must be enhanced. All activities must take place within the strict framework of the law. The powers of the CPSU and legislative, executive and judicial bodies should be made explicit. Law must assume its own force, rather than serving merely as a tool of the political leadership.

- State and party officials and bodies must be made subordinate to the law. Judicial officials and law enforcement agencies must be made wholly independent of party and state agencies.
- A meaningful system of constitutional law must be developed. In order to protect constitutionally endowed rights, a constitutional court must be established with full enforcement powers, including the power to annul legislation and administrative acts that are deemed unconstitutional.
- Laws must be fairly and uniformly enforced. Selective enforcement and professional discretion exist in all legal systems; however, the grounds for selectivity should not be based on political expedience.[70]

Following the 19th Party Conference commissions began drafting an impressive array of laws designed to achieve the goals which Gorbachev had articulated. Among the new legislation being drafted and debated were: USSR Law on Property, Fundamental Principles of Legislation on Land, Fundamental Principles on Leasing and Leasing Relations, Fundamental Principles of the Judicial System, Law on Uniform Tax System, Law on Socialist Enterprise, Law on Pensions, Law on Constitutional Review in the USSR, Law on the Status of People's Deputies, Law on the Status of Judges, Law on the Press, Law on Rights and Duties of Soviet Police, and Law on Religion and Freedom of Conscience.

Much of this legislation was enacted by the USSR Supreme Soviet over the course of the next two years. On December 1, 1988, 55 of the 174 articles of the constitution were amended by the USSR Supreme Soviet. Several of these amendments were necessary to legitimize changes in political institutions and processes. For example, Articles 108, 109, and 110 created a new "super" legislative body, the Congress of People's Deputies, which was elected in relatively competitive, free elections in 1989.[71] The 1988 amendments also elevated citizens' rights (while continuing the practice of enumerating citizens' responsibilities to the state), recognized the separation of legislative and executive functions, and did away with the CPSU's power to approve appointments to influential posts. Proposals for the elimination of Article 6 of the constitution, which recognized the Communist Party as "the leading and guiding force" in Soviet society, and for the creation of an executive presidency were raised at the 19th Party Conference but were not enacted until early 1990.

Also included in the constitutional amendments enacted in December 1988 were provisions for creating a Constitutional Supervision Committee.[72] The Constitutional Supervision Committee was composed of a chair, a deputy chair and twenty-five members, who were selected by the Congress of People's Deputies to serve ten-year terms.[73] The committee could consider an issue only when it was requested to do so by a governmental body or on its own initiative, but not by petition of individual citizens. If the committee found that the constitution had been violated by a statutory act adopted by the Congress of People's Deputies, or by a provision of a constitution of a union-republic, that finding did not nullify the act. However, such a determination mandated that the dispute be brought before the next session of the Congress of People's Deputies, and if it disagreed with the committee's finding by a two-thirds vote, then the act remained in force. Otherwise, it was revoked. All other statutory acts that the committee found to be in conflict with the USSR Constitution or that violated basic human rights and freedoms would "lose force," and either be referred to their originating body for revision, or brought before the Congress of People's Deputies for consideration. While the Constitutional Supervision Committee fell short of a fully functioning constitutional court, it did make some effort to translate constitutional provisions into legally protected rights.

Several measures were introduced to minimize party and government interference with the courts. Article 155 of the constitution was amended to strengthen the language pertaining to judicial independence.[74] The USSR Law on the Status of Judges, passed in August 1989, elaborated on Article 155 by forbidding attempts to interfere or to exert pressure in any form on a judge or people's assessor "with the intent of impeding a complete, full and objective handling of a particular case, or of securing an unlawful court decision."[75] (The law did not apply to attempts to influence police, investigators, procurators, or advocates, however.)

The procedure for selecting judges was also altered in an attempt to insulate judges from political pressures in their respective regions. Judicial terms were increased from five to ten years, and judges were selected by the soviet at the next higher level of government. The nomination of judges was removed from the province of the party and vested in judicial selection panels comprised of judges chosen for a five-year term by judges at the regional level.[76]

The Law on the Status of Judges also established the independence of the courts even from supervision and intrusions by the Ministry of Justice. Judges and lay assessors could not be charged with a crime without approval of the union-republic Supreme Soviet and all cases brought against judges fell within the exclusive jurisdiction of the USSR Supreme Court.

Another measure designed to enhance the independence of the court was the expansion of the powers and number of people's assessors (lay judges). Considerable debate was aired in legal journals during the period 1987–1989 on whether to expand the number of people's assessors or adopt the jury system. The Law on the Status of Judges enlarged the court to include two professional judges and three lay assessors, or one professional judge and four lay assessors.

One of the most significant changes incorporated into the Law on the Status of Judges was recognition of the presumption of innocence. The law states, "The accused is presumed innocent until his guilt is proven in the manner prescribed by law and established by a court judgment that has entered into legal force."[77] Another critical element of emerging Soviet law was the recognition of habeas corpus (inviolability of the individual) and strict controls on the ability of law enforcement agencies to search citizens' homes and monitor their communications. Discussion also focused on introducing adversarial procedure to diminish the influence of the Procuracy in criminal cases, but the Procuracy managed to preserve most of its powers.

In November 1989 the Supreme Soviet passed a new USSR Fundamental Principles of the Judicial System, which expanded the right to defense counsel during the preliminary investigation, created separate systems of patent courts and juvenile courts, and allowed republics to introduce jury trials in criminal cases involving especially grave crimes.[78] People's assessors were retained for less serious cases.

Following the 19th Party Conference some promising changes were also introduced or discussed in relation to criminal law. In the late 1980s, there was a trend toward the decriminalization of minor offenses, and an increasing willingness of procurators to halt criminal investigations before trial. Criminal prosecutions fell by approximately 30 percent in 1988.[79] The draft Fundamental Principles of Criminal Law, circulated in 1988, called for the decriminalization of several minor crimes and victimless offenses. Sentences were reduced for many crimes, the number of offenses for which the death penalty could be imposed was reduced, internal exile was eliminated as a form of punishment, and the infamous Articles 70 and 190-1 on anti-

Soviet agitation and propaganda and defaming the Soviet state were abolished.

Progress in developing a state governed by the rule of law under Gorbachev was impressive when viewed against Russian and Soviet legal traditions. The legislative acts designed to bolster the independence of the courts, coupled with the establishment of an independent organization to represent defense attorneys, adoption of the presumption of innocence, guarantees of habeas corpus, and expanded rights of defense counsel during the preliminary investigation indicated progress toward achieving some of the requisites of a *Rechtstaat*. Such changes alone, however, were insufficient to insure judicial independence and equality before the law. For such concepts to take root, they must become institutionalized and inculcated into the legal culture of a society.

A disturbing countervailing trend also became apparent. In late 1990, the president was granted wide-ranging emergency powers, including the power to declare martial law in cases of civil emergencies, and the power to ban disturbances of the public order, including strikes, demonstrations, publications, movements, and organizations that pursue "militant and anticonstitutional goals." The president could also impose "temporary presidential rule" over particular regions or republics, suspending the authority of their governments, revoking their legislation, and dissolving their parliaments. Furthermore, in May 1990 the Supreme Soviet passed a law which imposed criminal penalties of up to six years in prison for publicly insulting the president.

Perhaps the area in which the least progress was made in Gorbachev's "legal democratization" was in elevating the rights of the individual *vis-à-vis* those of the state. Vladimir Kudryavtsev, director of the prestigious Institute of State and Law, observed that the Soviet Union still had not developed a system in which individual rights take precedence.[80] Valery Savitsky, a noted constitutional scholar at the Institute of State and Law, remarked that the March 1990 constitutional amendments that recognized individual, collective and state ownership (in that order) "got it right for the first time."[81]

Reforming Russian law: lessons of the past

The experience with legal reform during the 1950s and 1960s under Khrushchev and in the 1980s and 1990s under Gorbachev show some marked similarities. As we noted in Chapter 1, the process of reform is not a continuous, incremental one, rather it proceeds in fits and starts. Certainly, a critical factor is the receptivity of the political leadership to reform.[82] Both Khrushchev's de-Stalinization campaign and Gorbachev's program of glasnost and perestroika created an environment conducive to the discussion of fundamental legal reforms. Whether or not these discussions resulted in substantive changes, however, depended on a number of other factors. Chief among them was the willingness of the professional legal community to support the reforms. As we saw in the debate over extending the right to counsel to the preliminary investigation and the presumption of innocence, the reforms under Khrushchev were slowed by resistance of the Procuracy, the KGB, and the Ministry of Internal Affairs, the three most conservative and powerful bureaucracies in the former Soviet legal system.

The fundamental ambivalence between the rights of the individual and preserving the power of the state was evident in both of these reform periods. Although there was widespread discussion in the 1950s concerning the need to enhance the rights of individual citizens vis-à-vis the state, few substantive changes were instituted. Khrushchev's campaign against the repressive policies of Stalin succeeded in lowering the arbitrariness and extra-judicial nature of Soviet law, but it did not end repression entirely. The Brezhnev regime's vigorous campaign against dissidents can be seen as a state-sponsored, institutionalized form of repression that incorporated due process only to provide a gloss of legitimacy to the proceedings. Fundamental to Brezhnev's conception of law was its role in protecting the interests of the state and society as a whole, not in protecting the rights of individual citizens.

Under Gorbachev, the debate resumed over elevating the rights of the individual, but little substantive progress was made in realizing these rights. As in the 1950s, progress was slowed by the bureaucratic might of conservative vested interests in the Procuracy, the KGB, and the Ministry of Internal Affairs, not to mention the Communist Party. Also slowing the progress of legal reform under Gorbachev were the destabilizing effects of his economic, social, and political reform. As the country fell deeper and deeper into crisis, the scope of reformist discourse broadened from revising the criminal code and expanding citizens' rights *within* the context of a socialist legal system, to a fundamental restructuring of Soviet society on the basis of a market economy and democratic political system. Naturally, as the debate widened, the impetus to achieve specific legal reforms lost momentum.

The legal profession, especially legal scholars, played a critical role in raising the issues and setting the reform agenda under both Khrushchev and Gorbachev. Legal scholars are the most likely jurists to be knowledgeable about West European and common law legal systems, having been exposed to works of Western legal philosophy and having participated in international scholarly conferences. For years under communist rule, one of the most popular courses in Soviet law schools was "Bourgeois Legal Theory." One Russian jurist observed, "We were supposed to read the works of Locke, Hobbs, Rousseau, and Mill so we could criticize them from a Marxist–Leninist perspective. But, everyone simply wanted to learn about these works and Western legal traditions because we wanted to introduce them in this country someday."[83]

As in the legal reforms of the eighteenth and nineteenth centuries, a prominent role was played by a Westernizing intellectual elite. Looking at the wide sweep of Russian legal history one can find little support for the indigenous development of such critical concepts as equality before the law, protection of civil liberties against encroachment by the state, supremacy of the law, and judicial independence. These concepts were, for the most part, imported from Western Europe and the mode of transmission was a Westernized intelligentsia, most notably professional jurists who had been exposed to these concepts and had internalized them.

The August 1991 attempted overthrow of Gorbachev greatly accelerated the process of political reform, resulting ultimately in the collapse of the USSR and initiating the difficult process of redefining the fundamental nature of the post-communist political and legal system. Since the abortive coup, the most pressing task for each of the former union-republics has been to draft a new constitution that sets forth the basic architecture of a new state and legal system. We now turn to a discussion of the problems encountered in drafting a new Russian constitution.

4   Forging a new constitution

Constitutions do not govern by text alone, even as interpreted by a
supreme body of judges. Constitutions draw their life from forces
outside the law: from ideas, customs, society and the constant
dialogue among political institutions.[1]

Louis Fisher
American constitutional expert

It was a painful sight for all who watched – whether behind the police
barricades leading down to the Moscow River or on CNN. Artillery
shells blasted gaping holes in the walls of the Russian parliament
building where several hundred supporters of Vice-President Aleksandr Rutskoi and Speaker Ruslan Khasbulatov were defying President
Yeltsin's decree to disband and submit to new elections. Thick black
smoke billowed from the windows of the upper floors, blackening the
white marble facade. A Russian woman, watching in disbelief
remarked, "This sort of thing doesn't happen in civilized countries."[2]
    At the root of the crisis between President Yeltsin and the Russian
parliament that resulted in the violent confrontation at the White
House in October 1993 was the conflict over the fundamental constitutional structure of the new Russian state. Constitutions, by their
very nature, establish political institutions and allocate power among
them. With the collapse of the Soviet Union in December 1991, the
necessity of ratifying a new Russian constitution became a matter of
utmost urgency. The demise of the Union left a ramshackle array of
institutions and laws, some left over from the Brezhnev era, and others
the product of Gorbachev's turbulent reforms. None of these institutions or laws commanded the authority normally associated with
modern democratic governments. The problem confronting Russian
leaders in the aftermath of the failed *coup d'état* of August 1991 and the
collapse of the USSR was how to resolve the fundamental questions
of allocating power that must inevitably be addressed in a new

constitution. These contentious issues had to be resolved in an atmosphere of political and economic turmoil. Furthermore, unlike the American constitution that was drafted behind closed doors by an elite group of white, well-educated, wealthy, male land-owners, the new constitution in Russia was being worked out in the glare of television lights and involved a vast array of interest groups, factions, political parties, and prominent political figures, seeking to maximize their particular interests.

Yet, the process of democratic reform in Russia badly needed the legitimacy and stability that only a constitution could provide. Law, especially constitutions, provides a degree of consensus and legitimacy to the fundamental distribution of power in societies – between various branches of government, and between national institutions and regional and local bodies. Such constitutional arrangements provide the stability necessary for democracies to function. In this chapter, we chart the debate surrounding the drafting of a new constitution for the USSR and Russia. We note the impediments to constitutional development and how they ultimately led to the violent clash between President Yeltsin and the Russian parliament. Finally, we analyze the new constitution of the Russian Federation, which was approved by the plebiscite of December 12, 1993.

The history of the constitution

The present constitution of the Russian Federation is the fifth such document to be ratified since the October Revolution of 1917. The first constitution of the Russian Soviet Federated Socialist Republic was enacted in 1918 in order to consolidate the victories of the Bolsheviks. The document stressed the revolutionary nature of the society, specified the rights of the "toilers and exploited peoples," placed all power in the soviets (Bolshevik-dominated councils), abolished private ownership of the land, and established the fulfillment of socialism as the immediate goal of the society.

The incorporation of new territories into the republic during and after the Civil War led to the formal adoption of a federation in 1922, and thus, to the need for a new constitution. That document, ratified in 1924, differed from its predecessor primarily in specifying and differentiating the powers of federal bodies and the powers of the constituent republics.

The "Stalin Constitution," ratified in 1936, redefined the USSR as "a socialist state of workers and peasants" and enshrined the CPSU as "vanguard." It reaffirmed socialist ownership of the means of production and created the Supreme Soviet (consisting of two houses – the Soviet of the Union and the Soviet of Nationalities) to replace the Congress of Soviets.

During Khrushchev's de-Stalinization drive in the mid-1950s and early 1960s, Soviet jurists began to urge the ratification of a new constitution that would reflect the achievements of the USSR and also would further extend the notion of citizens' rights. A drafting commission was established in 1962, but progress on the constitution was halted by Khrushchev's ouster two years later. The ruling group that removed Khrushchev was motivated by a conservative desire to restore dependability and stability to Soviet politics. In his first public speech upon assuming the title of general secretary of the party, Leonid Brezhnev promised to bring "stability of cadres," ending Khrushchev's policy of rapid personnel turnover. Brezhnev and his entourage denounced Khrushchev for "hare-brained schemes" and a failure to consult with relevant experts in making policy – whether agronomists for agriculture policy, the military for security policy, or jurists when undertaking legal reform. Thus, Brezhnev's conservative orientation played to the interests of the large bureaucracies and institutions that dominated the Soviet political landscape. For the most part, these bureaucratic interests favored the predictability of the status quo.

What little innovation the Brezhnev leadership promoted in the mid-1960s had degenerated a decade later into stagnation. As if to compensate for his increasingly authoritarian and decrepit leadership, Brezhnev began to orchestrate a "cult of the personality" around himself. Schools, factories, and army units were named for him. Entire art exhibits were devoted to portraits of the "great leader." Thus, it was in an atmosphere of rising authoritarian conservatism and renewed attacks against dissidents that Soviet jurists were again assembled to up-date the constitution. Observers both inside the USSR and in the West speculated that the primary motivation for enacting a new constitution was not to address inadequacies of the 1936 document, but to create a vehicle for the further aggrandizement of Brezhnev as "the Law Giver."[3] Work began on a new draft in the early 1970s and was completed in 1977 in honor of the sixtieth anniversary of the Bolshevik Revolution.

The 1977 Constitution of the USSR or "Brezhnev Constitution" did not differ radically from its predecessors; in fact, the preamble stressed the continuity of Soviet law. The document defined the USSR as a "socialist state of all the people" and formally recognized the CPSU as "the leading and guiding force in Soviet society."[4]

Like most constitutions, the Soviet constitutions embodied the highest statement of the goals and principles of the society. They defined the powers of various state bodies, including the executive, the cabinet, the legislature, the courts, the Procuracy, and other state bodies. Unlike most constitutions, however, the constitutions of the former USSR were not binding legal documents in the sense that their articles were cited in court determinations. Constitutional provisions in the USSR had legal force only when they were implemented in one of the codes of law of the various republics. Many constitutional provisions remained unrealized, due to the absence of implementing legislation. For example, Article 58 of the 1977 Constitution stated "Actions of officials that contravene the law or exceed their powers, and infringe the rights of citizens, may be appealed in a court in the manner prescribed by law."[5] However, no law was adopted to implement the provisions of this "guarantee" for more than ten years. Finally in 1987 the Supreme Soviet enacted the Law on Appeals, which expanded citizens' rights to seek judicial review of grievances against government agencies and officials.[6]

Soviet-vintage constitutions also were used as propaganda documents, supposedly guaranteeing numerous rights and privileges of Soviet citizens – such as the right to freedom of expression, freedom of assembly, or freedom of religious belief, when in fact the state imposed severe restrictions on all such "freedoms." The Brezhnev Constitution made an explicit linkage between citizens' rights and duties. Article 39 stated "Enjoyment by citizens of their rights and freedoms must not be to the detriment of the interests of society or the state, or infringe the rights of other citizens."[7] Article 59 declared: "The exercise of rights and liberties is inseparable from the performance by citizens of their duties."[8] The 1977 Constitution's provision for free speech also began with a qualification that, in essence, nullified it: *"In accordance with the interests of the people and in order to strengthen and develop the socialist system,* citizens of the USSR are guaranteed freedom of speech, the press, and assembly, meetings, street processions and demonstrations"[9] (author's stress). Thus, free speech was only allowed as long as it supported the interests of the regime.

The 1977 Constitution incorporated some provisions, especially in the area of criminal procedure, that reflected changes introduced during Khrushchev's de-Stalinization program in the 1950s. Article

151 declared that justice is administered solely by courts and Article 160 guaranteed that "No one can be adjudged guilty of committing a crime and subjected to criminal punishment other than by the verdict of a court and in accordance with [criminal] law."[10]

Neither the 1977 Constitution nor Brezhnev's legal policy provided much grounds for optimism that the Soviet Union was evolving into a *Rechtsstaat*. To the contrary, the Brezhnev leadership's increasingly brutal repression of dissidents, including their forced incarceration in psychiatric facilities, the proliferation of graft and corruption, especially among the high-ranking nomenklatura, the routine intrusion of party officials in court cases, and the concentration of political and economic power in the hands of an aging oligarchic leadership who considered themselves to be above the law did not bode well for the future development of rule of law in Russia.

Mikhail Gorbachev came to power in 1985, following the short tenures of Yuri Andropov and Konstantin Chernenko, determined to rejuvenate the Soviet system. Gorbachev, at 53, was the youngest leader since Stalin to head the party and the only lawyer since Lenin. Despite his background as a jurist, law and legal reforms were not at the forefront of Gorbachev's reform agenda. His immediate tasks were to consolidate his political authority and to stimulate the sagging economy.

Gorbachev recognized the impracticability of waiting for constitutional redrafting to undergird his policies. Instead, he articulated his policies of glasnost, perestroika, and democratization, implementing them with laws and decrees as necessary. Where the Soviet constitution proved to contradict his policies, he managed to persuade the majority of deputies in the Supreme Soviet to amend the document. The 1977 Constitution, like its predecessors, provided for amendment by a simple majority vote of the Supreme Soviet. Until 1989, this was largely a formality since the Supreme Soviet was a rubber-stamp body for the CPSU. In the fifty-three-year history of the body there had never been a dissenting vote cast.

In June 1988 at the 19th Party Conference Gorbachev began to espouse creation of a law-governed state requiring extensive revision of the constitution. It had become apparent that policy changes were outstripping constitutional revisions and that a whole new constitutional structure was needed. However, the process of drafting a new constitution would inevitably prove to be contentious and protracted. In the meantime, many constitutional amendments had to be made to accommodate the rapidly changing political and economic situation.

During the period 1977 to 1988 the Soviet constitution had been amended only once, in 1988 alone almost one-third of the constitution's 174 articles were amended.[11] These amendments shifted the locus of power from the party to reconfigured state bodies – most notably, the Congress of People's Deputies. Other amendments guaranteed an independent judiciary, created a Constitutional Supervision Committee, and expanded citizens' rights to judicial review.

More amendments were introduced in the period 1989 through 1991, including the establishment of an executive presidency, creation of a Constitutional Court, and the abolition of the Communist Party's monopoly on political power (Article 6).

In late 1989 Gorbachev appointed a Constitutional Commission, which he chaired, to begin work drafting a new constitution for the USSR. Members of the drafting commission included many leading jurists and other notable figures such as dissident Andrei Sakharov. The work of the drafting commission was slowed by various republics seizing the initiative to revise their own constitutions, often without consulting officials at the all-union level. The breakdown in relations between Moscow and the republics, which was characterized as "the war of laws," prompted Gorbachev in 1990 to attempt to renegotiate a treaty on the relations of the republics with the center.

Ironically, as the pace of discussions of constitutional issues picked up in 1989 and 1990 and as the country's political and economic situation grew increasingly unstable, Gorbachev expanded his presidential powers substantially. In 1990 the president was accorded greater powers to issue binding decrees especially in economic matters, the power to suspend the Congress of People's Deputies, and the power to declare "presidential rule," a special form of martial law. Work of the drafting commission proceeded almost uninterrupted until the demise of the Soviet Union in December 1991, but the thrust of the commission's recommendations on separation of powers, guarantees of civil liberties, checks and balances, and federal/republic power-sharing ran counter to the increasing concentration of power in the president's hands.

During the last two years of the Soviet state, the rapid pace of political and economic change itself impeded progress toward drafting a new constitution. Perhaps the most volatile area of the law was the rapidly evolving nature of federal relations. In 1989 the Baltic states declared themselves sovereign and the following year the Lithuanian Supreme Soviet declared the republic's independence from the USSR.

In the Baltic republics and elsewhere laws were being passed by legislatures that directly contradicted all-union legislation, resulting in what Russian commentators dubbed "law wars" or "anarchy of laws." Some decisions, such as Moscow Mayor Gavril Popov's plan for the privatization of state-owned housing in the city, were overturned by the USSR Supreme Court. In other cases, federal authorities acceded to local wishes and did not challenge new laws and decrees passed by subnational bodies. The ability of Gorbachev's government to enforce compliance in cases involving conflicts of law was so marginal that, in effect, most regional and local legislation was permitted to stand unchallenged. Yet, these developments further eroded the legitimacy of the existing constitutional framework of the Soviet system.

The August 1991 abortive *coup d'état* both hastened the collapse of the old order and reinforced the society's commitment to constitutional government. Throughout the three-day crisis, those who resisted the action of the Committee on the State of Emergency accused the coup's organizers of violating the constitutional system, specifically the illegal and unconstitutional removal of the president from office. The Committee on the State of Emergency attempted to legitimize the take-over by declaring a national emergency:

A mortal danger has come to loom large over our great Motherland. The policy of reforms, launched at Mikhail Gorbachev's initiative and designed as means to ensure the country's dynamic development and the democratization of social life, have entered for several reasons into a blind alley ... All democratic institutions created by the popular will are losing weight and effectiveness right in front of our eyes ... The country is sinking into the quagmire of violence and lawlessness.[12]

In his appeal broadcast to the people of Russia, President Yeltsin denounced the putsch as a "reactionary unconstitutional *coup d'état*" and demanded "a return of the country to normal constitutional development."[13] Law was a crucial weapon on the side of Yeltsin and the defenders of the White House. Few people wanted to revert to the days where the constitution and laws could be ignored at the convenience of whoever was in power at the time. Thus, the victory over the Committee on the State of Emergency was a victory for constitutionalism in Russia.

In the aftermath of the August 1991 coup, the majority of the republics voted to become independent, sovereign states. All-union political institutions were losing their authority and legitimacy as power flowed to the republics and regions. For constitutionalism to develop, a minimum degree of consensus is required as to the basic structures and values of the system. By late 1991 Soviet society was simply too fluid and wracked by political conflict for such consensus to develop. Ultimately, progress toward drafting a new constitution of the USSR and a USSR Federal Treaty was overwhelmed by the collapse of the Soviet Union as a state.

Post-Soviet constitutional development in Russia

The collapse of the Soviet state in late 1991 made the ratification of a new constitution most urgent for Russia. Since the USSR no longer existed as a legal entity its laws technically no longer had legal force.[14] To fill this void, President Yeltsin and the parliament concurred that the constitution and laws of the former RSFSR would continue to be observed until a new constitution and laws could be adopted. This was a necessary, but unsatisfactory situation, since the 1978 Constitution of the Russian Federation and most of the laws were products of the Brezhnev era and reflected the values of the now-repudiated communist system.

The collapse of the USSR and the secession of fifteen independent states did not resolve all of the aspirations of ethnic groups residing in the former USSR. Nationality groups below the level of the fifteen former union-republics also were demanding increased political and economic power. Resolving these conflicting issues was especially critical in the Russian Federation where more than 100 ethnic groups reside. Many constitutional scholars felt it was necessary to resolve these federative issues prior to the ratification of a new constitution. Thus, the adoption of a new Federation Treaty on March 31, 1992 represented a major step in the effort to redefine the relations between the Russian Federation and the various "subjects" of the Federation. Modelled after earlier draft union treaties that circulated in the USSR since 1991, the Federation Treaty spelled out the respective jurisdictions of Russia and the republics. The terms of the treaty were then incorporated into several constitutional amendments adopted in April 1992. The general thrust of the amendments was to decentralize power and grant concessions to ethnic minorities. Federal authority was maintained over currency, customs regulations, banking and credit institutions, communications, transportation, nuclear energy, space exploration, defense, security, arms production and procurement, administration of justice, and weights and standards among other areas. Concurrent powers were recognized in environmental protection, conservation, historic preservation, education, science, culture, sports, health care, social welfare and social protection, disaster relief and emergency situations, as well as natural resources, minerals, and forestry. The "subjects" of the Federation enjoy reserve powers.

Although the Federation Treaty represents a significant departure from the USSR's concentration of power in the center, the provision of concurrent federal–republic control of natural resources in particular prompted Tatarstan to refuse to sign the document. Checheno-Ingushetia also refused to recognize the treaty; the Chechens were pushing for total independence from Moscow. The threat of break-away regions and the lack of clear delineation of concurrent powers in the treaty meant that thorny constitutional questions had yet to be resolved.

Progress toward drafting a new constitution and laws was thus delayed by heated disputes over three major issues:

> the relative allocation of powers between the executive branch (presidency) and the legislative branch (parliament),

> the relative allocation of powers between central (federal) and subnational institutions, and

> the process for ratifying a new constitution.

In early 1992 the Russian Supreme Soviet convened a special commission for drafting a new constitution to govern the newly independent state. The commission was chaired by President Yeltsin, but the actual work of drafting the document was headed by Executive Secretary Oleg Rumyantsev, the noted Russian constitutional scholar. Included on the commission were many prominent jurists and legal scholars, including several who had been involved in earlier attempts to draft a new constitution for the USSR. During the drafting process, the commission was heavily influenced by legal scholars associated with the pro-reform Institute of State and Law. This group not only pushed for legal reforms, but also had considerable knowledge and expertise about the legal systems in the United States, France, Germany, the Scandinavian countries, as well as the reformist Central European states such as Poland and Hungary. On the other hand, the commission was also criticized by some prosecutors for not incorporating enough people actually working in the area of law enforcement.[15]

The commission released a draft constitution for consideration by the Sixth Congress of People's Deputies, which met in April 1992.

Despite meticulous efforts of the commission to balance executive and legislative powers, the document encountered sharp opposition from parliamentarians of various political persuasions. The commission's draft created a semi-presidential republic with a federal structure. The president would have substantial authority, including the right to name Cabinet members, veto legislation, issue decrees, call referenda, and make fundamental social, economic, and foreign policy decisions. The existing two-tiered system of the Congress of People's Deputies and the Supreme Soviet would be abolished in favor of a bicameral legislature.

Parliamentarians within the Congress of People's Deputies and the Supreme Soviet objected to limiting the power of legislative bodies and to the need for new elections to a reconfigured parliament. Leading the opposition of the "official draft" of the constitution was parliamentary speaker Ruslan Khasbulatov. A commentator in the newspaper *Megapolis-Express* characterized the dilemma confronting the commission as a no-win situation:

The opposition forces were by no means represented by the former nomenklatura alone. Whereas the Communists call Rumyantsev's draft "bourgeois," Professors Sobchak and Popov call it "socialist," the hard-line democrats call it "eclectic," and the national-patriots call it "Russophobic." You can't please everyone, especially when the issue at hand concerns the dividing up of power. The up-shot was that the authors of the draft, in an effort to divide power amicably, simultaneously deprived both the President and the parliament of what they consider their fair shares. Naturally, both sides presented their own arguments to the Congress, amendments that reflected different understanding of harmony and fairness.[16]

Ten days before the Congress convened to discuss the new constitutional draft, a second draft document prepared by Sergei Alekseev and Anatoly Sobchak was circulated. Both Alekseev and Sobchak were noted jurists and had been members of the commission working on a draft of a new constitution of the USSR in 1989. They were deeply dissatisfied with the Rumyantsev draft because they felt it insufficiently protected the civil rights and liberties of Russian citizens, inadequately provided for separation of powers which they considered essential to avoid a return to dictatorial rule, and was unclear on "national-state structure."[17] Furthermore, Sobchak and Alekseev argued that the drafting commission relied too much on the form and structure of the Brezhnev Constitution. Sobchak observed: "I see no fundamental difference between the point in Article 1 of the draft that proclaims 'the Russian state is a social state' and the same article in the Brezhnev Constitution, which proclaims that 'the Soviet Union is a state of all the people.' The words are different, but the meaning is the same."[18]

Sobchak's draft constitution relied heavily on the model constitution developed by Andrei Sakharov prior to his death in early 1990. That document called for the creation of a parliamentary republic in which the executive would have little independent authority. Sakharov's draft enshrined individual rights and permitted each ethnic group within the Russian Federation to negotiate its own status within the federation, rather than have one Union Treaty attempting to set a uniform standard of center/periphery relations for each regional and ethnic group. Finally Sobchak and Alekseev advocated the convening of a Constituent Assembly to ratify a new constitution, arguing that the Congress of People's Deputies was no longer a viable institution and lacked a popular mandate, having been elected by a flawed process in 1990.[19]

A third draft constitution was worked out by President Yeltsin's chief legal adviser, Sergei Shakhrai. That draft called for the creation of a republic with a strong executive presidency. Under the terms of Shakhrai's draft, the president would be elected for a six-year term. He would appoint a cabinet, without parliamentary approval or confirmation. The president would also have the right to introduce legislation in the parliament. He would have veto power over parliamentary legislation, although the parliament could overrule a veto with a two-thirds majority. The "presidential" draft, like the other two drafts, would establish a bicameral legislature. Parliament would not be able to impeach the president and the president could not disband the parliament.

Debate over these competing constitutional drafts often bogged down in trivialities, such as debating the legitimacy of the existing constitution of the Russian Federation. The Congress of People's Deputies argued for three days over whether to change references to Leningrad to St. Petersburg and whether to delete references to the USSR. As the debates grew more protracted and absurd, they tended to undermine the legitimacy of the congress to make such a momentous decision. *De facto* power was gravitating to the presidency as the country faced critical economic, political, and social problems and the parliament appeared determined to avoid taking action.

The debate over a new constitution raised many quandaries. How can the Russian Federation break from the legacies of the communist past? Should all pre-existing institutions be abolished? If so, by what authority? Should pre-existing institutions (namely, the Congress of People's Deputies) be permitted to ratify a new constitution? The pre-existing constitution of the RSFSR (1978) declared that the congress wields "supreme power," while relegating to the president the role of "the highest official" and "the head of executive power in Russia."[20] Changing this provision would be tantamount to the congress voting themselves out of office, or at a minimum calling for new elections, in which many of the deputies would not be re-elected. Yeltsin considered the congress "an artificial, supraparliament [whose] very existence is a permanent basis for disrupting the balance among the legislative, executive and judicial branches."[21] But, what other legitimate mechanisms could be employed to ratify a new constitution?

In an effort to circumvent the congress, the first deputy premier, Gennady Burbulis, proposed the convening of an Assembly of Russian Citizens or Constituent Assembly to ratify a new document.[22] Burbulis' proposal won the support of several pro-Yeltsin factions and parties including Democratic Russia, the Republic Party, Free Russia People's Party, and the Peasants' Party. Speaker of the parliament, Ruslan Khasbulatov, and Sergei Filatov, first vice-chairman of the Russian Supreme Soviet, denounced Burbulis' proposal for a Constituent Assembly on the grounds that it would infringe the power of the Congress of People's Deputies.[23] Furthermore, Filatov indicated that even when a new constitution is ratified, deputies to the congress should be allowed to serve out their terms to insure an orderly transitional period and legislative continuity.[24]

Opposition to a Constituent Assembly combined with the anticipated controversy over how to select delegates to such a gathering argued in favor of the president scheduling a national referendum on a draft constitution. On several occasions through 1992 and 1993 President Yeltsin threatened the intransigent members of the Supreme Soviet with a public referendum. Even if referendum results were not binding, under the terms of the existing constitution and the Law on Referenda, a strong public endorsement of a new constitution by the citizens of Russia would severely undermine the position of the parliament.[25]

The deadlock over resolving the constitutional issue was also perpetuating chaos elsewhere in the law and judicial administration. Since the Russian legal system is based on a codified system of laws, the drafting of a constitution takes on added significance. In the civil law tradition, the constitution establishes the foundation upon which all other bodies of law are built. Thus, Russian jurists were reluctant to press for major revisions in the criminal code, to adopt a new commercial code to govern economic relations, and to introduce a new land law and other codes, until a new constitution was in place. Meanwhile, the pace of policy changes had greatly outstripped changes in codification, leaving citizens and foreigners operating in a state of legal confusion. The anarchy of laws that prevailed also tended to strengthen the hand of the president and further eroded the balance of power between the legislative and executive branches. By mid-1992, it was becoming imperative that the constitutional impasse be resolved, since it was impeding the political and economic transition in virtually every sphere. Yet, with the current configuration of power, the president was unable to overcome his opponents in the parliament. This constitutional deadlock had degenerated into a full-blown crisis by early 1993.

October 1993 constitutional crisis

The constitutional order in Russia had become badly eroded by early 1993. The Supreme Soviet, led by Ruslan Khasbulatov, used its power to block Yeltsin's legislative initiatives. As a consequence, Yeltsin resorted to ruling by decree. However, Khasbulatov and Vice-President Aleksandr Rutskoi both denounced Yeltsin's decrees as unconstitutional and illegitimate. Commentators began to liken the impasse to the period of "dual power" (*dvoevlastiye*) that existed during the summer of 1917 when the Bolsheviks and the Provisional Government controlled competing councils that issued conflicting decrees and proclamations.[26] The previous experience with dual power led to a breakdown of law and order and ultimately resulted in the Bolsheviks' decision to seize power by force. No one wished to see history repeated.

The 8th Russian Congress of People's Deputies, March 10–13, 1993 refused to renew the emergency powers that it had temporarily granted Yeltsin in November 1991, making it more difficult for him to continue his market-oriented reforms. The congress deputies, the majority of whom were conservative critics of Yeltsin, had been elected in 1990 when the Communist Party still held a monopoly on political power. The agenda for the 8th Congress consisted of only two items: a resolution on implementing constitutional reform and a proposal to review compliance with the Russian constitution by the legislative and executive branches. Yeltsin tried to add two other items to the agenda: a proposed referendum on constitutional reform and a proposal to hold early elections to a new parliament and the presidency. On the eve of the Congress Yeltsin met with advisers to discuss ways to avert a showdown with the parliament. The president repeated his thinly veiled threat that if the Congress continued on its obstructionist course he would have to resort to "extreme measures."[27] He acknowledged that such measures, most probably the dissolving of the Congress, and introducing a state of emergency and direct presidential rule, would not be in accordance with the existing constitution.[28]

After a stormy appearance before the Congress on March 12, Yeltsin walked out. The congress went on to amend the constitution to protect its own interests. The Congress amended Article 121-6 to prevent the president from disbanding constitutionally elected bodies. Should the president attempt to dissolve any of these bodies without the congress' consent, it would constitute grounds for impeachment.

On March 13 the congress voted against holding a constitutional referendum, as Yeltsin had proposed. The existing Law on Referenda stated that a referendum could only be called at the request of one-third of the deputies and Yeltsin was 59 votes short. Complicating the issue of holding a national referendum to reaffirm the president's authority and economic policy, was the rising tide of ethnic nationalism in various regions of the Russian Federation. In Tatarstan, President Shaimeev announced that no referendum would be held in his republic regardless of what happened in the rest of the federation.[29] Other minority regions including Yakutia, Dagestan, and Khakassia threatened to follow suit.[30]

The chairman of the Constitutional Court warned that the country was "on the brink of catastrophe." He noted, "it is better to live under a bad constitution, than with no rules at all," an allusion to his desire to continue to operate under the 1978 Constitution of the RSFSR that would retain full parliamentary powers.[31]

Faced with an impasse of monumental proportions, Yeltsin addressed the country on March 20, 1993 and repeated his veiled threat to impose direct presidential rule. He announced a national referendum for April 25 and promised that he would abide by the results. Valery Zokin, speaking on behalf of the Constitutional Court, which had neither heard oral arguments nor considered briefs in the case, declared that the president's proposed action would violate the constitution and provide grounds for impeachment.[32] Three days later, Yeltsin backed away from a direct confrontation with the parliament. Yeltsin's decree made no mention of "special rule" nor of disbanding the parliament. It did call for a referendum on Yeltsin's presidency and on the proposed constitution. Presidential spokesman Vyacheslav Kostikov alluded to the fact that popular approval of the draft constitution was Yeltsin's chief objective in the dispute with parliament. His aim was never to impose direct presidential rule, but instead he wanted approval of the referendum as a fallback position, hoping that a popular mandate would bolster his position *vis-à-vis* the congress.[33] The stakes were high, however. Should Yeltsin not obtain majority support in the vote of confidence on his leadership, he declared that he would be duty-bound to step down.[34] The parliament reluctantly went along with Yeltsin's plans for a national referendum, but only after insisting that a question be included asking for voter confidence in Yeltsin's economic and social policies. The actual ballot contained four questions:

> *Question 1*
> Do you approve of President Yeltsin's leadership?
> *Question 2*
> Do you approve of President Yeltsin's social and economic
>   policies?
> *Question 3*
> Do you favor early elections for the presidency?
> *Question 4*
> Do you favor early elections for the parliament?

Yeltsin and his Russia's Choice faction mobilized voters with the slogan "Da. Da. Nyet. Da!" To the surprise of many political observers and members of the parliament, Yeltsin's support remained fairly high. More than 62 percent of the country's 105.5 million eligible voters took part in the referendum; 59 percent of the voters expressed confidence in Yeltsin's leadership and 53 percent approved of his socio-economic policies. Only 40 percent of eligible voters favored early presidential elections, while 74 percent favored early elections for the parliament.[35] However, in order to be binding, more than half of all eligible voters had to approve early elections, thus the referendum did not force out the conservative legislators. It did strengthen Yeltsin's hand and his claims to legitimacy for his leadership and reform program.

Following his strong showing in the April 1993 referendum, Yeltsin released yet another draft constitution. This document was further amended by a Constitutional Assembly convened during the summer of 1993 to provide input from Russia's eighty-nine "subjects" or regions.[36] Members of the Constitutional Assembly had been selected by regional administrators most of whom were loyal to the president. Not surprisingly, this draft called for the creation of a strong presidency.

The debate among three competing drafts of a new constitution exposed the key dilemmas confronting the transitional regime. How could popular will and the political clout of reform advocates neutralize the influence on the drafting process of former members of the Soviet nomenklatura who were fighting to protect their power, property, and influence? What is the proper forum for adopting a new constitution – a popular referendum, a constitutional convention, or parliamentary approval? Should the society continue to be bound by the Brezhnev-vintage constitution that vests all power in the Congress of People's Deputies and the Supreme Soviet, even though those bodies were dominated by former communists, most of whom had no claim to electoral legitimacy?

The course that Yeltsin and Russia was taking had few if any models to follow. The American and French Revolutions toppled colonial or monarchial regimes and sought a clean break from the past. In the Russian case, the revolution was being attempted from the top down. Rather than experiencing a clean break from the past, Yeltsin was attempting a "controlled" and orderly revolution. The stakes were high and there was no guarantee that if one side saw that it was losing the argument, it would not resort to violence to preserve its interests.

Another fundamental issue left unresolved in the three drafts was how to strike a balance between maintaining some national unity, while providing ethnic groups and regions some power to make their own policies. The forces favoring a strong union and those favoring granting more powers to the various regions and republics within the Russian Federation did not neatly coincide with supporters of Yeltsin or his opponents. Generally speaking, supporters of a strong presidency tended to support strong centralized institutions in Moscow. Yet, even Yeltsin recognized the important political powerbase that existed in the countryside and attempted to tap that support by convening the Constitutional Assembly to adopt the new constitution.

Less fundamental, yet nonetheless vexing, problems remained in the constitutional drafts.[37] None of the draft constitutions amply protected civil rights of citizens. Insufficient protections were also afforded for private property – largely because members of the various drafting commissions could not agree on whether or how to privatize the land and other assets of the country. As a carry-over from the seventy-four-year experience with communism, all three draft constitutions tended to make sweeping promises of social entitlements which the collapsing Russian state was in no position to deliver to its citizens.

The inability of the government to resolve these fundamental disputes and dilemmas resulted in a continued stalemate between the president and the parliament that eventually came to a head in September and early October 1993. On September 21 President Yeltsin issued a decree dissolving the parliament. Throughout the summer the parliament had stalled on approving Yeltsin's proposed legislation on private land ownership. Deputies approved a budget that would have resulted in continued soaring inflation rates. In the foreign policy field, the parliament took provocative actions on the Crimea dispute that further strained relations with Ukraine. These actions put the parliament and the president on a collision course.

When issuing his decree disbanding the parliament, Yeltsin noted that his actions were not consistent with the existing constitution, but he indicated that the constitution was no longer workable. The parliament refused to disband, so it was evicted by force on October 4. Parliamentary Speaker Khasbulatov and Vice-President Rutskoi eventually surrendered and were arrested, along with many of their supporters who had been barricaded in the White House.

In overcoming his opponents in the parliament, Yeltsin cleared the way for the ratification of a new constitution, the draft of which was circulated on November 9. Yeltsin announced a national referendum to approve the new constitution to be held on December 12. At the same time elections would be held to a newly reconfigured parliament.

The constitutional draft which was voted on in December incorporated the major elements of the earlier presidential draft constitution. Revisions inserted after the October 4th insurrection reduced the status of republics and regions and defined more clearly the relations between federal structures. For example, republics, territories, regions, federal cities, and autonomous areas were referred to as "subjects" rather than constituent units of the Russian Federation. The constitution, as ratified in December 1993, envisioned an essentially unitary system, with subnational units having regional representation, but within a strong unitary framework. In addition, several provisions strengthening the president were inserted prior to the release of the final draft document on November 9. For example, the president was given the power to appoint the prime minister, subject only to the "consent" of the lower house of parliament. The president appoints other ministers on the recommendation of the prime minister. The president also enjoys the right to preside over meetings of the government, giving him much more direct influence in the day-to-day administration of policy than is the case in France, for example.

The constitution clearly establishes the Russian Federation as a presidential republic. The parliament (Federal Assembly) is composed of two houses, the State Duma or lower house consists of 450 elected deputies and an upper house (Council of the Federation) consists of 178 deputies – two from each of the 89 regions of the Russian Federation.[38] Deputies to the State Duma are elected for a four-year term, but no term is provided for the Federation Council. In fact, it is not even clear in the constitution whether members of the Federation Council must be elected. The constitution states that the chamber will "be composed" and avoids using the word "elected," perhaps because the drafters were emulating the upper chamber of the German parliament, the Bundesrat, whose members are local officials selected indirectly in their respective regions. Nevertheless, deputies to the first Federation Council were elected along with deputies to the State Duma on December 12, 1993. In drafting the provisions on the separation of powers, Yeltsin's advisors clearly relied heavily on the French, German, and American models. The division of functions between the two chambers of the parliament, their bases of representation, and the introduction of and threshold clause and "split-list voting" to the lower house resemble features of the current German Basic Law.

The constitution, like that of the United States and France, provides for a strong, directly elected president. The president appoints the prime minister and this appointment is subject to confirmation by the legislature. All other members of the government (Cabinet) are appointed by the President upon the suggestion of the prime minister and are not confirmed by the State Duma. In addition to the posts of chair and deputy chair of the Cabinet, the president appoints the chair of the Central Bank, judges to the Supreme Court, Constitutional Court, and Superior Arbitration Court, and the prosecutor-general.

If the State Duma refuses to confirm the president's choice for prime minister three times, the president may dissolve the parliament and call new elections. This provision was added in reaction to the refusal of the Congress of People's Deputies to approve Yegor Gaidar, Yeltsin's candidate for prime minister in 1992. This provision was intended to coerce the parliament into eventually approving a presidential nomination rather than face new elections. However, the threat of a parliamentary rejection of a nominee could also prompt the president to name a prime minister who is more acceptable to the Duma.

Another provision inserted into the final draft of the constitution which forces the president to cooperate to some extent with the parliament stipulates that there cannot be a vote of no confidence within the State Duma during the first year of office. Furthermore, the State Duma cannot be dissolved if it is considering treason charges against the president and possible impeachment, if the president has declared a state of emergency in the country, or if the presidential term is within six months of expiring.

Like the French president, Yeltsin now has the authority to dismiss the government without the approval of the State Duma. The president is responsible for foreign policy and defense, he chairs the Security Council and has the authority to declare war and states of emergency. In the latter two instances, the president does not need to secure the approval of either house of the parliament; he is only obliged to inform them "without delay."[39]

Throughout his term in the presidency and especially during the last year of confrontation with parliamentary leaders culminating in the October 4 storming of the White House, Yeltsin was charged with violating the former constitution and threatened with possible impeachment. The new constitution spells out a detailed and very restrictive process of impeachment that makes it unlikely the president could be forced from office. Impeachment proceedings are initiated by the vote of no less than one-third of the deputies of the State Duma alleging treason or "other grave crime" on the part of the president. A committee is then formed by the Duma to evaluate the charges. Following this investigation, a formal bill of impeachment requires a two-thirds vote in the Duma. The Duma's actions are also subject to confirmation by both the Constitutional Court and the Supreme Court.[40] Finally, all of these decisions are handed over to the Council of the Federation that makes the final determination by a two-thirds vote. The entire process cannot exceed three months.

The powers of the parliament lie primarily in legislative initiative and oversight. Whereas most economic policy decisions lie with the government (including fiscal controls, credit, monetary policy and budgeting), the Duma must approve these policies. In addition, the

State Duma confirms the president's appointments for the posts of prime minister, chair of the Central Bank, comptroller, and human rights commissioner.

Supervision in the areas of foreign policy, armed forces, security affairs, and internal relations of constituent parts of the federation rests with the upper house, the Council of the Federation. The upper house also confirms appointments to the Constitutional Court, the Supreme Court, the Superior Court of Arbitration, and the prosecutor-general.

During its troubled transition to democracy, one of the chronic problems in Russia has been confusing, overlapping, and conflicting jurisdictions and competences of legislative and executive bodies at various levels of government. The new constitution does not substantially remedy this situation. The constitution does spell out the respective powers of the president and the parliament on legislation. Legislation can be initiated by the president, either chamber of the parliament and their deputies, the government, and legislative organs of the "subjects" of the Federation. The rights of legislative initiative are also vested in the Constitutional Court, the Supreme Court, and the Superior Court of Arbitration in matters under their jurisdictions. The president may veto legislation, although he does not have the power of a line-item veto that the presidential draft of the constitution had proposed. A presidential veto can be overridden by a two-thirds majority of the total members of the Federation Council and the State Duma.

Most of the confusion in the Russian legislative scene today is introduced by the liberal policy of empowering numerous institutions and bodies to issue binding decrees and other normative acts. The president has unrestricted authority to issue decrees, edicts, and directives and to call referenda. Presidential decrees are binding and have force of law unless they are specifically rescinded by the parliament. Both chambers of the parliament also have the power to issue decrees within their respective policy areas. To add to the confusion, the constitution also gives the government (including individual ministries) the power to issue decrees, edicts, and directives on issues related to policy implementation. However, the constitution fails to provide adequate procedures for preventing or adjudicating clashes between these various types of legislation.[41]

The principal arbiter of disputes between the executive and the legislature is the Constitutional Court, which has been enlarged from thirteen members to nineteen members. The court guarantees that all federal laws and decrees comply with the constitution. The court also is empowered to resolve jurisdictional disputes between federal bodies. Disputes between subnational bodies are entrusted to the Supreme Court, unless they pertain to constitutional issues. In addition, the president is granted the authority to mediate disputes between federal organs and various bodies in the constituent parts of the federation.[42]

One of the most potent weapons in the hands of the president is the power to suspend acts by executive officials in regions and republics when those acts contradict the constitution, federal law, or treaties signed by the Russian Federation. In earlier versions of the constitution, this power rested only with the Constitutional Court.

Article 71 spells out the area of exclusive federal jurisdiction, including control over federal property, the federal budget, federal taxes, transport, communications, power generation, currency, the treasury, financial institutions, postal service, armed forces, defense and security, foreign policy, and foreign economic relations. More controversial is Article 72 that specifies the realm of joint federal–regional jurisdiction. These powers include control over land use and disposal, mineral resources, water and other natural resources, public health facilities, social services, cultural, educational, recreational, and scientific facilities. In addition, federal and regional and local officials are jointly responsible for environmental protection, housing, law enforcement, "delimitation" of state property, and the establishment of general principles for the organization of local self-government. Yet, the constitution fails to specify the details of how such joint jurisdiction would work in practice. No doubt, the complexities of center–periphery relations in Russia argued in favor of a generally worded and vague statement. However, this lack of specificity will undoubtedly be the source of on-going tensions and disputes between federal officials in Moscow and leaders of the regions that are "subjects" of the Russian Federation.

Another deficiency of the new constitution is its weak provision and guarantee accorded to rights and liberties stated in Articles 17–64 and incorporated in several other articles of the document.[43] Many of these guarantees are so broad and absolute that they are unachievable. For example, Article 38 states, "Concern for children and their upbringing are the equal right and duty of the parents." Articles 39 and 40 guarantee pensions, social benefits, and housing, although the state is in no position to be able to deliver on these promises. Most disturbing to some Western observers is the provision enabling the president to declare a state of emergency, which would in effect suspend any or all of these civil rights of citizens.[44] Most democracies have provisions for states of emergency or police powers which are necessary for the survival of the state and society during times of civil or natural disaster. The existence of such provisions in the new Russian constitution should not by itself be alarming. Rather, it would only be alarming if such extraordinary powers were invoked frequently, especially to further some narrow partisan political interest.

The seemingly exhaustive list of rights and protections of Russian citizens contained in the constitution is, no doubt, a reaction to the repressive history of the Soviet and tsarist systems. Thus, there are specific prohibitions against torture, disseminating propaganda, and being subjected to medical, scientific, or other experiments without their voluntary consent (Articles 21 and 29). Furthermore, citizens are protected against the collection, storage, utilization, and dissemination of information about a person's private life without his or her consent (Article 24). Article 27 proclaims that each person may freely travel outside the Russian Federation and the right to return without impediment and also may travel and move one's residence freely inside the Russian Federation. Article 13 prohibits the adoption of a state ideology.

Some provisions of the new constitution clearly reject earlier socialist economic norms. Articles 9 and 36 recognize the right to private ownership of land and Article 34 states that each person has the right to engage in entrepreneurial activity.

The constitution also incorporates several of the amendments in Russian criminal law and procedure made during the period 1988 through 1991. These changes were enacted to facilitate a fair and unbiased judicial process, especially in criminal cases. Article 49 formally establishes a presumption of innocence. Article 50 prohibits double jeopardy. Article 51 states that a person may not be compelled to testify against himself. Citizens are guaranteed the right to a trial by jury (Articles 20 and 47) and to compensation for damages if they are victims of crime (Article 52). Finally, the constitution prohibits the expulsion or extradition of citizens to other states.

As in previous constitutions of the USSR, the section on rights also contains specific duties of citizens. Thus, the constitution establishes the obligation of citizens to pay taxes and duties, to protect nature, the environment and cultural monuments, and to protect the Russian Federation, including the obligation to serve in the armed forces

(Article 59). Unlike previous documents, however, the latter obligation includes alternative service for those people who, due to religious beliefs, cannot perform military service.

Chapter 9 of the constitution sets out the procedures for amending the constitution. Reacting to the excessive amending of the Russian constitution during the gridlock between President Yeltsin and the parliament in 1992 and 1993, the drafters favored much more restrictive amendment procedures. Amendments to Chapter 1 (Foundations of the Constitutional System), Chapter 2 (Human and Civil Rights and Freedoms) and Chapter 9 require a three-fifths vote of members of the Federation Council and the State Duma. A Constitutional Assembly is then convened and may amend the constitution with a two-thirds vote or alternatively the amendment may be ratified by a national referendum. In the case of a referendum, the amendment requires that a majority of voters support the amendment and that more than half of all eligible voters participate in the referendum. Amendments to Chapters 3–8 require ratification by the legislative organs of at least two-thirds of the subjects of the Russian Federation.

Conclusion

On the face of it, the new Constitution of the Russian Federation vests tremendous powers in the presidency and leaves the parliament with only marginal powers. Critics of President Yeltsin maintained that he was creating through quasi-legal means an authoritarian state structure. Oleg Rumyantsev charged that the document "legalizes [the president's] own dictatorship."[45] Vladimir Lysenko, a member of the president's Commission on Legislative Proposals, also spoke out against the concentration of so much power in the hands of the president.[46]

Yeltsin's decree calling for a plebiscite on the draft constitution was issued on October 15 and the draft document was made public on November 9, leaving only one month for debate and discussion of the constitution. Yeltsin's choice of terminology "plebiscite" rather than "referendum" was not accidental. According to the 1990 Law on Referenda, issues affecting the constitution required the support of a majority of all registered voters, rather than a majority of all those voting. This requirement made it extremely unlikely that any constitution would achieve support by means of a national referendum. In his March 1991 referendum creating the Russian presidency, Yeltsin received the support of 69.85 percent of the voters, yet this represented barely more than half of all registered voters due to low levels of voter participation. Faced with declining voter turnout and an intransigent parliament, Yeltsin had planned to convene a special Constitutional Assembly to enact a new document. However, after the October violent clash with the Russian parliament, the regions began to make unacceptable demands for sovereignty. Thus, Yeltsin proposed a constitutional plebiscite in which approval of the new constitution would require a simple majority of participating voters.

Results of the December plebiscite confirmed Yeltsin's forecast. Only 54.8 percent of registered voters bothered to cast ballots, and, of those, 58.4 percent supported the new constitution.[47] Had the constitutional ratification depended on the referendum it would have lost, since only about 31 percent of all eligible voters supported the new constitution. The month-long delay in publishing the official election results also led to accusations of vote rigging, but no wrong-doing has been substantiated.[48]

Critics of Yeltsin feared that with the ratification of the new constitution, Russia would become a constitutional autocracy, with the president wielding unchecked powers.[49] Western commentators expressed great concern that Russia was drifting toward authoritarianism. One commentator went so far as to charge that the new constitution would result in the reinstitution of a "totalitarian system."[50] However, these fears have since proven to be exaggerated.

The election of the new parliament in December 1993 appears to have moderated any attempt on Yeltsin's part to abuse his strong presidential powers. Although the pro-Yeltsin party Russia's Choice won the largest portion of the seats in the State Duma (21.3 percent), the bloc of seats controlled by Vladimir Zhirinovsky's Liberal Democratic Party, the Communist Party of Russia and the Agrarian Party together accounted for 40.4 percent of the seats in the Duma. Moderate reform and centrist parties control most of the remaining 38.3 percent of the seats. Given this tenuous balance in the parliament, Yeltsin has been reluctant to rule by decree and ignore his opponents. To do so would likely precipitate another constitutional crisis and erode the legitimacy of the constitution that grants him strong powers. All sides seem to realize that the new constitution, despite its flaws, is immeasurably better than continuing to operate under an antiquated Brezhnev-era document.

The development of constitutional government in Russia in recent years serves to remind us that constitutions are not static legal documents that spring into existence fully formed. Rather, constitutions, and the political institutions they create, must develop their own legitimacy and evolve over time in response to changing political, social, and economic conditions. It is encouraging that all parties in Russia today – even the extremists on the right – appear to recognize the legitimacy of the new constitution and are operating within its provisions. This is the best indication yet that Russia is on its way to constitutionalism. However, given its centuries-long tradition of dictatorial and arbitrary rule, it will be a long and perilous journey.

5 Citizens and the state: the debate over the Procuracy

Today there is law and order in everything. You cannot beat someone for no reason. If you do beat someone, it must be for the sake of order.

Maxim Gorky,
The Lower Depths (1903)

A single death is a tragedy, a million deaths is a statistic.[1]
Joseph Stalin, 1879–1953

A fundamental component of reform of the Russian legal system is redefining the status of individual citizens *vis-à-vis* the state. As we have noted, since ancient times, state authority has ruled supreme in Russia and was only marginally restricted by the power of law, the courts, or constitutions. Indicative of the state-centric conception of legal authority is the predominant role played by the Procuracy in the Russian legal system. In recent years, political pressures unleashed by the policies of glasnost, perestroika, and democratization have, however, posed a serious challenge to the role of the Procuracy. In the wake of the attempted August 1991 *coup d'état*, and the fragmentation of central organs of authority of the former USSR, the future role of the prosecutor's office in the Russian legal system is a hotly debated issue. At the heart of the debate is the question whether (or how) the rights and interests of citizens should be enhanced and the powers of the state curtailed.

History of the Procuracy

The Procuracy dates back to 1722, when Peter the Great created the post of procurator-general, subordinate to the Imperial Senate. The Procuracy was charged with the dual functions of supervising the activities of the Senate to protect against abrogation of its decrees and

104

regulations, and supervising the prompt and full execution of edicts. The introduction of the Procuracy was an attempt, in a single stroke, to incorporate in Russia a public law system similar to those that had developed in Western Europe over the course of centuries. Peter's attempt to introduce public law norms into Russia ultimately failed due to the absolutist and personal nature of power of the Russian monarchy and the absence of a workable foundation of private law in Russian society.

Catherine II extended procuratorial supervision to regional and local levels where procurators served as the "eyes of the tsar" in monitoring the activity of provincial governors and other officials. Procurators attended meetings of various administrative and executive bodies to insure that their actions conformed to law. When a breach of the law was discovered, it was reported to a superior procurator as well as to the provincial governor and, in some cases, to the minister of justice.

Procuratorial supervision of regional and local administration was resented by the provincial governors and was eliminated by the legal reforms of 1864. Those reforms confined the Procuracy to the prosecution of criminal cases and appealing criminal and civil court actions. Responsibility for criminal investigations was also taken away and given to pre-trial investigators who functioned as independent judicial officers, subordinate to the trial court. Thus, the Procuracy after 1864 resembled somewhat its French counterpart and its functions remained largely unchanged until the Bolshevik Revolution in 1917.

A decree of the Council of People's Commissars of November 24, 1917 abolished the Procuracy and all other tsarist legal institutions. The Bolsheviks favored informal control mechanisms, such as worker tribunals. However, just as Peter discovered 200 years earlier, Lenin found that the tribunals were inadequate to stem the rise of crime and abuses of power by local and regional officials. A People's Commissariat of Justice was created to prosecute criminals and to review local and regional actions of officials which conflicted with the decrees of the central government. The People's Commissariat of State Control and later the People's Commissariat of Workers' and Peasants' Inspection also were granted the power to indict or recommend the dismissal of regional and local officials who failed to execute laws faithfully.

In 1922 the Bolshevik Government reestablished the Procuracy and invested it with the power to supervise the legality of administrative officials, agencies, and citizens. In his famous letter on "Dual Subordination and Legality" Lenin noted that the Procuracy must be a single, unified, hierarchical organization, completely independent of local and regional authorities. Thus, from 1922 onward, the Procuracy resumed its pre-1864 character, as the "eyes of the state" to insure full and complete cooperation in executing the policies of the rulers.

The Procuracy's central position in the administration of justice after 1922 derived not only from its hierarchical and centralized organizational structure, but also from the wide range of functions it performed. The procurator was involved at every stage in the criminal process. The arrest of a suspect and the search for evidence required his written authorization. In Soviet criminal procedure, the prosecution of cases proceeded through two stages: preliminary investigation and trial. The procurator participated in both stages. In the most serious cases, investigators were often procuratorial officials. Also falling within the realm of procuratorial action were the review or appeal of criminal and civil cases, the supervision of prisons, prisoner complaints, parole, and the release of prisoners; supervision of the actions of the police and secret police; supervision of juvenile commissions; supervision of the courts; and supervision of the legal conduct of all government bodies, enterprises, social organizations, officials, and citizens. This latter function, the supervision of administrative and economic officials and bodies, is referred to as general supervision.

Under Joseph Stalin and his procurator-general, Andrei Vyshinsky, the Procuracy focused its energies almost exclusively on state-sponsored coercion. No longer did the Procuracy concern itself with citizens' complaints against administrative actions, rather it concentrated on weeding out all opponents of Stalin. Prior to the establishment of the infamous "special boards" in the Ministry of Internal Affairs, the Procuracy's primary responsibility was prosecuting political criminals and securing their speedy imprisonment or execution. It is estimated today that more than 40 million Soviet citizens died as a direct result of Stalin's terror.[2]

A second major responsibility of the Procuracy was overseeing the successful implementation of Stalin's industrialization and collectivization campaigns. Procurators undertook investigations not only of legal infractions and violations, but also to ensure proper execution of the party's policies. According to one Soviet jurist,

The view that the basic content of the work of the procurator in general supervision must be his direct "organizational-political" participation in carrying out economic campaigns was widely disseminated. In practice, this vague arrangement often led to converting the procurator into the authorized representative in sowing, harvesting, procurement and other economic campaigns.[3]

Some local procurators went so far as to prescribe the times and manner in which grain should be harvested or the manner in which production should be organized in a factory.[4] This economic focus of procuratorial supervision would continue throughout the Stalin years, and to a lesser extent until the late 1980s.

Following Stalin's death in 1953 and Khrushchev's denunciation of Stalin's abuses, discussions flourished concerning the need for legal reforms. Stalin's successors moved quickly to dismantle the infamous "special boards" and reorganize the security police apparatus. An editorial in *Pravda* in April 1955 criticized the Procuracy for "serious shortcomings" in failing to stop the "anti-state activities of individual officials."[5] Reflecting the new political climate, the emphasis in procuratorial supervision shifted from coercion and repression to prosecuting ordinary criminals and supervising legality.

One of the most significant developments of this period was a revival of interest in general supervision and the rights of the individual against state administration.[6] A Statute on Procuratorial Supervision in the USSR of May 24, 1955 expanded the Procuracy's terms of reference relative to general supervision. The statute for the first time spelled out procuratorial powers of protest, representation, and proposal. It also empowered procurators to demand official documents, records and information concerning possible violations of laws.

When a procurator encountered a ministerial decree or other "normative act" of an executive body that violated established laws, the procuracy filed a protest, citing reasons for the protest and demanding that the illegal act be rescinded or amended. In some cases, the Procuracy had the power to suspend implementation of the act, pending consideration of the protest. If the agency disagreed with the procurator's position and rejected the protest, the procurator could refer the matter to a procurator at a higher level. Procuratorial protests were successful in reversing illegal administrative actions in more than 96 percent of all cases in the first instance.[7]

Procuratorial representations were issued when prosecutors encountered numerous acts that they considered to be illegal or improperly handled by administrative officials. Because representations were not issued to a particular party, they did not command compliance or any particular response, rather they served merely as a warning to administrative officials. Procuratorial proposals were non-binding suggestions to administrative agencies and officials and were not usually based on legal violations.

Reflecting the reform orientation in Soviet law during the Khrushchev years, procuratorial actions primarily concerned grievances of individual citizens: violations of labor rights, illegal imposition of fines and other administrative sanctions, housing complaints, and complaints about officials overstepping their proper authority. However, this would change under the conservative leadership of Leonid Brezhnev. In 1968, in response to the Communist Party Central Committee criticism that the Procuracy was neglecting its role as the protector of the state's economic interests, the emphasis of procuratorial supervision shifted to representations reflecting the state's interests: theft of state property, substandard production, padding of plan-fulfillment records, and violations of labor discipline.[8] During the latter Brezhnev years procurators resumed their "micromanagement" of enterprises, factories, and farms to insure fulfillment of production plans and delivery schedules.

Throughout the post-Stalin period, the Procuracy also maintained its responsibility for investigating and prosecuting criminal cases. Under Brezhnev the Procuracy was particularly active in arresting and prosecuting dissidents. In June 1965, Brezhnev authorized the KGB to resume arresting critics of his regime. The process began in Leningrad and continued in the Ukraine with more than thirty arrests.[9] The crackdown culminated in September 1965 with the arrest of authors Andrei Sinyavsky and Yuli Daniel for having their books smuggled out of the USSR and published in the West. The arrest and trial of Sinyavsky and Daniel in 1965 together with the Soviet invasion of Czechoslovakia in 1968 gave rise to a period of vocal resistance to the Brezhnev regime. The Procuracy worked closely with the KGB in investigating, arresting, and prosecuting dissidents. By the time of Brezhnev's death in November 1982 the Procuracy had become greatly feared by Soviet citizens as an organization of state-sponsored coercion closely linked to the KGB.

The Procuracy grew in power and prestige during the post-Stalin period. In the late 1970s it employed more than 18,000 lawyers or some 12–13 percent of the legal profession. In addition, the Procuracy directly supervised another 18,000 criminal investigators, comprising over 14 percent of the legal profession.[10] N. S. Aleksandrov, former dean of the Juridical Faculty of Leningrad State University, reported that most law students wanted to become procurators. Traditionally, the top law students in each graduating class went to work for the

Procuracy, while less-distinguished graduates became jurisconsults, advocates, or judges – in that order.[11] The favored position of the Procuracy was also indicated by granting the procurator-general membership in the Central Committee of the Communist Party, the only practicing jurist to be represented in that body.

The Procuracy and perestroika

The Procuracy was slow in responding to the challenges of President Mikhail Gorbachev's reforms. As an institution, it initially reflected a conservative bias, resisting both change and public challenges to its authority. The early days of glasnost and perestroika unleashed an outpouring of public and press criticism of the functioning of Soviet law enforcement agencies, including the Procuracy. A series of articles in 1986 and 1987 in *Literaturnaya gazeta* by Arkady Vaksberg and Olga Chaikovskaya disclosed the widespread failure of prosecutors and other judicial officials to observe proper procedures, including the fabrication of evidence, coerced confessions, "telephone justice" (attempts by political officials to influence the outcome of cases), and the execution of persons who were later proven to have been innocent.[12] Vaksberg concluded that so many judicial and procuratorial officials make "legal mistakes" that they cannot be regarded as "atypical."[13] The then procurator-general, Aleksandr Rekunkov, a carryover from the Brezhnev regime, reacted angrily to these exposés, dismissing them as "sensational journalism." However, within weeks he was forced to admit in a *Pravda* article that certain local party and state officials consider themselves above the law.[14]

The Procuracy was roundly criticized at an October 2, 1986 meeting of the Politburo where Gorbachev noted that the Procuracy needed to be restructured. The thrust of the organizational changes was to enhance "the strict observance of laws" to ensure "social justice and the inviolability of the constitutional rights of citizens."[15] The Politburo also reaffirmed "the inadmissibility of any attempts to interfere in the investigation and trial of specific cases."[16]

The Procuracy came under attack again the following year. On June 4, 1987, the CPSU Central Committee adopted a resolution entitled "On Measures to Increase the Role of Procuratorial Supervision in Strengthening Socialist Legality and Law and Order."[17] The resolution criticized the Procuracy for failing to stop large-scale theft, bribery, racketeering, and report padding and other deceptive practices. The document also charged that insufficient attention was being devoted to safeguarding citizens' rights and interests. Consequently, the Central Committee deemed it necessary to restructure the functions and organization of the USSR Procurator's Office, its Collegium and procuratorial offices at the regional and local levels. In order to improve effective handling of citizens' complaints, the Procuracy began to organize its work along subject lines, creating special units to deal with economic violations, criminal investigations, violations of the social rights of citizens, ecological violations, etc.

As a result of the restructuring, procurators were vested with several new powers. These included the right to issue binding directives to reverse clear violations of law by administrative agencies and officials; to suspend unlawful acts, decisions, and directives against which procuratorial appeals have been lodged; and to charge economic managers with ensuring the observance of laws by their subordinate enterprises and organizations.[18]

The resolution also called for improving the selection, training, and professional standards of procuratorial personnel. Specifically, it recommended better training, especially in the fields of applied economics and management. Finally, the resolution directed the Procuracy to pay greater attention to nationality factors in staffing its offices, especially in the republics and non-Russian regions.[19]

With the legal reform, prestige and career benefits in the Procuracy fell steadily. Aleksandr Bastrykhin, director of the Procuracy's training institute for criminal investigators in Leningrad noted in 1991 that the prestige of procurators had fallen and that procuratorial salaries were not keeping pace with inflation.[20] Many prosecutors and investigators were leaving their posts for jobs with private enterprises, joint ventures or going to work as advocates (defense attorneys), who were free to set their own fees. Professor Vladimir Daev of Leningrad State University Faculty of Law confirmed that the popularity of a career in the Procuracy had fallen dramatically among law students.[21]

In the face of high-level criticism, Rekunkov was dismissed on May 27, 1988, and replaced by Aleksandr Sukharev, the former minister of justice of the Russian Republic. Sukharev's background was most unusual for a procurator-general, in that the bulk of his career had been spent in the Ministry of Justice, thus, he was a virtual outsider brought in to clean up the work of the Procuracy.

The 19th Party Conference of mid-1988 placed a heavy emphasis on developing the "rule of law state" in the USSR. In his address to the gathering, Gorbachev declared:

[We must] radically strengthen socialist legality and law and order, to eliminate the possibility of the usurpation of power and abuses, effectively counter bureaucratism and formalism, provide reliable guarantees for the protection of the constitutional rights and freedoms of citizens, and ensure the fulfillment of their duties with respect to society and the state.[22]

Gorbachev acknowledged problems in the Soviet legal system: "Restructuring has revealed with special clarity the conservatism of our country's present legal system, which in large part is still oriented not toward democratic or economic methods, but toward command-administrative methods of management, with their numerous prohibitions and petty regulations."[23] Gorbachev also noted that in recent years the Procuracy had assumed more and more responsibilities, which deflected it from its principal missions – the prosecution of criminal cases and general supervision of legality. He proposed transferring the bulk of criminal investigations from the Procuracy to an independent division within the Ministry of Internal Affairs.

About the same time, the Procuracy reverted to its pre-1969 policy of issuing more protests than representations, and the majority of those actions concerned violations of the rights of citizens. But it also became evident during this time that the majority of the public did not trust the Procuracy. The Procuracy was widely perceived as an organ of state coercion, not as an ombudsman for assisting citizens with their grievances against bureaucratic officials.

The reorientation of the Procuracy under Sukharev stirred up considerable resistance within the organization.[24] Procurators resented the rapid turnover of top-ranking prosecutors. In 1988 and 1989 alone, eight of the top twelve officials within the USSR Procuracy were replaced. This was indicative of personnel changes occurring throughout the country in regional and local procuracies as many older prosecutors took advantage of the opportunity to retire.

The notorious Gdlyan-Ivanov case further lowered morale within the Procuracy. In 1988 procuratorial investigators Tel'man Gdlyan and Nikolai Ivanov led a high-level investigation into official corruption and organized crime in Uzbekistan that resulted in the arrest and conviction of Leonid Brezhnev's son-in-law, Yuri Churbanov. Taking advantage of the publicity generated by the case, Gdlyan and Ivanov were elected to the USSR Congress of People's Deputies in March 1989. A few months later, the investigators attempted to link conservative Politburo member Yegor Ligachev to the widening corruption scandal, but Ligachev mounted a counter-offensive, charging that the investigators had violated procedures and gathered evidence illegally. A special commission of the Congress of People's Deputies was established in June 1989 to look into the affair. Charges against Gdlyan and Ivanov were eventually dropped following the August 1991 attempted *coup d'état*.

Under the influence of glasnost and perestroika substantial progress had been made in expanding citizens' rights, but many changes remained *de facto*. New legislation codifying the liberalized policies of the government took time to draft and enact, and in several instances, legislation expanding citizens' rights to free speech, press, and conscience encountered opposition from conservative politicians. The policy of glasnost succeeded in effectively removing most censorship restrictions. The Main Administration of Literature and State Publishing (Glavlit) was abolished in June 1986. Newspapers and magazines flourished, covering a wide range of political opinions. A progressive Law on the Press of the USSR, which granted editorial boards absolute control over editorial content of all publications and broadcasts, went into effect in August 1990.

The celebration of the millennium of Christianity in Russia in 1989 coincided with an easing of restrictions on churches and religious practice in the USSR. The Law on Freedom of Conscience and Religious Organizations in the USSR of 1989 granted religious groups control over their property and permitted them to engage freely in educational, evangelical, and charitable work, including maintenance of contacts with religious organizations abroad.

Finally, notable progress was made in the area of human rights. Gorbachev convened an international human rights conference in Moscow in February 1987. Andrei Sakharov, who had been released from house arrest in Gorky only three months earlier at Gorbachev's insistence, attended the gathering and praised the release from labor camps of many Soviet dissidents. The abuse of psychiatric "treatment" of political dissidents was terminated and the USSR was readmitted to the World Psychiatric Association. Restrictions on foreign travel and emigration were eased and resulted in a mass exodus. By 1989, Jews were leaving the Soviet Union at a rate of 100,000 every year.[25] Large numbers of Germans and Armenians also took advantage of the relaxed emigration policy to leave the country.

On December 1, 1990, Sukharev was relieved as procurator-general. He was replaced by Nikolai S. Trubin. The appointment of Trubin, a moderate with strong ties to Gorbachev, was consistent with Gorbachev's swing to a more hard-line position in late 1990. Trubin had been most outspoken on the need to preserve the Procuracy as a unitary, hierarchical, and central organ of state control and supervision. In his speeches and interviews he frequently alluded to the fact that the Procuracy was patterned on the French model. (However, France is not a federal state; it is a state with a strong, centralized, unitary government and administrative apparatus.)

At the same time, however, Trubin was realistic in observing that the Procuracy must "free [itself] from functions which do not belong to it."[26] In a 1991 article in *Pravda*, Trubin noted: "The legal position of the prosecutor must be reconsidered. The conception according to which the prosecutor oversees the examination of a case in court has been outgrown. The prosecutor, after all, is a participant in the court proceedings. The main substance of our work [in court] remains carrying out the state prosecution."[27] In another article, he proclaimed "The prosecution must have the same rights as the defense, and not one iota more."[28] Trubin favored the creation of a separate, investigative agency independent of the Ministry of Internal Affairs, the KGB and the Procuracy. He reasoned that since the Procuracy is charged with overseeing the legality of criminal investigations, it should not conduct any investigations itself.

While favoring some limitations on procuratorial activity, Trubin strongly defended maintaining the Procuracy's oversight of virtually all areas of government administration, including the soviets and state security organs. The 4th Congress of People's Deputies in December 1990 granted prosecutors at all levels the right to protest acts of their corresponding soviets which they consider unconstitutional or otherwise illegal. Previously, the Procuracy could only protest acts of the executive committees of soviets, but not acts of the soviets themselves. At the Congress, Trubin argued for even broader powers, namely the power to suspend acts of soviets pending their review by a court, however this power was not granted to the Procuracy.

In 1991 Trubin's leadership of the Procuracy began to encounter resistance from reform-minded procurators, especially at the republic level. In April, Valentin G. Stepankov, a 39-year-old procurator in Boris Yeltsin's home district of Sverdlovsk, was appointed procurator-general of the RSFSR. At the time of his appointment, Stepankov noted that power was gravitating to the republics, and the USSR Procuracy, if it survived at all, would exist only as a coordinating body, having primary jurisdiction only in prosecuting violations of all-union laws. Procurators in ethnic regions and republics were especially outspoken in pressing for greater autonomy from the USSR Procuracy. In the case of the three Baltic republics, dual procuracies existed – one answering to the USSR Procuracy and an "independent" Procuracy created by national forces in the republic's parliament.

Stepankov angered Trubin when he signed a separate protocol on May 27, 1991, recognizing the independent Procuracy of the Latvian Republic. This action caused a storm of controversy in the USSR Procuracy, where Stepankov was charged with violating the central, unified chain of command. Stepankov justified his actions on the grounds that the Procuracy's unified, hierarchical structure was breaking down anyway. In order to gain the trust and cooperation of Baltic officials in matters of extradition and countering transborder shipments of contraband, he felt he had no alternative but to recognize the working Procuracy in each republic.[29]

Stepankov also took the initiative to draft a new RSFSR Law on the Procuracy that granted the republic procuracy sole authority in supervising the execution of all laws of the Republic. The authority of the USSR Procuracy would be limited to enforcing all-union laws on the territory of the Republic "in coordination with the procurator-general of the RSFSR."[30] Even matters of personnel, training, and budget were removed from central determination.

Stepankov's stated objective was to use the Russian Procuracy as a tool for enforcing reformist legislation by the Russian parliament.[31] In this sense, he was seen at the time as a progressive. Yet on issues challenging the authority and jurisdiction of the Russian Procuracy (e.g. human rights, rights of accused persons, and expansion of court jurisdiction), he was quite conservative.

The Stepankov–Trubin struggle prior to the August 1991 coup attempt, created an uncomfortable situation for many regional and local procurators. For example, Dmitri Verovkin, procurator of Leningrad, was by career service and temperament a conservative in line with Trubin. He noted that legal changes had not kept pace with political reforms. For example, despite all the discussion of promoting a market economy, the criminal code of the Russian Republic still outlawed speculation and this anomaly was causing problems for law enforcement agencies.[32] Verovkin wanted to continue to prosecute violations of "price gouging," but recognized that to do so was "out of favor" politically.[33] Clearly, he was a man caught in the middle – more inclined toward Trubin's orientation, but afraid of alienating his immediate superior, Stepankov.

The Procuracy and the *coup d'état*

The USSR procurator-general's office appeared to throw its weight behind the Committee on the State of Emergency during the early hours of the attempted *coup d'état* of August 1991. Trubin was out of the country at the time, leaving First Deputy Procurator-General Aleksei Vasilyev as acting head of the agency. According to Stepankov's account of developments:

At 5:30 p.m. on August 19, a government telegram signed by acting USSR Procurator-General Vasilyev was sent out to local offices. If you discard all the verbal wrappings, its point came down to carrying out the decisions of the Committee on the State of Emergency. One of the first directives of USSR Procurator-General Trubin upon his return from abroad was a reminder that politically motivated strikes were banned. And this came at a time when the political mobilization of the masses was the most effective weapon against the putshchists.[34]

Stepankov and most of the procurators of the Russian Republic Procuracy resolutely aligned themselves with Yeltsin and those resisting the Committee on the State of Emergency and refused to obey Vasilyev's instructions. In some regions and cities (e.g. Kazan, Omsk, Magadan, and Kyzyl), procurators enthusiastically sided with the leaders of the coup, outlawing public demonstrations and announcing their intention to uphold decrees issued by the CSE. In other regions and cities (e.g. Kemerovo, Tyumen, and Nizhnevartovsk) procurators resisted the CSE and announced support for "the duly elected officials of the Russian Republic."[35] In most cases, they appear to have kept a low profile, perhaps because of the absence of Trubin and the split signals they were receiving concerning the Procuracy's position on the coup.

Soon after the collapse of the attempted coup and the arrest of its organizers, Vasilyev was dismissed "for showing a lack of principle and faint heartedness at a critical moment for the country and for having failed to provide correct legal assessment of the activities of the Committee for the State of Emergency."[36] Deputy Procurator-General I. P. Abramov, who was in charge of supervising activities of the KGB, was also dismissed. The same day it was announced that all CPSU activities were immediately terminated within the Procuracy and all procurators who had not done so were ordered to renounce their membership in the Communist Party.

In the wake of the abortive coup, and public criticism that although he was away he did not actively come out against the attempted overthrow of the government, Trubin resigned on August 29, 1991 and the Collegium of the USSR Procuracy was disbanded. The USSR Supreme Soviet accepted Trubin's resignation, but asked him to stay on until his successor could be named.

A purge of the Procuracy was underway. Aleksandr Katusev, chief prosecutor in the Soviet Army, was dismissed for supporting the coup. In Ukraine, the republic's Supreme Soviet voted to "depoliticize" the procurator's office. When the procurator-general of Ukraine, M. Potebenko, protested this action as illegal and contrary to the constitution, he was relieved of his post.[37] In Kazakhstan, President Nazarbaev called for radical reforms of the armed forces, the KGB, the Ministry of Internal Affairs, and the USSR Procurator's Office, "taking into account the republic's sovereignty."[38] Mikalai Ihnatovich, a leading investigator of criminal misconduct within the Procuracy, was named the new procurator-general of Belarus and immediately charged with investigating the Belorussian Communist Party's support for the coup.[39]

Meanwhile, Stepankov insisted that the Russian Republic Procuracy take charge of the investigation into the criminal activities of the organizers of the coup, bolstering his image as a champion of reform. He refused to turn over materials on the coup leaders to the USSR Procuracy: "I can't turn over materials to the Union Prosecutor's Office. I don't trust them."[40]

The August 1991 coup undermined the authority of all-union institutions and hastened the breakdown of the USSR along ethnic lines. Bowing to strong nationalist pressures in the Baltic republics, Trubin abolished the Latvian and Lithuanian prosecutors offices subordinate to him. The process of ethnic separatism continued throughout the Fall of 1991. Stepankov's strong stand against ethnic violence within the Russian Federation began to tarnish his pro-reform image. On October 23, 1991, Stepankov banned all political parties and public associations that advocated violating the territorial integrity of the Russian Federation.[41] It remains unclear what legal authority the procurator-general had to order such a ban. The action was aimed primarily at the separatist movements in Tatarstan and Checheno-Ingushetia. He also threatened to close any newspapers or media that "promote separatist tendencies."[42]

There were also evident internal rifts within the Procuracy surrounding the issue of whether the agency should continue to exist as a centralized, unitary organ, or be dismantled, much as occurred with the KGB. In early November the hard-liners in the USSR Procuracy made a last-ditch, desperate move to restore their waning authority. On November 5, 1991, Viktor Ilykhin, USSR State Prosecutor for State Security Matters, brought charges of treason against Gorbachev for granting independence to the Baltics. USSR Procurator-General Trubin immediately fired Ilykhin and repealed his order, but it was an indication of the chaos in the Procuracy that such an action could have been taken without having been preempted by the procurator-general.

On November 22, 1991, the RSFSR Supreme Soviet passed a resolution abolishing the office of the USSR Procuracy and transferred its functions to the RSFSR Procuracy. Trubin "realized his impotence and resigned," according to Stepankov.[43] After November 1, all financing for the USSR prosecutor's office ceased and some 39,000 employees were laid off. Some were subsequently hired by the Russian Procuracy, but most retired or sought employment elsewhere.

The events of the coup and its aftermath rapidly accelerated the pace of change in the USSR, and those changes also dramatically affected the Procuracy. The devolution of authority from the center to the republics broke down the Procuracy's centralized, hierarchical structure. Stepankov ordered a new draft Law on the Procuracy to be prepared that called for maintenance of a centralized, unified, and hierarchical Procuracy answering to the RSFSR procurator-general, rather than to the USSR procurator-general. All of the functions of the procuracy remained in place.

National and regional sentiments throughout the Russian Federation led to subnational bodies declaring sovereignty over their own affairs, including law enforcement. For example, in 1990, in the city of Kazan, 500 miles east of Moscow, the Tatar Supreme Soviet passed a Law on Sovereignty of the Republic. Under the strong-armed leadership of President Mintimer Shaimeev, former Communist Party chief of the Tatar Autonomous Republic, the pace of reforms in Tatarstan has been slow but orderly. While the Procuracy of the Tatar Republic is nominally subordinate to the Russian prosecutor's office, in practice, it functions with a great deal of autonomy.[44]

In Kazan and elsewhere the breakdown of the old system of law enforcement was associated with a dramatic increase in crime, especially organized crime. The overall reported crime rate rose steadily: 13.2 percent in 1990, 18 percent in 1991, and 30 percent in 1992. An alarming pattern of violent crimes involving use of firearms was reported in 1992 and 1993. Crimes involving weapons more than tripled in the first half of 1993, according to Interior Minister Viktor Yerin. Many of those crimes were the result of inter-gang warfare.

There are approximately 3,000 known criminal gangs in Russia organized into some 50 associations or syndicates.[45] In Tatarstan there are 111 gangs with an estimated total membership of more than 5,000.[46]

The legal commentator for *Pravda* implicated the reforms in the breakdown of authority, especially within law enforcement agencies themselves:

Criminal activities themselves are taking on fundamentally new character-istics previously unknown to us ... Today not only is there an enormous increase in the number of actively operating gangs, including gangs of young people who commit crimes that are simply outrageous and brutal to the point of absurdity, but a phenomenon that is totally new to us is appearing – gangs made up of former military men and personnel from the Ministry of Internal Affairs (police) and KGB (people who have been "expelled," "discharged," "cut back," "ordered out" and so on). Groups like this are especially difficult to combat.[47]

The failure of the coup also raised popular and elite expectations concerning the need to create a state functioning according to the rule of law, especially Western concepts of the rule of law. Pressures in this direction, emanating especially from the Russian parliament, threatened to redefine drastically the role and functions of the Russian Procuracy.

The draft of a new Russian Federation Constitution, published on October 11, 1991, in *Rossiiskaya gazeta*, called for limiting the Procuracy to the prosecution of criminal matters in courts. The procurator's power of general supervision would be assumed by a newly estab-lished People's Ombudsman (*Pravozashchitnik*), appointed by the Russian parliament to investigate actions of government agencies, enterprises, local organs, and officials when those actions violate the rights of citizens. The investigatory powers of the Procuracy were to be taken away and vested in a special agency for criminal investi-gation. Supervision of the courts – a power long resented by judges – was to be granted to the Supreme Court of the Russian Republic.

The drastically scaled-back Procuracy envisioned in the 1991 draft constitution of the Russian Republic coincided with the views of Rus-sian Minister of Justice Nikolai Fedorov. In a speech before Russian judges in late October 1991, Fedorov noted that the Procuracy as a higher supervisory body of state power was a uniquely Soviet institution, a "sacred cow" created by Stalin and Vyshinsky. He denounced procuratorial supervision of the performance of the courts as a "legal atavism" and general supervision as a "totalitarian snoop" (*zaglyadyvanie*).[48] He argued that the only proper role of the Procuracy is to prosecute criminal cases in court. Limiting the role of the Procuracy, would, in his view, strengthen the court system and bring the Republic's legal system into closer conformity with established European norms and legal experience.

The new Law on the Procuracy

As we noted in chapter 4, the drafting of a new constitution for the Russian Federation became bogged down in fights over the division of power between the center and the provinces, and between the executive and legislative branches. Rather than waiting for the resolution of these complex disputes, Stepankov pushed through the Supreme Soviet a new "Law on the Procuracy of the Russian Federation" in January 1992. The procurator-general hoped to reinforce the powerful position of the Procuracy in a new law before opponents could mount an attack on the agency.

The new legislation preserved the Procuracy as a single, unified, and centralized institution charged with "supervising the implementation of laws by local legislative and executive bodies, administrative control organs, legal entities, public organizations, and officials, as well as the lawfulness of their acts."[49] Article 2 specified that the procuratorial supervision extends to investigatory agencies, prisons and places of detention, and military units and their administrative offices. In each case, the Procuracy does not supplant the authority of the given agency, but is charged with seeing that proper procedures and laws are followed.

While the new law retained many of the broad supervisory powers of the Procuracy, provisions were introduced to depoliticize the institution. Article 4 stated that no political party organizations are permitted within the Procuracy. Procurators cannot be members of elected or other governmental bodies if they would have to supervise the legality of the acts and decisions of such bodies. As a result, procuratorial officials who were elected to national, regional, and local soviets had to resign those posts, including Stepankov, who was elected to the Council of Nationalities of the Russian Supreme Soviet and served from June 1990 to February 1991. Article 7 gave the procurator-general and his subordinate procurators the right to be present at sessions of the Congress of People's Deputies and the Supreme Soviet, and their counterpart bodies at subordinate levels.[50] Thus, procurators at the city level have the right to attend sessions of the city soviet. The procurator-general and procurators of the constituent republics also may address parliamentary bodies at corresponding levels concerning their interpretations of laws. Finally, the procurator-general and procurators of the constituent republics have the right to ask the courts at their respective levels to look into the constitutionality of various normative acts and to represent the Procuracy's interpretation of such acts in court.

The most important change in the new "Law on the Procuracy" was the elimination of procuratorial supervision over the activities of the courts. The law was consistent with the draft constitution of the Russian Federation and the position of the Justice Minister Fedorov, who favored enhancing judicial independence by making the courts subordinate only to the Supreme Court. Article 9, however, granted the Procuracy the right to investigate citizens' requests and grievances arising from court decisions as long as those cases are not under appeal or otherwise currently under court consideration. The Procuracy also retained its long-standing power to submit cassation protests (appeals) against unlawful or unfounded court decisions.

The Procuracy also lost responsibility for conducting criminal investigations. The preliminary investigation now falls to a special investigatory body, although the Procuracy retains supervisory authority over the lawful conduct of this new investigatory agency.[51] Article 2 noted that in exceptional cases specified by the criminal procedure code, the Procuracy carries out criminal investigations, but until the code is revised it is difficult to know exactly what these cases might be. The law only indicated one clear circumstance in which the Procuracy, rather than the new investigatory agency, has sole investigatory jurisdiction: criminal investigations into the activities of procurators.

The Law on the Procuracy of the Russian Federation retained the Procuracy's powers of general supervision over the legality of activities of local administrative agencies, ministries, departments, economic and control agencies, enterprises, institutions, organizations and associations, military administrative organs, political organizations and movements, and officials, as well as local soviets. Heavy lobbying by Stepankov and his deputies in the Russian Procuracy was apparently successful in rejecting the provision in the draft constitution for the creation of a People's Ombudsman.

Of particular interest to the international business community were those provisions in Article 20 and 21 that empowered procurators to undertake inspections of alleged legal violations of various bodies, officials and organs, including enterprises' business establishments and institutions, including foreign businesses. In the conduct of such inspections, procurators may enter the premises of enterprises, obtain access to documents and materials, and compel disclosure of necessary documents, materials, statistical and other data within ten days. The power of the Procuracy and the police to examine the files of joint ventures and wholly owned foreign corporations came to the fore in 1991 when searches of foreign company offices were conducted based on allegations of illegal currency transactions. The issue remains largely undefined in the present law: there are no stated provisions allowing a foreign corporation or joint venture partner to enjoin procurators from examining files, or for protecting trade secrets and other proprietary information. In such cases, the Procuracy is technically conducting an "inspection" (*proverka*) rather than a criminal "investigation" (*sledstvie*), and thus is not required to produce a search warrant.

The "Law on the Procuracy of the Russian Federation" was an attempt to balance the demands for greater judicial independence with the established legal culture of a centralized, unified, and powerful Procuracy with broad-ranging authority to supervise compliance with the laws of the Federation. While procuratorial authority over the courts and the conduct of criminal investigations were substantially reduced, the Procuracy retained much of its earlier scope and power. The Law on the Procuracy of the Russian Federation did not resolve the fundamental question of the proper position of the Procuracy within the Russian legal system. In the course of drafting a new constitution in 1992 and 1993, that question was revisited and again resulted in sharp differences of opinion within the legal community.

The debate intensifies

As the debate over the role of the Procuracy developed throughout 1992 and 1993, two dominant positions emerged – one favoring the maintenance of a strong, centralized and hierarchical Procuracy with a wide array of functions and another favoring strengthening the courts. The latter position argued that as long as the Procuracy dominates the legal system, the courts will never develop the legitimacy and independence nor receive the resources they need to become strong. Consequently, proponents of expanding the role of the courts (i.e. the Ministry of Justice and many legal scholars associated with the Institute of State and Law) tend to favor stripping the Procuracy of all of its functions except the prosecution of cases in court.

As proponents of legal reform have stressed the need to emphasize the development of the courts, the Procuracy has urged the preservation of its central place in the Russian legal system and the preservation of its broad powers. In April 1993 when a draft law was circulated calling for the creation of an independent investigatory agency, officials of the Procuracy, the Ministry of Internal Affairs, and the Ministry for Security (former KGB) quickly convened a press conference to voice their opposition to this plan.[52]

Even greater resistance was marshaled against attempts to abolish or curtail the Procuracy's powers of general supervision and this debate goes to the heart of the future of the Russian legal system. Stepankov and numerous other procurators have argued that court review of individual grievances is too complicated and costly for average citizens. N. A. Karavaev, deputy procurator-general, noted that at present the courts lack the necessary personnel and resources to handle large numbers of cases.[53] In many regions and districts of Russia today there is only one judge. In some instances one judge must cover as many as three districts to hear all cases – criminal, civil, family matters, probate, etc.[54] Furthermore, Karavaev noted that many of the newly elected judges are very young and inexperienced. He estimated that the development of an adequate court system may take fifteen to twenty years.[55]

More fundamentally, procurators argue that the current crisis conditions in the country require a strong, centralized agency to insure legality. This role has traditionally been played by the Procuracy. Despite Stepankov's earlier reputation as a pro-reform supporter of Yeltsin, after the coup he gravitated to a much more status quo or conservative position. Rather than promoting reforms, procuratorial powers were used more frequently to block reformist policies of Yeltsin and others when those policies lacked proper legislative foundation. The law and order orientation of the Procuracy found many allies among conservative deputies in the Russian parliament.

Since 1991, procurators have found themselves time and time again challenging the legality of government actions and policies. For example, when Gavril Popov, the mayor of Moscow, reorganized the capital into prefectures as a means of circumventing the old bureaucracy of city government, the Moscow prosecutor's office protested the decision as over-stepping his legal authority and Popov was forced to retreat. In 1991 and 1992 the Moscow Procuracy issued more than 100 protests against illegal acts of the city soviet. In more than one-half of the cases, the city voluntarily backed down.[56] In the remaining cases, the Procuracy took the matter to court and won in every instance. V. K. Goncharov, senior assistant procurator of Moscow, noted that political interference by the new generation of politicians was even worse than under the old regime dominated by the Communist Party.[57] According to Goncharov, many of the newly elected deputies to the soviets had an "insufficient appreciation" of the law or sought to use their newly acquired political influence in illegal ways.

In Nizhny Novgorod (Gorky) the city prosecutor, Aleksandr Fedotov, protested several of the actions of the provincial governor, Boris Nemtsov, including his proposed plan for large-scale privatization of industry in the city. In 1992 Fedotov's office lodged fifteen protests against actions of the governor and ten against actions of the city soviet or the mayor. Of these, only four went to court and the prosecutor's office won in all four instances.[58] Even high-level policies have been reversed by procuratorial protests. Stepankov's office issued protests against the order of the State Bank calling in all ruble notes issued prior to 1993.[59]

Perhaps because it is using its powers to challenge the legality (and even the constitutionality) of the acts of executive officers, most of whom are Yeltsin appointees, the Procuracy earned the reputation as a conservative, anti-reform institution with close links to the Russian parliament. This characterization is only partly correct.

Procurators from Stepankov down to the provincial and local levels repeatedly pointed out that the pace of political and policy changes is far outstripping the pace of enacting new legislation. In the case of Nemtsov's grand scheme for privatizing state property in Nizhny Novgorod, the prosecutor's office correctly protested on the grounds that as yet there was no legal basis for him to undertake such a program. Legislation on privatizing most large enterprises in Russia languished in the Russian parliament. As long as procurators are charged with seeing that all legislative and executive decrees and actions conform to the law and as long as that law lags behind political developments, the Procuracy will inevitably act as a conservative force blunting the reform process. Deputy Procurator-General Karavaev succinctly summarized the dilemma:

It may be true that the [1978] Constitution and laws lag behind public opinion and that resolving the constitutional dilemma may be impossible without first resolving the gridlock between the president and parliament. However, to conclude that this constitution is no longer valid and not to defend it and other laws of the country would lead to anarchy and that is not a viable answer.[60]

On the other hand, this conservative orientation coupled with Stepankov's desire to preserve the status and power of the Procuracy also resulted in the forging of close ties to Yeltsin's opponents in the Russian parliament. In November 1992 Stepankov convened a special emergency conference of prosecutors to express serious concerns over the on-going confrontation between the legislative and executive branches of the Russian government. In his opening remarks Stepankov decried the rapid rise in violent crime. He went on to argue for the maintenance of a centralized, strong, and independent prosecutor's office, calling it "the backbone of the Russian Federation."[61] He denounced attempts by some deputies and members of the president's office to limit prosecutors' rights and reduce the Procuracy's functions to simply prosecuting cases in court. He noted that the Procuracy had become so marginalized that it was not even mentioned in the new draft constitution worked out by the Constitutional Commission. "Given the unstable political situation, the incipient market, the upsurge in crime and the aggravation of relations between nationalities, only the prosecutor's office can be a reliable guarantor of law and order and legality. It follows from this that prosecutor's powers must be broadened and that they must be given real assistance in material-technical and personnel support."[62] Ruslan Khasbulatov, speaker of the Russian parliament and leading opponent of President Yeltsin, also spoke at the conference, echoing Stepankov's sentiments.

As the dispute between President Yeltsin and the Russian parliament erupted into open confrontation during early 1993, Stepankov and the Russian Procuracy appeared to side increasingly with the legislative branch. On April 22 the prosecutor's office announced that it had brought criminal charges against two of Yeltsin's top associates, State Secretary Gennady Burbulis and Defense Minister Pavel Grachev. The two were charged with illegally selling military property abroad.[63] Less than one week later, Stepankov addressed the Russian parliament to urge them to support the creation of a special commission to investigate corruption among government officials. The commission, which was accountable to both the Procuracy and the parliament, was granted special powers to conduct inquiries, interrogations, searches and the removal of documents from government offices, including those of the staff of the president and the Council of Ministers. Stepankov noted that the legislative branch was not immune to corruption, but acknowledged that the commission's attention would focus on the president's office and other executive branch agencies.[64] The principal targets of the probe were two additional Yeltsin aides: First Deputy Prime Minister Vladimir Shumeiko and head of the Federal Information Center, Mikhail Poltoranin. Shumeiko is the chief architect of Yeltsin's defense conversion program, while Poltoranin was widely blamed by conservative parliamentary deputies for supposedly biased television reporting prior to the presidential referendum of April 25, 1993.

The increasingly partisan role of the Procuracy in the political dispute between President Yeltsin and his adversaries in the Russian parliament seriously undermined the agency's credibility and jeopardized the chances of its survival under a new constitution. The presidential draft constitution limited the Procuracy to three functions: the supervision of the legality of criminal investigations (but not the actual conduct of those investigations); the prosecution of cases in court; and the challenging in court of illegal acts of state bodies.[65] In other words, the Procuracy would be stripped of its power of general supervision. Furthermore, the presidential draft constitution granted the courts the power and responsibility to supervise the legality of procuratorial activity, a reversal of earlier roles when the Procuracy supervised the courts.

Perhaps the biggest blow to the status of the Procuracy occurred in late May 1993 when the Military Collegium of the Russian Federation Supreme Court ruled that Procurator-General Stepankov and Deputy Procurator-General Yevgeny Lisov committed "flagrant violations of the law while investigating the criminal case involving the Committee for the State of Emergency."[66] The court indefinitely suspended the trial, pending the assignment of new prosecutors in the case. Stepankov and Lisov had published a book, *The Kremlin Conspiracy: The Investigation's Version*, that appeared prior to the trial and which the court ruled violated the constitutional principle of presumption of innocence. The court's ruling was called courageous by political commentators.[67] According to the *Izvestiya* commentator, the decision bodes well for the future of Russian justice, if not for the Procuracy:

One is surprised at the scrupulousness with which the military judges are following procedural rules governing the hearing of a criminal case. And it is even more striking that, for perhaps the first time, we are seeing a court ruling that makes direct references to the Constitution, human rights, the presumption of innocence and judicial independence. It is an impressive example of Russian justice.[68]

The ruling, together with Stepankov's apparent siding with the Russian parliament against Yeltsin in September and October 1993, resulted in the president asking for Stepankov's resignation, which he tendered soon after the crisis had passed. Within days, Aleksei I. Kazannik, a law professor from Omsk University, was named procurator-general. Kazannik had no prior experience in the Procuracy; his expertise was in environmental and administrative law. He did, however, have strong ties to Yeltsin. In 1990 when regional and local elections were held to newly established legislative bodies, Boris Yeltsin narrowly missed being elected. Kazannik volunteered to relinquish his seat so that Yeltsin could become a member of the Russian Supreme Soviet. Kazannik's appointment was widely viewed by procurators and legal scholars as a "reward" for this display of loyalty.

However, Kazannik surprised many within the Procuracy. Within his first month in office he called for the resignation of approximately one-half of Stepankov's top assistants. Lisov was reassigned as deputy procurator of the city of Moscow.[69] Kazannik ordered a review of all procuratorial employees even down to the local level, to assess how well they were performing their jobs.

Although he had no previous experience in the Procuracy, Kazannik was outspoken in supporting the preservation of the Procuracy's central role in the legal system. Deputy Procurator-General Orlov reported on Kazannik's first speech to the staff of the Procuracy upon assuming office: "I have never been a defender of bureaucratic interests. I have always considered the general interests of society. But now, for the first time, I will act to protect and defend the interests of the Procuracy because those interests are the interests of the general population."[70] According to Orlov, the "radical reformers" see the Procuracy as an instrument of repression from the former totalitarian regime. He responds to them: "Who didn't serve the totalitarian system then?"[71]

During the Fall of 1993, Kazannik mounted a strenuous effort to preserve the Procuracy's status in various drafts of a new constitution that were circulating in the capital. When the final presidential draft of the constitution appeared to limit the Procuracy's powers to prosecuting criminals, Kazannik lobbied Yeltsin and within one day the section delineating the Procuracy's powers was dropped. Kazannik argued successfully in favor of leaving out any listing of procuratorial powers from the constitution, which in effect meant that the Procuracy would continue to be governed by the 1992 "Law on the Procuracy."[72]

When asked whether they anticipated the need for a new law on the Procuracy in light of the approval of the new constitution, procurators responded that the newly elected parliament could be presented with the urgent need to draft and ratify many new pieces of legislation and that a new law on the Procuracy would be relatively low priority. This suits the interests of the Procuracy, since they fear that any reopening of the question of the Procuracy's jurisdiction and powers would result in a constriction of those powers.[73]

The 1993 Constitution makes only minor changes affecting the Procuracy. The procurator-general of the Russian Federation is nominated by the president and confirmed by the Federation Council and serves for a five-year term. Procurators of the republics are appointed to five-year terms by the Russian procurator-general and confirmed by the legislative bodies of their respective republics. Regional, district, and city procurators are appointed by the Russian procurator-general and do not require confirmation by any elective body. Thus, the Procuracy remains independent of regional and local soviets and their executive committees, which has been a point of considerable friction in the past.

The Procuracy was again cast into the midst of a high-level political squabble in early 1994. The State Duma passed a decree on amnesty that resulted in the release of the organizers of the October 1993 violence in Moscow.[74] President Yeltsin maintained that the action constituted a pardon, a power that only he enjoys, and ordered Kazannik "to retain the conditions for the detention" of the persons charged with organizing the coup. Kazannik responded that the prosecutor-general's office has no right to interpret legal acts, but must carry them out.[75] Kazannik resigned on February 28, 1994 rather than concede to President Yeltsin's wishes. He was replaced with the 36-year-old Aleksei Ilyushenko. Ilyushenko's fifteen-year career in the Procuracy began in Krasnoiarsk krai, but he eventually was elevated to the RSFSR prosecutor's office under Stepankov before being appointed to the President's Oversight Administration. The Federation Council initially refused to accept Kazannik's resignation and twice the body refused to confirm Ilyushenko's nomination. During the stormy confirmation debate, it was repeatedly noted that Ilyushenko had served as the head of the Interdepartmental Commission on Combatting Corruption that had investigated charges against former Vice-President Rutskoi.

Faced with lack of confirmation of his appointment, Yeltsin had two options: either to appoint someone else or to permit Ilyushenko to serve indefinitely as acting procurator-general. He chose the latter option. In his reduced capacity, Ilyushenko was prohibited from appointing local and regional procurators. In other respects, however, he undertook an active role in restructuring the Procuracy and mobilizing forces in the war on crime.

Meanwhile in late 1994 discussion resumed over a new draft law on the Procuracy circulated in the Russian parliament. At this point it is unclear whether any renewed attempt to dramatically reduce the powers of the Procuracy could win sufficient support to pass the Duma. Even if such a law should be passed, it is unlikely that Yeltsin would sign it.

The recent disputes and partisan wrangling point out clearly the extent to which the Procuracy and the rest of the Russian legal system remains highly politicized. If the Procuracy is removed from its dominant position in the Russian legal system, it will fall to the courts to fill the void. It remains uncertain, however, whether the courts are up to the task, given the absence of a history of courts with the power and independence to constrain the state and the low level of public awareness of the law and willingness of citizens to seek judicial protection of their rights and interests. For now it would appear that the Procuracy has managed to preserve its central place in the Russian legal system. The election victory of conservatives in the Russian parliament combined with the steady increase in crime is likely to further solidify that position. In chapter 6 we analyze the myriad of challenges facing the Russian judiciary today.

6   In search of a just system: the courts and judicial reform

> For more than 73 years we had no real judicial branch of
> government. The courts were just an extension of Party power.
> Anyone who came before the court had little chance of a fair trial.
>
> Boris Zolotyukin,
> Chair, Committee on Juridical Reform,
> Russian Parliament (1992)[1]

With the exception of the relatively brief period from 1864 to 1917, courts have not enjoyed much status or independence in Russia and the Soviet Union. The first courts evolved in Russia in the late fifteenth and early sixteenth centuries largely as a mechanism for enforcing the tsar's policies and for resolving disputes between subjects. The notion that the crown could be held accountable to the law – a fundamental feature of English law since the Magna Carta in 1215 – was never accepted by the monarchy nor by the Bolsheviks after the Revolution of 1917. The central problem confronting the judiciary today is establishing the the fundamental norm of an independent judiciary whose decisions are based solely on law, rather than political expediency, and are binding even on organs of the state.

Organization of the courts

With the collapse of the USSR in late 1991, the judiciary underwent substantial revision. Under the former constitution of the USSR there were all-union courts (e.g. the USSR Supreme Court, the Supreme Arbitrazh Court, and military courts) and union-republic courts and their subordinate courts at the regional, city and district levels. The all-union courts of the former USSR ceased to exist as of December 31, 1991 and no counterpart institutions were incorporated in the treaty establishing the Commonwealth of Independent States. Thus, the current judicial system in Russia is based on the former system of the Russian Republic courts.

At the pinnacle of the judicial system in Russia is the Ministry of Justice. The Ministry of Justice administers the judicial system of Russia and is responsible for drafting relevant legislation on the courts, judges, and substantive law codes. In addition, the ministry undertakes the training of judicial personnel and gathers and analyzes court statistics. The ministry is assisted in its work by departments of justice in the eighty-nine constituent republics and regions of the Russian Federation.

In December 1991 President Yeltsin created the State Legal Affairs Administration of the President of Russia (GPU) headed by his chief advisor on legal reform Sergei Shakhrai. The GPU, with a staff of 304 and a personnel budget of 4.6 billion rubles, is charged with coordinating legal policy between the president's office and other executive and legislative bodies, drafting laws for the president, and advising him on the implementation of laws. In addition, the GPU has been granted authority over issues of civil defense, pardons, state awards, citizenship disputes, political asylum, and nationality relations.

The GPU in many respects duplicates the responsibilities of the Ministry of Justice and has led to considerable inter-institutional rivalry. Nikolai Fedorov, former minister of justice, diplomatically described the GPU as "an unusual entity in the system of state power."[2] Hostilities rose with the release of GPU's first draft piece of legislation, a law "On Criminal Liability for Deliberate Noncompliance with Laws of the Russian Federation." Yeltsin had long been frustrated by overt resistance to his decisions and decrees, especially at the regional and local levels. The draft law called for punishment up to seven years imprisonment for officials who refused to enforce presidential decrees. Fedorov was highly critical of the law, likening it to policies of the Third Reich[3] and stating that it even exceeded Stalin's repressive policies of 1937.[4] "It is hard to imagine that such a draft could have been put together by lawyers," he remarked.[5]

Critics also dispute the assignment to the GPU of supervisory authority over the armed forces, police, state security agency, the prosecutor's office, and the courts of arbitration. Just what the legal basis is for such "oversight" remains unclear and may contravene the constitution. While the Ministry of Justice and the GPU play a major role in the operation of the judicial system, they do not have formal supervisory power over the courts. That responsibility is assigned to the Supreme Court of the Russian Federation.

The Supreme Court hears cases on appeal from inferior courts and in a limited number of cases of "exceptional importance," the court has original jurisdiction. The court includes twenty justices and forty-five lay assessors. The court is divided into three chambers or collegia – for civil cases, criminal cases, and military cases. The court procedure governing cases before the Military Collegium is the same as that governing criminal or civil cases in the other two collegia. In all three chambers cases are heard by a panel of three judges, and in cases of original jurisdiction, one judge and two lay assessors.

The Supreme Court is charged with supervising subordinate courts and resolving disputes between them. The court regularly issues instructions to inferior courts directing them in the handling of various types of cases or pointing out mistakes and shortcomings in their practice. Due to its supervisory role over judicial policy and administration, the court also enjoys the power of legislative initiative.

Subordinate to the Russian Federation Supreme Court are courts of the constituent national republics, regions (*oblast*), and territories (*krai*), as well as the cities of Moscow and St. Petersburg. These courts hear cases on appeal (and protest) from lower courts and also routinely serve as the courts of first instance in major cases. Like the Supreme Court, provincial courts have separate chambers (divisions) for civil and criminal cases.

At the lowest level of the judicial hierarchy are the city and district courts (formerly known as "people's courts"), that exist in towns and in rural districts, as well as in urban districts of large cities. These courts function as the courts of first instance for the vast majority of civil and criminal cases.

On July 1, 1995 a new system of commercial courts was introduced, governed by a new Commercial Procedure Code. These courts replace the former system of arbitration (*arbitrazh*) tribunals. The commercial courts resolve commercial disputes, including disputes involving foreign companies and foreign entrepreneurs. The jurisdiction of the commercial courts extends to a wide array of issues, including disputes associated with privatization, taxes, bankruptcy, reorganization, and administrative proceedings related to commercial activities.

At the lowest level there are eighty-two regional (oblast), republic and territorial (krai) commercial courts. Above these courts are ten federal commercial courts which function as courts of cassation. The Higher Commercial Court of the Russian Federation oversees the commercial courts and hears cases on appeal.

Structure of the Courts of the Russian Federation

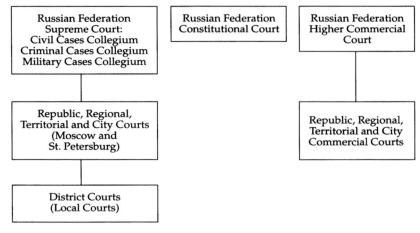

After the Russian Revolution of 1917, courts were abolished and replaced with informal tribunals to handle various conflicts and administrative disputes. Tribunals were favored because they resolved disputes on the basis of the "revolutionary consciousness" of ordinary workers, removing decisions from the elite corps of professional jurists. Special tribunals were created for housing, transport, labor, and military affairs. Of these non-judicial tribunals only two types continue to exist: military tribunals and comrades' courts.

Military tribunals are organized hierarchically into a separate branch of the Russian judiciary, regulated by a special statute. Military tribunals at all levels are federal courts. They have jurisdiction in all criminal matters (and civil cases arising from criminal actions) committed by members of the armed forces, police, security police, prison personnel, and others officially employed in the law enforcement and security fields.[6] Appeals of tribunal decisions can be lodged only against actions of the courts of original jurisdiction. Like the regular district court, military tribunals consist of one judge and two lay assessors. In all other cases, the court consists of three professional judges.

Comrades' courts are informal citizens' bodies, elected in housing units and places of employment to resolve infractions of social norms or punish minor criminal acts. For example, comrades' courts frequently impose small fines on residents guilty of disturbing the peace of an apartment building, or found guilty of vandalism. In factories, comrades' courts punish cases of minor theft of enterprise equipment or materials. In their peak of activity during the Khrushchev years, some 197,000 comrades' courts were disposing of more than 4 million cases per year.[7] However, the legal profession succeeded in limiting the jurisdiction of the comrades' courts, complaining that they routinely meted out prejudicial, arbitrary justice and meddled in nonjudicial matters. Although they were out of favor with professional lawyers, comrades' courts existed up to 1992 considering tens of thousands of cases each year. With the demise of the USSR and the CPSU, the functions of the comrades' courts have been assumed by justices of the peace courts or other local bodies.[8]

The Constitutional Court

Separate from the hierarchy of regular courts is the Constitutional Court of the Russian Federation. The Constitutional Court, established in July 1991, is the most promising indication yet of the Yeltsin government's commitment to a law-governed society. The Russian Constitutional Court grew out of Gorbachev's effort in 1990 to establish a separate and independent judicial system to adjudicate constitutional conflicts horizontally between the various branches of government and vertically between central institutions and subnational units.[9] The Supreme Soviet of the Russian Federation approved the enabling legislation creating the court in late spring 1991, but sharp political differences over the extent of the court's powers and selection of justices delayed its realization. The law establishing the Constitutional Court called for fifteen judges to be elected by the Russian parliament for a limited life term (until age 65). Of the twenty-three candidates nominated, the parliament could agree on only thirteen; the other two seats remained vacant. The thirteen judges selected from among their number Valery Zorkin to serve as chief justice.

Zorkin was born in 1943 and raised in the Soviet Far East. He graduated from Moscow State University in law, continuing to pursue an advanced degree (*kandidatskaia*) in law. Zorkin joined the law faculty at Moscow University, teaching courses on the history of law and the theory of law. Upon completion of the doctoral degree he was named professor of law in the Department of Constitutional Law and Jurisprudence of the Academy of the USSR Ministry of Internal Affairs.

Among the other twelve justices initially elected to the Constitutional Court there was one woman. Six justices, in addition to Zorkin, held the doctorate of law, four had the *kandidatskaya*, and two held the basic university law degree. Prior to their selection to the

Constitutional Court, the justices had distinguished themselves in academe and legislative service, while one served as a prosecutor in Siberia. The justices were assisted by a staff of 43 people and a professional staff of 156, organized into departments reflecting major branches of law (land law, constitutional law, criminal law, international law, administrative law, etc.).

The Russian Constitutional Court was modeled on the constitutional courts of Western Europe, especially the German Federal Constitutional Court. The Constitutional Court is the only court empowered to review constitutional questions and access to the court is relatively unrestricted; most cases require no previous hearing. Decisions of the court are final and not subject to appeal.

While the Law on the Constitutional Court clearly stated that the body "does not review political questions" and that the court may rule "only on questions of law," the boundary between law and politics in Russia was ambiguous. Given the court's mandate to adjudicate disputes between the executive and legislative branches and between the federal and subordinate units of government, it was inevitable that the court would become embroiled in political disputes. Article 9 of the law granted the court the right to initiate legislation in parliament, further blurring the political and legal realms of the court's activity. In December 1992 the law was amended, allowing the court to examine political cases.

The Russian Constitutional Court initially only considered one case at a time, which severely restricted the number of cases that could be considered in a year. During its first full year of operation, the court considered only nine cases. By contrast, the US Supreme Court hears between 75 and 150 cases per year. The German Federal Constitutional Court also hears about 150 cases per year. Chief Justice Zorkin noted that the court was receiving "hundreds of complaints" daily from ordinary citizens.[10] While the vast majority of these petitions failed to meet the court's requirements for standing and access, some 16,000 petitions and complaints were handled informally. By the end of its first year, the Russian Constitutional Court had forty cases pending on its docket.[11] A new Law on the Constitutional Court of the Russian Federation of July 21, 1994 now permits the courts to handle multiple cases simultaneously.

The expanding caseload is the result, in part, of the court functioning as a court of original jurisdiction (except in individual rights cases which require prior vetting) and the absence of well-developed gate-keeping procedures. The rapidly expanding caseload of the court also reflects its increasing popularity among citizens.

The biggest potential threat to the court's legitimacy is the tendency for it to be drawn into political disputes. During its first year of operation it became apparent that parties who had lost an issue in the political arena were turning to the court to support their positions. For example, the court was asked by a group of parliamentary deputies to challenge more than twenty edicts of parliamentary speaker, Ruslan Khasbulatov, including his attempted takeover of the newspaper *Izvestiya*. Conservatives also sought relief from the court, as in the case of the right-wing extremist group, the National Salvation Front. The NSF challenged Yeltsin's December 1992 decree banning the organization, arguing that it represented an over-reaching of the president's executive authority. The court agreed to hear the case in early 1993.

The cases heard by the court during its first year in existence helped to build its credibility and legitimacy. The first case declared unconstitutional President Yeltsin's merging the Ministry of Internal Affairs and the Ministry of Security. Although the court's ruling came as a surprise to Yeltsin and his chief legal advisor, Sergei Shakhrai, Zorkin persuaded them to abide by the ruling. To have ignored the court's decision would have severely undermined the fledgling institution.

In the next two cases, the court ruled that the parliament had exceeded its constitutional authority in attempting to limit the activities of the Copyright Agency and the Competition and Anti-Monopoly Committee. Thus, the court in its first three cases, managed to steer a careful course between the executive and legislative branches.

Two of the early cases considered by the court concerned grievances of ordinary citizens who had been improperly fired from their jobs. In one case, several workers were denied the right to judicial review of their firings. In the other case, two workers were terminated just prior to retiring in an effort to save their employer's pension fund. The success of these workers' petitions quickly earned the court the reputation as a defender of citizens' rights and resulted in a flood of new petitions.

During its first year in operation, the court's authority was openly challenged in only one case – the Tatarstan Referendum of March 1992. The court ruled that the referendum on independence for the Tatar Autonomous Republic contravened the Constitution of the Russian Federation and ordered the referendum canceled. The political leaders in Kazan dismissed the court's decision as a "judicial travesty" and went ahead with the referendum.[12] The court has no independent means to insure compliance with its rulings and President Yeltsin was unwilling to worsen relations with the Tatars by attempting to enforce the court's decision by coercive methods.

Undoubtedly the most important case to be considered by the court during its first year concerned the suspension of the Communist Party of the Soviet Union and the nationalization of its assets following the August 1991 attempted *coup d'état*. Yeltsin's decrees on the CPSU were politically motivated, but they also raised important legal issues that the Constitutional Court could not avoid.

Yeltsin's opponents charged that the Russian president had exceeded his authority in outlawing the Communist Party and seizing its assets. Chief Justice Zorkin echoed this position in a *Moscow News* interview of November 17, 1991.[13] Supporters of the president's actions argued that the CPSU was not a normal political party, but a pseudo-government that had been imposed by force and repudiated at the polls in the election of Yeltsin as president in 1991 and by popular resistance during the coup. They also provided the court with detailed information on the party's illegal transfers of funds abroad and widespread corruption. Furthermore, the presidential side sought to link the Communist Party as an organization and its leaders to the illegal attempt to seize power in August 1991.

The politically charged trial spilled into the press as former President Gorbachev refused to appear despite a summons and was eventually barred from traveling abroad, in a futile attempt to force him to testify. Zorkin heatedly denounced Gorbachev's defiance of the court, casting doubts on his neutrality to hear the case.

A carefully constructed compromise decision was announced in the CPSU case in late 1992. The court ruled by a 9 to 3 vote that Yeltsin was within his constitutional powers in banning the leading organs of the Communist Party, but that local and regional branches of the party had the right to exist and to regain their confiscated property.[14] A strongly worded dissenting opinion by Justice Luchin argued that the president had exceeded his competence and that the court had decided the case on the basis of "expediency rather than law."[15] The middle-of-the-road decision in the CPSU case reflected Zorkin's chief concern – preserving the integrity and legitimacy of the Constitutional Court as an institution.

However much the CPSU case enhanced Zorkin's image and that of the court, it also created sharp rifts among the justices and reinforced Zorkin's tendency to engage in extra-judicial comment on cases pending before the court. Zorkin's political outspokenness reached a crescendo in the spring of 1993 when he denounced Yeltsin's threat to assume special powers. He appeared in a press conference with several other officials to denounce the president for threatening another *coup d'état*. When the issue came before the court, Zorkin did not recuse himself, but voted with the majority that the substance of the president's televised address advocated unconstitutional means to resolve the presidential–parliamentary deadlock. Yet in his speech, Yeltsin took no concrete action nor issued any legal act. He merely indicated some threatened possible courses of action to break the legislative–executive logjam. This cast the Constitutional Court into the position of ruling on the constitutionality of Yeltsin's statements of intent, which were largely hypothetical. Furthermore, Zorkin and other members of the court were, in effect, issuing a decision without benefit of either oral argument or the submission of written briefs. The overtly partisan role played by Zorkin and other justices served to undermine the legitimacy of the Constitutional Court.

By mid-1993 Zorkin appeared fully aligned with the parliament and its speaker, Ruslan Khasbulatov, against Yeltsin. Zorkin's increasingly partisan and vocal opposition to the president eroded the court's cohesion and public respect for the court. In June 1993 the deputy chairman of the Constitutional Court, Nikolai Vitruk, and Justice Anatoly Kononov both urged Zorkin to refrain from engaging in political activities. Vitruk went so far as to call for Zorkin to resign.[16]

Yeltsin's decree of September 21, 1993 dissolving the parliament and the subsequent storming of the White House on October 3 shocked many observers. Yeltsin was, in effect, carrying out the action he had threatened in March. Chief Justice Zorkin appeared alongside Khasbulatov at a press conference and announced an emergency session of the court to examine Yeltsin's actions. Later that same night he announced to deputies of the Supreme Soviet that the Court considered Yeltsin's decree unconstitutional and grounds for impeachment. (It was later disclosed that four justices, Nikolai Vitruk, Anatoly Konorov, Ernst Ametistov, and Tamara Marshchakova voted against Zorkin's interpretation.) Zorkin, although appearing to side with Khasbulatov and Rutskoi, proposed early elections to both the parliament and the presidency as a compromise political solution to the constitutional impasse.

On October 5, after the surrender of Rutskoi and Khasbulatov and their supporters, the Russian Federation Constitutional Court announced that it would limit its deliberations to hearing petitions from citizens and organizations. The next day Zorkin was persuaded to resign as chief justice, declaring that it was impossible for him to perform his duties under existing conditions. Zorkin's resignation as chairman preserved the hope that the Constitutional Court could weather the turmoil and reemerge as a legitimate judicial institution.

On October 17, 1993 President Yeltsin issued a decree suspending the Constitutional Court pending the adoption of a new constitution. The decree charged the court with playing "a negative, essentially complicit role in the tragic development of events in the city of Moscow on October 3–4, 1993."[17] The decree indicated the possibility of abolishing the Constitutional Court and replacing it with a consti-tutional collegium (chamber) within the Russian Federation Supreme Court. Ultimately, however, a compromise position was reached to enlarge the court to nineteen judges – an addition of six new judges to the previous thirteen.[18] In October 1994 Yeltsin nominated six prominent jurists to the high court. They included: Mikhail Mityukov, deputy chairman of the State Duma and a leader of the Russia's Choice political faction; Vladimir Tumanov, a Duma deputy rep-resenting the pro-reform Party of Russian Unity and Concord; Valery Savitsky, a prominent constitutional scholar who supported Yeltsin's decrees combating organized crime; Olga Khokhryakova, a specialist on labor and social security law, from Yeltsin's native city Ekaterin-burg; Mikhail Krasnov, an advisor to Yeltsin's aide Yuri Baturin; and St. Petersburg judge Vladimir Yaroslavtsev. The motivating factor in Yeltsin's selections was clear – to balance the judges on the current bench who are very critical of him with justices who are much more pro-reform and pro-Yeltsin. Three of the nominees were approved by the Federation Council, but Mityukov, Savitsky, and Krasnov were rejected. During the debate preceding the balloting, several deputies expressed reservations about the candidates being too closely associ-ated with Yeltsin and too heavily weighted toward Moscow. In a hopeful sign, both the Federation Council and the president commit-ted themselves to resolving the make-up of the court within the frame-work of the new constitution.[19] The passage of a new Law on the Constitutional Court enacted on July 21, 1994 has also helped solidify its place in the Russian legal system.

The biggest threat to the Constitutional Court remains the possibil-ity of it being politicized by one or another political faction. Certainly the development of a workable system of judicial review of consti-tutional provisions will take time to gain legitimacy and authority. A credible start has been made. The future of the court depends on it remaining above the political fray. It can only be hoped that the most contentious constitutional issues have been worked out with the adoption of a new constitution and that the Constitutional Court will provide some stability in the midst of an otherwise chaotic situation in the country.

Judicial procedure

Judicial procedure currently in place in Russia is a curious mix of the European civil law tradition and socialist legality with a smattering of indigenous ancient Russian practices. Russian law belongs to the larger family of civil law systems that are ultimately derived from the rules, principles, and practices elaborated in the ancient Roman Forum. Anglo-American students of Russian law, who are accustomed to the common law systems derived from England, are at a disadvantage in understanding Russian law and legal procedure, while European scholars find the fundamentals of the Russian legal system quite familiar.

Historians have suggested that civil law encouraged autocracy, while common law promoted democracy. The common law principle was enshrined in the maxim *Rex no debet esse sub homine sed sub Deo et Lege* (The king should not be under any man, but under God and the Law), while the principle of civil law was *Quod principi placuit legis habet vigorem* (The will of the sovereign has the force of law). Generally, civil legal systems grant greater authority to state officials than do common law systems.

Civil law and common law also differ markedly in the origins of laws. In common law systems, judges make law by establishing precedent decisions. Laws thus change organically, growing as a result of piecemeal judicial decisions. In civil law systems, all laws are the official enactments of executive or legislative bodies. These laws are gathered into codes and periodically updated and standardized. Greater importance is attached to official documents and reports in civil law systems, and administrative officials are given broader discretionary powers.

As in other civil law systems of Western Europe, Russian courts traditionally functioned on the basis of inquisitorial procedure, rather than adversarial procedure. The function of the court proceeding is to inquire into the events that resulted in either the civil suit or criminal offense. All parties actively engage in this fact-finding inquiry, most notably the judge. In a civil law system the judge is not the independent, neutral arbiter that one associates with courts in common law countries, rather the judge is an active participant in all aspects of the trial. Judges may call for evidence and question witnesses – generally before either the prosecution or the defense.

Compared with courts in the West, judicial procedure in Russia is quite informal. Judges routinely interrupt prosecutors, defense attorneys, or witnesses. Spectators in the courtroom often react audibly to statements of the accused or witnesses, sometimes calling out blatantly prejudicial remarks such as "He's a scoundrel, just look at him!"[20] Public interjections such as this are usually permitted by the judge and cannot be protested by the defense. Evidence is handled quite casually. Court reporters provide only a summary of the proceedings, rather than a verbatim account.

Given their central role in the judicial system, judges became the object of official pressure during the Soviet period. Lenin and his associates were cynical about law and the legal system. Lenin is reported to have quipped, "Law is policy." In his view, law and the courts merely served the interests of the state, which, in turn, protected the interests of the dominant class in society. There was no such conception as an independent judiciary. As we noted earlier, courts were abolished in 1917 and replaced with informal, revolutionary tribunals. When the courts were gradually reinstituted, judicial appointments went to loyal Bolsheviks (often with no formal legal education) and their performance was closely monitored by the party through its powers of nomenklatura. Virtually all judges above the local level were party members. Judges not only were expected to determine innocence or guilt, but also to educate the accused and all present in the courtroom. When pronouncing sentence, judges often berated the accused for failing to uphold socialist values, for being drunk in public, or for setting a bad example for children. Soviet judges were an important instrument of socialization and, as in other careers involving socialization of societal norms, women were heavily represented on the bench. A study in mid-1970s found that approximately 60 percent of all those "employed in dispensing justice" were women.[21]

As we noted in Chapter 3, the seeds for the reform of Soviet judicial procedure were sown in the 1950s in reaction to Khrushchev's secret speech and denunciation of Stalin. Khrushchev criticized Stalin for, among other things, violating "Leninist norms" of collegiality and consultation in the drafting of legal policies and procedures. Soviet jurists took advantage of the opportunity to press for basic reforms in Soviet criminal law and procedure. Chief among the concerns of Soviet jurists was the abolition of the doctrine of analogy. Since 1922 Soviet judges were empowered to convict persons for committing "socially dangerous acts," even though the acts were not identified as crimes in the criminal code. Under the doctrine, persons could be convicted of an offense analogous to a criminal offense. In 1937 alone, the analogy principle was applied in more than 500 cases.[22] Between 1938 and 1952 there were four attempts by Soviet jurists to abolish the principle of analogy in new drafts of the criminal code but they all failed to be ratified. Analogy was finally eliminated in 1958 when a new Fundamental Principles of Criminal Law was enacted. Article 3 of the RSFSR Criminal Code of 1960, reflecting the changes in the Fundamental Principles, stated: "Criminal responsibility and punishment applies only to people guilty of committing a crime – that is, intentionally or carelessly committing a socially dangerous act *specified in criminal law*"[23] (italics of the author).

During the reform movement of the 1950s, Soviet jurists succeeded in eliminating other draconian elements of the Stalinist system. The powers of the secret police were reduced, the special tribunals of the secret police that had condemned millions to death or to labor camps were abolished, searches and arrests required warrants, only courts could impose criminal penalties, and the rights of the accused during the preliminary investigation were expanded.

In the 1950s the major law schools of the USSR, Moscow State University and Leningrad University, were on the forefront of the reform movement. It was at this time that Mikhail Gorbachev was a student at Moscow University Law Faculty. The revision of legal codes and the debates they engendered at the time were undoubtedly important in shaping his views on the importance of an independent judiciary, rule of law, and equality before the law.

During the Brezhnev era an unofficial bifurcation of the Soviet judicial system developed. In non-political cases, Soviet court procedure appeared to function with increasing professionalism. By the early 1960s, more than 95 percent of all judges had a higher legal education.[24] Increasingly, the political leaders deferred to legal professionals in the making of policy. The legal profession took steps to bring the Khrushchev-era "popular justice" under control and replace it with "socialist legality." V. M. Chkhikvadze, former director of the Institute of State and Law, noted that "socialist legality" stresses guaranteeing the procedural and substantive rights of citizens and ensuring the professionalism of the courts.[25] Minor criminal cases were transferred from comrades' courts to regular people's courts, so that the accused could enjoy full rights to a defense. The consideration of "parasite" cases was also transferred from administrative tribunals to the courts. Citizen input in law enforcement and adjudication was restricted and brought under provisions of the new criminal procedure code.

The same judicial system that was capable of professional and fair handling of routine cases, however, was also capable of being used as an arbitrary and repressive tool to punish critics of the regime. Beginning in the early 1960s and extending throughout the Brezhnev era, there was a resurgence of a dictatorial trend in Soviet law. The powers of the police were expanded, new legislation severely restricted public demonstrations, dissidents were rounded up, tried, and sentenced to labor camps or psychiatric hospitals, and capital punishment was reintroduced for a wide variety of offenses, resulting in a rapid increase in the number of executions.

Even in this arena, however, by the 1970s KGB officers usually took the trouble to secure a search warrant before ransacking the apartment of a dissident. Criminal trials of such noted critics as Vladimir Bukovsky, Yuri Orlov, and Anatoly Shcharansky were carefully conducted according to criminal procedure, even if the outcome was a foregone conclusion.

By the mid-1970s, declining economic performance coupled with the conservative bureaucratic leadership style of the Brezhnev regime combined to shift the emphasis of socialist legality from protecting the interests of individual citizens to protecting the economic interests of the state. The 25th Party Congress in 1976 stressed the need for legal regulation of economic activity to increase production, to strengthen the economic system, and to counter fraud, theft of socialist property, and the padding of accounts and plan-fulfillment reports. R. A. Rudenko, the then procurator-general, noted that the Procuracy had been ordered to strengthen its supervision of legality in all economic organizations.[26] The 1979 Statute on the Procuracy incorporated several new provisions relating to economic violations. For example, Article 3 stated that "the fight against violations concerning the protection of socialist property" is one of the fundamental responsibilities of procurators.[27] Laws protecting socialist property and setting punishments for economic crimes were substantially strengthened in the January 1983 revision of the Criminal Code of the RSFSR.

Repeatedly during the Brezhnev years, political and economic concerns prompted law enforcement officials to launch massive anti-crime campaigns. Under the pressures of a campaign against economic crimes, law enforcement and judicial officials were less likely to observe proper investigatory procedures and insure due process for the accused. As one Western expert on the Soviet legal system noted, "Anti-crime campaigns ... tend to blur the line between administration, governed by considerations of expediency, and adjudication, governed by impersonal, general rules."[28] During one of the highly publicized anti-bribery campaigns of the 1960s, a Soviet defense attorney lamented, "If you have a bribery case these days, you might as well give up."[29]

The juridization process since Stalin's death led some observers both inside and outside the USSR to conclude that judicial independence was not only desirable (in contrast to Lenin's cynical rejection of judicial independence) but had been achieved in practice. It was only with the introduction of glasnost in 1986 that the extent of political influence over the activities of the courts came to light. Encouraged by Gorbachev's policy of glasnost, journalists began to publish exposés of "telephone justice" in which party and government officials meddled in the activities of the courts.

Glasnost uncovered not only interference in the courts, but also favoritism in the courts' handling of cases of party members and government officials. For example, an article by Arkady Vaksberg reported how the investigators and judges in Chelyabinsk saved a young man whose father "works in the executive committee of the regional soviet and whose mother has an influential friend in high places" from criminal prosecution for causing the death of a tenth-grade student.[30] Politicians were accused in the press of using the courts to punish their critics. In Kazakhstan, a two-year sentence was passed on the chief accountant of a state farm who had refused to sign some dubious expense accounts designed to cover the cost of a banquet laid on by the first party secretary of the district.[31] In Uzbekistan a teacher exposed illegal actions by several local officials in the Kashkadar'ya region and was subsequently sentenced to five years on trumped-up charges of slander.[32]

Widespread debate among Soviet jurists also focused on the abolition of the death penalty. Numerous press reports began to appear in 1987 detailing cases of the erroneous application of the death penalty. In 1987 it was reported that the death penalty was imposed in forty-seven cases, including twenty-six cases of violent crimes, five cases of economic crime or abuse of public office, and six cases of war crimes.[33] All those condemned to death were men. In the second half of 1987, after the appearance of several critical articles in *Moskovskiye novosti*, *Nedelya*, and *Ogonek*, there were no additional death sentences handed out for economic crimes.[34] Those articles cited cases in which innocent people were wrongly accused, and sometimes the victims of attempts by law enforcement officials to fabricate evidence. In one case in Vitebsk (cited in chapter 3), a man was wrongly accused of the rape and murder of several dozen women over a fifteen-year period.[35] Local police, responding to pressures to solve the case, fabricated evidence that resulted in the conviction of an innocent man. Fortunately, another man, being held on other charges confessed to the murders and the condemned man was released before the sentence was carried out. The case resulted in the dismissal and eventual conviction of eight former officials in Belorussian law enforcement agencies.[36] The "Vitebsk Affair" was apparently not an isolated case, *Literaturnaya gazeta* and *Sovetskaya Rossiya* reported similar cases in Latvia and Krasnodar' krai.[37]

One of the earliest goals of legal perestroika was to guarantee greater independence of judges. The USSR Law on the Status of Judges, passed in 1989, made it a criminal offense, punishable by up to three years' incarceration to exert pressure on a judge or people's assessor "with the intent of impeding a complete, full and objective handling of a particular case, or of securing an unlawful court decision."[38] (The law did not apply to attempts to influence police, investigators, procurators, or advocates, however.)

The law altered the procedure for selecting judges in an attempt to insulate them from political pressures in their respective regions. Judicial terms were increased from five to ten years, and judges were selected by a soviet at the next higher level of government. The nomination of judges was removed from the province of the party and vested in judicial selection panels comprised of judges chosen for a five-year term by judges at the regional level, although it is likely that party officials influenced the composition of the judicial panels. Even with these provisions, proposals were debated for giving judges tenure for life to insure their independence.

Judicial independence from political officials also depends on such pragmatic considerations as allocation of housing for judges. Under previous arrangements, local judges received their housing and other benefits through local party and government bodies. Former Russian

Minister of Justice V. Abolentsev noted one case in which a judge was threatened with losing his apartment if he did not rule a particular way.[39]

The Law on the Status of Judges prohibits the dismissal or reprimanding of judges whose decisions are overturned on appeal. Judges may be disciplined only when they make illegal decisions or act in bad faith and where their actions have significant consequences.[40] According to official records released by the Supreme Court, in 1993, forty-five judges were relieved of their positions for behavior that discredited them. In some 3 percent of all cases, judicial decisions had to be changed due to judicial misconduct.[41]

In the past, judges were sometimes subject to criminal prosecution to punish them for failing to follow the directives of party officials. The Law on the Status of Judges provides that judges may be prosecuted only with the consent of the supreme soviet of the republic. In the case of a Supreme Court judge, the initiation of criminal proceedings requires the approval of the Russian parliament. Furthermore, the law removes the right to prosecute judges from local prosecutors, vesting such power in the procurator-general. These changes have gone a long way toward insuring greater independence of judges from the local authorities.

The court of first instance in most civil and criminal cases consists of one judge assisted by two people's assessors.[42] People's assessors are ordinary citizens, 25 years old or older, elected at general meetings of factories, collective farms, or residential blocs for a term of two years. During their terms, assessors may be called upon for not more than two weeks court duty each year. People's assessors are released from their jobs with pay to serve in court and in many cases they are reimbursed for their travel expenses. People's assessors function as "lay judges" with the power to decide guilt or innocence, but also have all the rights and powers of the professional judge, including the right to review all investigatory documents, call and question witnesses, examine evidence, set punishment, and award damages. Judicial determinations are made in private by a vote of the judge and the two lay assessors. In most cases, lay assessors tend to defer to the professional training and experience of the judge, but instances have occurred where the two lay assessors outvoted the professional judge. In appellate cases, where questions under review are procedural or involve technical points of law, cases are decided by panels of three professional judges. However, all courts in the Russian Federation are considered to have original jurisdiction and, therefore, utilize the services of lay assessors, with the exception of the Constitutional Court.

Appellate procedures

Appellate courts in Russia enjoy broad powers of review over the decisions of trial courts in criminal matters. Five types of appeals (or protests) can be distinguished: appeals of actions of criminal investigators, cassational appeals, cassational protests, private appeals, and private protests. The first type of appeal, against the actions of a criminal investigator, is usually intended to challenge procedural violations in the gathering of evidence in a criminal case. The suspect (or his or her legal counsel) may lodge a complaint either orally or in writing with the Procuracy. The substance of the complaint must be looked into within a set period of time, normally three days. Failure to follow established procedures during the preliminary investigation often results in a ruling of inadmissibility of evidence in court and can result in a retrial or acquittal.

The review of court decisions by higher courts before they enter into force is referred to as "cassation" in Russia. Cassation can be sought by either the prosecution or the defense sides. When the action is brought by the prosecution, it is called a cassation protest; when it is sought by the defendant, it is called a cassation appeal. Private cassation appeals or protests can also be lodged by other interested parties (e.g. the victim). Appeals and protests may relate to both the verdict and the sentence. Grounds for the annulment or modification of a trial court's judgment include both procedural errors and factual errors. Although the appellate court may modify the judgment of the trial court, it is prohibited from increasing the punishment or applying a provision of the criminal code for a more serious crime.

A cassation appeal or protest must be lodged within seven days from the day the trial court judgment is rendered. The filing of an appeal or a protest automatically suspends execution of the court's judgment or ruling. The appellate court has broad powers to uphold the judgment, annul the judgment and return the case for further investigation or retrial, annul the judgment and terminate the case, or modify the judgment. If a retrial is ordered by the appellate court, the case will be returned to the court of original jurisdiction but will be heard by a different judge and new lay assessors.

The jury trial experiment

During the Gorbachev years there were repeated proposals to expand the number of lay assessors to provide for even more citizen input into judicial affairs and to further reduce the likelihood of political intrusions into court decisions.[43] Calls were also heard for the restoration of jury trials that had existed in Russia from 1864 to 1917. A law on jury trials went into effect in 1993 and the first case was heard by a jury in December 1993.

Jury trials are being reintroduced on an experimental basis after a hiatus of seventy-six years. With the assistance of the US Agency of International Development (USAID) and the American Bar Association, Western experts have been brought in to consult with their Russian counterparts. Their first task was to develop a bench book to assist judges in the conduct of a jury trial. The bench book specifies elements of procedure for the submission of evidence, examination of witnesses, presentation of evidence, and instructions to jurors that are not covered in the existing Code of Criminal Procedure.

Jury trials are being introduced only in the most serious cases – cases involving punishment exceeding ten years incarceration or the death penalty. Because it is an experiment, defendants are now given the option of choosing whether to have their cases heard by a jury or by a regular court, consisting of one professional judge and two lay assessors. The jury trial program began in five regions: Moscow, Stavropol, Ivanovo, Ryazan, and Saratov and in early 1994 was extended to four more districts: Altai, Simbirsk (Ulyanovsk), Krasnodar, and Rostov-on-Don.

The jury is composed of twelve Russian citizens (and two alternates) between the ages of 25 and 70. People with criminal records are prohibited from serving on a jury. Citizens selected for jury duty may ask to be relieved due to a disability or a professional conflict of interest, otherwise service is mandatory. Jurors decide questions of guilt or innocence, while judges decide questions of law. The jury reaches its decision based on a majority vote, with a vote of seven to five necessary for conviction. The jury meets separately from the judge to deliberate. It is up to the judge, guided by the Criminal Code, to set punishment; however, the jury may, if it chooses, recommend leniency in a case.

The first jury trial took place in mid-December 1993 in the provincial city of Saratov. The case concerned a fight over a card game that resulted in the deaths of three people. Two brothers, Artur and Aleksandr Martynov, survived the fight and were charged with murder. They both requested to be tried by a jury. The Martynovs admitted to killing the three men, but argued that they acted in self-defense. The prosecution's case was severely damaged when the judge ruled that much of the evidence against the Martynovs had been gathered illegally and could not be used in court, prompting the prosecutor to make a motion for reducing the charges against the accused. After two days of hearing the case, the jury voted to convict the Martynov brothers on a reduced charge of excessive use of force in self-defense. The jury also voted unanimously to recommend leniency in sentencing. As a result, Artur was sentenced to one and one-half years and Aleksandr to one year. Some observers noted that under the previous system they would very likely have been found guilty of murder and could even have been sentenced to death.[44]

Opinion on the desirability of jury trials is quite divided. Prosecutors are much more likely to oppose jury trials and the "subjective" judgment that citizens may bring to a case. The chief procurator in Saratov, Nikolai Makarov, voiced a common concern: "Criminality has grown so much, I am more than certain that the jury won't even consider the legal niceties that are taken into account by professionals when they come to sentencing, which might allow for an appeal before the Supreme Court."[45] Concerns of jury bias based on ethnicity or nationality were alleviated somewhat in the Martynov case. The Martynovs are gypsies, a nationality group that is often despised by Russians and other ethnic groups. The fear that a jury would be prejudiced when hearing cases involving gypsies or other minority groups proved to be unfounded in this case.

Russian prosecutors also fear that guilty parties may be acquitted due to defense counsel playing to a sympathetic jury. (However, the judge has the right to vacate an unfounded conviction by a jury.) Other critics of the introduction of jury trials cite problems of inadequate resources to support the introduction of jury trials. For example, in the Stavropol and Moscow regions, no courtrooms exist in which there is space for a jury to be seated.[46] In some districts there are insufficient numbers of judges; not infrequently there is only one judge to handle all criminal cases arising in three districts.[47] To facilitate the introduction of jury trials, ninety-nine new judges were to be named in the nine regions in which the experiment was slated. However, these appointments were delayed because the Russian Supreme Soviet, which had to approve the nominations, ceased to exist as of October 2, 1993.[48]

There have also been problems with the selection of jury pools. Rather than selecting jurors randomly from voters' lists, as specified in the law, officials in Ryazan province followed past practice for naming lay assessors – they solicited names from local enterprises and collectives.[49] Such a practice undermines the objectivity of the jury.

Budgets are also inadequate to pay jurors for their time, to insure their anonymity and safety, or to compensate judges adequately. Salaries of judges have not kept pace with inflation, prompting many judges to take positions in private practice or as legal consultants to private enterprises, which offer much higher salaries. Prosecutors complain that many judges, especially at the district level, are young and inexperienced. A high-ranking prosecutor summed up the attitude: "Maybe we do need stronger courts, but it may take 15 to 20 years to build such a system."[50]

Inadequate court facilities and support services also threaten to undermine the effectiveness of the courts. During seventy-four years under the communist regime, officials paid little attention to the court system. Many local courts meet in old buildings without elevators and in which even the heating and plumbing frequently do not work properly. According to Minister of Justice Fedorov, more than 1,000 courts are located in buildings that should be condemned.[51] Court reporters record proceedings using shorthand. Computers, word processors, and dictaphones are non-existent. Most courts do not have a working photocopy machine and even typewriters are difficult to obtain. Trials often encounter long delays due to shortages of police guards and vehicles to shuttle defendants from jail to court.

Defense attorneys tend to favor the jury trial experiment, noting that it can provide a check on the state prosecution to abide by investigatory and criminal procedure. Aleskei Galaganov, president of the Russian Bar Association, observed, "In our view, trial by jury will be a serious obstacle to erroneous judgments."[52] Sergei A. Pashin, head of the Department of Judicial Reform and Legislation in the office of the president and one of the drafters of the reform, stresses that jury trials will bring about a greater degree of equality of sides in criminal proceedings: "I hope that jury trials will change the face of our justice. Instead of inquisitorial justice, we will see the prosecution and defense challenging each other in court to prove the guilt or innocence of the accused."[53]

The guarantee of equality of parties before the court, promised in Article 429 of the criminal procedure code, is not yet fully realized in many Russian courts, even in the jury trial experiment. While prosecutors open the trial with a reading of the indictment and extensive findings of the preliminary investigation, defense counsel are not granted the right to an opening statement to outline their case. Judges appear reluctant to give up their traditionally assertive role, including examining witnesses and objecting to defense questions even when no objection has been raised by the prosecution. Furthermore, defendants, as in the British tradition, are forced to sit in a "defendant's box" surrounded by guards which limits the ability of defense counsel to consult with their clients and can stigmatize the accused.

The long-standing traditions in Russian law favoring the state prosecution may be changing to a degree with the adoption of jury trials, but they have not been totally eliminated. The evolution of a new judicial system in which citizens' rights are no longer subordinate to those of the state requires more than structural and procedural reforms; it requires a fundamental change in legal culture and that will take at least a generation.

The Russian bar

Instrumental in the transformation of the Russian legal system will be the *advokatura* or Russian bar – attorneys who provide representation to citizens in civil and criminal cases. Following long-standing Soviet practice, advocates are organized into "colleges" of about 150 lawyers each. These colleges maintain consultation bureaus in virtually every town and city throughout the country. Each bureau has a staff of approximately twenty advocates. At the consultation bureaus citizens may seek legal advice on a vast array of questions: divorce, custody, inheritance, property rights, housing disputes, product liability complaints, labor conflicts, and so forth. The colleges also provide legal defense for people accused of criminal offenses. The constitution provides that a defendant is guaranteed the right to legal counsel and that legal assistance will be provided free of charge if the defendant cannot afford a lawyer. Prior to 1988 legal fees were set by state authorities. However, fees were so low that many advocates were forced to demand under-the-table payments, "gifts," and other "favors" in exchange for their services. After 1988 advocates were permitted to set their own fees.

There were approximately 27,000 advocates in the Soviet Union. Until February 1989 advocates were not represented by a professional organization, although there had been repeated calls for an organization to represent their interests. The creation of the Union of Advocates, however, for the first time gave defense attorneys an institutional basis for pressing their demands for legal reform. However, the organization and its powers remain disputed. A December 1990 draft of a new Law on the Advokatura proposed keeping the structure of colleges of advocates under the direction of the Ministry of Justice. The Union of Soviet Advocates organized a public protest march in Moscow which drew some 600 attorneys. The advocates demanded the right to be a self-governing profession, free of the ministry's control or supervision.

Increasingly, Russian attorneys are establishing their own law firms, independent of the colleges and consultation bureaus. Such private law firms began on an experimental basis in Moscow and St. Petersburg and are rapidly spreading throughout Russia.

Another point of controversy is whether law school graduates should continue to be required to complete a one-year *stazhirovka* or internship prior to becoming a licensed advocate. Although the one-year internship is technically still required, it is not being enforced today.

With the collapse of the USSR, the former Union of Soviet Advocates has fragmented into three organizations. The International Union of Advocates endeavors to unite all advocates of the former Soviet Union. Closely associated with it is the Russian Union of Advocates. Both associations favor preserving the existing system of colleges and consultation bureaus. A rival organization, the Association of Russian Advocates, draws on support from provincial lawyers who resist the collegiate structure and dominance of Moscow and St. Petersburg lawyers in the other organizations.

The International Union and its affiliate Union of Russian Advocates claim a membership of about 40 percent of all advocates, while the association's membership represents approximately 30 percent of the profession.[54] The remaining advocates apparently are not affiliated with any professional organization.

While Russian advocates are eager to assert their professional independence and right to self-governance, their lack of solidarity appears to be jeopardizing their professional interests. The former collegiate structure is rapidly unraveling and the ability of any of the professional associations to control its members, including certifying the qualifications of advocates, is seriously in doubt today. Furthermore, the internal rifts within the *advokatura* lessen its ability to press for substantive changes in the law, such as the right for greater access to their clients early in criminal proceedings and the right to participate in the preliminary investigation. As in other areas of Russian society, the rapid collapse of former institutions threatens to replace a hyper-centralized command and control structure with a fragmented and anarchic situation.

Reform of the criminal code

For several years, Soviet and Russian jurists have noted the need to recodify criminal law. The present code is the product of the Khrush-chev reforms of the late 1950s and only partially addressed problems of the previous Stalinist code. Work was begun in 1987 on a compre-hensive revision of the criminal code. In 1985, legal scholars at the Institute of State and Law, anticipating the more tolerant atmosphere of the Gorbachev era, drafted a "Theoretical Model of a Criminal Code" that greatly influenced the direction of efforts to reform the criminal code. Work on the new draft criminal code was completed in mid-1988 and it was widely circulated for discussion. However, adoption of the revised criminal code was set back by political insta-bility and ultimately by the collapse of the USSR in late 1991. A new draft criminal code for the Russian Federation was published in Janu-ary 1992, but has yet to be adopted officially.

Chief among the concerns of jurists during the drafting were extending the right of counsel during the preliminary investigation, restricting the application of the death penalty, formally adopting the presumption of innocence, as well as decriminalizing a number of victimless offenses.

A long-standing grievance of Russian defense attorneys is that they were denied access to materials during the preliminary investigation in criminal cases. Given the importance of the preliminary investi-gation and the extremely high conviction rate of persons who are for-mally charged, advocates have long argued that they need to be involved in every stage of the criminal investigation and trial. During the period of legal reform under Khrushchev, the right to counsel during the preliminary investigation was extended to minors and people judged to be mentally incompetent, but not to ordinary adult suspects. The new draft of the Criminal Code of the Russian Feder-ation of January 1992 would extend the right to counsel during the preliminary investigation to all people.[55]

The draft also drastically scales back the number of offenses for which the death penalty can be imposed. Under the previous criminal code of the former USSR, the death penalty, by shooting, was applied in cases of treason, espionage, terrorist acts, sabotage, and intentional homicide committed under aggravating circumstances (e.g. murder for profit, murder to cover up a previous crime, murder of a pregnant woman, or especially brutal murder). Capital punishment was also employed to punish officials in flagrant cases of economic crimes (e.g. accepting bribes on a grand scale, theft of state property, embezzlement, and extortion). For instance, in 1985, the head bookkeeper of a construction firm in the Ukraine was accused of forming a criminal conspiracy with a number of stores in Kiev to steal state property. Over a period of years, the group systematically embezzled more than 327,000 rubles ($225,000). The Kiev regional criminal court sentenced the bookkeeper to death. His accomplices were sentenced to long terms in labor colonies.[56] As we have noted, press accounts in 1987 of the erroneous application of the death penalty, however, brought an end to executions for economic crimes.[57] The new draft criminal code would permit the death penalty only for murder, espionage, treason, terrorist acts, and sabotage. In practice, the vast majority of death penalty cases involve murder. For example, in the first six months of 1992, ninety-five people were sentenced to death; ninety-four for murder and one for threatening the life of a police officer.[58] A law of April 29, 1993 limits use of the death penalty to especially serious crimes and only applies to men aged 18 to 65.

The new draft criminal code specifically includes a presumption of innocence. While the 1958 code stated that the accused does not have to prove his or her innocence, it stopped short of placing the burden of proof on the prosecution. In part, the reluctance to adopt a formal presumption of innocence reflects the very nature of the Russian criminal investigation. Having completed an exhaustive preliminary investigation, the prosecutor submits a "summary of accusations" to the trial judge for review. If serious doubts exist in the prosecution's case, the matter will not be recommended to go forward to trial. Thus, any case that comes to trial carries an unofficial, yet powerful presumptive bias against the accused. One Western observer characterized a trial in the USSR as "an appeal from a pre-trial investigation."[59] It is the recognition of this accusatory bias that prompts Russian lawyers to argue for defense counsel during the preliminary investigation.

The 1992 draft code proposed decriminalizing a number of offenses, most notably political crimes, economic crimes, and victimless crimes. Although the draft code has not been enacted, several of its provisions were introduced via amendment to the existing criminal code. Article

70 of the code which specified up to seven years deprivation of free-dom for anti-Soviet agitation has been deleted. Article 154 of the former code made it a crime to "resell goods for the purpose of making a profit" and was amended in October 1990.[60] Articles of the code making various moral offenses crimes have also been altered. For example, Article 121 was amended in June 1993 to decriminalize homosexual acts among consenting adults.

The draft criminal code fails to eliminate several troubling carry-overs of Khrushchev's experiments with popular justice: the com-rades' courts, social accusers and social defenders, and "traveling ses-sions" of courts. Social accusers are "representatives of social organizations or workers' assemblies" who may appear before the court on their own initiative, not as part of the prosecution, to express an opinion as to whether the charge has been proved and to rec-ommend punishment. Social defenders play a similar role in testifying to the character of the defendant. Traveling sessions of criminal courts, although rare, are still permitted to enable larger numbers of citizens to witness proceedings. For example, in 1990, due to widespread public pressure authorities in Kazan agreed to hold a rape trial in a soccer stadium.[61]

Finally, the revised criminal code increases sentencing limits for crimes committed "by an organized group." For example, an attack by a group is punishable by imprisonment from six to fifteen years (Articles 91 and 146) and the seizure of hostages draws a sentence of five to fifteen years (Article 126-1).[62]

Crime in Russia

One of the unfortunate results of the reform process in the former USSR is the breakdown of public order and a rapid increase in violent crime. Murders increased in 1993 by 27 percent, on top of a 22 percent increase the previous year.[63] Rapes increased by 15 percent in 1993.[64] In the past few years there has been a virtual explosion of property crimes, especially theft and robbery. These categories of crime increased 75 percent from 1991 to 1992.[65] Crimes involving weapons rose by 250 percent in Russia in 1993, while crimes resulting in serious bodily injury jumped by 24 percent.[66]

An increasing portion of violent crimes appear to be linked to the rise of Mafia-type organized crime syndicates. In a single week in July 1993 gangland-style gun battles killed seven people in Moscow.[67] Four were killed near a luxury car dealership selling Alfa-Romeos and

Jeeps. Newspaper reports suggested the attack was prompted by the dealership's refusal to pay thousands of dollars in protection money to a criminal gang. Recently, bankers have become a prime target for gangland-style killings. Interior Minister Viktor Yerin estimated that there are about 3,000 organized criminal gangs forming about 50 criminal syndicates in Russia.[68] According to one estimate, two-thirds of all commercial and financial enterprises in Russia and 40 per cent of individual businessmen are engaged in some form of corruption.[69]

Organized crime is increasingly infecting Russian youth. Tempted by easy money, many young people have given up on attending school and instead are involved in semi-legal or criminal activities, selling everything from chewing gum to pirated copies of rock music tapes at outdoor kiosks. Profits for young "entrepreneurs" can range from 45,000 to 120,000 rubles per day ($15–$40) – approximately three times the national average daily wage for an adult worker. In Moscow alone, educators estimate that some 80,000 youngsters have stopped attending school.[70]

Pavel Romanov, deputy head of the Moscow Internal Affairs Administration's Department for Combating Juvenile Crime, notes: "The criminal world often uses children for its purposes, knowing that until they are 14 they are not liable to criminal punishment. Minors are contracted to fence stolen items and sell drugs and weapons."[71] In the first half of 1993 juvenile arrests for selling drugs increased some 350 percent over the same period the previous year. Juvenile arrests for extortion increased four-fold. A disproportionate share of juvenile offenders are recent newcomers to Moscow and other Russian cities. One-sixth of all juvenile crimes in Moscow are committed by newly arrived youngsters from Azerbaijan, Ukraine, Moldova, and Dagestan.[72]

Russian specialists disagree as to the causes of the alarming increase in crime and breakdown of public order. Some attribute the trend to the deliberate dismantling of or crippling of security organs, such as the police and the KGB. Due to plummeting prestige and salaries, many criminal investigators have left their posts. At present one-third of all criminal investigators within the Procuracy have been on the job less than one year.[73] Given their relative low salaries and lack of experience and equipment, it should not be surprising that less than one-half of all reported murders are solved. Thus, the deterrent effect of law enforcement has been seriously eroded. Efforts by law enforcement agencies to combat organized crime have been hampered by woefully inadequate resources and training. Mobsters often have more powerful weapons than the police. Low salaries for police investigators and others involved in law enforcement also make them ready targets for bribes. Vladimir Rushailo, chief of the Moscow police department observed, "Even if we manage to jail an influential member of the Mafia, his fellow-bandits immediately unleash a campaign pressuring victims, witnesses, judges, public assessors. And they do this quite freely. Clearly, the criminals are much more inventive than the lawmakers."[74]

Other scholars indicate that the period of rapid inflation and the flooding of the private economy with desirable and expensive consumer goods has created an incentive for criminals to acquire cash quickly, resulting in a precipitous rise in armed robberies and thefts. Another factor that undoubtedly has encouraged the rise of organized crime is the continued existence in Russia of monopolies in the production, distribution, and transport of desirable goods. The monopolies are the direct legacy of the communist regime in which the state controlled everything. Today many of the same monopolistic patterns still exist, often manipulated by the same party officials who previously managed wholesale and retail trade and transport under the Soviet regime. The break-up of organized crime syndicates will come only with the break-up of these monopolistic networks.

Increases in random anti-social acts have also been recorded during this transitional period in Russia. Russian criminologists have noted an increase in petty vandalism and a flagrant disregard for public order. Drivers routinely disregard traffic signals. Petty theft is rampant – whether auto parts taken from parked cars, light bulbs stolen from stairways in apartment buildings and resold on the streets, or supplies taken from factories and stores and traded to friends. Sociologists attribute these trends to a breakdown of the structure of Russian society and have labeled the behavior *naglost'* – a form of insolence, acting out of citizens' anger at the economic and social dislocations they are experiencing.

A disproportionate share of crime and anti-social activity in cities such as Moscow is attributed to "outsiders" – especially people from the southern non-Russian areas of the Russian Federation. Following the October 1993 violent resistance to President Yeltsin and the forced disbanding of the Russian parliament, a state of emergency was declared in Moscow and several other cities. People without proper residency permits were forced to leave Moscow and other cities. Over an eight-day period, more than 12,000 people were expelled from the capital.[75] As a direct result of the state of emergency and the deportations, the crime rate fell in the city by 26.6 percent.[76] While the restrictions raised troubling questions about human rights, they were overwhelmingly popular with Muscovites.[77]

The outbreak of crime has prompted proposals for other changes to the criminal code to enable the police to crack down on street crime. For example, Deputy Minister of Internal Affairs Aleksandr Kulikov proposed reinstituting criminal liability for begging and vagrancy. The police also want expedited procedures for hearing minor criminal cases (involving penalties of less than three years). A proposal has also been floated to extend the period of preliminary detention under Article 122 of the Code of Criminal Procedure without obtaining special authorization from the Procuracy from three to thirty days. Especially in the case of organized crime and economic crimes involving several jurisdictions, three days has proven to be an inadequate period of time for investigators and prosecutors to coordinate their activities in evaluating a crime and preparing the case for requesting court-ordered pre-trial detention.

Conclusions

Efforts to reform the Russian judicial system and criminal law have encountered many of the same tendencies and challenges seen in other areas of legal reform. Once the political leadership signaled its willingness to examine questions of legality, the impetus for judicial reform shifted to the professional legal community, especially legal scholars associated with the Institute of State and Law and the State Legal Affairs Administration of the president's office. Academic legal experts, most notably those in Moscow and St. Petersburg, tend to be more knowledgeable about European legal systems and have internalized a set of legal values including notions of rule of law, procedural due process, equal treatment, and judicial independence that pertain in Western legal systems but are not yet fully realized in Russia.

Among the practicing jurists, advocates have been the most supportive of substantive and procedural reforms because they have the most to gain. Unfortunately, defense attorneys have blunted their effectiveness in pushing reforms due to internal wrangling and jurisdictional conflicts. Prosecutors, the police, and criminal investigators have tended to resist reform efforts or accept them only grudgingly, fwhen forced to do so by political pressure from on high. Prosecutors fear that reforms will erode the Procuracy's central position in the legal system. Not only do prosecutors jealously guard their turf, but they also fear that the reforms will undermine the existing judicial system before a new system is able to replace it. The creation of a judicial vacuum, they fear, will only promote crime and disorder.

The prosecutors and others in law enforcement are not alone in these concerns. The recent explosion in the crime rate has fueled a strong public backlash. In the December 1993 elections, the right-wing Liberal Democratic Party, under the leadership of Vladimir Zhirinovsky, made a strong showing in parliamentary elections, in part, by advocating a strong law-and-order, anti-crime platform. The path of judicial reform is not a continuous and incremental one, rather it has been marked by many shifts and turns resulting from the clash of strong doctrinal, political, and bureaucratic interests.

Despite the progress that has been made in recent years, Russian law and the judicial system still manifest a fundamental ambivalence toward the state. Law is still widely viewed as a means of social engineering, of enforcing government policy, and instructing and guiding the population, rather than as a means by which citizens can protect their rights. Judge Ametistov, one of the justices of the Constitutional Court, observed: "The court and law in Russia were not tools for protecting people but for suppressing them. But in the last years, the situation has changed. More and more people now come to the court to protect themselves."[78] The development of rule of law and a just judicial system in Russia requires a more assertive citizenry and legal profession willing to use legal means to guarantee their rights but also willing to accept, rather than circumvent, laws and court rulings. Ametistov notes, "Unfortunately, everything depends not on the law or the legal system but on individuals. It will be possible, but only after one or two generations of lawyers, when the Old Guard and their pupils leave."[79]

7   Law and the transition to a market economy

> In terms of economic growth, the only thing worse than a society
> with a rigid, overcentralized, dishonest bureaucracy is one with a
> rigid, overcentralized honest bureaucracy.
>
> Samuel P. Huntington,
> Professor of Government, Harvard[1]

Since the introduction of economic reforms under Gorbachev's policy
of perestroika, law has played a major role in setting the course and
pace of economic reform. Nevertheless, the legal framework for economic reforms in Russia today is far from being adequate. There exists
a plethora of laws governing economic activities, but they are often
inconsistent, conflicting, and overlapping and have emanated from
many different authorities at various levels in the Russian Federation.
Some substantial bodies of law and legal codes of the former USSR
are still in force, even with the demise of the Soviet Union.[2] Other
areas of law – for example, commercial law and tax law – for all practical purposes do not exist and leave businesses and officials operating
in a legal state of nature, bordering on anarchy. The conflicting and
confusing legal situation in the Russian economy poses one of the
most significant impediments to foreign investment and to the effective utilization of IMF and World Bank funds earmarked for stimulating privatization and economic reform. In this chapter we review the
principal pieces of emerging Russian economic law and note the
impediments that must be overcome in order for conversion of the
economy to be successful.

Legal reforms and the economy under Gorbachev

During the period 1985 through mid-1988 Gorbachev gradually
undertook measures to revitalize the Soviet Union's stagnating economy. Gorbachev's policies, often referred to under the general term

perestroika (restructuring), initially sought to stimulate economic performance, improve the technological level of production, increase the
efficiency in utilization of resources, and improve work discipline
through application of both coercion and positive incentives.

One of the chronic problems confronting the Soviet economy since
the time of Stalin was poor work discipline. A study conducted by
Soviet researchers in 1983 found that only one-fifth of the labor force
worked the full last hour of the workshift.[3] Gorbachev recognized that
one of the reasons for frequent absenteeism on the job was that workers were alienated from their jobs. He urged renewed efforts to realize
the aims and objectives of the 1983 Law on Work Collectives, enacted
under Andropov, which granted workers the right to participate in
managerial decision-making in their enterprises. The 1987 Law on the
State Enterprise incorporated many of the same provisions.[4] The law
called for the election of enterprise directors, and also made
enterprises self-financed – state subsidies would be phased out and
unprofitable enterprises would be declared insolvent and closed. One
of the problems with self-financing, however, was that enterprises
were not yet granted the freedom to determine the price of their products, nor did they have absolute autonomy to decide what to produce
or where it should be sold. Thus, enterprises tended to be caught in
a catch-22, where they still received state orders to produce goods the
price of which they had no control over. By 1989 the centralized
system of government orders and delivery directives was breaking
down; enterprises were producing what they deemed to be most
profitable and delivering them wherever they could anticipate reliable
payment. Often economic relations took the form of barter deals,
where television sets produced by a factory were exchanged for
potatoes or vegetables produced by nearby farms and workers were
paid in goods rather than rubles.

Another persistent problem of the Soviet economy was underutiliz-
ation of labor reserves. With projections for a serious decline in
growth rate of the Soviet labor force by the year 2000, the Gorbachev
administration moved quickly to attempt to rationalize the assignment
of workers within the economy. A 1985 joint decree of the USSR Council of Ministers and the Central Council of Trade Unions on "work
place attestation" sought to curb labor hoarding by Soviet enterprises.
The decree also encouraged enterprises to scrap obsolete equipment.[5]

Under the terms of Gorbachev's policy of self-financing, in 1987
Soviet enterprises for the first time became responsible for covering
all operating expenses, including payroll and benefits. The result was

layoffs. By 1993 unemployment rose to 800,000, slightly over 1 percent of the workforce.[6] By mid-1995 unemployment reached an estimated 9.6 million, or 13 percent of the workforce.[7]

Gorbachev also introduced new legislation in 1985 and 1986 to step up supervision and punishment of economic crimes, including poor work discipline, substandard production, theft of state property, and intoxication in the workplace. On July 1, 1986, a decree went into force that increased the financial liability of workers for damages caused by them to the enterprise in which they work.[8]

The Gorbachev leadership also launched a vigorous campaign against black market activities and organized crime. A 1986 decree "On Intensifying the Struggle against Derivation of Non-Labor Incomes" increased penalties for the unauthorized use of state-owned vehicles, machinery, or equipment in an attempt to stop blackmarket activities.[9]

In 1987 and 1988 several other new enactments redefined ownership and property rights in the USSR. The Law on Joint Ventures, for the first time since the Revolution, enabled foreign corporations to own capital assets in the Soviet Union. Initially, the Law on Joint Ventures limited Western partners to 49 percent of the shares, insuring the Soviet partner a dominant position. Such restrictions, however, discouraged foreign companies and the restriction was lifted in 1991. The Law on Cooperatives enabled Soviet entrepreneurs to open private (or cooperative) businesses. Initially, the coop law was quite restrictive, limiting the number of partners to ten. The purpose in the Law on Cooperatives was to legalize private family businesses. Soon after its enactment in 1988, privately operated cafes, restaurants, beauty parlors, and other services opened in Moscow and St. Petersburg. To a significant degree, the Law on Cooperatives simply legalized private services that had been flourishing as blackmarket activities in the "second economy" since early in the Brezhnev period.

Despite these innovations, by late 1991 economic reforms had seriously outpaced enactment of laws to legitimate those reforms. The precipitous collapse of the former USSR left its constituent republics singularly unprepared to enact legislation and create new institutions to make and implement economic policy. Despite its facade of federalism, the Soviet Union centralized economic decision-making in Moscow to an extent not often appreciated in the West. Even relatively minor production decisions were made by central planners and ministerial officials in the capital, rather than by enterprise managers. Similarly, state farm managers received orders from the Ministry of Agriculture informing them of timetables for planting, applying fertilizer, and harvesting – regardless of local growing conditions. As these centralized institutions lost power, the surviving republics transferred decision-making powers to analogous republic institutions. Thus, the Central Bank of the Russian Federation took over the role of the Soviet State Bank (Gosbank) and the Soviet Foreign Trade Bank (Vneshekonombank) and the Russian Ministry of Finance replaced the functions of the former USSR Ministry of Finance. Previous laws continued to be enforced, even while republic legislatures discussed the need to draft new laws and legislation to replace those of the former USSR.

The pace of the government's privatization efforts accelerated substantially from 1993 through 1995. As of late 1993 there were some 21,500 industrial enterprises operating in Russia, of which 14,000 (65 percent) were still state owned.[10] In the retail sector, only 15 percent of the nation's 593,000 shops and small businesses had been privatized by 1993.[11] By mid-1995 some 70 percent of the Russian economy had been transferred to collective or private ownership and income from the sale of state enterprises was expected to net 8.7 trillion rubles ($1.9 billion) in 1995.[12] Slowing progress toward privatization was the difficulty in finding potential buyers for the largest, heavy industrial complexes that dominated the Soviet economy. Confronting drastic cuts in government orders, outmoded equipment, and shortages of capital to renovate, these enterprises and associations remain among the last to be commercialized. Yet, the government was reluctant to declare such enterprises bankrupt and close them for fear of creating massive unemployment. For example, in Ekaterinburg the gigantic metal-working complex Uralmash once employed some 35,000 people. Closing Uralmash would be devastating to the local and regional economy, yet sustaining it and other such rust-belt industries with government subsidies was draining the state budget. The solution of the State Property Committee has been to split off the most productive and promising portions of former industrial associations, selling shares in them at auctions. Unsold shares, generally of the least promising enterprises, remain in the hands of the government.

Forms of legal organization in Russia

Russian law recognizes a variety of legal forms for the organization of economic activities. Even during the seventy-four-year period of communist rule, Soviet law differentiated state enterprises, collectives, and social organizations. Now, with the privatization of large sectors of the economy, Russian lawyers have had to expand their range of legal entities to accommodate a wide variety of commercial ventures never before existing in the country.[13]

State enterprises

State-owned enterprises, factories, and other establishments still account for a sizable portion of the Russian economy today, despite the privatization program. Certain key sectors of the economy – railroad, utilities (except telephones), defense, postal services – are prohibited from privatization. In other public service areas, such as education and health care delivery, limited private enterprise exists alongside an extensive system of state services. Thus, even if the privatization program of Yegor Gaidar and his successor Viktor Chernomyrdin are successful, state-owned industries will continue to occupy a major role in the Russian economy for the foreseeable future.

Russian enterprises are governed by the "Law on Enterprises and Entrepreneurial Activity" of December 1990. This law set forth the very general structure and legal regime for both private and public enterprises and, thus, was quite vague in its formulation. The law established state enterprises as separate juridical persons and limited liability for their actions to the total value of their assets. The Soviet Enterprise Law of 1987 had mandated worker participation in enterprise decision-making through the general meeting of the labor collective and the election of an Enterprise Council. A fierce struggle was waged over the rules surrounding enterprise governance, because by 1992 many enterprise managers feared that rank-and-file workers were assuming too much power. An "industrial lobby" composed mostly of enterprise managers pushed for favorable treatment, especially in any attempt to privatize enterprises through the distribution of shares. At the same time, liberal reformers in Moscow were attempting to open the managerial structures of Russian enterprises to encourage foreign investment. These efforts were strenuously resisted by managers and the still powerful nomenklatura of various economic ministries.

Lease enterprises

Before full-scale privatization was attempted, the Gorbachev leadership promoted leasing arrangements in order to encourage technological innovation and efficiency within state enterprises by creating incentives for workers. Under the terms of leasing arrangements specified in a degree of the USSR Supreme Soviet of April 1989 and a subsequent act, "Fundamental Principles of Legislation of the USSR and the Union Republics on Lease," people could lease some or all of an enterprise's assets (buildings, machinery, etc.) to produce goods and then sell them either back to the enterprise or sell them on the general market. Lease enterprises were recognized by the state as separate legal entities from the enterprises in which they existed. The duration of lease agreements was usually no less than five years and as long as fifteen years. At the conclusion of the lease period, lessees could negotiate a new lease or, in most cases, they had the option to buy the enterprise's assets.

Leases were intended to be awarded on the basis of competitive contracts, however, the legislation initiating leasing explicitly directed enterprises to give priority to workers within their respective enterprises who could, by a two-thirds vote, organize themselves into self-governing work brigades for the purposes of the lease activity. In practice, few if any lease enterprises resulted from competitive bidding – instead, they were created by "insiders" both workers and management who saw leasing as a quick means to capture the most profitable portions of an enterprise, while ridding themselves of less profitable activities. By 1992 the government had grown concerned that insider leasing deals were threatening the privatization program and terminated further leasing arrangements. However, by this time more than 9,451 enterprises, employing 8 percent of the labor force, were operating under leasing arrangements.[14] They accounted for 13 percent of total production, 44 per cent of retail trade and catering.[15] By 1995 almost all lease enterprises had been converted to one of various forms of corporate ownership.

Industrial associations

During the 1970s Soviet economic planners attempted to facilitate interindustrial cooperation and efficiency by bringing factories together into industrial associations, patterned loosely on Western multinational corporations. The experiment with industrial associations proved to be only a mixed success. While the creation of industrial associations did enlarge the size of industrial enterprises, enabling smaller, less efficient factories the advantage of research and design bureaus of their larger affiliates, it also created a new layer of bureaucracy between the enterprise and the ministry.

In the last months of Soviet rule, it became clear that privatization was going to occur, either due to government policy or to spontaneous collapse and reorganization of the economy. Several of the ministries supervising industrial sectors, fearing loss of their governing role, transformed themselves into industrial associations. Thus, the former Ministry of Machine-Tool and Instrument-Making Industry became Stankoinstrument, a joint-stock company. The former minister now serves as president of the company and most of his deputies occupy high-level managerial positions. These industrial concerns continue to act as a powerful lobby force opposing the break-up of interrelated industries and in favor of continued government subsidies. The companies also preserved the monopolistic control over various sectors of the economy that was a hallmark of the Soviet economy. In most cases, enterprises within the former industrial associations continued to exist as legal entities under terms of the Russian Enterprise Law of 1990, however, some opted to change their status to joint-stock companies or lease enterprises. The associations were also recognized under Soviet law as separate juridical entities.

The governance structure of industrial associations was quite arbitrary. Often the association would assign one-half of its share to its constituent enterprises, while one-half would be held by the association acting as trustee for the state. The general meeting of the association in most cases consisted of representatives of its constituent enterprises, which would elect a Management Board and half of the members of a watchdog Supervisory Council. The state would select the other members to serve on the Supervisory Council. The real power in governing the activities of industrial associations and their constituent enterprises rested with the president and the Management Board. Thus, the move to "corporatize" Soviet industry through the creation of joint-stock companies merely transferred ownership of a huge portion of the country's industrial base to former ministers and other members of the party–state nomenklatura. At the same time, these same people were no longer accountable to the Council of Ministers, nor were they accountable to shareholders or the public.

As of the end of 1991, there were more than 3,000 industrial associations in Russia. They accounted for almost 40 percent of industrial production and more than 6.5 million workers.[16] Each industrial association linked together numerous enterprises – as many as 1,000 enterprises and factories – into one corporate structure.

The cartel-like nature of industrial associations is most visible when they are analyzed in relation to a given sector in the economy. Thus, for oil production Rosneftigas controls 99.8 percent of Russian oil production, while Gasprom controls 93 percent of natural gas production. Ugol Rossii controls 97.7 percent of coal production, and Stankoinstrument controls 88.7 percent of machine tool production.[17] The associations have not been shy about using their clout to discourage competition within their respective sectors, by opposing efforts by the government to decentralize ownership through genuine privatization programs.

Cooperatives

Even under the communist regime, cooperatives existed in agriculture, consumer services, and housing as separate entities. Unlike state enterprises, which received direct orders and directives from ministries and state-planning agencies, cooperatives received advice or recommendations from higher state bodies. The cooperatives were supposedly self-governing. In reality, however, the activities of cooperatives were strictly controlled through the party's nomenklatura power. In addition, cooperatives were required to sell their products to the state at prices determined by central authorities. The property of cooperatives (land, buildings, and equipment) was given to the cooperatives by the state or, in some cases, provided on the basis of a long-term lease.

In 1988 a new Law on Cooperatives went into effect. The intent of the new legislation was to broaden the terms of cooperatives to incorporate activities that were going outside legal economic channels in the black and gray markets. In addition, the new legislation, which was subsequently amended in 1989 and 1990, granted cooperatives a greater degree of independence from the state in line with Gorbachev's policy of perestroika. Initially, the Law on Cooperatives limited coops to ten partners. The law carefully avoided the appearance of condoning private enterprises in the sense that it mandated that all members of the coop be shareholders, rather than simply employees in a private business owned by an independent businessman. The intent was to legalize family businesses, primarily in the service sector: cafes, restaurants, tailor shops, beauty salons, etc. The restrictive terms of the law naturally resulted in widespread abuses. The later revisions of the law lifted many of these unenforceable restrictions on cooperatives.

The governing body of cooperatives is the general meeting of its members. All members have one vote, regardless of their contribution to the activities of the coop. The general meeting decides issues of membership, election of officials, changes to the charter, liquidation of assets, setting of fees, and distribution of profits. The general meeting also elects a chairman or a board of directors.

In the service sectors and in agriculture, cooperatives play a major role in privatizing economic activity. As of late 1993, approximately 95 percent of Russia's state and collective farms had been privatized.[18] Approximately two-thirds of them are now joint-stock companies or cooperatives, yet little has changed in the actual management and operation of these farms. In addition, there are now approximately 300,000 privately owned family farms.[19] Together with the garden plots that people rent outside of major cities, private farming accounts for nearly two-fifths of total agricultural output. In the service sector, cooperatives account for 15 percent of all businesses, while in housing almost 50 percent of the units are privately (cooperatively) owned.[20]

With the collapse of the USSR, a new law, the Russian Law on Consumer Cooperatives of 1992, provided a legal foundation for the continued operation of cooperatives. The new law basically repeated the same provisions of the pre-existing legislation with few amendments or expansions. Most of the economic activities that are referred to as "private enterprise" in Russia are, in fact, governed by the Russian Law on Consumer Cooperatives. For example, cooperatives are collective bodies – people working for cooperatives are share-holders. The law does not specify a formula for the distribution of shares, however. Shares are commonly distributed either in terms of the amount and quality of labor performed or the share of initial capital contributed to the cooperative, or some combination of both.

Private (commercial) enterprises

The 1990 Russian Law on Ownership established equality for all forms of property – private, state, municipal, and collective. The law established the right of Russian citizens to operate private businesses, under terms set forth in the Enterprise Law. The law establishes that private enterprises can engage in any activity not prohibited by law. Prohibitions exist in the manufacture of weapons or ammunition, production or processing of precious metals, and production of tobacco or alcoholic beverages.

There are several types of legal business entities in Russia, each of which has different licensing requirements. Many of these forms of business organization also exist in other countries, in fact, legal provisions for some types of businesses were directly borrowed from German and American commercial law.

Individual entrepreneurs may now obtain legal recognition of their businesses as a sole proprietorship. However, they may not employ hired labor in any form. Private businesses of this type exist primarily in the field of consumer services and handicrafts, but have also been formed recently by independent computer consultants, dentists, translators and interpreters, among others. The advantage of licensing as an individual entrepreneur is that the licensing process is quite simple and taxes on earnings are lower than for other forms of private enterprise. The law suggests that the owner of such a business may enjoy limited liability, but this is not altogether clear.[21]

Businesses that employ workers must register as one of several forms of private or collective enterprises. A General Partnership or "full partner company" is an association among "citizens" for the purpose of engaging in an economic activity. The partnership is not a juridical person, rather each participant is an independent legal personality and must bear full liability for obligations of the enterprise.[22]

A Limited Partnership or "mixed partner company" distinguishes "actual partners" from "contributing members." A mixed partner company is recognized as a legal person. General partners bear personal responsibility for the activities and obligations of the enterprise, while contributing members' liability is limited to their contribution. The limited amount of charter capital was 10,000 rubles as of April 1994.[23]

The joint-stock company, first created by Decree No. 601 of the Russian Council of Ministers in 1990, has become the most popular form of business entity in Russia. Russian law recognizes two forms of joint-stock companies: closed joint-stock companies and open joint-stock companies. Closed joint-stock companies are privately operated and their shares must be traded internally. Open joint-stock companies may issue shares and sell them to the public without any restrictions. The transfer of shares within a closed company requires the consent of the majority of shareholders.

In both forms, joint-stock companies are recognized legal persons and must be registered with the Ministry of Finance. The purchase of more than half of a company's shares must be approved by the State Committee on Antimonopoly Policy and Promotion of New Economic Structures. As of April 1994 the minimum capital necessary to establish an open joint-stock company was 100,000 rubles and 10,000 rubles for a closed joint-stock company.

There can be only two classes of shares in a joint-stock company: preferred and common stock, with the preferred not exceeding 10 percent of the charter capital and with only common shares carrying voting rights. The joint-stock company may issue bonds with a minimum redemption date of one year. The joint-stock company is also required to maintain a reserve fund in the amount of 10 percent of the charter capital and is subject to certain disclosure provisions such as making available for inspection the accounts, reports, and audits, and publishing a quarterly report to the Ministry of Finance.[24]

Governance of joint-stock companies is generally set out in their bylaws. Normally the bylaws allocate ultimate authority to the shareholders' meeting, which in turn delegates decision-making power to the board of directors, the governing board, and the auditing committee. The shareholders' meeting has exclusive right to alter the bylaws, elect directors, liquidate the company, and to increase or decrease its authorized capital. Meetings of shareholders must be held at least once a year.

The board of directors is elected by the general meeting for a two-year renewable term. The board is empowered to make important decisions, affecting both personnel and production matters. The director of the company is selected by the board from among its members. The general director nominates executives to head the various divisions of the company, but these nominations are subject to the approval of the Board of Directors. Together the general director and these top-ranking officials, comprise the governing board, which is responsible for managing the day-to-day affairs of the company.

Most of the privatized industries of the former Soviet Union have opted to become closed joint-stock companies.[25] This has enabled former state enterprise directors to retain their leadership posts in their respective companies, while gaining substantial new powers and freedom to enlarge their financial stake in its operations. Of course, the creation of a joint-stock company implies that the company ceases to be a state enterprise and is, therefore, no longer eligible to receive government subsidies. As we will discuss below, the corporatization of Russian industry has resulted in transfer of state enterprises to the hands of a relatively small group of industrial and former Communist Party officials, but has left those industries starved for investment capital. As a result, recently privatized industries have engaged in selling off portions of their businesses to raise badly needed funds. Others have courted foreign investors, in exchange for a portion of the company's production.

Dilemmas of privatization

Perhaps the single biggest challenge confronting the Russian economy
has been how to convert state-owned enterprises to private (or
collective) ownership efficiently and equitably. Stanislav Shatalin and
Grigori Yavlinsky first proposed the rapid and massive privatization
of Soviet industry in their 500 day plan in mid-1990. After much vacil-
lation, Gorbachev announced that he favored the general direction of
the plan, but disagreed with the strict timetable. Given the enormity
of the task or privatizing the entire Soviet economy in only 500 days,
one Russian wag noted, "You don't understand. They're talking about
Biblical days, not calendar days!" A much more moderate program,
which preserved the powerful role of industrial ministries, was
adopted by Prime Minister Nikolai Ryzhkov and implemented in 1991
by Ryzhkov's successor Valentin Pavlov.

Some of the most notable initiatives in the area of privatization came
at the republic and regional levels. In June 1991 the Russian Federation
adopted the Law on Privatization of State and Municipal Enterprises.
The law established the State Committee for the Management of State
Property, under the direction of Anatoly Chubais, to develop guidelines for the rapid privatization of state-owned assets in the Russian
Federation, patterned after Germany's Treuhandanstalt. Progress in
privatizing industry in Russia, in contrast to the USSR, can be attributed to the influence of Russian President Boris Yeltsin and his leading economic adviser Yegor Gaidar. The Privatization Law in Russia
called for the conversion of most large state enterprises into joint-stock
companies. The biggest disputes remained unresolved, however, over
how this goal should be accomplished.

One of the recurrent stumbling blocks to rapid privatization was
the issue of fairness. Seventy-four years of Soviet rule obliterated virtually all private wealth in the country. The only people who accumu-
lated considerable sums of personal savings tended to be high-ranking
members of the party and state elite, who were widely accused of
having abused their offices for their own personal gain. To reward
them by permitting them to buy up the choice assets of the former
USSR violated many citizens' notion of fairness. A similar problem
stalled efforts to privatize housing. The mayor of Moscow proposed
in 1991 simply to transfer ownership of all housing controlled by the
city to the tenants in those apartments.[26] Such a policy was immediately challenged, however, including a case that went to the USSR
Constitutional Supervision Committee. The objections to Mayor

Popov's proposal was that former Communist Party officials and other members of the former elite had luxurious apartments in desirable neighborhoods, while ordinary workers were left with nondescript two-room flats in sterile high-rise projects on the outskirts of the city. And what of the thousands of people who had no adequate housing and were on the city's twelve-year waiting list for a separate apartment? Even today, an estimated 20 percent of urban residents live in communal apartments, in which each family has a room in a former pre-revolutionary townhouse, but must share the bathroom and kitchen with residents in the other rooms.[27] Nationwide, an estimated 2.5 million young families are living in substandard conditions.[28]

Approximately 5.5 million dwellings were privatized in 1993. The pace of housing privatization has been much faster in reform-minded cities, such as Moscow, St. Petersburg, and Nizhny Novgorod, but considerably slower, especially in the industrial cities of the Urals and Siberia. The majority of housing is being distributed to its occupants free of charge. With privatization progressing rapidly, privately owned housing now accounts for almost half of all housing.[29] The other side of the coin is that the collapse of government revenue has resulted in the virtual termination of new housing construction by the state.

Another category of people with large amounts of disposable income in order to take advantage of privatization are members of organized crime rings. However, Russian authorities are reluctant to reward these groups by handing over whole industries to them. In fact, organized crime groups have been reluctant to invest in industry, preferring instead to obtain vast amounts of income quickly from extortion, kickbacks, gambling, and prostitution. Proceeds from these activities are converted into foreign currency by Mafia-controlled banks and quickly taken out of the country.

Similarly, there is a strong public backlash against foreign investors who take advantage of Russia's privatization program. One of the earliest foreign buyouts in St. Petersburg sparked a scandal that was felt throughout the country. A famous factory, dating back to the time of Peter the Great and the founding of the city in 1703, had for centuries been known for its high quality production. In 1991 Mayor Sobchak encouraged foreign investors to enter the Russian market to revitalize stagnating industries. When a foreign company bought a controlling share of the factory it was trumpeted as a great success for Sobchak's policy. However, when the foreign engineers examined the factory, they advised that it be bulldozed and a whole new state-of-the-art factory be built. Such an investment exceeded the company's short-term abilities. In addition, a recession in Europe had reduced demand for their products. Consequently, the company officials decided to close the plant until conditions for such a large-scale investment looked brighter. In the meantime, some 1,600 employees were laid off.[30]

Given the difficulties of finding adequate investors to buy Russian industrial enterprises, the government has favored a number of programs for the sale of state-owned property to Russian citizens through vouchers, auctions, and issuance of stocks or shares. The idea behind all of these programs is to distribute shares in the former state-controlled companies to workers, creating a new middle class, which will have a strong vested interest in stability and reform. The economic dilemma is that ordinary citizens lack the experience, expertise, and the capital needed to rejuvenate stagnating industries. Below we summarize the major facets of the government's privatization program.

Two decrees, issued by President Yeltsin late in 1991 and early 1992, set out the goals and procedures for the Russian privatization program.[31] These acts set the priority on the immediate privatization of wholesale and retail trade facilities and small state enterprises. The privatization of medium and large-scale enterprises has proven to be much more controversial, however. In the Summer of 1992, the Russian parliament, in which a sizable faction of deputies represented the interests of industrial ministries, enterprise associations, and powerful industrial managers, demanded that any privatization program contain preferential provisions for insiders and retain the former ministerial apparatus. Acting Prime Minister Gaidar and Yeltsin's chief of the State Property Committee, Anatoly Chubais, pushed for a more open scheme of privatization that would enable outside investors (including foreigners) greater access to privatizing industries. At the same time, they favored a drastically streamlined administrative apparatus.

Privatizations of medium and large state enterprises to date have largely been undertaken under provisions of Yeltsin's 1992 decree on joint-stock companies which incorporated the Statute on Commercialization of State Enterprises and their Companies. This Commercialization Statute set forth an accelerated procedure for the conversion of state enterprises into joint-stock companies. The statute, in one bold stroke, removed these newly formed companies from the jurisdiction of ministries and other organs of state administration.[32]

The privatization program differentiated several categories of businesses; some were prohibited from being privatized, others could only be privatized with the approval of various federal or local authorities, and some types of businesses were subject to mandatory privatization. The first category, enterprises that were excluded from privatization, included radio and television stations, ports, enterprises producing or refining diamonds, gold and other precious metals, public utilities, water resources, and cultural and historic sites.

Armaments industries, the energy sector, commercial banks, printing plants and publishers, and portions of the atomic energy sector may be privatized only with the consent of the government of the Russian Federation. A wide array of industrial enterprises with a dominant market position, employing more than 10,000 workers or having fixed assets in excess of 150 million rubles must obtain permission from the State Property Commission to privatize. This category of industries includes the bulk of transportation services (air, sea, and rail), large construction firms, education and research institutions, the medical and pharmaceutical industries, and oil refining. In this category of enterprises, the State Property Committee can retain a controlling block of shares for up to three years.[33]

Some facilities and enterprises can only be privatized with the consent of local governments. Most often such "municipal privatizations" apply to waste treatment plants, water purification plants, recreation and community centers, pharmacies, and public baths. The bulk of mandatory privatizations were wholesale and retail trade establishments, restaurants, cafes, light industries and consumer industries, small construction firms, food processing plants, and motor transport companies (trucking and taxis). The government's privatization program called for the conversion of approximately 30 percent of the economy by the end of 1993 and another 30 percent by the end of 1995. The focus of early privatization efforts was on the mandatory category of enterprises.

Serious privatization was impossible without first a major liberalization of pricing. As long as central authorities continued to set prices at low levels – often below the cost of production – there would be no incentive for entrepreneurs to acquire a factory or shop. The massive freeing of prices on most goods and services in January 1992 removed this hurdle in many sectors, although food processing (especially bakeries) continued to be under centrally set low pricing arrangements.

Much more difficult has been the task of devising a plan for the privatization of some 4,000 large enterprises, that is, those enterprises employing more than 1,000 workers and holding fixed capital of over 50 million rubles. Since Stalin's time, Soviet economic planners placed great emphasis on creating ever larger production units. In 1979, enterprises, associations, and combines employing more than 1,000 workers accounted for more than 70 percent of all industrial output, employed almost three-quarters of the industrial labor force, and garnered more than 80 percent of all capital funds.[34] Some of the largest enterprises and industrial associations, such as the giant machine-tool company Uralmash in Ekaterinburg, boasted 30,000 to 40,000 employees at their peak of operation in the mid-1980s.

The privatization of large enterprises became the focus of a protracted struggle in 1992 with the working out of the Privatization Law and its subsequent implementation. The two major protagonists in this struggle where insiders, who favored preferential treatment for managers and workers, and government officials, who pressed for more open access to ownership. Based on the unhappy experience of privatization under the pre-existing laws of the USSR, the Privatization Law of 1992 prohibited the sale of shares of enterprises to other enterprises or institutions that were more than 25 percent controlled by the state. This provision was incorporated into the law to prevent industries from buying up interests in one another, thus creating a web of conservative, economic interests to scuttle any real attempt at genuine privatization.

Under the terms of the Privatization Law, employees in enterprises targeted for privatization by the State Property Committee would buy shares in their enterprises at a 30 percent discount. Recognizing the limited ability of most workers to take advantage of this provision, due to the absence of savings, the law enabled them to make installment purchases over a three-year period.

Most controversial was the change in the method of setting a value on the assets of enterprises. The initial Privatization Law envisioned "market" valuation. However, after heavy lobbying from industrial interests, the Interim Methodological Guidelines for the Valuation of Properties Marked for Privatization (Supplement No. 2) of January 1992 replaced market valuation with "residual" or book value. Furthermore, no inflation factor was incorporated into the valuation formulae. The result of these two changes was that enterprises were valued at far below market levels. Anatoly Chubais, head of the State Property Committee, illustrated the effect of these decisions by noting that largely due to inflation and devaluation of the ruble a Volga taxi cab in August 1992 was valued at 2,000 to 3,000 rubles – between 10 and 15 dollars!

The change in the methodology of valuation represented a great boon to insiders who were acquiring controlling interests in enterprises (purchased with discounts) at grossly deflated prices. The result was a virtual giveaway of state property.

In June 1992, the Yeltsin government announced enactment of its State Program for Privatization. Under the terms of that program, employees in state enterprises could opt for one of three methods of acquiring interests in their respective industries on preferential terms.

Variant 1. Under this plan, all employees would receive free of charge one-quarter of the shares in their enterprise in the form of preferred, non-voting stock. In addition, employees could buy an additional 10 percent of the shares (with full voting rights) at a 30 percent discount. Managerial personnel (the manager, deputy managers, chief engineers, and chief accountant) would be given the option of purchasing an additional 5 percent of the shares at the nominal price.

Variant 2. Under this option, employees could purchase up to 51 percent of the shares in their enterprises at the nominal price, with no voting restrictions.

Variant 3. Designed only for large enterprises with more than 200 employees and more than 1 million rubles in assets, this variant permitted workers to buy up to 20 percent of the shares at a 30 percent discount. The workers then could opt to contract with a group of insiders (usually previous managers) to manage the enterprise's operations. In exchange, the managing group would receive voting rights to the 20 percent of the shares owned by the enterprise's employees.

The decision of an enterprise to select either of the last two variants must be ratified by two-thirds of the employees at the general meeting of the enterprise. Should the workers fail to endorse either Variant 2 or Variant 3, the enterprise would have no choice but to be privatized according to the provision of Variant 1.

The shares of commercialized enterprises not sold to insiders would be sold to outside investors through state and/or municipally operated property funds. Most often, the sale of unsold shares takes place through auctions. Monthly auctions have been held at which up to 10 percent of an enterprise's shares have been offered for sale to the general public and foreign investors. Ten percent of the proceeds from these sales is returned to the employees' "personal privatization account" within each enterprise.

During the course of its implementation, the government's privatization program was clearly altered to favor insider interests, especially those of top-level managers. This has proven to be a mixed blessing. On the one hand, the privatization program now in effect concentrates wealth and industrial and political power in the hands of the same group of managers that is quite conservative and resistant to change. On the other hand, these managers have acquired considerable expertise in operating within the anarchic conditions of the collapsing Soviet economy; they have well-developed informal communications, supply and delivery networks. Most important, they know who to bribe and how to avoid entanglements with the rapidly growing organized crime syndicates. While the government came away from this compromise solution with less than it had hoped, it succeeded in constructing mechanisms for the corporatization of state-owned industries that have some chance of success, whereas, a method of privatization that closed out existing managers would have been doomed to failure. In addition, it is hoped that the new incentives provided by a dynamic market and the need for both investment capital and profits will encourage even old-school Soviet managers to make wise decisions. Finally, the State Program has eliminated all restrictions on the transfer of stocks, including preferentially acquired shares. Secondary markets have sprung up throughout Russia, dealing in enterprise shares and public vouchers. The government hopes that these secondary markets will represent a sufficiently large block of shares to moderate any adverse effects of insider control of the newly privatized industries.

The government's program for privatization of medium and small-size firms and enterprises not subject to corporatization, as specified above, calls for the liquidation of assets through auctions or competitive tenders. Target prices are set for each property and authorized by the State Property Committee or appropriate local property community. The sale price may not fall more than 30 percent below the target price. Initially, the terms of the Presidential Decree mandated that there must be more than one bidder, but this was subsequently altered to enable single, non-competitive bids when they came from employees within the enterprise. As a result of unfortunate experiences with foreign buyouts, such as the factory in St. Petersburg mentioned above, terms for both auctions and competitive tenders may include a variety of stipulations and restrictions: requiring the enterprise to continue operations for a set period of time, requiring the enterprise to produce certain goods, prohibiting the enterprise from staff reductions for a period of up to one year, requiring the enterprise to maintain certain levels of investment, and requiring the enterprise to continue the provision of various social programs (housing, polyclinic, day care facilities, etc.).

As with large enterprises, insiders were granted considerable benefits and preferences in auction and tender privatizations of medium and small enterprises. Employees were given the possibility of purchasing the enterprise on installments over a three-year period. In addition, employees were granted 30 percent discounts off the purchase price resulting from the auction or bid. Finally, the portion of revenue from shares sold to outsiders and distributed to employees of the enterprise was raised to 30 percent in the case of an auction and 20 percent in the case of a competitive tender sale.

The pace of privatization of small-scale enterprises has been quite uneven. In all, some 175,000 stores and small enterprises are subject to mandatory privatization.[35] The government's State Program called for 60 percent of these to be privatized by the end of 1992. In reality, privatizations were occurring at a much slower rate – as of late 1993, only about 15 percent of all small businesses had been privatized.[36]

In Nizhny Novgorod, the pace of privatization has been much greater. In fact, Nizhny Novgorod is often cited as an example for the rest of the country. The local "governor" Boris Nemtsov and his chief economic strategist Grigori Yavlinsky have undertaken an aggressive and innovative approach to privatization. By August 1992 more than 200 of the city's retail outlets and 377 enterprises had been successfully privatized.[37] In Moscow, 7,533 businesses had been sold by July 30, 1992. In St. Petersburg, the pace of privatization has been notably slower with only 112 privatizations by mid-1992.[38] The factors that would appear to favor rapid privatization include active, strong leadership support for privatization, the openness of the process, the absence of restrictive conditions, and assumption of the debts of the privatized enterprises.

During the seventy-four years of Soviet rule virtually all private wealth was either nationalized or destroyed, leaving Russian citizens with few resources to take advantage of these new investment opportunities afforded by privatization. Recognizing this fact, the Yeltsin government sought to broaden participation in privatization through the issuance of vouchers. Vouchers were also expected to create demand for shares and build public support for the privatization program, with the ultimate goal of creating a middle class with vested interests in the privatization of the economy. A presidential decree of April 1992 called for vouchers to be distributed to all citizens by the fourth quarter of the year. The first tranche of privatization vouchers was to be issued to every Russian citizen, regardless of age, between October 1 and December 1, 1992.

Unlike the voucher programs in Czechoslovakia and Poland, the Russian voucher program did not differentiate voucher purchases from cash purchases of shares or preferential insider purchases. The nominal value of each voucher was set at 10,000 rubles and a privatizing enterprise was required to accept vouchers at that value in exchange for shares. The value of the vouchers was calculated based on the cost of 35 percent of the shares in all enterprises to be privatized, divided by the number of citizens to receive vouchers. Vouchers were freely exchangeable and a lively market immediately developed in the sale and purchase of vouchers at fluctuating market rates. Private banks created mutual fund accounts and lured investors to buy shares in these accounts with their vouchers. Many citizens simply held on to their vouchers because they did not know what to do with them. They did not trust the banks, nor did they know what was a good or safe investment. Unfortunately, due to the absence of adequate securities exchange oversight and licensing many unscrupulous companies promising fantastically high interest rates bought up vouchers and disappeared with peoples' life savings.

Another problem plaguing the voucher program was the relatively modest nominal value of the vouchers. At the time of issue, the vouchers equaled only $60 per person and on the markets they were bringing in only $35 each. Due to inflation and devaluation of the ruble, the value of a voucher had slipped to only $5.55 by mid-1994. Delays in issuing vouchers compounded by inadequate information for citizens as to how to invest their vouchers resulted in seriously prolonging their issuance, which merely exacerbated the effects of inflation and the plummeting value of the ruble. The last voucher auctions were held in mid-1994. Since July 1, 1994 all share purchases had to be made in cash.

Reform of agriculture and land law

Privatization of land initially proceeded at a much slower pace than industrial privatization, in part because of the powerful influence of state farms that oppose reforms in the agricultural sector, but also because of a deep-seated cultural aversion of private ownership of large tracts of land. We have noted that under ancient Russian law, private land ownership was not widely recognized as a property right. During the height of imperial power under the tsars, land rights were granted by the tsar to faithful subjects and with the extension of these land rights, so too extended serfdom. The injustices of this system gave added weight to arguments against private land ownership, arguments that were exploited most profoundly by the Bolsheviks during and after the October Revolution.

As Gorbachev's policy of perestroika began to unfold in 1987 and 1988, modest reforms were attempted in agriculture, designed to expand the realm of private initiative in the food and consumer goods sectors. A decree of September 25, 1987 called for expanding the *podryad* (contract) system of assignment and remuneration, by requiring that all farms and food enterprises be fully self-financed by 1988–1989.[39] A second decree, issued on the same date, sought to stimulate production on private plots and incorporate this production into the general economy.

A new draft Model *Kolkhoz* Statute was announced on January 1, 1988. The draft called for greater farm autonomy, transition to self-financing by 1988–1989, and self-management. Under the provisions of the statute, members of collective farms were granted a greater degree of participation in the affairs of the collective, including the right to select chairmen and set their salaries. Private plots of collective farm members were no longer limited in size, nor was the number of livestock that members were permitted to keep. The Model *Kolkhoz* Statute was an attempt to bring collective farm law into conformity with the Law on the State Enterprise by granting farm workers the same participatory rights enjoyed by industrial workers, while putting them under the same responsibility to cover their own operating expenses.

The 1990 Law on Ownership went further by establishing the principle of equality in law of various types of ownership: state, collective, and private, including the private ownership of land. Throughout 1990 agrarian interests debated a proposed new Law on the Peasant Household. A draft of the law first appeared in July 1990 and it was enacted on November 22, 1990. It was supplemented by the Russian Law on Land Reform (also passed in November 1990). The goal of the legislation was to end state subsidies of collective and state farms, by transferring ownership to the farmers. The most hotly contested issues concerned the distribution of shares and provisions for farmers to leave the collective. A group representing farm management succeeded in stipulating that the general meeting of the farm's workers must approve all requests to leave the farm. Likewise, the Law on the Peasant Household gave the general meeting the power to determine the distribution of the farm's assets. The net result of these actions was to discourage private entrepreneurial farmers, since the land and equipment that a former member of a collective or state farm would receive would not be large enough to support a viable individual farm. The Law on the Peasant Household also stipulated that land shares distributed to farmers could not be resold for ten years to prevent profiteering from land sales.

The RSFSR Land Code of 1991 provided that local soviets could sell or give away land with two restrictions: the land had to be used for specified purposes (small-scale farming, housing construction, etc.) and the purchaser or grantee could not sell or transfer the land from that specified use for ten years.

Frustrated by the slow pace of privatization in the agricultural sector, President Yeltsin issued a series of decrees beginning in late December 1991 repealing sections of the RSFSR Land Code and facilitating the transfer of state-owned land. Yeltsin's Decree on Urgent Measures to Implement Land Reform in the RSFSR of December 27, 1991 required that all farms be commercialized by the end of March 1992. Under the terms of the decree, collective and state farms could reorganize themselves in one of several ways: (1) they could liquidate themselves and distribute shares and equipment to all members; (2) they could sell the assets of the farm to an industrial enterprise and become employees of an enterprise; (3) they could form an association with all farmers as members; (4) they could convert themselves into joint-stock companies with each farmer receiving a share of the company's assets; or (5) they could divide all the assets among the farmers who would then voluntarily form a cooperative. The result of President Yeltsin's action was a flurry of criticism from farm managers and agricultural interests. Eventually, the government backed down and created a sixth option: permitting the collective and state farms to retain their existing legal status, but with the provision that they would now own their land, rather than the state owning the land.

Technically it was possible, under the Decree on Regulation of Land Relations of October 1993, for members of collective farms to demand the partition of the land or to receive compensation. In practice, such actions were rare, however. The previous restriction requiring land-owners to sell their land back to the state was finally eliminated as was the 10-year moratorium on land sales.[40]

A decree of April 1993 directed local governments to inventory land available for distribution to citizens, implement a system of registration of land titles, and issue titles. Decree 503 of May 1993 provided regulations for the private purchase and sale of land plots and created a procedure for assessing transfer taxes on land sales. Decree 1767 of October 1993 "On the Regulation of Land Relations" permitted free disposition of land, including the right to sell, lease, or mortgage land owned by natural or juridical persons. The decree also required registration of land interests, and established that localities may sell land through auction or other competitive procedures.

Since 1993 efforts have been made to draft a new land code that would supersede all previously existing decrees and laws on land in one comprehensive body of law. Such a draft was brought to the Supreme Soviet in July 1993 and passed, only to be vetoed by President Yeltsin. The code included a 10-year moratorium on the resale of land given by the state. A slightly revised version of the proposed 1993 Land Code was prepared by the Ministry of Agriculture and the Land Reform and Land Resources Committee (Roskomzem) but was rejected by the Council of Ministers in early 1994. A third draft was accepted by the Council of Ministers in June 1994 and introduced in the State Duma in July. The president's office strenuously objected to the draft on procedural grounds, arguing that Yeltsin had issued a directive that a land law would be introduced through the president's office.

The new Civil Code of the Russian Federation, approved by the State Duma and signed by the president in November 1994, also established the right to private ownership of land. However, like its predecessors, it retains the concept of "purposeful use," tying rights to the land to the uses made of it.

Under existing land legislation, companies and other juridical entities may not own land, but may obtain limited rights to use or lease land. A presidential decree of August 1992 grants privatized enterprises who acquire property through auctions or tender the right of "permanent use" or the right to lease with the option to acquire permanent use. The distinction between permanent use and ownership center on restricted ability to resell the property. Under the "permanent use" provision, enterprises could not freely sell their land, but were forced to sell it back to the state.

By the end of 1993 about 95 percent of the collective and state farms in Russia were reorganized, most of them (about two out of three) opting for joint-stock status.[41] The legal change in status had little effect, however, on the day-to-day operation of the farms. The reforms succeeded in denationalizing farms, while not fully privatizing them. By early 1994 more than 270,000 private family farms existed in Russia and they, together with private garden plots, accounted for approximately 40 percent of all total agricultural output.[42] Personal household garden plots produced over one-quarter of Russia's agricultural output in 1991 and accounted for approximately 20 percent of total livestock.[43]

The reasons for the reluctance of Russian farmers to attempt to farm privately are complex. Many farmers, accustomed to years of working in a collective or state farm, are risk-adverse and prefer the guaranteed salary of working for an enterprise or joint-stock company. Others cite the critical dependency of private farmers on sources of supply of seed, fertilizer, equipment, herbicides, gasoline, and transportation. Even if they were willing to assume the risks of planting, raising a crop, and selling it on the open market, they are reticent to do so when the necessary supplies, equipment, and materials for successful farming are so unreliable. Finally, those who attempted to leave collective and state farms were often actively discouraged from doing so by political pressures from farm managers. Although the Law on the Peasant Household stipulated that farmers wishing to leave the collectives were to be given land of average quality, in reality many were granted marginal land, far from the village or equipment center.[44] Many collectives and state farms simply refused to give independent farmers their share of livestock and equipment and instead paid them a lump-sum payment for their share at grossly undervalued rates and in rapidly depreciating rubles, leaving the new farmer with inadequate resources to buy his own equipment or livestock.

Meanwhile, in order to continue the supply of produce to the cities, the government retained the system of compulsory deliveries through 1993. The state negotiated with collective and state farms for the delivery of a certain amount and assortment of produce to be delivered, and in return the state paid in advance, provided production credits, and guaranteed supplies of necessary inputs, thus reducing the risk to the large farms. Small independent farmers were not eligible for this program, however.

By mid-1993 the state budget was no longer able to supply sufficient subsidies to meet its commitments. Following President Yeltsin's suspension of the parliament on September 21, 1993 state subsidies and credits to agriculture stopped entirely. Furthermore, the government announced that it would not be able to pay farmers the agreed upon price for their produce.[45] Agricultural interests groups, most notably the Agrarian Union, lobbied heavily against the plan favored by the State Property Committee that would have forced the break-up of large farms into small family farm units. Yeltsin's decree of October 27, 1993 attempted to rectify many of the mounting legal and logistical problems of privatization of agriculture.[46] The decree gave farmers' collectives possession of their land and property shares, making them freely transferable. The price of equipment and other property was indexed for inflation and the 10-year moratorium on land sales was revoked. Finally, the decree ended as of January 1, 1994 all state subsidies and stated that all future state purchases of agricultural commodities would be made at market prices. Gone was the disincentive resulting from state-negotiated low prices for agricultural produce, while inputs (fertilizer, gasoline, etc.) had to be purchased at expensive market rates. However, the marketization of the agrarian sector was not popular with farmers. In a scene reminiscent of the early collectivization in the 1930s, some farmers refused to harvest their crops in 1993 rather than sell them to the state at prices below those for which they had contracted. The strength of rural resistance to the government's policy of forcing the privatization of farming, was registered most profoundly at the polls in the parliamentary elections of December 1993. The Agrarian Party polled 10.4 percent of the vote for the State Duma, and came in fourth.[47]

Privatization of housing

Housing, like agriculture, has proven to be a complex and contentious sector for privatization. The underlying dilemma facing local and national policy-makers alike, is the issue of fairness. In 1991 Gavril Popov, mayor of Moscow, proposed the overnight privatization of housing in the city by simply transferring ownership of apartments and other residential properties to their occupants. The USSR Constitutional Supervision Committee ultimately ruled that the mayor lacked the jurisdiction to dispose of state property. But the opposition lay primarily in the fact that Popov's action would have granted ownership of the best apartments to former Communist Party officials, government ministers, army generals, and others from the ranks of the top nomenklatura who had managed to obtain the best properties due to political connections. The rapid privatization of housing would not resolve the problems of the thousands of people in Moscow and millions of people around Russia who were on waiting lists for a separate flat and were now residing with relatives or in cramped and unpleasant communal apartments or industry-owned barracks.

The Housing Privatization Act of 1991 attempted to address the equity issue by granting legal title to apartment residents, with the full right to sell, lease, and bequeath the property. Under the provisions of the Act, residents were granted up to a certain amount of space free of charge (the amount was to be determined by local authorities) and space in excess of that amount would have to be purchased by the occupant at a price determined by a government assessor. Predictably, this system is fraught with the potential for corruption and has been the subject of considerable resentment among average citizens. In addition to rewarding those people who due to political connections occupied spacious and well-located apartments, the new law saddled residents with the costs of utilities and upkeep of their units, resulting in a net increase in the monthly housing costs of the average Russian. Nevertheless, during the first five months of 1992 more than 400,000 apartments were converted to private ownership.[48] The success of the program was particularly evident in Moscow, where some 160,000 units were privatized in the first nine months of 1992 alone.[49]

Bankruptcy

One of the central elements of Gorbachev's initial policy of perestroika was "self-financing." No longer would state-owned enterprises be able to continue running up huge deficits and be bailed out by state subsidies. Although self-financing was an important part of official governmental economic policy since 1987, there was no legal basis for declaring enterprises bankrupt and forcing the liquidation of its assets. Several drafts of a new bankruptcy law were submitted to the president and parliament. Finally, a new Law on Bankruptcy went into effect March 1, 1993. The law provides a general framework for insolvencies, statutory definitions, and various procedures for satisfaction of creditor claims, including liquidation (voluntary or involuntary), reorganization, and composition. The greatest resistance to a workable system of bankruptcy came from the industrial lobby, which argued that rigid enforcement of the policy of self-financing would result in massive layoffs and a precipitous fall in production of essential goods.

Given the deadlock with the parliament, President Yeltsin issued a decree on declaring state enterprises bankrupt on June 15, 1993. The

decree limits government intervention when the state holds a 50 percent stake in the enterprise and when the enterprise has been unable
to meet its obligations to its creditors for a period of at least three
months or when its long-term debts are twice as large as the enterprise's assets.[50] Management of enterprises declared bankrupt would
be assumed by the State Committee for the Management of State Property, which could reorganize the enterprise or declare it bankrupt and
liquidate its assets by auctioning off any or all of the enterprise's
property.

Certain conditions reduce the attractiveness of liquidated assets to
interested potential investors, however. Parties wishing to purchase
part or all of a liquidated enterprise must assume the debt of that
enterprise, must guarantee employment for 70 percent of the workers
in the liquidated industry and provide for maintenance and retraining
of fired workers.[51] In some cases, the government can even stipulate
that the enterprise continue to produce certain essential items. Need-
less to say, these conditions are not attractive to most investors.

Taxation

One of the most perplexing problems confronting governments
attempting to make the transition from a government owned, centrally
planned economy to a private, market economy is the collapse of
government revenue collection. Under the previous system, the state
set prices and determined wages and salaries, thus ensuring that costs
did not exceed income, including revenues necessary for operating
the massive state bureaucracy. With privatization, the state is no
longer able to skim off wages or capture revenue through manipulat-
ing prices. Instead, like established capitalist states, the government
now must raise revenues through taxation.

The tax system in Russia, like other elements of the rapidly evolving
economy, has developed chaotically. Many economic transactions
occur "off the books," so no income is reported. The large factories
that once provided a huge portion of the government's operating revenue have suffered from lack of demand for their products and many
have had to cut back on production or stop production entirely. As
a result, the budget deficit of the Russian government during the
period 1992–1993 averaged approximately 7.2 percent of the gross
domestic product.[52]

The Russian Federation government, and regional and local governments, desperate for cash have begun to levy taxes. Personal income
taxes in Russia range from 12 to 30 percent, while companies are

charged 39 percent in payroll taxes and 38 percent in corporate profits taxes.[53] Unlike these taxes that require voluntary reporting and payment, a 35 percent value-added tax was introduced in 1991. Other taxes include export and import taxes, transport, road use, vehicle sales tax, vehicle ownership tax, vehicle resale tax, water taxes, land taxes, housing taxes, police tax, education tax, environment tax, dog and cat ownership taxes, taxes on currency transactions, stock market transactions, taxes on registrations of enterprises, and tourist taxes. Fees are also assessed for commercial use of the word "Russia" or the double-headed eagle symbol. In all, more than 100 different taxes exist in Russia. If an entrepreneur in certain types of businesses diligently paid taxes, he or she could end up having taxes exceed total income by 20 to 30 percent![54] Not surprisingly, there is massive and pervasive tax evasion in Russia. In fact, the tendency for governments to impose so many indirect taxes and fees in the past few years has been in an attempt to capture revenues that were otherwise going unreported and uncollected. The irony is that the complex array of taxes encourages tax fraud and discourages growth and investment, especially foreign investment. In order to rectify this situation, the State Duma passed a federal law that went into effect on October 1, 1995 that lowers the number of taxes to twenty and steps up enforcement.[55] Despite this legislation, tax evasion is likely to remain a chronic problem for the government.

Price liberalization and inflation

Centrally set prices that had been a hallmark of the Soviet economy represented a significant impediment to economic reform and private entrepreneurial activity. As long as prices were determined by bureaucratic officials and those prices were artificially low, there was little incentive for producers to increase production. The prices on some goods were below the costs of production. For example, a loaf of bread in 1987 cost 16 kopeks or approximately one half cent, so low that youngsters, unable to buy soccer balls in stores, were sometimes seen playing soccer with old loaves of bread. Western estimates indicate that food subsidies alone cost the Soviet economy some 130 billion rubles per year and accounted for some 30 percent of the state budget.[56] Largely due to price subsidies, by 1989 the Soviet economy was running a deficit of some 100 billion rubles ($17 billion), which represented approximately 10 percent of the gross domestic product.[57]

On January 2, 1992 the government began to free prices on most commodities, allowing prices to float up to market levels. Some consumer goods, such as bread and medicines, continued to have controlled price increases, as did essential producers' goods (energy, steel, transportation). As a result, retail prices shot up 245 percent in one month.[58] For the year of 1992, inflation approached 3,000 percent as prices rose rapidly to meet pent-up demand. The government responded in 1993 by reducing credits to large state enterprises and making deep cuts in spending on social programs. These stringent policies, associated with acting Prime Minister Yegor Gaidar, elicited strong criticism and calls for his resignation. In late 1993, Gaidar was forced to resign as acting prime minister and Viktor Chernomyrdin, a long-time minister in the oil and gas industry, assumed the post as chief economic adviser to President Yeltsin. Despite Chernomyrdin's pointed rejection of "shock therapy" he has continued to follow in Gaidar's path of maintaining a tight monetary policy, cutting back on subsidies to state enterprises and forcing inflation down. By early 1994, the inflation rate was down to 8.7 percent per month, the lowest rate since prices were unfrozen and significantly below the IMF's target rate.[59]

The political and social costs of the government's policy of economic stringency are considerable, however. Spending on social programs in 1993 fell by 20 percent over the previous year.[60] The number of hospital beds and doctors declined by about 5 percent in 1993, infant mortality rose by 5 percent, and life expectancy for males dropped from 62 to 59 years of age in a single year.[61] Incidence of diphtheria and measles more than doubled.[62] Meanwhile, unemployment rose to 5 to 6 percent.[63] The deputy minister of labor estimates that another 4 to 5 million employees are working shortened work shifts or are on extended leave because industries lack funds to pay them.[64] In late 1993 and early 1994 many workers, from coal miners to hospital employees and professors, held demonstration strikes to protest at not being paid. In many cases, workers are owed three or four month's pay. Workers' frustrations were also registered at the polls, most notably with the strong showing of Vladimir Zhirinovsky's Liberal Democratic Party and other conservative parties that favor a continuation of state subsidies and investment in social programs.

Conclusion

The difficulties the Russian economy has encountered during the transition to a market system have been exacerbated by the haphazardness and inadequacy of the legal infrastructure and law enforcement mechanisms. To date, comprehensive legislation has not been enacted in such crucial areas as torts, contracts, taxation, labor relations and dispute resolution. Similarly, Russian property law and the process of titling of private property is quite rudimentary. No just system of protection of property rights or resolution of economic contracts has yet been constructed that most investors take for granted elsewhere in the world.

The State Duma adopted Part One of a new Civil Code of the Russian Federation on October 21, 1994. Although the Federation Council failed to pass the legislation (largely due to disagreements over provisions relating to land and other property rights) they did not act within the requisite fourteen days. The chair of the Duma sent the bill to the president for his signature. He signed it on November 30, 1994 and it took effect January 1, 1995.

A compelling argument for the need for a new Civil Code was that not only was Russia in a rapid process of economic transformation, but the myriad of decrees, laws, and regulations governing the marketization process were conflicting, contradictory, and imprecise. The new code supersedes these legislative acts. Part One of the Civil Code deals with general provisions, property rights and estate rights, as well as general rules governing obligations and contracts. Part Two, which is still being worked out, will contain rules governing various types of obligations (contracts and torts), inheritance law, and conflicts of law. The new Civil Code unequivocally states that all civil legislation falls within the exclusive jurisdiction of the Russian Federation in accordance with Article 71 of the Constitution of the Russian Federation.

Article 1 of the new Civil Code reaffirms the principles of the inviolability of property, freedom of contract, and the unacceptability of arbitrary interference in private affairs. Article 212 declares "equality in forms of ownership," in accordance with Article 8 of the constitution. Counterbalancing these principles are the legitimate concerns of the state: anti-monopoly provisions, rules against unfair competition, protection of the interests of consumers, and requirements of public safety.

Finally, Part One of the new Civil Code attempts to clarify terminology designating "enterprise" to mean state and municipally owned economic entities. The Law on Introduction into Operation of Part One of the Civil Code provides that "enterprises" may be reorganized into companies (*obshchestva*), partnerships (*tovarishchestva*), or cooperatives (including a sole proprietorship). Firms that refuse to reorganize themselves must operate under a legal regime based on "operative management" (subsidiary liability) until July 1, 1999.

Given the absence of the necessary laws, the chaotic nature of the tax system which invites (or requires) tax fraud, and the seeming absence of enforcement of laws on economic crime, it should not be surprising that a large portion of economic transactions go on outside the law and unreported. Certainly the activities of organized crime syndicates are beyond the reach of government officials. But also, in the petty retail sector, most transactions are handled informally for cash. Similarly, privatizations are occurring spontaneously throughout the former Soviet Union, even when the legal basis for such actions is not fully in place.[65]

One story helps to illustrate the chaotic (and somewhat charming) nature of economic life in Russia today. An acquaintance, a former physics technician at Moscow State University, frustrated that his salary was not keeping pace with inflation, decided, like several of his associates, to go into private business. Through a family member, who was working in New Delhi, this young man learned that in India he could buy good quality wool sweaters for approximately $5 a piece. He and his friends traveled to India in the Fall of 1993 to buy a shipment of sweaters, which they intended to sell on the streets of Moscow. Since it was already October, they reasoned that they should pay extra to ship the sweaters by air freight, since they would arrive too late if they were shipped by rail. Aeroflot agreed to fly the shipment of sweaters to Moscow and promised delivery in one week. The budding entrepreneurs returned to Moscow and anxiously awaited the arrival of their goods. After three weeks went by they began to worry that their sweaters had been lost or stolen. (Cargo insurance is unheard of in Russia for these types of commercial dealings.) Finally, after one month the sweaters arrived at Sheremetrovo International Airport.

By this time, however, cold weather had already set in and these academics-turned-businessmen were having trouble selling their wares. On November 7, the former revolutionary holiday, there is a gigantic flea market held at Lenin Stadium, site of the 1980 Olympic Games, and our intrepid businessmen planned on selling the sweaters there. In true Russian form, they got together the night before to drink vodka in celebration of their impending business coup. As a result of the previous night's celebrations, these would-be entrepreneurs overslept. By the time they arrived at the stadium all the rental stalls were already taken. So, they set up their goods in the parking lot outside the stadium. They were soon approached by the police who informed them that it is illegal to sell goods outside the stadium. "This is a very serious offence," they were told, "the fine could be as high as 400,000 rubles ($400) and your goods could be confiscated." It is likely that the police were attempting to scare the business partners into paying a bribe, but, being academics, they did not understand this and were arrested. However, several days later when their case came to trial, the judge was quite lenient. They were fined only 4,000 rubles ($4) and their goods were not confiscated. In fact, when the judicial officials returned the sweaters to the men, people waiting for their cases to come to trial in the court house began to buy the sweaters and the young businessmen managed to clear $260 for the day!

8   Legal reform in the republics

> The worst legacy we have from the Stalin era is the way we think.
> And we cannot obtain new thinking on credit.
>
> Oazug Nantoy,
> *Moldovan reformer*[1]

The challenges and course of legal reform in Russia has been paralleled in many respects by reform efforts in other newly independent states of the former USSR. Each nation has had to struggle with building an independent and just court system, revise existing laws, or draft new codes governing virtually every branch of the law. Several of the nations emerging from the former USSR have adopted new constitutions that delineate the powers of newly established parliaments and executive offices. To varying degrees these new countries have concerned themselves with protecting human rights, overcoming centuries-long legacies of authoritarian rule and absence of civil liberties. Many of the newly independent states have begun to privatize state-owned assets, including the land, and debated how this can be done equitably. Finally, most of these countries have had to address the issue of their multiethnic nature – how much power should reside in central institutions, how much power should remain at the local and regional levels? What rights should be granted to Russians and other non-indigenous peoples residing in these newly independent states? And most importantly, how can governments keep centuries-old interethnic hatreds from erupting into violence?

While the conditions these nations face are in many ways similar, their responses have by no means been uniform. In this chapter we survey recent developments in the reform of the legal systems in the newly independent states of the former Soviet Union and note similarities and differences in their approaches to reforming their legal systems. We begin with the three states that have had the most contact with Western legal systems: Latvia, Lithuania, and Estonia.

The Baltic States: fast-track reforms

Lithuania first emerged as a grand duchy in the early thirteenth century and, in close association with Poland, came to dominate a large, multiethnic state, ruled by a privileged aristocracy until 1795. In contrast to the princely absolutism of the Russian Empire, Lithuanian rulers were constrained by a powerful landed aristocracy and constitutions that granted towns a large degree of autonomy. The grand princes of Lithuania were elected constitutional monarchs who granted extensive rights and privileges to their subjects. In 1795 Poland and Lithuania were partitioned; the bulk of Lithuania's lands were annexed by Russia and the remaining territory was acquired by Austria and Prussia. However, in order to placate the powerful Lithuanian landed aristocracy, a statute was enacted that permitted a limited degree of self-governance, civil liberties, and a separate system of law.[2]

In 1840 the Lithuanian Statute was repealed in favor of Russian law. Under Aleksandr III, the Russian language became mandatory in all schools, the Roman Catholic Church was suppressed, parochial schools were forced to close, and attempts were made to institute the Cyrillic alphabet. Thus, the promising development of Lithuanian legal culture was snuffed out only to reemerge with full independence in 1918.

Taking advantage of the chaos engendered by the Russian Revolution, the Lithuanians declared their independence on February 16, 1918. The Constitution of 1922 proclaimed Lithuania an independent sovereign state ruled on the basis of democratic, liberal principles.[3] The constitution established a unicameral parliament elected for a term of three years by direct, proportional ballot. The government was responsible to the parliament and headed by the prime minister. The head of state (president) was a largely figurehead position elected by the parliament. Finally, the constitution granted full rights to minorities – mostly Germans, Poles, Russians, and Jews – residing in the republic.

In 1926 the democratic constitutional system was altered to address recurrent governmental instability. Control of the parliament was fragmented among numerous parties and factions, resulting in frequently shifting coalition governments. The constitution was altered again in 1938 to allow the president to dissolve parliament and govern by decree. Furthermore, the president could appoint and dismiss the government at will. This system existed for just one year, until Lithuania was forcibly annexed into the USSR by the 1939 Nazi–Soviet Pact.

On August 25, 1940, a new Soviet-style constitution was adopted, which abolished former legal and political institutions and granted a monopoly to the Communist Party. RSFSR law codes, including codes of criminal and civil law and procedure, were introduced and continued to be observed until 1957 when all three Baltic republics adopted their own codes, patterned on those of the Russian republic.

Lithuania was the first republic to reassert its sovereignty on March 11, 1991, well before the August *coup d'état*. While Lithuanians were able to agree on the desirability of independence, few other issues have been resolved amicably. Underlying legal reform developments in Lithuania was the early rise of a powerful national independence movement, Sajudis, which swept the communists from power in the March 1990 elections. Immediately following the vote, a temporary constitution, the Provisional Fundamental Law, was adopted. However, the legitimacy of the law existed only so long as there was a general consensus in the parliament. Such a consensus existed until November 1991 when right-wing deputies formed an informal coalition with left-wing groups. The coalition held sufficient strength to block most pieces of legislation and made it impossible for the pro-reform parties to hold a stable majority in the Supreme Council.

Chairman of the Supreme Council and the leader of Sajudis, Vytautas Landsbergis, believed that the only way to break the deadlock was to establish a strong executive presidency. A referendum was held on May 23, 1991 to establish a directly elected president. Although 69.5 per cent of those voting supported Landsbergis' plan, turnout was low (only 57.5 percent) and the measure failed to receive support from the majority of all eligible voters – thus it failed to be passed.

With the defeat in the referendum, the debate over establishing a powerful executive shifted to the commission drafting a new constitution. The Supreme Council impaneled a fourteen-member commission to prepare a draft of a new constitution in December 1991. For months members of the commission haggled over the drafts, but they were unable to resolve their basic disagreements over the powers of the president. The draft favoring a strong parliament, although supported by all but three commission members, failed to win widespread public support. The "minority" draft was supported by Sajudis and nine other parties and called for the creation of a strong executive presidency, patterned on the American model.

In the absence of a clear majority in the Supreme Council, Sajudis resorted to boycotting sessions until a date was set for new parliamentary elections. The result was a paralysis of legislation in the Supreme

Council. The factions also split over voting systems, with Sajudis favoring direct election and the former communists favoring proportional representation. Charges of corruption and disclosures of collaboration with the KGB by several Sajudis deputies weakened public support for Landsbergis' leadership, including his position on the draft constitution.

Meanwhile, Lithuania's economy continued to decline, in part due to chronic fuel shortages resulting from Russia's decision to impose an energy embargo on the fledgling state. In 1992 industrial production declined by 48 percent, the GNP dropped 61 percent, and inflation rose by 1,163 percent.[4] Crime increased 14 percent and organized crime groups proliferated.[5] The public's growing resentment over these developments was reflected at the polls in the Fall 1992 parliamentary elections. The Democratic Labor Party (formerly the Communist Party) gained 73 of 141 seats in the parliament, pro-Landsbergis forces won only 52 seats, with the rest being split among a number of centrist and independent parties.[6] The electoral defeat for his faction prompted Landsbergis to accept a compromise on the draft constitution.

On October 25, 1992 voters approved a new constitution that was a compromise between the supporters of a strong presidency and those in favor of a powerful parliament. The constitutional debate, however, had been protracted and at times bitter, undermining attempts to reconcile factional differences. After adoption of the new constitution, Algirdas Brazauskas, former Communist Party chief and leader of the Democratic Labor Party, offered to form a grand coalition with Landsbergis' faction. However, Landsbergis rejected the offer.

In the February 1993 presidential elections Brazauskas defeated Stasys Lozoraitis, former Lithuanian ambassador to the United States, with a comfortable 60 percent.[7] Rather than run against Brazauskas, Landsbergis and his supporters formed an opposition party named Homeland Union, which supported restitution of nationalized property to its former owners and efforts to privatize small and medium-sized businesses.

Having resolved most of the nagging constitutional questions, Brazauskas began to address the two other critical problems: the economy and crime. In mid-1993 the government of Lithuania passed legislation permitting the prosecutor's office to impose "preventive detention" for up to two months for individuals suspected of involvement in organized crime. The economy continued to decline in 1993 with GDP falling 35 percent, industrial production down 46 percent, and construction dropping 38 percent.[8] Economic pressures resulted in public dissatisfaction with the government of Prime Minister Adolfas Slezevicius, which narrowly survived a no-confidence vote on June 16, 1994. The two issues most responsible for public discontent are scandals surrounding the privatization of some of Lithuania's most prized factories and enterprises and the erosion of personal income due to rampant inflation. In late 1994 the parliament was debating a draft law that would revoke "illegal" privatization that benefited members of the former Communist Party nomenklatura and another law that would index savings held in Lithuanian banks as of February 26, 1991 by a factor of at least 100. The IMF strongly discouraged both measures as economically catastrophic, yet public opinion strongly supported both laws. This episode illustrates that even in the most progressive states of the former USSR economic austerity measures combined with fragmented parliamentary parties can result in destabilization of governments and nationalistic backlashes.

In 1995 a draft Law on Public Trading in Securities was completed and brought to the Lithuanian parliament for adoption. The law would provide badly needed regulation of the securities market, including licensing of stock brokerages and banks.

Although Latvia only became an independent country in 1918 its legal culture dates back to Germanic and Swedish occupations lasting from the sixteenth to the early twentieth centuries. Latvia's first constitution, ratified in February 1922, established the basic principles of the independent and sovereign republic.[9] The document set forth procedures for elections and defined the powers of the parliament, the presidency, the Cabinet of Ministers, courts, and other governmental bodies.

With the seizure of Latvia by the Soviet Army in 1940 and the nation's forced annexation into the USSR, a new constitution was imposed. Based on the model of Stalin's 1936 constitution, the document recognized the monopoly of the Communist Party in all spheres of life. Yet another constitution was introduced in 1978, reflecting changes resulting from the adoption of the 1977 "Brezhnev" Constitution in the USSR.

Latvia declared its independence on August 21, 1991 and the 1922 Constitution was reinstated as the republic's fundamental law, pending a more thorough constitutional revision.[10] Given the overwhelming political, social, and economic difficulties confronting the country, the inadequacies of operating with a seventy-year-old constitution and the realities of thousands of Russian troops in Latvia, the transition to full constitutional rule would take time.

The Declaration of Independence passed by the Supreme Soviet of the Latvian SSR of May 4, 1991 set out nine points leading to "the re-establishment of the *de facto* independence of the Republic of Latvia" and the outlines of new governing institutions, including a parliament to be elected by universal, direct, secret vote on the basis of proportional representation. Consistent with the 1922 Constitution, the Supreme Council (parliament) was identified as the principal institution of state power. The document proclaimed primacy of social, economic, cultural, and political rights, guaranteeing these and all other internationally recognized human rights. These guarantees apply equally to Latvian and non-Latvian residents in the republic. The Declaration of Independence of Latvia also affirmed Latvia's commitment to develop relations with the USSR in accordance with the Peace Treaty of August 11, 1920.[11] Finally, the document called for the formation of a commission to revise the constitution "so that it corresponds to the present political, economic, and social situation in Latvia."[12]

Until new codes of law could be developed, existing Soviet-era legislation continued to be recognized and enforced in most fields. In a few areas, such as laws on religion, the press, citizenship, and various articles of the criminal code relating to economic and political crimes, Soviet laws were rejected and not enforced.

Further delaying progress toward ratification of a new Latvian constitution was the presence of Soviet/Russian military forces and the need to elect a new parliament. Many Latvians questioned how free elections could be held with large Russian troop concentrations in the country. To facilitate the electoral process, the Supreme Council in 1991 began to draft a new law on elections and a law on political parties. The law, however, raised the complex issue of citizenship and the rights of resident non-Latvians in Latvia. A strict citizenship requirement, limiting participation to people who were citizens of Latvia prior to the 1940 Soviet takeover and their descendants, would have made almost half of all residents of Latvia ineligible to vote. According to the 1989 census, Latvians constituted only 52 percent of the population, while Russians constituted 34 percent, Belorussians 4.5 percent, Ukrainians 3.5 percent, Poles 2.3 percent, Lithuanians 1.3 percent, Jews 0.9 percent, Gypsies 0.3 percent, Estonians 0.1 percent, Germans 0.1 percent, and others 1.0 percent.[13]

After much wrangling, a Law on Citizenship was enacted by the Saeima on July 22, 1994. The law stipulated that only those citizens of prewar Latvia and their descendants would be granted citizenship automatically, regardless of nationality. Others had to apply for citizenship. These policies were vehemently denounced by Yeltsin's government as discriminatory to Russians and other non-Latvians.[14] Yet, numerous human rights groups sponsored by the United Nations, the European Union and other international bodies have visited Latvia and the other Baltic states in recent years and have concluded that Latvia's citizenship and language laws generally comply with international legal norms.[15]

In June 1993 Latvia's first national elections were held. Parties of the moderate Right won the largest number seats in the Saeima and formed a government under Prime Minister Valdis Virkavs. The new parliament elected as president, Guntis Ulmanis, an economist and grandnephew of Karlis Ulmanis, the president of Latvia during its interwar period of independence. The Latvian constitution does not accord the president much power, but Ulmanis has sought to make it more than a mere figurehead post and has stressed national solidarity in order to endure the hardships of the transition.

Ulmanis' position has also been strengthened by recurrent cabinet instability in the government. In July 1994 a ruling coalition government made up of representatives of Latvia's Way and the Latvian Farmer's Union was forced to resign when the farmers' group left the coalition. Ulmanis attempted to persuade parliamentarians to support a coalition of conservative parties, but this proposal lacked sufficient backing to prove viable. Finally, in mid-September, Latvia's Way, which holds one-third of the seats in the parliament, managed to form a new government. The emergence of stable democratic government, necessary for undertaking systematic legal reforms, remains uncertain in Latvia as long as numerous parties must rely on forming coalitions in order to govern.

Like Latvia, Estonia asserted its full independence from the USSR during the August 1991 *coup d'état*. An *ad-hoc* Constituent Assembly was appointed to serve as a temporary body and charged with drafting a new constitution, which would be submitted to the public for a referendum. As in the two other cases in the Baltics, there was a fundamental split between those favoring a presidential republic and those favoring a parliamentary republic.

The Constituent Assembly supported a plan for the creation of a parliamentary government headed by a prime minister, rather than a presidential system. A conservative coalition headed by Arnold Ruutel, chairman of the Supreme Soviet, lobbied for the creation of a strong presidency. Ruutel was interested, no doubt, in preserving his post as chief executive and was joined by former members of the Popular Front and the communists – all of whom feared losing their positions if parliament took over most governing authority. The parliamentary faction prevailed. The final draft constitution called for a unicameral State Assembly (Riigikogu) with a figurehead president. Despite a last minute attempt to derail constitutional approval by a group calling itself "Restitution," the constitution passed overwhelmingly on June 28, 1992, with some 91 percent of the voters supporting the draft.

With a new constitution in place, new parliamentary elections were held in September 1992. A coalition of five reform-oriented parties, calling itself Pro Patria, gained the largest bloc of seats and formed a government under Prime Minister Mart Laar. The parliament elected Lennart Meri to be the first post-Soviet president of Estonia.

A second issue on the June 28 ballot asked whether non-citizens of Estonia who had applied for citizenship prior to June 5 should be permitted to vote in the forthcoming parliamentary elections. The measure failed with only some 47 percent of the vote.[17]

The issues of adoption of a new citizenship law and rights of non-Estonians dominated the political scene throughout 1992 and 1993. In February 1992 the Supreme Council passed enabling legislation reinstating the 1938 Law on Citizenship. The law limited citizenship to those who were citizens of Estonia prior to World War II and their descendants, regardless of ethnicity. In order to obtain citizenship, persons must reside in Estonia for at least two years, demonstrate minimum competence in the Estonian language and swear allegiance to the state and the constitution. Delegations from both the Council of Europe and the Conference on Security and Cooperation in Europe visited Estonia and concluded that Estonia's citizenship laws met Western standards. Nevertheless, the 39 percent of the population who were not Estonian felt the laws were discriminatory, especially the Russians, who constituted 30 percent of the population.[18]

The perceived discrimination against Russians residing in Estonia became a major issue in Estonian–Russian relations. President Yeltsin even attempted to link the issue of Russian troop withdrawals to Estonian citizenship laws.[19] The controversy escalated in 1993 over the issue of participation of non-Estonians in the municipal elections. While the constitution guarantees the right to vote in municipal elections to all Estonian residents, regardless of citizenship, there was disagreement over whether non-citizens also had the right to run for office. The parliament resolved the matter by excluding non-citizens from seeking elected office.

Shortly thereafter, the parliament passed a law on aliens that required non-citizens to apply for residency permits. Non-Estonian residents with ties to the former Communist Party, the KGB, and the USSR armed forces and their descendants were precluded from receiving residency permits. Sparked by anger against the law on aliens, non-Estonian residents in Narva, who constituted 90 percent of the local population, proposed a referendum on territorial autonomy. The referendum passed by a close margin, but was invalidated by the Estonian Supreme Court, which cited numerous election irregularities.[20]

While the issues of citizenship and naturalization were hotly debated in Estonia, the economic situation began to stabilize in 1993. The government's tough monetary, budgetary, economic stabilization, and privatization policies began to show results. Inflation was slowing, the kroon remained one of the most stable currencies in Europe, and production, although down substantially from pre-independence levels, appeared to have bottomed out.

The political transition in Estonia remains rocky, however. The government of Mart Laar was replaced in September 1994 by a no-confidence vote "for improper conduct of affairs of state."[21] The parliament rejected the president's first proposed candidate for head of government, Siim Kallas, president of the Bank of Estonia, because he promised to continue Laar's radical reforms. The president's second nominee, Andres Tarand, former minister of the environment and founder of the Green Movement in Estonia, offered a more moderate program. Had the parliament rejected Tarand's nomination and been unable to name a candidate of its own, according to the constitution, new elections would have had to be called and a substantial amount of pending legislation would have been further stalled.

New draft legislation such as a Law on Forms of Business Associations and a new draft Civil Procedure Code are attempting to reshape the economic environment of Estonia to facilitate the privatization of the economy. Recent efforts have also resulted in a relaxation of Estonia's strict citizenship requirements. In June 1995 the government of Estonia proposed amending the law on foreigners to remove a provision requiring the expulsion of all non-citizens who did not apply for residency and job permits by July 12.[22]

The three Baltic states, capitalizing on their history of interwar independence, their legacy of Western legal culture, and renewed sense of national identity have made great strides in reforming their political and legal systems. Problems still lay ahead. All three states suffer from a fragmented party system, with many parties represented in their parliaments, thus requiring the formation of coalition governments. Coalition governments have proven to be quite fragile, especially when having to confront such difficult problems as privatization of state enterprises, economic austerity measures, and citizenship and the rights of resident aliens. That these states have succeeded thus far in surmounting these difficult issues bodes well for their future development.

Ukraine and Belarus: uncertain sovereignty

Until 1992 Ukraine never existed as an independent state and thus never developed a distinctly Ukrainian legal tradition. For most of its modern history, the Ukraine was incorporated into the Russian Empire and then the USSR, and its legal culture closely parallels that of Russia.

During the brief period of legal reform under Khrushchev, tentative steps were taken by Ukrainian jurists to expand the rights of citizens *vis-à-vis* the state. With the renewed repression of the Brezhnev regime, however, discussion of civil liberties was driven underground where it came to be associated with other dissident demands, most notably the rights of ethnic minorities within the USSR, especially Ukrainians.

One of the chief voices expressing the need for legal reform and the protection of citizens' rights was the underground publication, the *Ukrainian Herald*. The *Ukrainian Herald* began publication in early 1970 to voice demands for democratic rights in the Ukraine. Its statement of purpose, printed in its first edition, included the presentation of information on "violations of the freedom of speech and other democratic freedoms which are guaranteed in the Ukraine, on the violations of national sovereignty (instances of chauvinism and Ukrainophobia), and attempts to misinform the public on the condition of Ukrainian political prisoners in prisons and labor camps and on various acts of protest."[23] In 1972 the newspaper published a letter signed "A Group of Soviet Citizens," which denounced the return to Stalinist repression during the 1960s and 1970s. The author cited the invasion of Czechoslovakia, the harassment of Aleksandr Solzhenitsyn along with "the suppression of national consciousness, multiple arrests of leading representatives of the Ukrainian intelligentsia, threats, blackmail, persecution, and countless mass searches."[24]

By the mid-1970s the chief standard bearer of human rights, including the right to national self-determination, was the Ukrainian Helsinki monitoring group. The organization publicized acts of repression directed against Ukrainian nationalists and appealed to international organizations to persuade the USSR to abide by its treaty commitments under the Council for Security and Cooperation in Europe. Leaders of the Ukrainian Helsinki Watch Group, including Petro Sichko and his son Vasyl, were routinely arrested and convicted of "anti-Soviet slander and agitation."

The introduction of Gorbachev's policies of glasnost and perestroika did not immediately end the repression of Ukrainian nationalists and advocates of human rights. The cause of legal reform in Ukraine was impeded by the continued presence of Volodymyr Shcherbitsky, the long-time party chief of the republic, who not only did not support Gorbachev's reforms, but also brutally suppressed any and all manifestations of popular front activity. Shcherbitsky, the last Brezhnevite in the top leadership, managed to hold to his seat in the Politburo until September 1989.

While the 19th Party Conference of 1988 was heralded as an important watershed event for legal reform in the Soviet Union, Ukrainian jurists were much more reserved in their assessments of it. Gorbachev's call for the creation of a law-based state (*Rechtsstaat*) implied the acceptance of the existing power structure of the Soviet single-party state. The resolution on legal reform adopted at the conference stated: "Over the next few years it will be necessary to ensure the supremacy of the law in all spheres of society and strengthen the mechanism of the maintenance of socialist law and order on the basis of the development of people's power."[25] *Izvestiya* noted that the goal was "to create a socialist state based on law" but "within the context of . . . the one-party system."[26]

Only gradually did members of the Ukrainian intelligentsia succeed in forming a popular movement in support of democratization and republic sovereignty. The movement came to be known as Rukh. As support for Gorbachev's reforms gathered momentum in 1988 and 1989, the Ukrainian leadership was forced to accede to demands for legal reform and increased rights of self-governance. Rukh, together with other pro-reform groups, formed a coalition known as the Democratic Bloc and in the March 1989 elections managed to win about one-quarter of the seats in the Ukrainian Supreme Soviet, despite manipulation by the party.[27] Leonid Kravchuk, a moderate reformer, was elected chairman of the Ukrainian Supreme Soviet and gradually shifted toward embracing Ukrainian sovereignty and creation of a democratic, law-governed society in the Ukraine.

The leadership of Rukh seized the opportunity to shape the legal reform agenda. In February 1989, Rukh released a draft document delineating several basic concepts to a law-based society. These included: "the State exists for the people, not the other way around; the people are the source of law; the law stands above the state, its institutions, public organizations, and individual citizens; and the interests of the majority are protected by a system of representation."[28] Equality before the law and the interests and rights of minorities should also be guaranteed and protected. Central to Rukh's program was the position that genuine sovereignty of the Ukraine was inseparable from the realization of a law-based state.

The realization of such goals also necessitated the dismantling of the "Stalinist-Brezhnevist administrative-command system" and its replacement with full democracy, political pluralism, a mixed economy, social justice, separation of powers, independence of the courts, and supremacy of law. These principles were set forth at the first congress of Rukh in September 1989.[29]

Demands for sovereignty escalated throughout 1990, as the Supreme Soviet voted in July by a margin of 355 to 4 in favor of Ukraine's sovereignty. At the second congress of Rukh resolutions were passed demanding full independence and the outlawing of the Ukrainian Communist Party. In October 1990 mass demonstrations and strikes spread throughout the country, demanding greater independence from Moscow.

The government responded to these demands by taking the first steps toward creating an independent legal system for the republic. A new procurator-general of the Ukraine was appointed, independent of the USSR procurator-general and answerable only to the Ukrainian Supreme Soviet. A Constitutional Court was established by a law of June 3, 1992 and its judges were expressly prohibited from being members of a political party or members of parliament. Modeled after the German Constitutional Court, the Ukrainian court has exclusive jurisdiction to strike down unconstitutional laws and other normative acts of legislative and executive bodies. The Constitutional Court is also empowered to rule on the constitutionality of abstract or hypothetical questions. The president, the chair of the parliament or one-fifth of the deputies of parliament may request the Constitutional Court to rule on the question of whether certain statutes, decrees, or other actions (including legislation adopted but not yet implemented) are valid or not.[30]

The selection of justices to the Constitutional Court of Ukraine is complex and heavily politicized. The parliament elects the justices from a list of candidates. Half of the candidates are recommended by the parliament and half by the president. The Ukrainian Constitutional Court is designed to consist of fifteen justices, including a chair. However, as of mid-1994 only five of the fifteen seats had been filled due to obstructionist tactics of Narodna Rada, the democratic bloc in the Ukrainian parliament.

The Ukrainian Supreme Soviet also formed a Constitutional Commission to draft a new fundamental law. Work on the draft constitution was slowed by the insistence of the Communist Party that the new document reflect the "socialist choice" that Ukrainians supposedly made in 1917. The Communist Party also opposed the creation of a strong presidency, favoring a parliamentary republic.

While the work on the constitutional draft proceeded slowly, many new laws were enacted, reflecting the changing political and economic conditions in the country. In early 1991 the Ministry of Justice was reportedly working on drafts of almost seventy new laws dealing with demonopolization, property rights, bankruptcy, and rights of citizens.[31] Two of the first laws to be ratified concerned freedom of conscience and religion and the rehabilitation of victims of political repression. President Kravchuk noted in mid-1991 that the Supreme Soviet had adopted 220 legal acts in the previous 12 months and that 46 of these related to "the constitutional foundations of Ukrainian statehood and democracy."[32]

To substantiate its independence and to signal its commitment to international norms of human rights, the Ukrainian government applied for membership in the Conference on Security and Cooperation in Europe in May 1991. The Ukraine also joined the International Covenant on Civil and Political Rights.

Following the aborted *coup d'état* in Moscow, the Ukrainian Supreme Soviet proclaimed the independence of Ukraine on August 24, 1991. This declaration was subject to approval in a December 1 referendum. An overwhelming majority (90.3 percent) of the voters (84.1 percent of those eligible to vote) supported the declaration of independence and 61.5 percent favored Kravchuk as president.[33] Four days later, the Ukrainian parliament voted to nullify the 1922 treaty incorporating Ukraine into the USSR. Ukraine's secession from the Soviet Union doomed Gorbachev's desperate efforts to hold the USSR together with a re-negotiated Union Treaty.

Independence increased the urgency to adopt a new constitution. In June 1992 the Constitutional Commission completed its work and submitted a draft document to parliament. The draft constitution called for the creation of a strong executive presidency together with a bicameral legislature. Before it could be ratified, however, the constitution was overwhelmed by economic and political developments. The effects of shock therapy have been much more pronounced in Ukraine than in Russia, resulting in an estimated 85 percent of the population living below the poverty level.[34] The gross national product fell by some 11 percent in 1993 on top of another 15 percent the previous year.[35] The country was paralyzed by a miner's strike in June 1993, which worsened the political situation and resulted in a vote of no confidence in the government in September 1993.

The economic crisis precipitated a political struggle between the parliament and the president, between the president and the prime minister, and between Ukraine and Russia. In an effort to stabilize the parliamentary–presidential impasse, a new electoral law was passed, which introduced the plurality (first-past-the-post) principle, to minimize party fragmentation and reduce the number of competing factions in the parliament. The draft constitution was revised twice, once in July 1992 and again in October 1993. The first change, providing for a unicameral rather than a bicameral assembly, was made largely to placate the existing deputies by preserving the status quo. The July revision of the draft constitution called for some judges to be appointed by the national assembly rather than all judges being appointed by the president, and changed the term for which judges are selected.[36] The continual revision of the draft constitution delayed the vote on its ratification to March 1994 and, thus, postponed new parliamentary and presidential elections.

The October 1993 draft constitution establishes a judicial branch consisting of the Constitutional Court, general courts, and arbitration courts. Justices of the peace, which have replaced the comrades' courts, are publicly elected for a term of five years. Judges of the Supreme Court are appointed by the parliament, while judges serving on all other levels are appointed by the president. The draft also provides for judicial immunity, but also gives citizens the right to sue for damages caused by judicial error.[37] The constitution provides for jury trials, but it is still unclear whether these extend only to certain categories of cases.

Rather than transform the Ukrainian Procuracy into an Attorney General's office, the 1993 Constitution places the Procuracy within the judicial branch and retains many of its earlier powers: prosecuting cases in court, supervising the legality of executive branch actions, overseeing searches, investigations and detentions, and consideration of citizens' grievances. The latter function overlaps that of a newly created office, the Parliamentary Representative for Human Rights.

Meanwhile, Ukrainian jurists have been working on a vast amount of new legislation and laws pertaining to privatization of large and small enterprises, privatization of land, foreign investment, the creation of securities and stock exchanges, a Law on Trusts, a new Civil Code, a law on the Constitutional Court, a new Law on the Procuracy (which strips it of its supervisory powers over the courts), and a revised Criminal Code. As in Russia, Ukrainian jurists are also experimenting with reintroduction of jury trials and various mechanisms of judicial appointment to insure greater judicial independence.

Due to changes in civil and criminal procedure, cases in the first instance are now tried by one judge in a bench trial, by a three judge collegium, or in certain cases by two judges and three people's assessors. Jurors now are empowered not only to decide innocence or guilt, but also vote and sentencing. To handle the mushrooming volume of administrative cases, a new subdivision of administrative judges has been developed at the district and city levels.

The Supreme Rada adopted a Law on the Commercial Court in June 1991. The law creates a two-tier system of commercial courts: regional and city courts and the Higher Commercial Court of the Ukraine. The commercial courts boast a staff of 1,238 judges and in its first four years of existence handled some 359,000 claims.[38]

The Ukrainian Law on the Status of Judges of February 1993 attempts to protect the court from unlawful interference. It also seeks to raise the qualifications of judges and guarantee adequate funding for the courts and judges.

As in Russia, the Ukrainian law stipulates that judges may not be members of any political party. In addition to meeting age, educational, and work experience guidelines, prospective judges must pass a qualifying examination administered by judicial qualifying commissions composed of judges and attorneys. Judges in lower courts are elected for a ten-year term by the corresponding council of people's deputies.[39] The independence of judges is still problematic because of their relatively low salaries and dependence on local governments for a broad range of benefits: housing, education for their children, vacations, and utilities.

A significant new weapon of the courts in Ukraine is their ability to find persons in contempt for obstructing the administration of justice.[40] This power was instituted to put an end to the practice of "megaphone justice" in which strikes and demonstrations were undertaken to apply pressure on the courts.

Finally, the Law on the Status of Judges removes the Ministry of Justice's "organization management" of the courts. Instead the ministry is charged merely with "organizational support."[41] One area where the ministry will be hard pressed is finding adequate facilities for Ukrainian courts. Soon after independence the Ukrainian Supreme Court was using auditoriums of various state enterprises for court sessions involving especially serious criminal cases. However, this practice came to an end when those enterprises began to demand fees for use of their facilities.[42]

One of the myriad of problems confronting the Ukraine is the Crimean issue. The Crimean peninsula was awarded to Ukraine in 1954 by Nikita Khrushchev. At that time, the transference of control over the territory was of little consequence since both Russia and the Ukraine were parts of the USSR. However, now that Ukraine has achieved independence, the Crimea, the majority of whose population is Russian, wants either to reunite with Russia or to be independent and sovereign. In late 1992 the legislature of the Crimean Autonomous Republic declared independence from Ukraine and held elections for a new post of president of the Crimea. The Ukrainian Supreme Soviet refused to acknowledge the legality of these actions and has taken measures to coerce the breakaway region back under Kiev's control. The unresolved status of Russians living in Crimea and the contentious issue of dividing the Black Sea fleet has complicated Ukrainian relations with the Russian Federation.

The worsening economic crisis in Ukraine and the divisive issue of Ukrainian–Russian relations came to a head in the Spring 1994 parliamentary and presidential elections. Ukraine's economic crisis deepened in 1994, with GDP falling between 30 and 40 percent, high inflation rates, stagnant privatization, and a tax policy that is driving away foreign investors and hard currency.[43] The country appeared deeply polarized along ideological positions on the "Russian question" – that is, whether Ukraine should renew close economic ties with Russia or should seek to integrate itself more into the economies of Western Europe. The Western Ukraine strongly voted for President Leonid Kravchuk and parties favoring the latter, pro-European position; while the eastern half of the country favored Leonid Kravchuk and renewed ties to Moscow. Ukraine's Communist party, which had only been permitted to reemerge six months prior to the election, won 86 seats, most of them in the eastern and southern sections of the country. Kuchma's victory, with 52.1 percent of the vote, signaled a major reorientation of the direction of policy in Ukraine and major rethinking of the draft Constitution, further delaying progress toward meaningful legal reform.

Like Ukraine, Belarus never experienced independence during its early history. The Belorussian National Republic was declared in March 1918, but was shortly thereafter incorporated into the Bolshevik Soviet state. Given its lack of sovereignty, Belarus was late in developing a sense of national identity. For many Belorussians the most formative period of national consciousness occurred under Stalin. Belorussia was granted the status of a union-republic in 1926 and Belorussian language and culture were actively promoted thereafter.

Rising nationalism in mid-1990 led to the republic declaring its sovereignty and after the August 1991 *coup d'état*, the Supreme Soviet voted to declare itself independent of the USSR. The realization of its independence has been more troublesome in Belarus than in any other of the newly independent republics of the former USSR. With a Supreme Soviet elected in 1990 and heavily dominated by communists and members of the nomenklatura, progress toward a new political and legal system was stymied. In early 1992 a petition calling for early elections was signed by more than 442,000 voters, yet after much haggling, the Supreme Soviet banned the referendum. Meanwhile, the republic continued to function based on the 1978 Brezhnev-era constitution.

The refusal of the legislative branch to assume a constructive role resulted in power flowing to the executive, headed by Vyachaslav Kebich. As the impasse became more serious in the summer of 1992, the government began to rule by decree. What legislation was passed by the Supreme Soviet, such as a law on bankruptcy, a law on military service, and a special decree halting the privatization process on the grounds that it fostered corruption, was never fully implemented.[44]

The intransigence of the Supreme Soviet, especially its decision to ban a referendum on early elections and the shift toward anti-market economic policies, threatened to increase tensions in the country and exacerbate differences over drafting a new constitution. Legislative reluctance to support economic reforms continued into 1993 with the Supreme Soviet passing a law on land ownership and governing the distribution of vouchers for privatization. The land law was a victory for collective and state farms. It recognized the right of collectives and state farms to own and use land and limited the redistribution of land to smallholdings and private homes, thus preventing the forced transference of state land to private ownership.

The drafting of a new constitution for Belarus languished throughout 1992 and early 1993 due to political strife within the parliament and between the parliament and the executive branch. A draft was completed in May 1993 and presented to parliament, which adopted 88 of the 153 articles. One of the most contested issues was whether Belarus would adopt a presidency. Support or opposition to the creation of a presidency shifted back and forth between the conservatives and the pro-reform factions, depending on who appeared at the time to be the person most likely to win that post.

Meanwhile, crime rose precipitously – by 21 percent in the first half of 1993. Premeditated murders increased 46 percent; aggravated assaults 42 percent; muggings 59 percent, and robberies 8 percent.[45]

Finally on March 15, 1994, by a majority vote, the Belorussian Supreme Soviet adopted a new constitution. The document proclaimed the Republic of Belarus a "unitary, democratic, socially oriented state based on the rule of law," exercising supreme and full power over its territory and pursuing independent domestic and foreign policies.[46] The constitution creates a president, who is head of state and head of the executive branch of government. The president is empowered to appoint members of the Cabinet of Ministers. The most important cabinet ministers (prime minister, and ministers of foreign affairs, internal affairs, finance and defense and the chairman of the State Security Committee) must be confirmed by the Supreme Soviet. The president also serves as commander-in-chief and can impose martial law in cases of emergency. The president does not have the power to dissolve the parliament. The Supreme Soviet can remove the president by a two-thirds vote if it determines that he has violated the constitution, committed a crime, or cannot serve for reasons of health.[47]

In order to discourage personalities from playing a dominant role in Belorussian politics, the president is prohibited from being a member of a political party while in that office. The president is limited to a maximum of two five-year terms. The new constitution is a compromise document that attempts to balance the power of a strong presidency with an effective parliament that can act as a watchdog over the president's actions.

The first round of elections for the presidency were held on June 23, 1994. Six candidates managed to get sufficient signatures to be on the ballot. With the exception of Alyaksandr Lukashenka, all of the candidates presented pro-reform agendas. The 39-year-old Lukashenka was the most conservative of the field. He centered his campaign on denouncing corruption among top political elites and advocated an end to privatizing and reunification with Russia. Although he was favored to win, Prime Minister Vyacheslau Kebich garnered only 17.3 percent of the vote in the first round of elections, while Lukashenka polled almost 45 percent. The new constitution requires that at least 50 percent of the eligible electorate vote and that a candidate needed more than 50 percent of the vote, thus a runoff was scheduled for July 10. Capitalizing on strong support from pensioners and collective farmers, Lukashenka won by a landslide with 81.1 percent against Kebich's 14.1 percent.[48] Lukashenka's surprising victory gave many pause for concern, especially since it followed the strong showing of Vladimir Zhirinovsky's Liberal Democratic Party in the December 1993 elections in Russia. (Lukashenka has previously visited Russia at Zhirinovsky's invitation.) The election was a clear repudiation of the old guard and a popular reaction against the painful economic policies of earlier leaders, rather than an endorsement of Lukashenka's policies.

Once in office, Lukashenka's policies also became more coherent and less conservative. In October he proposed a program of urgent measures to end Belorussia's economic crisis by hastening the transition to a market economy. His program called for using strict monetarist methods to stabilize the Belorussian ruble, stop the decline in production, and rebuild international economic relations with Russia.[49] He also pushed through amendments to the law on local self-government, which strip local and regional soviets of their powers and transfer their functions to executive officials appointed directly by the president. The result is the formation of a rigidly centralized pyramid of power with the president at the top. Lukashenka justified the move as necessary to overcome local resistance to his reforms, as he attempted to lead Belarus on a rapid transition to a market economy.[50] Lukashenka's resort to appointed officials in the provinces is reminiscent of Yeltsin's reliance on appointed "governors" that also drew heated criticism. Observers in Minsk remarked that Lukashenka, having turned from supporting egalitarian socialism into a champion of capitalist market reforms, nevertheless remains a devotee of authoritarian methods. This assessment tended to be substantiated later in the year when articles accusing several of the president's top advisers and cabinet ministers with corruption were censored. Newspaper editors were ordered not to run the stories, so instead they published their editions with gaping blank spots where the stories would have appeared.[51]

A new Law on Economic Insolvency and Bankruptcy was introduced in 1995. The law spells out procedures for liquidation and reorganization, collection of assets, avoidance of preferential and fraudulent transfers, filing and review of creditor claims, and distribution of assets. Belorussian legislators and jurists are currently working on a draft Civil Code, modeled in part on the one in the Russian Federation.

Transcaucasus and Moldova: ethnic conflict and instability

Progress toward substantive legal reforms in the three states of the Transcaucasus region and Moldova has been hampered by extreme interethnic violence and secessionist movements. The break-up of the USSR, followed by the retreat of Soviet military forces from the region and the appropriation to the warring parties of large quantities of sophisticated weapons has led to an intensification of the crises in these countries. Under conditions of civil war, efforts to build stable democratic governments and functioning legal systems have all but been abandoned. Meanwhile, crime, especially organized crime, runs rampant.

Of the three states in the Transcaucasus region, Armenia has been the most stable. The Armenian Pan-National Movement, under the leadership of President Levon Ter-Petrossyan, commands a significant majority in the parliament. Land was privatized in 1991 and 1992, which helped in alleviating food shortages, but Armenian industrial output has fallen precipitously since the break-up of the Soviet Union. Armenia is dependent on outside sources for the vast majority of its energy. Shortages of coal, oil, and gas, as well as industrial products and food have been exacerbated by a rail blockade imposed by Azerbaijan in 1989. For three years, Armenians, even in the capital of Erevan, have lacked heat and running water for extended periods of time. Living conditions have degenerated to "medieval," with people being forced to burn books to keep warm and to cook. The shortage of government funds resulted in abandoning plans to rebuild the towns in northern Armenia devastated by the earthquake of December 1988. More than 500,000 people remain homeless.[52]

Despite his popularity and a comfortable majority in the parliament, Ter-Petrossyan has encountered resistance to his proposed social and political reforms. In 1993 and 1994 opposition parties in parliament delayed adoption of a government budget, a Law on Citizenship, and the drafting of a new constitution. On July 5, 1995 Armenian voters elected a new parliament and approved a new constitution that creates a strong presidency. The constitution empowers the president to appoint and dismiss the prime minister and other members of the government. He can also disperse the National Assembly and call special elections. The president appoints the justices to the Constitutional Court and can issue decrees.

The new constitution includes a tripartite judicial system: ordinary courts, specialized courts, and a Constitutional Court. The courts of general jurisdiction are comprised of trial courts at the local level, appellate courts, and a higher Court of Appeal. Specialized courts deal with juvenile affairs, administrative disputes, military affairs, and commercial transactions. The Constitutional Court is comprised of nine justices that only hear cases involving constitutional questions.

The new constitution also guarantees private property and human rights and the rights of ethnic minorities "to preserve their traditions and to develop their language and culture."[53] But the continued tensions over Nagorno-Karabakh raise doubts about whether minority rights guaranteed in the constitution will be realized.

In neighboring Azerbaijan, the war over control of the Armenian enclave Nagorno-Karabakh destabilized the government of President Ayza Mutalibov, who was elected in September 1991. Mutalibov, the former Communist Party chief of the republic, was much criticized for consenting to Azerbaijan's joining the Commonwealth of Independent States (CIS). In early 1992 he was forced to resign when Armenian forces slaughtered some 400 Azeri civilians in a village in Nagorno-Karabakh.

The resulting presidential elections saw Abulfaz Elchibey, the highly respected scholar of Islamic history, elected president with almost 60 percent of the vote.[54] Elchibey's electoral victory was not, however, a victory of pro-democratic reform. One of the first decisions of the new leadership was to order the execution of six police officers accused of desertion. The officers were denied the right to counsel and were executed without benefit of a trial. Elchibey also issued a decree empowering the police to arrest and detain people for up to thirty days and to search their homes without search warrants.[55] These actions prompted one member of parliament to observe, "Not all the actions of the new national-democratic leadership of the republic are strictly in accordance with democratic rules, but at least we managed to avoid a civil war."[56] For the next year, Elchibey ignored his parliament and ruled by decree. He did, however, manage to obtain passage of a law on privatization of state enterprises. The law envisioned a two-year program for the sale of all government assets, including state farms. However, political turmoil in the country precluded serious efforts to implement provisions of the new law.

By June 1993 Elchibey's dictatorial leadership combined with continued losses of territory to the Armenians in and around Nagorno-Karabakh, resulted in an armed insurrection and his fleeing the capital in Baku for his home region of Nakhichevan. A coalition government was formed under the leadership of Geiger Aliev, former Communist Party first secretary. Several months later, Aliev defeated two other candidates, and was elected president with 98.8 percent of the vote.[57]

The inability of Aliev's government to stem Armenian territorial advances soon eroded his support. Aliev responded with repressive measures against his critics, such as the December 1993 law on military censorship, which permitted the temporary closure of publications that revealed military secrets or comments disrespectful of state officials.[58] After an attempted coup against Aliev in the Fall of 1994, the president imposed a state of emergency in the capital, Baku, enforced a curfew, and purged several of his top advisers in the Procuracy and the Ministry of Internal Affairs.[59]

In Georgia, the primary destabilizing factors have been internal civil wars and secessionist movements. In early 1992 Georgian President Zviad Gamsakhurdia, who had been under siege in the parliament building in Tbilisi for several weeks by rebel military forces, fled to Armenia and was replaced by a Military Council. The council suspended the constitution, declared a state of emergency and announced the establishment of a Coordinating Council, composed of members of moderate political parties, that was to function as a provisional parliament pending elections. The council extended an invitation to former Soviet Foreign Minister Eduard Shevardnadze to assume the post of president.

Shevardnadze quickly dissolved the Military Council and the Coordinating Council and replaced them with a new State Council to include representatives from a broad spectrum of political parties and ethnic minorities. Shevardnadze was elected chairman of the State Council and the body arrogated to itself the right to issue decrees. Parliamentary elections were held in October 1992 and Shevardnadze ran unopposed for the post of president.

Meanwhile in western Georgia, in the Abkhaz Autonomous Republic, the regional parliament unilaterally declared its independence from Georgia, precipitating a bloody civil war. The Abkhaz parliament building was burned to the ground by forces loyal to the Georgian government. The parliament was suspended and replaced by a Military Council dominated by ethnic Georgians.

Georgia was facing another ethnic challenge on its northern border with Russia, in the area of South Ossetia. The Ossetians were demanding the right to unite with their fellow Ossetians living just across the border in southern Russian.

Confronting these two severe challenges to the integrity of Georgia and a resurgence of paramilitary actions by supporters of Gamsakhurdia, Shevardnadze demanded from parliament, and was grudgingly granted, the power to enact decrees. He utilized this power to expedite his economic reforms and to appoint and dismiss members of his cabinet without having to consult with parliament.

By September 1993 the situation in Georgia had deteriorated to the point that Shevardnadze threatened to resign. In desperation the parliament granted Shevardnadze even more wide-ranging emergency powers and agreed to suspend its meetings for three months. When the parliament came back into session in November, Shevardnadze began to lobby for the adoption of a new constitution to be followed by new parliamentary elections. After months of acrimonious debate, the Georgian parliament finally approved a new draft constitution on August 24, 1995. The constitution provides for an executive presidency and a unicameral parliament. The president is to be elected by popular vote to a five-year term. The president retains the power to nominate key government officials and presides over the cabinet. The constitution fails to address, however, the issue of Georgian relations with the breakaway regions of Abkhazia and South Ossetia.

The political and social turmoil in Georgia has resulted in a collapse of virtually all public order in the country. Industrial production is down over 66 percent from 1990 levels and industries are operating at not more than 15 percent capacity;[60] 40 percent of the work force is estimated to be unemployed and some 90 percent of the population are living below the poverty line.[61] In such conditions, it is little wonder that constitutional and other legal reforms have not been forthcoming and are not likely to appear in the foreseeable future.

As in the three states of the Transcaucasus region, Moldova has been wracked by civil war and violence since the break-up of the USSR and this has greatly retarded efforts to undertake meaningful legal, political, and economic reforms. The territory of Moldova was first annexed into the Russian Empire in 1812 and its name changed to Bessarabia. In 1918 Moldova was united with Romania and remained a part of that country until 1940 when the territory was seized by the Red Army. The Soviet annexation of Moldova was followed by massive deportations, forced Russification, and an in-migration of large numbers of Russians, Ukrainians, and other non-Moldovans. The Moldovans, who speak a dialect of Romanian, were also forced to adopt the Cyrillic alphabet, an extraordinarily unpopular policy.

Sparked by Gorbachev's reforms, especially the greater freedom afforded by glasnost, the Moldovans began in mid-1988 to express ethnic demands. Initially their concerns focused on environmental issues and the return to the Latin alphabet. These demands soon broadened, however, into open criticism of the leadership of Semen Grossu, one of the last of Brezhnev's republic party secretaries, who continued to rule over the republic in an authoritarian fashion.

Moldova declared its independence on August 27, 1991, soon after the abortive *coup d'état* in Moscow. Under the leadership of President Mircea Snegur, the republic began to make tentative moves toward economic reform and distancing itself from Russia. However, the complex ethnic make-up of Moldova hindered a peaceful transition. Moldovans comprise only approximately 65 percent of the population, with Ukrainians 14 percent, Russians 13 percent, and Gagauz 3.5 percent. The population was deeply divided over whether Moldova should pursue its independence, be reunited with Romania, or reabsorbed into the Russian Federation. The Russians occupying the left bank of the Dniester river, fearing the loss of their majoritarian status with the break-up of the USSR, proclaimed the formation of the "Dniester Moldovan Soviet Socialist Republic" in December 1991. The Russia's Fourteenth Army, located in the Dniester region, began to undertake military action to secure control over those regions on the left bank in which Russians were a significant portion of the population.

Interethnic conflict between the newly independent state of Moldova and the Russian Federation was exacerbated by Russian provision of economic and military support to the insurgents. Even such distinguished Russian legal and political figures as Oleg Rumyantsev, Yevgeny Ambartsumov, Sergei Stankevich, and Andrei Kozyrev alluded to the incorporation of the Transdniester region into the Russian Federation.[62] Delegations from the Council of Europe, CSCE, and the United Nations visited Moldova and concluded that it was adequately providing for the rights of ethnic minorities within the republic. Moldovan schools were bilingual and minority rights for Russians, Ukrainians, and Gagauz were guaranteed in the draft constitution. In contrast, in the Transdniester Republic local authorities reinstituted policies of linguistic Russification. Russian script replaced Latin script, Russian textbooks were reintroduced, and many Moldovan schools were closed.

Throughout 1992 and 1993 military clashes in the region preoccupied the government and stalled progress toward adopting a new constitution and legal codes, including new laws on the electoral system, judicial system, banking, land reform, privatization, labor and social protection, foreign investment, customs, police and the security services, and local government.

The situation stabilized toward the end of 1993, but talks leading up to the withdrawal of Russian military forces were only undertaken on the condition of Moldova's joining the Commonwealth of Independent States and resolution of the Transdniester conflict. A new electoral law was enacted and work on the draft of a new constitution was completed and scheduled for adoption in 1994. As in many other transitional societies, new parliamentary elections were complicated by the proliferation of political parties. More than thirty parties registered for the 1994 elections. The Agrarian Democratic Party, a moderate party which favors close ties with Russia, won 45 percent of the seats in the parliament and formed a ruling coalition with Unity, which received 24 percent.[63] The pro-Romanian People's Front and the Congress of the Intelligentsia together polled only 17 percent. The victorious parties pledged to resolve the conflict in the Dniester region and in the Gagauz region in the southern part of the country, and to ensure equal rights for all citizens regardless of nationality. On July 28, the Moldovan parliament adopted a new constitution. The Basic Law declared "Moldova is a sovereign and independent, united and indivisible state."[64] It establishes the government as a republic with "semipresidential rule." The supreme representative body and sole legislative authority is the 101-member Moldovan parliament, while the president is head of state and the guarantor of the country's independence, unity and territorial integrity. The presidential term is four years and the president is prohibited from being a member of any political party. The constitution grants the Transdniester and Gagauz regions special status. While opposition parties vehemently opposed special status for these regions, the ruling parties argued that such an accommodation was necessary in order to bring about an end to the violence and normalization of economic relations with the Russian Federation.

Central Asia: toward Islamic or secular law?

By comparison to the Transcaucasus, Central Asia has enjoyed considerable tranquillity and success in bringing about legal reforms and drafting new constitutions. The chief question confronting several of these states is whether they want to reject the communist past. Gorbachev's revolutionizing policies of glasnost, perestroika, and demokratizatsiia barely scratched the surface of these societies. Throughout Central Asia, former Communist Party chiefs still wield supreme political power and the legal reforms that have been enacted may prove to be more window dressing than actual.

Voices for genuine legal reforms are equally divided between those who wish to introduce Western concepts of rule of law, separation of powers, constitutional government, and civil liberties and those who wish to re-introduce Islamic law and traditions. Thus, we find in each of these states a three-way struggle for the hearts and minds of citizens. One way represents the past with its alluring predictability and stability. The other two offer very differing visions of the world and the future course these countries might take. Below we briefly summarize developments in each of the newly independent Moslem states of Central Asia.

The five newly independent states of Central Asia traditionally ranked among the poorest and least developed of the former USSR. Prior to their incorporation into the Soviet state during the early 1920s, none of the states, with the exception of Uzbekistan, had any experience with independence. Even after seventy-four years of Soviet rule, ethnic, regional, religious, and clan loyalties seemed to supersede those of nation. The break-up of the USSR, thus, caught the leaders and citizens of Central Asia unprepared politically, economically, or psychologically for the tasks of nation-building.

The largest of the five Central Asian states, Kazakhstan, with a population of almost 17 million and a territory five times the size of

France has historically been closely affiliated with Russia and the Russian Empire. Kazakhs constitute only 40 percent of the population, while Russians make up 38 percent, Germans 6 percent, and Ukrainians 5 percent.[65] The Kazakh Communist Party, led by Nursultan Nazarbaev, staunchly followed the Moscow line. When the collapse of the party looked increasingly inevitable, Nazarbaev ran for and was elected president in April 1990. However, even after the 1991 abortive *coup d'état*, the Kazakh leadership remained loyal to Gorbachev and his attempts to renew the Union Treaty. When the USSR was faltering, Kazakhstan was the last to declare its independence and one of the first states to join the CIS.

Nazarbaev became a convert to market economic reforms relatively late in the Gorbachev period. But by 1992 he embarked on a rapid program of marketization and privatization, including housing and service enterprises. Nazarbaev's popularity has remained fairly high in the republic throughout its transition. The parliament, which was elected in 1990, contains several opposition parties, but most of them have tended to defer to Nazarbaev, rather than engage in confrontational strategies. Exceptions are the Nevada-Semipalatinsk movement (a joint American–Kazakh group opposed to nuclear testing) and the Social Committee for Ecology and the Aral Sea. Several other parties or movements have adopted strong nationalist or religious orientations. The large number of Russians in Kazakhstan and rising nationalism has also sparked the formation of several Russian parties and movements, although most Russians in Kazakhstan support the Socialist Party, a reincarnated organization from the discredited Communist Party.

By late 1993 the parliament voted to dissolve to prepare for new elections to a newly configured body. Local legislative bodies followed suit. During the interim, Nazarbaev was granted additional legislative power. In the March 7 parliamentary elections the "President's Union" won 45 of the 177 seats, while the People's Congress of Kazakhstan won 15 seats, the Socialists 12, and the Harmony Slavic movement 4.[66] Fifty-eight percent of the deputies elected to parliament are Kazakhs, 27.2 percent are Russians, and there are a few Ukrainians, Germans, Jews and one Uighur, Korean, Uzbek, Bulgarian, Pole, and one Ingush.[67]

Although the economic reforms resulted in a 25 percent reduction in national income in 1992 and 1993, Kazakhstan's rich natural resource wealth, combined with political stability, has been attracting major foreign investments. The worsening economic situation has resulted in President Nazarbaev continually shuffling his cabinet and even resorting to requesting the resignation of his entire cabinet in October 1994.

Legal reform in Kazakhstan has been hampered by the failure to ratify a new constitution. A draft constitution was under consideration in the Fall of 1992 and was eventually ratified in 1993. In the opinion of Western observers, it had several troubling aspects. For instance, the constitution reportedly required that the president be ethnically Kazakh and proclaimed the official language of the republic to be Kazakh, although Russian was recognized as the "language of inter-ethnic communication."[68] The constitution also transfers some powers from the parliament to the executive. Several laws enacted since independence also tend to reinforce Nazarbaev's hold on power. For example, the October 1992 Law on Protecting the Dignity and Honor of the President makes it a criminal offense punishable by three years imprisonment or two years' wages to insult the president publicly. The Law on National Security Organs of June 1992 grants security services the right to summons citizens for questioning, the right to tap telephone lines, and the right to enter and search businesses, apartments, and other premises only subsequently informing the procurator within 24 hours. Other laws have been more progressive and sought to realize and protect human rights. For example, the new Law on Immigration permits citizens of Kazakhstan to change their place of residence freely. The Law on Freedom of Religion of January 15, 1992 establishes freedom of religion, equal treatment of citizens regardless of attitude toward religion, and declares a clear separation of state and religious organizations.

Parliamentary opposition to President Nazarbaev rose to a crisis point in late 1994 and early 1995. In March 1995 the Constitutional Court ruled that the parliamentary elections were invalid because of numerous procedural irregularities. President Nazarbaev used this ruling as grounds for dissolving the parliament. He also called for a national referendum to extend his term of office for five more years. Official reports of the referendum declared that 95 percent of those voting approved the extension of the president's term.[69]

In reaction to this unstable situation, the president ordered work to begin on yet another draft constitution for Kazakhstan. The 1995 document shifts even more powers to the presidency, including the power to appoint the prime minister and all other ministers. The constitution replaces Kazakhstan's Constitutional Court with a weaker Constitutional Council, whose members will be jointly appointed by the president and the parliament. The president may call for a national referendum on proposed constitutional amendments, thus overriding parliamentary opposition. Local and regional interests are neutralized in this draft constitution, reflecting Nazarbaev's concern that too much local self-government might encourage centrifugal ethnic and religious tensions. Finally, the draft constitution gives the president the power to veto decisions of the Constitutional Court in cases relating to the constitutionality of laws and other acts passed by the government. Such a provision seriously undermines the independence of the court.

In the area of commercial law, Kazakhstan has enjoyed substantially greater success than in reforming political structures. A law on joint-stock companies, which applies to both foreign and domestic businesses, was introduced in 1994 patterned on comparable German laws. A new civil code is being drafted modeled on the new Russian code and has also been influenced by the Uniform Commercial Code. The Law on Competition resembles Western anti-trust laws. While the Law on Property has succeeded in transferring land to citizens, collectives and corporate owners, subsoil rights remain the exclusive property of the state. Mineral rights are consequently governed by a Law on Leasing.

Privatization in Kazakhstan has proceeded slowly and generally only has transformed the retail trade and small-scale production sectors of the economy. State enterprises remain the primary producers in heavy industry, mining, energy, and chemicals.

Yet to be enacted is a draft Arbitration Procedure Code which defines the procedures to be followed by newly created economic or commercial courts. The June 1995 draft code treats many issues superficially, including such crucial concepts as evidentiary questions, standing, and jurisdiction of the courts.

The picture of mixed success of legal reform in Kazakhstan is illustrative of President Nazarbaev's strategy: to create a stable political and economic environment in order to attract Western investors to develop Kazakhstan's wealth of minerals, oil, gas, and other resources. Such a strategy requires that commercial law be revised in a form familiar and favorable to Western investors. On the other hand, political stability can best be achieved in Nazarbaev's view by the concentration of powers in the hands of the president. This process does not bode well for the future development of democratic, pluralist institutions in Kazakhstan nor does it offer much hope for the development of an independent judiciary.

With 20.7 million citizens, Uzbekistan is the most populous country in Central Asia. President Islam Karimov, the former Communist Party chief, assumed the top executive title in 1990. Despite proclamations of support for pluralist democracy, Karimov rules Uzbekistan in much the same manner that past party chiefs ruled over their subjects. Karimov capitalized on threats of Islamic fundamentalists to justify anti-democratic measures, especially aimed at the nationalist movement, Birlik. In 1992 the Uzbek legislature voted to revoke Birlik's official registration, effectively banning the largest legal opposition group in the country. The leadership of Birlik was also subjected to intense criminal investigation by the State Prosecutor's Office for alleged legal violations.

On December 8, 1992 Uzbekistan adopted a new constitution, which proclaims the goal of becoming a pluralist democracy. The document guarantees freedom of conscience and freedom of travel. It creates the office of a powerful presidency, including the right of the president to appoint regional governors who report directly to him. The president is directly elected for a five-year term and may be re-elected once. The president has the power to dissolve the parliament, and appoint cabinet members, judges and other high-ranking officials. He also serves as commander-in-chief of the armed forces and may declare a state of emergency.

Although the new constitution proclaims numerous rights of Uzbek citizens, Article 20 qualifies the exercise of those rights by stating that citizens "must not violate the legitimate interests, rights and liberties of other persons, the state and society."[70] Also troubling is continued observance of a February 1990 ban on public demonstrations. On at least four occasions police have opened fire on unarmed demonstrators. The December 1992 Law on Public Organizations prohibits parties based on religious or ethnic bases, effectively outlawing the Islamic Renaissance Party. Like Kazakhstan, Uzbekistan also has a law prohibiting "insulting the dignity and honor of the president."

In 1993 the ban on opposition parties was lifted, but all political parties were forced to register with the Ministry of Justice. Birlik, whose headquarters had been confiscated by the government the previous year, lacked an official address and was prohibited from registering, permanently barring it from operating in the country. Other opposition groups encountered overt harassment and physical assaults or arrest on trumped-up charges. For example, six leaders of the opposition who had attempted to organize an alternate parliament were arrested, tried and sentenced to terms of ten to fifteen years in labor camps.[71] In the Fall of 1994 more than forty people were rounded up and charged with plotting a *coup d'état* against Karimov's government. Responding to pleas from the Human Rights Watch, Amnesty International, and the Society for Human Rights Observance in Central Asia several of the suspects were released, but others remain charged and subject to trials.

The repressive policies of President Karimov have forged an alliance between pro-Western reformers and Islamic nationalists, some of whom support Islamic fundamentalism. Nevertheless, in the December 1994 elections Karimov's party, the People's Democratic Party, continued to hold the largest bloc of the seats in the Oly Majlis (parliament). Failing to achieve political change at the polls Islamic fundamentalist forces threaten to take their challenge to the streets. Karimov's solution has been to enforce stability by stamping out all opposition, consequently, the outlook for progressive constitutional reforms in Uzbekistan today is not bright.

Like Kazakhstan, however, Uzbekistan has sought to revise its commercial laws to attract Western investment. On May 4, 1994 the Uzbek parliament passed a Law on Foreign Investment which set forth legal foundations for foreign investment in the republic. The law provides guarantees for foreign investors including the right to purchase, sell, and transfer property freely, and the right to transfer profits abroad "without any restrictions." The law, which was patterned on the Russian Law on Foreign Investment, was designed to promote economic development and greater integration into the world economic system.

In contrast to the authoritarian leadership in Uzbekistan, President Askar Akaev of Kyrgyzstan has tried to promote pluralist democracy and market reforms. Akaev is the only president of the five Central Asian states who was not a former Communist Party official. He was elected in October 1990 and has repeatedly expressed the hope that Kyrgyzstan would become the Switzerland of Central Asia. In 1992 the government undertook an ambitious program to privatize state assets and introduce market mechanisms. However, the Kyrgyz economy is closely linked to Russia's and suffered major setbacks due to the breakdown of established supply relations with the break-up of the USSR. In the period 1992–1993, national income in Kyrgyzstan fell by some 49.3 percent.[72] Next to Armenia and Tajikistan, Kyrgyzstan has suffered a sharper economic collapse than any other states in the CIS. As a result of its close ties to Russia, Kyrgyzstan has been one of the leading nations in trying to develop greater integration among the five Central Asian states and the CIS.

The economic crisis in Kyrgyzstan coupled with President Akaev's activist approach to economic reform has spurred resistance in the parliament and resulted in the parliament jealously protecting its involvement in economic policy-making. For his part, the president has sought the institution of a strong executive presidency with extraordinary powers to rule during the on-going economic crisis.

After a year-long tortuous process of drafting a new constitution, the parliament and President Akaev finally were able to work out the details and a new constitution was adopted on May 5, 1993. The parliament, which includes a sizable contingent of former communists and Kyrgyz nationalists, rejected the president's request for authority to appoint members of the government. The final document gives parliament the right to approve presidential nominees and a major role in making economic decisions. The president of the Republic, who is directly elected for a five-year term, serves as head of state. According to the new constitution, the president must be fluent in Kyrgyz, the official language of the state. (Russian language is, however, granted equal status with Kyrgyz.) New elections to the 105-member Zhogurku Kenesh (parliament) were scheduled for 1995.

Efforts by the conservative parliament to stall holding new elections and to diminish the powers of the president resulted in a crisis in 1994. In September 1994 Akaev disbanded the parliament to force new elections. He also proposed a referendum on several changes to the constitution which would strengthen his position. Chief among the changes was a proposal to reconfigure the parliament into a much smaller, professional body of only thirty-five members which would be in charge of day-to-day legislative work. The president also favored a measure permitting him to take important political decisions to the voters in a referendum, thus by-passing the parliament.[73] The Kyrgyz are accustomed to following their leaders and in the October referendum voters overwhelmingly supported Akaev's proposed constitutional changes. A computer specialist remarked, "Even if he has no bread in his house, a Kyrgyz will say his government is good."[74]

The collapse of the Soviet economic system and the threat of political opposition have resulted in a hardening of President Akaev's stance toward political opponents and an out-migration of Russians from the republic, taking with them their expertise in critical areas of medicine, education, engineering, and law. Neither development is good news for the prospects of building stable democratic political institutions in the country. In December 1993 the Kyrgyz parliament enacted a new Law on the Legal Status of Foreign Citizens in the Republic of Kyrgyzstan. While the law failed to recognize dual citizenship, it extended to non-Kyrgyz citizens the same rights and privileges as citizens in the hopes of stopping out-migration from the republic. Another positive development in mid-1995 was the removal of the "Judicial Presence" section of the constitution. The "Judicial Presence" functioned as a judicial oversight board appointed by the president, and severely undermined the independence of the judiciary. However, despite these developments and in spite of such hopeful and optimistic beginnings, the Kyrgyz commitment to democratic development and rule of law appears to be floundering.

In Turkmenistan, the power structure has remained virtually unchanged from the mid-1980s. The Communist Party of Turkmenistan, renamed the Democratic Party, holds power over all aspects of the country's political life. President Saparmurad Niyazov has developed a cult of personality that surpasses even that created by Stalin in the 1930s and 1940s. Schools, farms, factories, and army units were named after him. Niyazov, while agreeing to join the CIS, has actively pursued wider economic and diplomatic relations, especially with Turkey, Iran, and Pakistan. He has tried to capitalize on the country's natural resources, particularly its natural gas, to attract foreign investment.

In May 1922 Turkmenistan became the first Central Asian state to adopt a new constitution. The document grants the president wide-ranging powers and reorganizes the system of local administration. Following the adoption of the constitution new elections were held. Niyazov ran unopposed and received 99.5 percent of the vote.[75] Given the hold Niyazov has over the country, opposition groups are small in number and frequently the target of official harassment, often under the guise of an "anti-crime campaign."[76] The media remain a monopoly of the government and only rudimentary legal reforms have been undertaken.

The Turkmenistan case demonstrates a fundamental irony of economic and legal reform in Central Asia: authoritarian regimes that provide stability and marginalize opposition groups are able to provide economic and political stability that is attractive to foreign investors. Similarly, non-democratic governments are able to introduce new constitutions with a minimum of fuss, but in most cases, those constitutions do not represent major steps forward in creating societies that function on the basis of rule of law. Rather they are slightly polished versions of their Soviet-era predecessors.

Finally, in Tajikistan a civil war is threatening the very existence of that country. At the time of the coup and collapse of the USSR the first party secretary of the Tajikistan Communist Party was Rakhmon

Nabiev. Nabiev had been elected president in a landslide election in November 1991 and he interpreted this victory as an affirmation of communist rule. Throughout 1992 and 1993 the anti-communist opposition, which included pro-reform democrats, Tajik nationalists, and Islamic fundamentalists held demonstrations trying to force Nabiev to resign. In order to achieve some calm, the president agreed to form a "government of national reconciliation" by including opposition members in his cabinet. In the provinces, especially in the southern regions of the country, opposition forces maintained a stronghold. Violence erupted in mid-1992 and continued throughout the rest of the year. At one point, Nabiev was captured by a gang of young oppositionists and forced to resign. Weapons smuggled across Tajikistan's border with Afghanistan assisted both sides in quickly escalating the crisis. In just six months, the fighting claimed some 50,000 lives and caused half a million local inhabitants to flee their homes.[77] A new government, led by acting president Imomali Rakhmonov, proved no more capable of controlling its armed forces than did its predecessor. Rakhmonov's government was willing to use force to control the press and harass opponents. All non-communist newspapers and broadcast stations were closed, several pro-reform journalists were arrested or went into exile, and the leader of the Tajik nationalists, Mirbobo Mirrakhimov, was arrested.

Meanwhile, the destabilization of Tajikistan's southern border with Afghanistan, combined with the collapse of the economy (national income fell by some 56.7 percent in 1992 and 1993) has provided ideal conditions for a flourishing international drug trade.[78] Central Asia was traditionally a drug-producing region. As industrial production and large-scale agriculture have suffered, farmers are turning to growing opium poppies, hemp, and other narcotic-producing plants to supplement their incomes. Border outposts, manned with the assistance of Russian soldiers and border patrols, have proved ineffective in stemming the flow of drugs from Afghanistan through Tajikistan and on to Moscow and the West. Conditions in Tajikistan appear far from stable and legal reforms must await the resolution of fundamental political, economic, and ethnic disputes that are tearing the country apart. In the absence of Russian (or CIS-sponsored) occupation, it is difficult to foresee the Tajiks stabilizing the situation anytime soon.

Without exception, the process of transition to democracy and a market economy in the newly independent states of the former USSR has proven to be painful and fraught with difficulty. The states that have fared the best have had some history with pluralist democracy and a tradition of rule of law on which they could rely. The Baltic states were able to return, at least initially, to their pre-Soviet constitutions and laws. The strife torn areas of the Transcaucasus and Central Asia have few such democratic or legal traditions to assist them in their transitions.

Another factor that differentiates these republics' experience is the degree of economic collapse they have suffered. Economic deprivations naturally fuel discontent and can ultimately result in extreme forms of nationalism. As we saw in the case of Kyrgyzstan, although some states may begin with a desire to establish pluralist democracy, the specter of economic collapse tends to strengthen former Communist Party elites and ultra-nationalists, neither of which supports the goals of democratization.

For the foreseeable future, the course of legal reforms in the republics will continue to be determined by the contending forces of nationalism, interethnic animosity, economic collapse, religious revival, and the determined efforts of some to adopt Western notions of rule of law, constitutional government, and the protection of human rights. For most of these fledging states, the post-communist transformation will be long and arduous and the outcome of that process is neither sure nor predictable.

9 Legal reform and the transition to democracy in Russia

> What matters above all is not whether a law is bad or good. What matters is whether or not the law exists. A bad law is nevertheless a law. Good illegality is nevertheless illegal.
>
> Aleksandr Zinoviev,
> *The Yawning Heights*[1]

The transition from a communist society to a democratic state has proven to be a tortuous process throughout Eastern Europe and the former Soviet Union. Fledgling democratic institutions struggle to establish legitimacy and authority among a citizenry and officials long accustomed to working outside the system. Multiple, fragmented political parties divide the political spectrum into tiny cells that are forced to form coalitions in order to obtain parliamentary majorities. More often than not, these coalitions prove fragile and result in parliamentary instability and immobilism. Meanwhile, badly needed legislation languishes. The parliament, when unable to function as a normal democratic legislative body, becomes a forum for the fragmented party interests to proclaim their positions and play to public opinion by raising divisive, controversial issues, rather than building coalitions across party, ethnic, and ideological lines.

Faced with parliamentary immobilism, the president and other executive authorities are forced to rule by decree, which inevitably results in a cascade of accusations of a return to authoritarian rule.

The problems of creating stable democratic political institutions in Russia have been exacerbated by the precipitous decline of the Russian economy in recent years and the consequent collapse of the social infrastructure. Everyone expected that the transition to a market economy would be painful, but most people underestimated the extent of the shock. In the first heady days of economic reform, Russians openly spoke of joining the ranks of "civilized" countries like Finland, Austria, and Ireland. Many unrealistically assumed that economic stabilization and recovery could be achieved in a matter of a few years. The combined shock of a 45 percent reduction in GNP, an even larger reduction in industrial output, 3,000 percent inflation, only modest increases in wages, and an exploding deficit rapidly eroded people's enthusiasm for "shock therapy" and lent credibility to extremist views of nationalist demagogues.[2]

The crash of the Soviet economy also resulted in the collapse of the social infrastructure. Universities and other cultural institutions have been unable to pay their staffs for months at a time. Priceless pieces of artwork in Russian museums deteriorate for lack of adequate funds to maintain them. Intellectual talent leaves the country or becomes undervalued, as writers, musicians, and composers are forced to take low-level jobs in the private sector. Russian television, once known for its staid programming, now boasts talk shows and MTV. Billboards hawk Snickers candy bars, Barbie dolls, and Marlboro cigarettes when Russian citizens can barely afford to put food on their tables. Cash-strapped local governments cannot afford to repair and maintain buses, parks, public buildings, and streets. Law enforcement officers, like other state employees, have seen their salaries eroded by inflation. Many have left for employment as private security officers, others are forced to accept bribes or collect extortion money in order to maintain a minimal standard of living for their families. A recent report issued by the Duma indicates that approximately one-fourth of all persons convicted of bribery worked in law enforcement.[3]

Law and the desire for constitutional governance is, however, the one bright spot in this otherwise rather bleak picture. Political parties across a broad spectrum, most of the military, leaders of Russia's many ethnic groups, President Yeltsin, and the media agree on one basic principle: they do not want to go back to an authoritarian society in which power is held in the hands of only a few and in which there is no real rule of law. The desire to create a "rule of law state" has been at the heart of the political transformation of Russia and the success or failure of legal reform in Russia will determine, to a great extent, the prospects for the emergence of a viable democracy in that country.

Even if Russia experiences a resurgence of communists, as has occurred in several East European states, it does not necessarily signal an end to the process of democratization and development of rule of law. For the reborn communist parties in Eastern Europe and the newly independent states of the former USSR also uphold the principles of democratic election, political opposition, and rule of law.

As we have noted throughout this volume, legal reform in Russia today is being shaped simultaneously by numerous forces: the traditional values and legal culture of Russia, enduring remnants of Marxist–Leninist ideology that emphasized the value of the collective over the individual but also insured peace and interethnic harmony, norms and expectations derived from seventy-four years under the socialist social welfare state, Western influences often introduced under the aegis of bilateral and multilateral aid and technical assistance programs, and a rising tide of national identity and desire for sovereignty among peoples of the former USSR.

Russian legal culture, typical of many traditional societies, does not accord law and legal institutions high status and prestige.[4] Authority, including legal authority, is viewed as often arbitrary and something to be "gotten around" rather than complied with. Bribery flourishes in this culture, as it has for centuries, where local officials expect remuneration for favors, authorizations, or special dispensations.

At the same time, attitudinal surveys of Russians indicate overwhelming support for the long-term goals of legal reform and constitutional rule. For instance, a 1994 survey found that "legality" and "law and order" were consistently ranked at the top of a list of values by Russian citizens.[5] The high priority accorded these values did not vary whether the respondents favored the right-wing figure Vladimir Zhirinovsky, President Yeltsin, or radical reforms Yegor Gaidar and Grigory Yavlinsky. In the minds of most Russians rule of law was more prized than other values in the survey such as "a free market economy" or "genuine democracy."[6]

How do we explain this contradiction? On the one hand Russia has a traditional culture that does not value law, yet Russians today aspire to a system in which legal rights and interests of citizens are protected, in which the state's authority is circumscribed by law, and in which law enforcement agencies are able to maintain law and order. The fact that Russians have come to value rule of law represents a major break-through for the prospects of democratic development in the country. However, reflecting on their centuries-long legacy of arbitrary abuse of power, citizens are still uncertain and cynical about whether legal guarantees have any meaning.

The chaos resulting from restructuring the political, economic, and social fabric of transitional societies has also engendered a trend threatening the development of a rule of law state: the desire for strong leadership and stability, even if it impinges upon individual freedom. The three most highly revered institutions in post-communist countries today are the army, the church, and the presidency.[7] In Russia, 62 percent of all respondents expressed trust in the army, whereas only 7 percent trusted political parties.[8] In a recent poll, 28 percent of the respondents favored some form of dictatorial government (communist or neo-national). Yet it is heartening that even under current conditions of an alarming increase in crime and breakdown of public order, 54 percent of the respondents still favored democratic rule, and the second most trusted institutions next to the army were the courts.[9]

Another element of Russian political culture is evident in the course of recent legal reforms: political power (including the power to undertake reform) comes from the top. Most Russians look to the government to initiate the reforms. Reform comes from on high, just as it always has – whether Peter the Great's efforts to modernize early Russia or the Bolshevik's efforts to develop a "New Soviet Man." The recent legal reforms began in earnest only in 1988 in response to Gorbachev's address to the 19th Party Conference in which he made the creation of a law-governed state a top priority. Without a green light from the leadership, it is unlikely that reform efforts would have encountered much success.

As under Peter I and Catherine II, reforms initially were only allowed to proceed in so far as they did not impinge on the power of the state. In fact, the principal reasons the tsars considered legal reform in the first place was to make the execution of their rule more efficient. The legal reforms of the past decade have encountered the same limitations. As long as the legal reform process is being propelled from top-level political leaders, it is subject to their strictures and limitations. What is distinctive about the latest wave of legal reform is that the momentum of the reform got out of the leaders' control. In part, this was due to the fragmentation of political power between Gorbachev and Yeltsin, between Yeltsin and the parliament, and between the federal institutions of power and the republics. Since no one official or institution held dictatorial power to stop or control the process of legal reform, those reforms proceeded and were even able to capitalize on various factions in these disputes for support. On the other hand, the breakdown of established legislative authority also retarded the enacting of badly needed reformist legislation.

The prominent role that top-level political leaders have played in initiating the legal reforms in Russia has been vital in overcoming bureaucratic resistance. Perhaps the most hierarchical and powerful vested interests in the law enforcement community, the Procuracy and the Ministry of Internal Affairs, initially opposed restructuring the legal system, especially if those reforms would restrict their authority or limit their powers. After the 19th Party Conference, they could no longer oppose reforms overtly, to do so would have meant directly challenging the general secretary. Instead, they had to rely on bureaucratic foot-dragging and other forms of passive resistance.

The process of reforming the legal systems of the newly independent states of the former Soviet Union points up an interesting anomaly: states with authoritarian post-communist leaderships have been able to undertake legal reforms more expeditiously than have more democratic governments. Authoritarian leaders, anxious to legitimate their power with the patina of constitutional rule, have enacted new post-Soviet constitutions in Uzbekistan, Turkmenistan, Tajikistan, Georgia, Armenia and several other former republics. States with a more diverse and fragmented political landscape engaged in protracted and heated disputes over drafting new constitutions. In these cases, it was almost inevitable that parliaments (usually dominated by former members of the CPSU and its nomenklatura) strove to preserve parliamentary supremacy, while popularly elected presidents sought to shift power to the executive.

One might well ask where the ideas and conceptions that are so much a part of legal reform originated. To a significant degree, the idea of constitutional rule, the observance of human rights, norms of judicial due process, and justice have been imported into Russia from the West. With the gradual opening up of the Soviet Union in the wake of Khrushchev's de-Stalinization in the mid-1950s, Soviet jurists became increasingly aware of Western legal norms and procedures. One of the most popular courses in Soviet law schools was Bourgeois Legal Theory, in which students were permitted to read the works of Locke, Rousseau, Hobbes, Mill, as well as legal philosophers and practitioners such as Montesquieu, Weber, Kelsen, Holmes, and Cardozo, so that their views might be criticized from a Marxist–Leninist perspective. With the advent of glasnost numerous jurists noted that the ideas they were exposed to in this course were instrumental in shaping their notions of what "rule of law" meant.

The relaxed international climate afforded by détente in the 1970s also permitted increasing interaction between Soviet jurists and their counterparts abroad. Delegations of Soviet jurists visited the West and hosted Western legal scholars. Some even undertook collaborative research projects. Thus, the conduit for Western legal values and ideas tended to be jurists, especially legal scholars in major cities such as Moscow and St. Petersburg/Leningrad. When presented with an opportunity to expand their influence over the course of legal reform they did not hesitate to do so. The 19th Party Conference in mid-1988 provided them all the incentive necessary to lobby for fundamental reforms in the Soviet legal system.

A second force that played a pivotal role in shaping the process of legal reform was the political dissident movement. For centuries, political dissidents have been revered in Russia as the moral compass of society. The political trials of the writers Sinyavsky and Daniel in 1965, the expulsion of Nobel Laureate Aleksandr Solzhenitsyn, the 1968 crushing of Dubcek's experimentation with "socialism with a human face" in Czechoslovakia, and the arrest of Andrei Sakharov, the father of the Soviet hydrogen bomb, had a profound effect on the intelligentsia of the USSR. Foremost among the demands of the dissidents during the Brezhnev era were that the regime recognize civil liberties of Soviet citizens, criminal procedure for search and seizure, the right to a fair trial, the right to free speech and assembly, and an end to arbitrary harassment and punishment by the police and KGB. Like the jurists, the political dissidents of the 1960s and 1970s set the political and legal reform agenda in demanding a "rule of law state" that was eventually articulated by Gorbachev in 1988.

The central role of dissidents in the legal process is most poignantly illustrated by the case of Andrei Sakharov. Having been released from house arrest in 1987, Sakharov was elected to the Congress of People's Deputies in 1989 and drafted a constitution that provided for extensive protection of civil liberties. Although he died on the eve of the crucial December 1989 session of the congress where he planned to present the document, many of its provisions were later incorporated into the new Constitution of the Russian Federation of 1993.

In recent years Western aid and technical assistance has focused on building democratic institutions in Russia and the other newly independent states of the USSR. The American Bar Association, with funds provided by the Agency for International Development, was instrumental in the reintroduction of jury trials in Russia. The FBI is providing law enforcement agencies with equipment and training to help in combating organized crime. American and European judges, prosecutors, criminal investigators, and defense attorneys have met with their counterparts to offer advice on raising professional standards. In all of these interactions, Western concepts and values of law and justice are being transmitted.

The experience of the past few years of reform also confirms our earlier observation that the process of legal reform is not a steady one, rather it is marked by stops and starts. Periods of progress lead to backlash and periods of retrenchment. Dismantling the former legal infrastructure of Soviet law and its political institutions has inevitably created a vacuum. New political institutions, laws, and judicial bodies cannot be created overnight to fill the void. Unfortunately, this condition of a vacuum of power invited an explosion of spontaneous quasi-legal and illegal activities. Crime flourished and became increasingly organized. Now the newly created institutions are having to contend with sophisticated and diverse crime syndicates that have penetrated virtually every arena of Russian life. The leaders of organized crime groups in Russia today have a vested interest in stalling further political, legal, and economic reforms. Market competition poses a real threat to the continued lucrative businesses they have spawned and extortion schemes that feed off of others' businesses. Targeted murders of bankers and private entrepreneurs have discouraged Western capital from flowing into the country. Journalists and police investigators who seek to expose organized criminal activity have also been the targets of violence, as we saw in the recent murders of Vladislav Listyev and Dmitri Kholodov.

The response of the authorities to the wave of violent crime in major Russian cities today also poses a serious threat to the prospects of legal reform. In 1993 the mayors of Moscow and St. Petersburg expelled all people living in those cities who did not have valid residence permits. Thousands of citizens were forced to leave Moscow and St. Petersburg and the crime rate fell dramatically in both cities. However, efforts by authorities to crack down on crime can jeopardize the civil liberties of citizens. It is sensitivity to this fact that has dissuaded President Yeltsin from imposing a curfew in Moscow. He has, however, proposed extending the period for which a suspect can be held without a charge and without the right to counsel from 72 hours to 30 days.[10]

There is no doubt that Russia's progress toward creating a rule of law state has been rough and will continue to be so in the future. Yet, there are signs of progress and hope. The rudiments of a democratic system of government are now in place. In October 1993 the world watched while Russian special military forces shelled the parliament building to dislodge stalwart opponents of President Yeltsin. The "defenders of the White House" represented a coalition of reactionary political forces dominated by former members of the Communist Party apparatus who understood that enactment of a new constitution and new elections would catapult them from power.

Since those bloody days in Moscow in late 1993 much progress has been made. A new constitution has been ratified. Although many charged that it would allocate near dictatorial powers to the president, that has not proven to be the case. The December 1993 elections brought to a new parliament deputies who appear more willing to work together to resolve conflicts. In 1990, soon after the Communist Party lost its monopoly on power, several hundred political parties and factions were registered in the USSR. As we have seen in Italy and other countries, the proliferation of parties leads to cabinet instability and the immobilism of legislative bodies. Twenty-six parties attempted to get candidates on the ballot for the December 1993 parliamentary elections, but only 13 succeeded in obtaining the necessary 100,000 signatures. Of these, three failed to receive a minimum of 5 percent of the total vote and thus, did not win seats. The ten parties with deputies in the State Duma have become loosely organized into three major coalitions or blocs. The conservatives, composed of Zhirinovsky's Liberal Democratic Party, the Agrarian Party, and the Communist Party, constitute approximately 40 percent of the deputies. The pro-reform faction, made up of members of Russia's Choice, the Yabloko group, and others, account for approximately 35 percent of the deputies in the Duma. The remaining 25 percent of the deputies are moderates who align themselves with the conservatives on some issues and the liberals on other issues. The result has been a surprisingly stable and healthy situation, in which no one group has sufficient strength to push through legislation without seeking support elsewhere. Consequently, the reform-minded liberals and the conservatives have gravitated to the middle of the political spectrum and in so doing have tended to abandon their earlier extremist rhetoric.

Similarly, we have witnessed moderation of legislative–executive relations. President Yeltsin has managed to work with the new parliament. Recognizing the unpopularity of acting Premier Yegor Gaidar, the author of shock therapy, Yeltsin named the moderate former chief of the oil and gas industry, Viktor Chernomyrdin, to the post. Similarly, Yeltsin has had to take parliamentary opinions into consideration when making nominations to the Constitutional Court and other high-level bodies. Several of his nominees were rejected by the parliament, yet compromise candidates were eventually identified and the Constitutional Court has resumed its deliberations. Working together, the president and the parliament succeeded in approving budgets for both 1994 and 1995 despite the fact that those budgets necessitated painful cuts in government subsidies and services. With the new constitution in place, the groundwork has been laid for extensive legislative drafting. Parliamentary committees and the president's office have been cooperating on the preparation of literally hundreds of new codes and draft laws designed to provide greater stability amid the chaotic legal climate of Russia today.

These are positive signs, especially when one considers that only a few months earlier the president and the parliament were embroiled in a stalemate that erupted into violence. The unstable political system was functioning on the basis of an oft-amended communist era constitution that vested a virtual monopoly of power in the legislative branch. The Constitutional Court had ceased to function, having become ensnared in the conflict between the president and parliament. The lack of stable leadership and the failure of representative government combined to further the erosion of central authority in Moscow and federal institutions. Power devolved to the regions and republics of the Federation where the fate of democratic and legal reforms depended in large measure on the personal whim of regional leaders. In some regions, such as Nizhny Novgorod, Vladimir, and Tambov, reforms have enjoyed considerable success. In other regions, such as Tatarstan, Chechnya, and Bashkiria, nationalistic former communist party leaders have a tight hold on the reins of power and are reluctant to do more than pay lip service to reforms.

The post-October 1993 reforms are also impressive when viewed in a comparative perspective. It is useful to remind ourselves that democracy took centuries to evolve in Western Europe. Stable democracies depend upon supportive public attitudes such as tolerance for diversity, the development of parties, the creation of effective representative assemblies, the rule of law, and the emergence of courts whose decisions are honored by citizens and officials as being legitimate and binding. Each of these developments is potentially contentious and takes time to emerge. From the signing of the Declaration of Independence in 1776 until the adoption of the Constitution in 1789, the government of the United States functioned under the Articles of Confederation, which were imperfect at best in resolving basic issues of governance. Even after the adoption of the Constitution the US Supreme Court had to select its cases carefully mindful that controversial decisions would not be enforced and, thus, undermine its authority. The resolution of states' rights versus those of the federal government eventually resulted in a devastating civil war.

Furthermore, the process of democratization in Western Europe and the United States took place largely removed from public view. The drafters of the American constitution were all white, male landowners. Although they were divided over issues of states' rights versus federal powers and the issue of slavery, on most issues they agreed. The majority of the population remained unaware of what was transpiring in Philadelphia and how it might affect their interests. In the case of constitutional development and legal reforms in Russia, the process has gone on in the glare of television lights in a society in which everyone is aware of his or her interests. The fact that Russia has been able to enact a new constitution and develop new democratic political and legal institutions, however imperfect, is perhaps the best sign for the future of democracy and rule of law in Russia.

Certainly many problems confront Russians today and they will not be readily overcome. Most pressing is the need to develop a body of commercial law that elevates the concept of contracts to a central place in Russian law. Sir Henry Maine noted that contract formed the foundation of modern capitalist and democratic society because it enabled citizens to engage freely in private relations within the context of a government structure that protects the public interest.[11] It is through acting on one's private interest that one learns both the lessons of legal efficacy (the need to defend one's rights) and establishes the efficacy of the state's rule of law. Similarly, Russia badly needs to develop a system of tort law.[12] Both of these developments would elevate the status of courts as the principal arbiters of justice in Russia, thus undermining the traditional cultural value placed on political expediency, connections, favors, and bribes. The development of contracts and torts will also raise the awareness of citizens of their legal rights and the need to defend their own rights and interests in court, rather than rely on the state to do it for them.

The outbreak of crime in Russia today is a symptom of the collapse of order. But it is also a reflection of the former system, in which the Communist Party acted much like a Mafia organization, not only monopolizing political power, but also dictating where and how desired goods should be distributed. Local party chiefs, many of whom abandoned the party in 1991 and 1992 and have since become chiefs of rival organized crime groups, are adept at distributing scarce goods for a price. Until market reforms drive organized crime out through competition, the state must mount a vigorous anti-crime and anti-corruption effort. However, anti-crime measures may infringe upon the civil liberties of citizens and ultimately undermine the goal of creating a state that functions on the basis of justice, due process, and rule of law. Yet, to fail to address the problem of organized crime is to doom the process of democratic, legal, and market reforms to failure.

Fighting crime also requires that law enforcement agencies receive greater support and experiment with new methods of organizing their efforts. In the provincial city of Tambov, 250 miles southeast of Moscow, the militia has enjoyed considerable success in reducing violent crime.[13] Police services were decentralized to precinct offices with "militia posts" prominently located in high crime areas. Policemen patrol the streets to increase visibility and enable residents to get acquainted with them. In order to deter bribe-taking, the salaries of militiamen in Tambov were raised to three times the average wage in the region. Local authorities are also building attractive new housing units for law enforcement officials and have recently completed construction on two recreational complexes for use of militiamen. In 1994, robberies in Tambov decreased by 11 percent, automobile thefts dropped by 50 percent, and only 8 percent of murders go unsolved.[14]

The alarming collapse of the social, cultural, technological, health, and educational institutions of Russia mandates basic restructuring of the revenue collection system. Privatization occurred so rapidly that the government lost a huge portion of the assets which generated vital government revenues. The 1995 budget projects a deficit of 73.18 trillion rubles ($15.4 billion).[15] Undoubtedly, the Russian citizenry is unaccustomed to paying direct taxes and tax evasion is high. The government needs to rely on indirect taxes, such as VAT and employment taxes, to generate revenues to salvage these floundering institutions. To permit internationally prominent institutions such as the Hermitage art museum, Moscow State University, the Bolshoi ballet, and the St. Petersburg Philharmonic to deteriorate would be a blow to the pride of the entire nation. If the quality of education, health care, housing, and social services continues to decline, the public may find authoritarian leaders' offers of stability (at the cost of sacrificing democracy and rule of law) appealing. In August 1991 and again in October 1993 the military came to the defense of the elected leadership. But today some 100,000 military officers' families have no housing and are forced to live in tents erected on military bases. Some air force officers and their families are reported to be living in grounded aircraft abandoned on obsolete runways. How long they will be willing to endure such hardships coupled with the blow to their professional esteem is unknown. Government funds must be earmarked to address these hardships before they generate a powerful anti-democratic backlash.

The transition to democracy and a system of rule of law in Russia has not been easy. While most Russians agree on the ultimate goals they wish to achieve, namely a democratic, rule-of-law state, they must first endure the short-term hardships of transition. Under conditions of economic collapse, interethnic violence, and social chaos there is the very real danger that the short-term traumas of the transition process will deflect Russians from the ultimate goal of achieving a democratic society governed by rule of law.

Democracy is still in its infancy in Russia and more than anything else it requires time to mature and develop. Overcoming the obstacles to legal reform and democracy in Russia may take generations, but with each year the chances of success improve. Each election, each court decision, the enactment of each new law helps to enlarge the reservoir of democratic legal experience. Russia is forging a new legal culture that elevates the status of the individual, that values fair and impartial courts, that demands that government agencies and officials abide by laws and proper procedures, and that respects human rights. In the process of reforming the Russian legal system citizens are learning the very values that make democracy possible. During this transition phase the laws themselves and their enforcement may be less than perfect, but what is important is that they are functioning, however imperfectly. Laws matter. Rights are now being recognized and new generations of Russians are growing up in a rapidly evolving culture in which justice and rule of law are not empty slogans masking authoritarian rule and the arbitrary exercise of power.

Constitution of the Russian Federation

We, the multi-ethnic people of the Russian Federation,

United by our common destiny of our land,

Seeking to advance human rights and freedoms and promote civil peace and accord,

Preserving a historically established state unity,

Guided by universally recognized principles of equality and self-determination of peoples,

Honoring the memory of our ancestors, who bequeathed to us their love and respect for our homeland and their faith in goodness and justice,

Renewing the sovereign statehood of Russia and acknowledging the immutability of its democratic foundations,

Seeking to ensure Russia's well-being and prosperity,

Realizing our responsibility for our homeland for present and future generations,

Considering ourselves a part of the world community,

Adopt this CONSTITUTION OF THE RUSSIAN FEDERATION.

PART 1

Chapter 1. The principles of the constitutional system

Article 1

1. The Russian Federation – Russia shall be a democratic, federative, law-based state with a republican form of government.
2. The names Russian Federation and Russia shall have one and the same meaning.

Article 2

Human beings and human rights and freedoms shall be of the highest value. Recognition of, respect for, and protection of the human and civil rights and freedoms shall be the duty of the state.

Article 3

1. The multi-ethnic people of the Russian Federation shall be the bearers of its sovereignty and the sole source of authority in the Russian Federation.
2. The people shall exercise their power directly and also through bodies of state authority and bodies of local self-government.
3. Referendums and free elections shall be the highest expression of the people's authority.
4. No person shall have the right to appropriate power in the Russian Federation. Seizure of power or appropriation of authority shall be prosecuted in accordance with federal law.

Article 4

1. The sovereignty of the Russian Federation shall extend to its entire territory.
2. The Constitution of the Russian Federation and federal laws shall have priority throughout the territory of the Russian Federation.
3. The Russian Federation shall ensure the integrity and inviolability of its territory.

Article 5

1. The Russian Federation shall be made up of republics, territories, regions, cities with federal status, the autonomous region and autonomous areas, all of which are equal members of the Russian Federation.
2. The republics (states) shall have their own constitutions and laws. Territories, regions, cities with federal status, the autonomous region and autonomous areas shall have their own statutes and laws.
3. The federative make-up of the Russian Federation shall be based upon its state integrity, a uniform system of state authority, the separation of jurisdiction and powers between the bodies of state authority of the Russian Federation and bodies of state authority of the members

of the Russian Federation, and the equality and self-determination of the peoples within the Russian Federation.

4. All members of the Russian Federation shall be equal in their relations with federal bodies of state authority.

Article 6

1. Citizenship in the Russian Federation shall be acquired and revoked in accordance with federal law and shall be uniform and equal regardless of how it was obtained.

2. Each citizen of the Russian Federation shall have, throughout its territory, all rights and freedoms and shall carry equal duties as provided for in the Constitution of the Russian Federation.

3. No citizen of the Russian Federation shall be deprived of citizenship or of the right to change it.

Article 7

1. The Russian Federation shall be a social state, the policies of which shall aim to create conditions ensuring adequate living standards and the free development of every individual.

2. Citizens of the Russian Federation shall be guaranteed the protection of: their work and health, a minimum wage; state support for the family, motherhood, fatherhood, childhood, invalids, and aged people; the development of a system of social services; and the provision of state pensions, allowances, and other social security guarantees.

Article 8

1. A unified economic space, the free movement of commodities, services, and finances, and support for competition and freedom of economic activity shall be guaranteed in the Russian Federation.

2. Private, state, municipal, and other forms of property shall be equally recognized and protected in the Russian Federation.

Article 9

1. Land and other natural resources shall be used and protected in the Russian Federation as the foundation of life and the activity of the peoples living in the corresponding territory.

2. Land and other natural resources may become private, state, municipal, and other forms of property.

Article 10

State power in the Russian Federation shall be exercised on the basis of its separation into legislative, executive, and judicial branches. The bodies of legislative, executive, and judicial power shall be independent from one another.

Article 11

1. State power in the Russian Federation shall be exercised by the president of the Russian Federation, the Federal Assembly (Federation Council and State Duma), the government of the Russian Federation and the courts of law of the Russian Federation.
2. State power in the members of the Russian Federation shall be exercised by the bodies of state authority established by them.
3. The jurisdiction and powers between the bodies of state authority of the Russian Federation and the bodies of state authority of the members of the Russian Federation shall be delineated by this constitution, the Federation Treaty and other treaties on the delineation of jurisdiction and powers.

Article 12

Local self-government shall be recognized and guaranteed in the Russian Federation. Local self-government shall be independent within the limits of its powers. The bodies of local self-government shall not be part of the system of the bodies of state authority.

Article 13

1. Ideological pluralism shall be recognized in the Russian Federation.
2. No ideology shall be established as a state or compulsory ideology.
3. Political diversity and a multi-party system shall be recognized in the Russian Federation.
4. All public associations shall be equal before the law.
5. The creation and activity of public associations whose purposes or actions are directed at forcibly changing the foundations of the constitutional system, disrupting the integrity of the Russian Federation,

subverting the security of the state, creating armed units, or inciting social, racial, ethnic, or religious strife, shall be prohibited.

Article 14

1. The Russian Federation shall be a secular state. No religion shall be declared an official or compulsory religion.
2. All religious associations shall be separate from the state and shall be equal before the law.

Article 15

1. The Constitution of the Russian Federation shall be the supreme law and shall be in force throughout the territory of the Russian Federation. No laws or other legislative acts passed in the Russian Federation shall contravene the Constitution of the Russian Federation.
2. Bodies of state authority and bodies of local self-government, officials, citizens, and their associations shall abide by the Constitution of the Russian Federation.
3. All laws shall be made public on an official basis. No law shall be passed if it has not been made public. No regulatory legal acts affecting human or civil rights, freedoms and duties shall be effective if they have not been made public officially.
4. Universally acknowledged principles and standards of international law and international treaties of the Russian Federation shall be a part of its legal system. Should an international treaty of the Russian Federation establish rules other than those established by law, the rules of the international treaty shall be applied.

Article 16

1. The provisions of this chapter of the Constitution shall constitute the fundamental principles of the constitutional system of the Russian Federation and shall not be changed except in accordance with the procedure established by this constitution.
2. No other provisions of this constitution shall contradict the fundamental principles of the constitutional system of the Russian Federation.

Chapter 2. Human and civil rights and freedoms

Article 17

1. Within the Russian Federation human and civil rights and freedoms shall be recognized and guaranteed under universally acknowledged principles and rules of international law and in accordance with this constitution.
2. Basic human rights and freedoms are inalienable and belong to each person from birth.
3. The exercise of human and civil rights and freedoms may not infringe on the rights and freedoms of other persons.

Article 18

Human and civil rights and freedoms shall be instituted directly. They shall determine the purpose, content and application of the laws, the work of legislative and executive authority and local self-government and shall be guaranteed by the justice system.

Article 19

1. All people shall be equal before the law and the court.
2. The state shall guarantee equal human and civil rights and freedoms without regard to sex, race, nationality language, origin, property or official status, place of residence, attitude toward religion, persuasions, affiliation with social associations, or other circumstances. Any form of restriction of civil rights on the basis of social, racial, national, language, or religious affiliation shall be prohibited.
3. Men and women shall have equal rights and freedoms and equal opportunities to exercise them.

Article 20

1. Each person shall have the right to life.
2. The death penalty, until its abolition, may be prescribed by federal law as an exceptional penalty for particularly grave crimes against life with the granting to the accused of the right to have the case heard by a court with the participation of jurors.

Article 21

1. The dignity of the individual shall be protected by the state. Nothing may serve as a justification for its diminution.
2. No person shall be subjected to torture, violence, or other cruel or degrading treatment or punishment. No person may be subjected to medical, scientific, or other experiments without his/her voluntary consent.

Article 22

1. Each person shall have the right to freedom and personal inviolability.
2. Arrest, taking into custody and holding in custody shall only be authorized by a judicial decision. Without a judicial decision no person may be subjected to detention for a period of more than 48 hours.

Article 23

1. Each person shall have the right to the inviolability of private life, personal and family secrecy, and the protection of honor and good reputation.
2. Each person shall have the right to privacy of correspondence, telephone conversations, postal, telegraph, and other messages. The restriction of this right shall only be allowed on the basis of a judicial decision.

Article 24

1. The gathering, storage, use, and dissemination of information concerning the private life of an individual without the individual's consent shall not be allowed.
2. The bodies of state authority, the bodies of local self-government and their officials shall be obliged to provide each person access to documents and materials that directly affect his rights and freedoms unless otherwise specified in the law.

Article 25

The home shall be inviolable. No person shall have the right to enter a home against the will of the person(s) residing in it except in cases determined by federal law or on the basis of a judicial decision.

Article 26

1. Each person shall have the right to determine and indicate his nationality. No person may be forced to determine or indicate his nationality.
2. Each person shall have the right to use his native tongue and to choose freely the language of communication, upbringing, education, and artistic creation.

Article 27

1. Each person who is legitimately within the territory of the Russian Federation shall have the right to move freely and to choose where to live temporarily or permanently.
2. Each person may freely leave the boundaries of the Russian Federation. A citizen of the Russian Federation shall have the right to return to the Russian Federation without hindrance.

Article 28

Each person shall be guaranteed freedom of conscience and freedom of religion, including the right to profess individually or jointly with others any religion or to profess none, to freely choose, hold, and propagate religious and other beliefs and to act in accordance with them.

Article 29

1. Each person shall be guaranteed freedom of thought and speech.
2. No propaganda or agitation inciting social, racial, national, or religious hatred and enmity shall be allowed. The propaganda of social, racial, national, religious, or language supremacy shall be prohibited.
3. Nobody may be forced to express his opinions and persuasions or renounce them.
4. Each person shall have the right to freely seek, receive, transmit, produce, and disseminate information in any legitimate way. The list of data that constitute state secrets shall be fixed by federal law.
5. Freedom of the mass media shall be guaranteed. Censorship shall be prohibited.

Article 30

1. Each person shall have the right to association, including the right to establish trade unions to safeguard his/her interests. Freedom of activity of public associations shall be guaranteed.
2. No person may be forced to join, or to maintain membership in, any association.

Article 31

Citizens of the Russian Federation shall have the right to assemble peacefully without arms, to hold meetings, rallies, demonstrations, processions, and to picket.

Article 32

1. Citizens of the Russian Federation shall have the right to participate in the management of state affairs both directly and through their representatives.
2. Citizens of the Russian Federation shall have the right to elect and be elected to bodies of state authority and bodies of local self-government and to participate in referendums.
3. Citizens found by a court not to be sui juris or held in places of detention under a court sentence shall not have the right to elect or be elected.
4. Citizens of the Russian Federation shall have equal access to state employment.
5. Citizens of the Russian Federation shall have the right to participate in the administration of justice.

Article 33

Citizens of the Russian Federation shall have the right to appeal personally and to send individual and collective appeals to state bodies and bodies of local self-government.

Article 34

1. Each person shall have the right to freely use his abilities and property for entrepreneurial or any other economic activity not prohibited by law.

2. No economic activities aimed at monopolization or unfair competition shall be allowed.

Article 35

1. The right of private ownership shall be protected by law.
2. Each person shall have the right to own property and to possess, use and dispose of it both individually and jointly with other persons.
3. No person may be deprived of property except by a judicial decision. Compulsory alienation of property for state needs may only be carried out on the condition of prior and equal compensation.
4. The right of inheritance shall be guaranteed.

Article 36

1. Citizens and their associations shall be entitled to have land in private ownership.
2. The possession, use, and disposal of land and other natural resources shall be exercised by the owners freely unless this inflicts damage on the environment and/or infringes the rights and legitimate interests of other persons.
3. The conditions or procedures for land use shall be determined on the basis of federal law.

Article 37

1. Labor shall be free. Each person shall have the right freely to dispose of his abilities to work and to choose an occupation.
2. Compulsory labor shall be prohibited.
3. Each person shall have the right to work in conditions that meet the requirements of safety and hygiene, to remuneration for labor without any discrimination and not below the minimum wage established by federal law, as well as the right to protection against unemployment.
4. The right to individual and collective labor disputes with the employment of methods specified by federal law for their resolution, including the right to strike, shall be recognized.
5. Each person shall have the right to rest and leisure. A person working under a labor contract shall be guaranteed the length of working time, days off, holidays, and paid annual leave prescribed by federal law.

Article 38

1. Motherhood, childhood, and the family are under state protection.
2. The care of children and their upbringing shall be the equal right and duty of parents.
3. Able-bodied children who have reached the age of eighteen years shall take care of parents who are unable to work.

Article 39

1. Each person shall be guaranteed social security in old age, in the event of sickness, disability or loss of a family's primary provider, for the raising of children and in other cases specified by law.
2. State pensions and social benefits shall be established by law.
3. Voluntary social insurance, the creation of additional forms of social security and charity shall be encouraged.

Article 40

1. Each person shall have the right to housing. No person may be arbitrarily deprived of housing.
2. Bodies of state authority and bodies of local self-government shall encourage housing construction and create conditions for the exercise of the right to housing.
3. Housing shall be provided free or for a reasonable charge out of state, municipal, and other housing stocks to low-income and other persons indicated in the law who are in need of housing in accordance with procedures set by law.

Article 41

1. Each person shall have the right to health protection and medical assistance. Medical assistance in state and municipal health-care institutions shall be provided to citizens free of charge out of the resources of the appropriate budget, insurance premiums, and other receipts.
2. Federal programs for the protection and improvement of the health of the population shall be financed. Measures to promote state, municipal, and private systems of public health shall be taken. Activities conducive to improving the health of the individual, the development of physical culture and sports, and environmental, hygienic, and

epidemiological well-being shall be encouraged in the Russian Federation.

3. The withholding by officials of facts and circumstances that pose a threat to a person's life or health shall entail responsibility in accordance with federal law.

Article 42

Each person shall have the right to a favorable environment, reliable information on its condition and compensation for damage inflicted on his/her health or property by violations of environmental laws.

Article 43

1. Each person shall have the right to education.

2. Preschool, basic general, and secondary vocational education in state or municipal educational institutions and at enterprises shall be guaranteed to be accessible to all citizens free of charge.

3. Each person shall be entitled on a competitive basis and free of charge to receive a higher education in a state or municipal educational institution or at an enterprise.

4. Basic general education shall be compulsory. Parents or guardians shall ensure that children obtain a basic general education.

5. The Russian Federation shall establish federal state educational standards and support various forms of education and self-education.

Article 44

1. Each person shall be guaranteed freedom of literary, artistic, scientific, technical, and other types of creative work and teaching. Intellectual property shall be protected by law.

2. Each person shall have the right to participate in cultural life, to make use of cultural institutions, and to enjoy access to cultural activities and values.

3. Each person shall be obliged to care for the preservation of the historical and cultural heritage and cherish historical and cultural monuments.

Article 45

1. The state protection of human and civil rights and freedoms in the Russian Federation shall be guaranteed.

2. Each person shall be entitled to defend his/her rights and freedoms in every way not prohibited by law.

Article 46

1. Each person shall be guaranteed the judicial protection of his/her rights and freedoms.
2. Decisions and actions (or inaction) by bodies of state authority or bodies of local self-government, public associations or officials may be appealed in court.
3. Each person shall be entitled, in accordance with international treaties of the Russian Federation, to apply to inter-state bodies involved in the protection of human rights and freedoms if all available internal means of legal protection have been exhausted.

Article 47

1. No person may be deprived of the right to have a case examined in the court or by the judge to whose jurisdiction it is referred by law.
2. A person accused of committing a crime shall have the right to have a case heard by a court with the participation of jurors in the cases provided for by federal law.

Article 48

1. Each person shall be guaranteed the right to receive qualified legal assistance. In cases provided for by law legal assistance shall be provided free of charge.
2. Each person arrested, taken into custody, or accused of committing a crime shall have the right to use the assistance of a lawyer (defense attorney) from the moment of arrest, being taken into custody, or the bringing of a charge, respectively.

Article 49

1. Each person accused of committing a crime shall be presumed innocent until his/her culpability is proved in the manner specified by federal law and established by a court sentence which has become effective.
2. Defendants shall not be obliged to prove their innocence.

3. Irreconcilable doubts about the culpability of a person shall be interpreted in the defendant's favor.

Article 50

1. No person may be tried twice for the same crime.
2. Using evidence elicited in violation of federal law shall be inadmissible in administering justice.
3. Each person convicted of a crime shall have the right to a review of the sentence by a higher court in the manner specified by federal law, as well as the right to ask for a pardon or the lessening of a sentence.

Article 51

1. Citizens shall not be obliged to testify against themselves, their spouses, or close relatives as specified by federal law.
2. Federal law may establish other cases in which citizens are relieved of the duty to give testimony.

Article 52

The rights of victims of crimes or abuses of authority shall be protected by law. The state shall provide victims access to justice and compensation for damage inflicted.

Article 53

Each person shall have the right to compensation by the state for damage inflicted by illegal actions (or inaction) of bodies of state authority or their officials.

Article 54

1. Laws establishing or heightening responsibility shall not have retroactive force.
2. No person may be held responsible for an act which at the time of its commission was not considered to be a violation of the law. If after the commission of a violation of the law the criminal responsibility for it has been abolished or mitigated, the new law shall apply.

Article 55

1. The enumeration in the Constitution of the Russian Federation of fundamental rights and freedoms shall not be interpreted as a denial or diminution of other generally recognized human and civil rights and freedoms.
2. Laws abolishing or diminishing human and civil rights and freedoms shall not be issued in the Russian Federation.
3. Human and civil rights and freedoms may be restricted by federal law only to the extent necessary for upholding the foundations of the constitutional system, morality, or the health, rights, and lawful interests of other persons or for ensuring the defense of the country and state security.

Article 56

1. Individual restrictions on rights and freedoms, with an indication of the scope and time limits of their operation, may be imposed during a state of emergency to safeguard citizens' safety and uphold the constitutional system in accordance with federal constitutional law.
2. A state of emergency throughout the Russian Federation and in its individual areas may be declared under circumstances and in the manner specified by federal constitutional law.
3. The rights and freedoms specified in Articles 20, 21, 23 (Part 1), 24, 28, 34 (Part 1), 40 (Part 1), and 46–54 of the Constitution of the Russian Federation shall not be subject to restriction.

Article 57

Each person shall be obliged to pay statutory taxes and levies. Laws imposing new taxes or worsening the position of the taxpayers shall not have retroactive force.

Article 58

Each person shall be obliged to protect nature and the environment and to treat natural wealth with care.

Article 59

1. Defense of the Fatherland shall be the duty and responsibility of citizens of the Russian Federation.

2. Citizens of the Russian Federation shall perform military service in accordance with federal law.

3. In cases where the performance of military service runs counter to a citizen's persuasions or religion, and also in other cases specified by federal law, a citizen of the Russian Federation shall have the right to replace military service with alternative civilian service.

Article 60

A citizen of the Russian Federation may independently exercise his/her rights and duties in full from the age of eighteen.

Article 61

1. A citizen of the Russian Federation may not be expelled from the Russian Federation or extradited to another state.

2. The Russian Federation shall guarantee its citizens defense and protection outside its boundaries.

Article 62

1. A citizen of the Russian Federation may have the citizenship of a foreign state (dual citizenship) in accordance with federal law or an international treaty of the Russian Federation.

2. A Russian Federation citizen's possession of the citizenship of a foreign state shall not detract from his/her rights or freedoms and shall not release him/her from the duties arising from Russian citizenship unless otherwise specified in federal law or an international treaty of the Russian Federation.

3. Foreign citizens and stateless persons in the Russian Federation shall enjoy rights and bear responsibilities on a par with the citizens of the Russian Federation, except in cases specified by federal law or an international treaty of the Russian Federation.

Article 63

1. The Russian Federation shall grant political asylum to foreign citizens and stateless persons in accordance with universally acknowledged rules of international law.

2. Extradition from the Russian Federation to other countries of persons being pursued for their political persuasions, or for actions (or

inaction) that are not recognized as a crime in the Russian Federation, shall not be allowed. The extradition of persons accused of committing a crime, and the transfer of convicts for serving their punishment in other states, shall be carried out on the basis of federal law or an international treaty of the Russian Federation.

Article 64

The provisions of this chapter shall be the basis of the legal status of the individual in the Russian Federation and may not be changed except in the manner specified in this Constitution.

Chapter 3. The organization of the Federation

Article 65

1. The Russian Federation shall consist of the members of the Russian Federation:

the Republic of Adygeya (Adygeya), the Republic of Altai, the Republic of Bashkortostan, the Republic of Buryatia, the Republic of Daghestan, the Ingush Republic, the Kabardin-Balkar Republic, the Republic of Kalmykia – Khalmg Tangch, the Karachai-Circassian Republic, the Republic of Karelia, the Republic of Komi, the Republic of Marii El, the Republic of Mordovia, the Republic of Sakha (Yakutia), the Republic of North Ossetia, the Republic of Tatarstan (Tatarstan), the Republic of Tuva, the Udmurtian Republic, the Republic of Khakassia, the Chechen Republic, the Chuvash Republic – Chavash Republic;

The Altai Territory, the Krasnodar Territory, the Krasnoyarsk Territory, the Maritime Territory, the Stavropol Territory, the Khabarovsk Territory;

The Amur Region, the Arkhangelsk Region; the Astrakhan Region, the Belgorod Region, the Bryansk Region, the Vladimir Region, the Volgograd Region, the Vologda Region, the Voronezh Region, the Ivanovo Region, the Irkutsk Region, the Kaliningrad Region, the Kaluga Region, the Kamchatka Region, the Kemerovo Region, the Kirov Region, the Kostroma Region, the Kurgan Region, the Kursk Region, the Leningrad Region, the Lipetsk Region, the Magadan Region, the Moscow Region, the Murmansk Region, the Nizhny Novgorod Region, the Novgorod Region, the Novosibirsk Region, the

Omsk Region, the Orenburg Region, the Oryol Region, the Penza Region, the Perm Region, the Pskov Region, the Rostov Region, the Ryazan Region, the Samara Region, the Saratov Region, the Sakhalin Region, the Sverdlovsk Region, the Smolensk Region, the Tambov Region, the Tver Region, the Tomsk Region, the Tula Region, the Tyumen Region, the Ulyanovsk Region, the Chelyabinsk Region, the Chita Region, the Yaroslavl Region;

Moscow, St. Petersburg – cities of federal importance;

The Jewish Autonomous Region;

The Aga Buryat Autonomous Area, the Komi-Permyak Autonomous Area, the Koryak Autonomous Area, the Nenets Autonomous Area, the Taimyr (Dolgan-Nenets) Autonomous Area, the Ust-Orda Buryat Autonomous Area, the Khanty-Mansi Autonomous Area, the Chukchi Autonomous Area, the Evenk Autonomous Area, the Yamal-Nenets Autonomous Area.

2. Admission into the Russian Federation or the establishment within it of a new member shall be performed in the manner specified in a federal constitutional law.

Article 66

1. The status of a republic shall be defined by the Constitution of the Russian Federation and the constitution of the republic.

2. The status of a territory, region, city of federal importance, autonomous region, or autonomous area shall be defined by the Constitution of the Russian Federation and the statutes of the territory, region, city of federal importance, autonomous region or autonomous area adopted by the legislative (representative) body of the relevant member of the Russian Federation.

3. Upon submission by the legislative and executive bodies of an autonomous region or autonomous area, a federal law on the autonomous region or autonomous area may be adopted.

4. The relations of autonomous areas that form part of a territory or region may be governed by federal law and a treaty between the bodies of state authority of the autonomous area and, respectively, the bodies of state authority of the territory or region.

5. The status of a member of the Russian Federation may be altered by the mutual consent of the Russian Federation and the member of the Russian Federation in accordance with a federal constitutional law.

Article 67

1. The territory of the Russian Federation shall comprise the territories of its members, inland waters and the territorial sea, and the airspace between them.
2. The Russian Federation shall have sovereign rights and exercise jurisdiction on the continental shelf and in the exclusive economic zone of the Russian Federation in the manner specified by federal law and the rules of international law.
3. The boundaries between members of the Russian Federation may be changed with their mutual consent.

Article 68

1. The state language of the Russian Federation throughout its territory shall be the Russian language.
2. The republics shall have the right to establish their own state languages. In the bodies of state authority, bodies of local self-government, and the state institutions of the republics they shall be used alongside the state language of the Russian Federation.
3. The Russian Federation shall guarantee all of its citizens the right to the preservation of their native tongue and the creation of conditions for its study and development.

Article 69

The Russian Federation shall guarantee the rights of indigenous ethnic minorities in accordance with universally acknowledged principles and rules of international law and the international treaties of the Russian Federation.

Article 70

1. The state flag, emblem, and anthem of the Russian Federation, their description and manner of official use shall be established by a federal constitutional law.
2. The capital of the Russian Federation shall be the city of Moscow. The status of the capital shall be established by a federal law.

Article 71

The authority of the Russian Federation shall encompass:
    (a) the adoption and amendment of the Constitution of the Russian Federation and federal laws and supervision of their observance;
    (b) the organization of the federation and territory of the Russian Federation;

(c) the regulation and protection of human and civil rights and freedoms; citizenship in the Russian Federation; the regulation and protection of the rights of national minorities;

(d) the establishment of a system of federal bodies of legislative, executive, and judicial authority, the manner of their organization and work; the setting up of federal bodies of state authority;

(e) federal state property and the management thereof;

(f) the establishment of principles of federal policy and federal programs in the area of state, economic, ecological, social, cultural, and national development of the Russian Federation;

(g) the establishment of legal principles for a single market; financial, foreign exchange, credit and customs control, issuance of money, the principles of pricing policy; federal economic services, including federal banks;

(h) the federal budget; federal states and levies; federal funds for regional development;

(i) federal energy systems, nuclear power engineering, fissionable materials; federal transport, railways, information, and communications; space activity;

(j) the foreign policy and international relations of the Russian Federation, international treaties of the Russian Federation; issues of war and peace;

(k) the external economic relations of the Russian Federation;

(l) defense and security; defense production; the specification of the procedure for selling and purchasing arms, ammunition, military equipment, and other munitions; the production of poisonous substances, narcotic drugs, and the procedure for their use;

(m) the determination of the status and defense of the state border, territorial sea, airspace, exclusive economic zone and continental shelf of the Russian Federation;

(n) the organization of courts; the procurator's office; criminal, criminal-procedural and criminal-executive legislation; amnesties and pardons; civil, civil-procedural, and arbitration-procedural legislation; the legal regulation of intellectual property;

(o) federal conflict of laws;

(p) the meteorological service, standards, the metric system and the computation of time; geodesy and cartography; names of geographic features; official statistical and bookkeeping systems and procedures;

(q) government awards and honorary titles of the Russian Federation;

(r) the federal government civil service.

Article 72

1. The joint authority of the Russian Federation and the members of the Russian Federation shall comprise:

(a) ensuring the conformity of the constitutions and laws of republics, the statutes, laws, and other normative legal acts of territories, regions, cities of federal importance, the autonomous region, and autonomous areas to the Constitution of the Russian Federation and federal laws;

(b) the protection of human and civil rights and freedoms; the protection of the rights of national minorities; the ensuring of law and order and of public security; a regime of border zones;

(c) questions related to the possession, use and disposal of lands, minerals, water, and other natural resources;

(d) the demarcation of state property;

(e) nature management; environmental protection and the ensuring of environmental safety; specially protected natural areas; the protection of historic and cultural monuments;

(f) general issues of upbringing, education, science, culture, physical culture, and sports;

(g) coordination of issues of public health; protection of families, mothers, fathers, and children; social protection, including social security;

(h) the carrying out of measures to cope with catastrophes, natural calamities, epidemics and related clean-up operations;

(i) the establishment of general principles for taxation and levies in the Russian Federation;

(j) administrative, administrative-procedural, labor, family, housing, land, water, and forest legislation; legislation on mineral resources and on environmental protection;

(k) personnel of the courts and law enforcement agencies; the legal profession, the office of notary public;

(l) the protection of the ancestral habitat and traditional way of life of small ethnic communities;

(m) the establishment of general principles for the organization of a system of bodies of state authorities and local self-government;

(n) the coordination of the international and external economic relations of the members of the Russian Federation, and the fulfillment of the international treaties of the Russian Federation.

2. The provisions of this article shall apply equally to republics, territories, regions, cities of federal importance, the autonomous region, and autonomous areas.

Article 73

Outside the Russian Federation's scope of authority and the powers of the Russian Federation arising from the joint terms of reference of the Russian Federation and the members of the Russian Federation, the members of the Russian Federation shall enjoy full state power.

Article 74

1. The establishment of customs frontiers, duties, levies, or any other barriers to the free movement of goods, services, and financial resources shall not be allowed within the Russian Federation.
2. Restrictions on the movement of goods and services may be imposed in accordance with a federal law if it is necessary for ensuring the safety and protection of life and health of people, or to protect nature or culture.

Article 75

1. The monetary unit in the Russian Federation shall be the ruble. Issuance of money shall be carried out exclusively by the Central Bank of the Russian Federation. The introduction and issue of other money in the Russian Federation shall not be allowed.
2. Protecting and ensuring the stability of the ruble shall be the principle function of the Central Bank of the Russian Federation, which it shall discharge independently from other bodies of state authority.
3. A system of taxes to be collected for the federal budget, and the general principles of taxation and levies in the Russian Federation, shall be established by federal law.
4. State loans shall be issued in the manner specified in federal law and shall be accepted on a voluntary basis.

Article 76

1. Within the Russian Federation's terms of reference, federal constitutional laws and federal laws shall be adopted that shall have direct effect throughout the entire territory of the Russian Federation.
2. Within the joint terms of reference of the Russian Federation and the members of the Russian Federation, federal laws, and the laws and other normative legal acts of the subjects of the Russian Federation adoptable in conformity with them shall be issued.
3. Federal laws may not contradict federal constitutional laws.

4. Outside the Russian Federation's scope of authority and the joint terms of reference of the Russian Federation and the members of the Russian Federation, republics, territories, regions, cities of federal importance, the autonomous region, and autonomous areas shall exercise their own legal control, including the adoption of laws and other normative legal acts.

5. The laws and other normative legal acts of the subjects of the Russian Federation may not contradict federal laws adopted in accordance with parts one and two of this Article. In the case of a conflict between a federal law and another act issued in the Russian Federation, the federal law shall prevail.

6. In the case of a conflict between a federal law and a normative legal act of a member of the Russian Federation issued in accordance with Part Four of this Article, the normative legal act of the member of the Russian Federation shall prevail.

Article 77

1. The system of bodies of state authority of republics, territories, regions, cities of federal importance, the autonomous region, and autonomous areas shall be established by the subjects of the Russian Federation independently in accordance with the fundamentals of the constitutional system of the Russian Federation and the general principles of organization of the representative and executive bodies of state authority as specified by a federal law.

2. Within the Russian Federation's jurisdiction and its powers arising from the joint terms of reference of the Russian Federation and the members of the Russian Federation, federal executive bodies and the bodies of executive authority of the members of the Russian Federation shall form a single system of executive authority in the Russian Federation.

Article 78

1. Federal executive bodies for the discharge of their functions may create their own territorial bodies and appoint the appropriate officials.

2. Federal executive bodies may, by agreement with the bodies of executive authority of members of the Russian Federation, delegate to them the discharge of a part of their functions unless this action is contrary to the Constitution of the Russian Federation or federal laws.

3. The executive bodies of members of the Russian Federation may, by agreement with federal executive bodies, transfer to them the discharge of a part of their functions.

4. The President of the Russian Federation and the government of the Russian Federation shall ensure, in accordance with the Constitution of the Russian Federation, the discharge of the functions of federal state authority throughout the territory of the Russian Federation.

Article 79

The Russian Federation may participate in inter-state associations and delegate to them a part of its functions in accordance with international treaties unless this entails a restriction of human and civil rights and freedoms or is contrary to the fundamentals of the constitutional system of the Russian Federation.

Chapter 4. The President of the Russian Federation

Article 80

1. The President of the Russian Federation shall be the head of state.

2. The President of the Russian Federation shall be the guarantor of the Constitution of the Russian Federation and human and civil rights and freedoms. In a manner specified in the Constitution of the Russian Federation the President shall take measures to protect the sovereignty, independence, and state integrity of the Russian Federation and ensure the coordinated action and interaction of the bodies of state authority.

3. The President of the Russian Federation, in accordance with the Constitution of the Russian Federation and federal laws, shall determine guidelines for the domestic and foreign policy of the state.

4. The President of the Russian Federation, as the head of state, shall represent the Russian Federation domestically and in international relations.

Article 81

1. The President of the Russian Federation shall be elected to office for a term of four years by the citizens of the Russian Federation on the basis of universal, direct and equal suffrage by secret ballot.

2. A citizen of the Russian Federation who has attained the age of thirty-five years and has been resident within the Russian Federation for ten years shall be eligible for the office of President.

3. The same individual shall not be elected to the office of President of the Russian Federation for more than two consecutive terms.

4. The procedure for the election of a President of the Russian Federation shall be determined by federal legislation.

Article 82

1. Before beginning the execution of his office, the president of the Russian Federation shall take the following oath:

"I do solemnly swear that in executing the office of president of the Russian Federation I will respect and protect human and civil rights and freedoms, observe and defend the Constitution of the Russian Federation, protect the sovereignty, independence, security and integrity of the country, and faithfully serve its people."

2. The oath shall be taken in a solemn ceremony in the presence of the members of the Federation Council, deputies of the State Duma and judges of the Constitutional Court of the Russian Federation.

Article 83

The President of the Russian Federation shall:

(a) appoint, with the consent of the State Duma, the Chairman of the Government of the Russian Federation;

(b) be entitled to preside over sessions of the government of the Russian Federation;

(c) accept the resignation of the Russian Federation government;

(d) nominate for approval by the State Duma the Chairman of the Central Bank of the Russian Federation and bring before the State Duma the issue of removing the Chairman of the Central Bank of the Russian Federation from office;

(e) appoint, based on proposals by the Chairman of the Government of the Russian Federation, Deputy Chairmen of the government of the Russian Federation and federal ministers and remove them from office;

(f) nominate judges to the Constitutional Court, Supreme Court, and Court of Arbitration of the Russian Federation and the Prosecutor-General of the Russian Federation for appointment by the Federation Council; submit to the Federation Council a proposal for the dismissal of the Prosecutor-General of the Russian Federation; and appoint judges to other federal courts;

(g) organize and chair the Security Council of the Russian Federation, the status of which shall be defined by federal legislation;

(h) approve the military doctrine of the Russian Federation;

(i) organize the Executive Office (Administration) of the President of the Russian Federation;

(j) appoint and dismiss the plenipotentiary representatives of the President of the Russian Federation;

(k) appoint and dismiss the top commanders of the Armed Forces of the Russian Federation;

(l) appoint and recall, after consultations with the corresponding committees or commissions of the houses of the Federal Assembly, diplomatic representatives of the Russian Federation in foreign countries and international organizations.

Article 84

The President of the Russian Federation shall:

(a) call elections to the State Duma in accordance with the Constitution of the Russian Federation and federal legislation;

(b) dissolve the State Duma under the circumstances and in accordance with procedures stipulated by the Constitution of the Russian Federation;

(c) call a referendum in accordance with procedures stipulated by federal constitutional law;

(d) submit bills to the State Duma;

(e) sign and make public federal laws;

(f) give to the Federal Assembly an annual state of the nation message and a message on guidelines for the domestic and foreign policies of the state.

Article 85

1. The President of the Russian Federation may use reconciliatory procedures in order to settle differences between the bodies of state authority of the Russian Federation, as well as between the bodies of state authority of Russian Federation members. If no agreement is achieved, he may send the case to the appropriate court.

2. The President of the Russian Federation shall be entitled to suspend the acts of executive bodies of Russian Federation members if they

contradict the Constitution of the Russian Federation, federal laws, or the international obligations of the Russian Federation or constitute a breach of human and civil rights and freedoms, until the matter is decided by the appropriate court.

Article 86

The President of the Russian Federation shall:
(a) be in charge of the foreign policy of the Russian Federation;
(b) conduct negotiations and sign international treaties of the Russian Federation;
(c) sign instruments of ratification;
(d) accept the credentials and letters of recall of the diplomatic representatives accredited to his office.

Article 87

1. The President of the Russian Federation shall be Commander-in-Chief of the Armed Forces of the Russian Federation.
2. In the case of aggression against the Russian Federation or the direct threat thereof, the President of the Russian Federation shall introduce martial law throughout the territory of the Russian Federation or in some parts thereof and immediately inform the Federation Council and the State Duma of this action.
3. The martial law regime shall be determined by federal constitutional law.

Article 88

The President of the Russian Federation shall, under the circumstances and in accordance with the procedures stipulated by federal constitutional law, announce a state of emergency within the territory of the Russian Federation or some parts thereof and immediately inform the Federation Council and the State Duma of this action.

Article 89

The President of the Russian Federation shall:
(a) decide questions of the Russian Federation citizenship and the granting of political asylum;

(b) confer state awards of the Russian Federation, honorary titles of the Russian Federation, and top military and special titles;
(c) grant pardons.

Article 90

1. The President of the Russian Federation shall issue decrees and directives.
2. Decrees and directives of the President of the Russian Federation shall be binding for execution throughout the territory of the Russian Federation.
3. Decrees and directives of the President of the Russian Federation shall not contradict the Constitution of the Russian Federation or federal laws.

Article 91

The President of the Russian Federation shall have immunity.

Article 92

1. The President of the Russian Federation shall commence to execute the office of President with the taking of the oath and shall terminate the execution of the office when his term expires and the next President-elect takes the oath.
2. The President of the Russian Federation shall discontinue the execution of the office before its expiration in cases of resignation, continued inability to discharge the powers and the duties of the office for reasons of health, or removal from office by impeachment. New presidential elections shall be held no later than three months after the early termination of the execution of the office.
3. In case of the inability of the President of the Russian Federation to execute presidential powers and duties, they shall devolve to the Chairman of the Government of the Russian Federation. The acting President of the Russian Federation may not dissolve the State Duma, call a referendum or submit proposals on amendments to the Constitution of the Russian Federation or revisions of its provisions.

Article 93

1. The President of the Russian Federation may only be removed from office by the Federation Council on the grounds of accusations of high

treason or of another grave crime advanced by the State Duma, provided the Supreme Court of the Russian Federation qualifies the President's actions as criminal and the Constitutional Court of the Russian Federation concludes that the established procedure for the accusations has been observed.

2. The decision of the State Duma to advance accusations against the President of the Russian Federation and the decision of the Federation Council to remove the President from office shall be passed by two-thirds of the votes of the total number of deputies in each house on the initiative of at least one-third of the State Duma deputies, provided there is a corresponding conclusion by a special commission set up by the State Duma.

3. The decision of the Federation Council to remove the President of the Russian Federation from office shall be adopted no later than three months after the State Duma advances its accusations. If the Federation Council fails to adopt such a decision by this deadline, the accusations against the President of the Russian Federation shall be considered dismissed.

Chapter 5. The Federal Assembly

Article 94

The Federal Assembly – the Parliament of the Russian Federation – shall be the supreme representative and legislative body of the Russian Federation.

Article 95

1. The Federal Assembly shall consist of two houses – a Federation Council and a State Duma.
2. The Federation Council shall be composed of two representatives from each member of the Russian Federation – one from its representative and one from its executive body of state authority.
3. The State Duma shall be composed of 450 deputies.

Article 96

1. The State Duma shall be elected for a term of four years.
2. The procedure for forming the Federation Council and the procedure for electing the deputies of the State Duma shall be determined by federal legislation.

Article 97

1. Any citizen of the Russian Federation who has attained the age of twenty-one years and is qualified to vote may be elected a deputy of the State Duma.

2. No individual shall be a member of the Federation Council and a deputy of the State Duma simultaneously. A deputy of the State Duma shall not be a deputy of any other representative bodies of state authority and/or bodies of local self-government.

3. The deputies of the State Duma shall work on a professional, permanent basis. The deputies of the State Duma may not hold any government office or take other paid jobs, excluding teaching, science, and other creative pursuits.

Article 98

1. The members of the Federation Council and deputies of the State Duma shall be inviolable during the entire term of their office. They may not be taken in custody, arrested and searched, excluding in cases when caught locus delicti, as well as examined, excluding in cases stipulated by federal legislation in order to ensure the security of other individuals.

2. Inviolability shall be lifted by the corresponding house of the Federal Assembly on the recommendation of the Prosecutor-General of the Russian Federation.

Article 99

1. The Federal Assembly shall be a permanently working body.

2. The State Duma shall be convened for its first session on the thirtieth day after its election. The President of the Russian Federation may convene a session of the State Duma at an earlier date.

3. The first session of the State Duma shall be opened by the eldest deputy.

4. The jurisdiction of the previous State Duma shall end the moment the new State Duma begins its work.

Article 100

1. The Federation Council and the State Duma shall have their sessions separately.

2. The sessions of the Federation Council and the State Duma shall be public. In the cases stipulated by their code of procedure, they may hold their sessions in camera.

3. The houses may hold joint sessions to hear the messages of the President of the Russian Federation, the messages of the Constitutional Court of the Russian Federation, and statements by the leaders of foreign states.

Article 101

1. The Federation Council shall elect its Chairman and Deputy Chairmen from among its members. The State Duma shall elect its Chairman and Deputy Chairmen from among its deputies.

2. The Chairman of the Federation Council and his deputies, and the Chairman of the State Duma and his deputies shall preside over the sessions of their respective houses and supervise the observance of their regulations.

3. The Federation Council and the State Duma shall form committees and commissions and hold hearings on the issues within their respective terms of reference.

4. Each of the houses shall adopt its code of procedure and decide matters pertaining to the regulation of its activities.

5. To supervise the execution of the federal budget the Federation Council and the State Duma shall form an Accounting Chamber. Its composition and procedure of work shall be determined by federal legislation.

Article 102

1. The Federation Council shall have power:

   (a) to approve changes of borders between members of the Russian Federation;

   (b) to approve the decree of the President of the Russian Federation on the introduction of martial law;

   (c) to approve the decree of the President of the Russian Federation on the introduction of the state of emergency;

   (d) to decide the possibility of using the Armed Forces of the Russian Federation beyond its territory;

   (e) to call the elections of the President of the Russian Federation;

   (f) to remove the President of the Russian Federation from office by impeachment;

(g) to appoint the judges of the Constitutional Court of the Russian Federation, the Supreme Court of the Russian Federation and the Supreme Court of Arbitration of the Russian Federation;

(h) to appoint and remove from office the Prosecutor-General of the Russian Federation;

(i) to appoint the Deputy Chairman of the Accounting Chamber and half of its auditors and to remove them from office.

2. The Federation Council shall adopt resolutions on the matters that are within its jurisdiction in accordance with the Constitution of the Russian Federation.

3. The resolutions of the Federation Council shall be adopted by majority vote of the total number of its members, unless a different procedure is stipulated by the Constitution of the Russian Federation.

Article 103

1. The State Duma shall have the power:

(a) to approve the nominee of the President of the Russian Federation to the office of the Chairman of the Government of the Russian Federation;

(b) to decide questions pertaining to the vote of confidence with regard to the Government of the Russian Federation;

(c) to appoint the Chairman of the Central Bank of the Russian Federation and to remove him from office;

(d) to appoint the Chairman of the Accounting Chamber and half of its auditors and to remove them from office;

(e) to appoint an Officer for Human Rights, who will act in accordance with a federal constitutional law, and to remove him from office;

(f) to declare amnesty;

(g) to lodge accusations against the President of the Russian Federation for the purpose of removing him from office by impeachment.

2. The State Duma shall adopt resolutions on the matters that are within its jurisdiction, in accordance with the Constitution of the Russian Federation.

3. The resolutions of the State Duma shall be adopted by majority vote of the total number of its deputies, unless any other procedure is stipulated by the Constitution of the Russian Federation.

Article 104

1. The President of the Russian Federation, the Federation Council, members of the Federation Council, deputies of the State Duma, the

Government of the Russian Federation, and the legislative (representative) bodies of the members of the Russian Federation shall have the right to initiate legislation. The Constitutional Court of the Russian Federation, the Supreme Court of the Russian Federation, and the Supreme Court of Arbitration of the Russian Federation shall be entitled to initiate legislation on the matters within their respective terms of reference.

2. Bills shall be submitted to the State Duma.

3. Bills on the imposition or elimination of taxes, tax exemption, the issue of state loans and changes in the financial obligations of the state and other bills pertaining to the expenditures that are covered out of the federal budget may be submitted provided there is a consent of the Government of the Russian Federation.

Article 105

1. The federal laws shall be adopted by the State Duma.

2. The federal laws shall be adopted by majority vote of the total number of deputies to the State Duma, unless a different procedure is stipulated by the Constitution of the Russian Federation.

3. The federal laws adopted by the State Duma shall be submitted for consideration by the Federation Council within a period of five days.

4. A federal law shall be considered adopted by the Federation Council if more than half of the general number of its deputies have voted for it or if it has not been considered by the Federation Council within fourteen days of its submission. If the Federation Council rejects a federal law, the two houses may set up a reconciliatory commission to settle the dispute. After that, the federal law shall be due for repeat consideration by the State Duma.

5. In case of the disagreement of the State Duma with the decision of the Federation Council, a federal law shall be considered adopted if in the repeat voting at least two-thirds of the total number of the State Duma deputies have voted for it.

Article 106

Due for the mandatory consideration by the Federation Council shall be the federal laws adopted by the State Duma on the following matters:

(a) the federal budget;

(b) federal taxes and levies;

(c) financial, currency, credit and customs control and the issue of money;

(d) ratification and denunciation of the international treaties of the Russian Federation;

(e) the status and protection of the state border of the Russian Federation;

(f) war and peace.

Article 107

1. The federal law shall be forwarded to the President of the Russian Federation within five days of its adoption for signing and making public.

2. The President of the Russian Federation shall sign the federal law within fourteen days and make it public.

3. If the President of the Russian Federation rejects a federal law within fourteen days of its submission, the State Duma and Federation Council shall subject it to repeat consideration in accordance with the procedure stipulated by the Constitution of the Russian Federation. If after a repeat consideration the federal law is approved in its previous edition by majority vote of at least two-thirds of the total number of the Federation Council members and State Duma deputies, it should be signed by the President of the Russian Federation within seven days and made public.

Article 108

1. Federal constitutional laws shall be adopted on the matters stipulated by the Constitution of the Russian Federation.

2. The federal constitutional law shall be considered adopted if it has been approved by at least threequarters of the total number of the Federation Council members and by at least two-thirds of the total number of State Duma deputies. The adopted federal constitutional law shall be forwarded to the President of the Russian Federation for signing and publicizing within fourteen days of adoption.

Article 109

1. The State Duma may be dissolved by the President of the Russian Federation in the instances provided by Articles 111 and 117 of the Constitution of the Russian Federation.

2. In the event of the dissolution of the State Duma, the President of the Russian Federation shall set the date of elections. The newly elected State Duma should be convened no later than four months after the dissolution.

3. The State Duma may not be dissolved for the reasons laid down in Article 117 of the Constitution of the Russian Federation within the first twelve months of its election.

4. The State Duma may not be dissolved from the moment when it lodges charges against the President of the Russian Federation until the adoption of a corresponding decision by the Federation Council.

5. The State Duma may not be dissolved during a time when martial law or the state of emergency is in effect throughout the entire territory of the Russian Federation, and during a period of six months before the office of the President of the Russian Federation expires.

Chapter 6. The Government of the Russian Federation

Article 110

1. The executive power of the Russian Federation shall be vested in the Government of the Russian Federation.

2. The Government of the Russian Federation shall be composed of the Chairman of the Government of the Russian Federation, Deputy Chairmen of the Government of the Russian Federation, and federal ministers.

Article 111

1. The Chairman of the Government of the Russian Federation shall be appointed by the President of the Russian Federation with the consent of the State Duma.

2. The nomination concerning the candidate for the office of Chairman of the Government of the Russian Federation shall be submitted by the newly elected President of the Russian Federation within two weeks of his entering into office or after the resignation of the Government of the Russian Federation, or within a week of the rejection of a candidate by the State Duma.

3. The State Duma shall consider the candidate for the office of Chairman of the Government of the Russian Federation proposed by the President of the Russian Federation within a week of the submission of the nomination of the candidate.

4. After the State Duma rejects three candidates to the office of Chairman of the Government of the Russian Federation, the President of the Russian Federation shall appoint the Chairman of the Government of the Russian Federation, dissolve the State Duma, and call new elections.

Article 112

1. The Chairman of the Government of the Russian Federation shall submit to the President of the Russian Federation his proposals on the structure of the federal bodies of the executive power not later than one week after his appointment.
2. The Chairman of the Government of the Russian Federation shall propose to the President of the Russian Federation his candidates to the offices of Deputy Chairmen of the Government of the Russian Federation and federal ministers.

Article 113

The Chairman of the Government of the Russian Federation, in accordance with the Constitution of the Russian Federation, federal legislation and decrees of the President of the Russian Federation, shall determine guidelines for the activity of the Government of the Russian Federation and organize its work.

Article 114

1. The Government of the Russian Federation shall have power:
    (a) to prepare and submit to the State Duma the federal budget and ensure its execution; submit to the State Duma a report on the implementation of the federal budget;
    (b) to ensure the pursuit in the Russian Federation of a uniform financial, credit, and monetary policy;
    (c) to ensure the pursuit in the Russian Federation of a uniform state policy in the fields of culture, science, education, health protection, social security, and ecology;
    (d) to manage federal property;
    (e) to carry out measures aimed to ensure the defense and state security of the country and the pursuit of the foreign policy of the Russian Federation;

(f) to carry out measures aimed to ensure legality, protect human rights, personal freedoms and property, maintain public order, and combat crime;

(g) to exercise other powers stipulated by the Constitution of the Russian Federation, federal laws, and decrees of the President of the Russian Federation.

2. Regulations for the activity of the Government of the Russian Federation shall be determined by a federal constitutional law.

Article 115

1. On the basis and in pursuit of the Constitution of the Russian Federation, federal laws, and normative decrees of the President of the Russian Federation, the government of the Russian Federation shall adopt resolutions and directives and ensure their implementation.

2. The resolutions and directives of the Government of the Russian Federation shall be binding for execution in the Russian Federation.

3. The resolutions and directives of the Government of the Russian Federation may be denounced by the President of the Russian Federation if they contradict the Constitution of the Russian Federation, federal laws and decrees of the President of the Russian Federation.

Article 116

The Government of the Russian Federation shall submit a letter of resignation to the newly elected President of the Russian Federation.

Article 117

1. The Government of the Russian Federation shall be entitled to give the offer of resignation, which is either accepted or rejected by the President of the Russian Federation.

2. The President of the Russian Federation may adopt a decision on the resignation of the government of the Russian Federation.

3. The State Duma may give the Government of the Russian Federation a vote of no confidence. The resolution on the vote of no confidence to the Government of the Russian Federation shall be adopted by majority vote of the total number of the State Duma deputies. After the State Duma gives the Government of the Russian Federation a vote of no confidence, the President of the Russian Federation may announce the resignation of the Government of the Russian Feder-

ation or reject the decision of the State Duma. If within the next three months the State Duma again gives the Government a vote of no confidence, the President of the Russian Federation shall announce the resignation of the Government of the Russian Federation or dissolve the State Duma.

4. The Chairman of the Government of the Russian Federation may ask the State Duma to put the question of trust in the Government of the Russian Federation to a vote. If the State Duma gives a vote of no confidence, the President, within seven days, shall adopt a decision on the resignation of the Government of the Russian Federation or the dissolution of the State Duma and the holding of new elections.

5. In the event of the termination of its office or resignation, the Government of the Russian Federation, on instructions from the President of the Russian Federation, shall continue to work until a new Government of the Russian Federation is formed.

Chapter 7. Judicial power

Article 118

1. Justice in the Russian Federation shall be administered by the courts of law only.

2. Judicial power shall be effected by means of constitutional, civil, administrative, and criminal judicial proceedings.

3. The judicial system of the Russian Federation shall be established by the Constitution of the Russian Federation and federal constitutional law. The creation of emergency courts shall be prohibited.

Article 119

Citizens of the Russian Federation who have reached the age of twenty-five, have a higher legal education, and have a record of work in the legal profession of no less than five years, may become judges. Federal law may set additional requirements for the judges of the Russian Federation courts.

Article 120

1. Judges shall be independent and subject only to the Constitution of the Russian Federation and federal law.

2. Should a court discover in considering a case that a decision taken by a state or some other governmental body contravenes a law, it shall accept a decision which is in accordance with the law.

Article 121

1. Judges shall be irremovable.
2. The powers of a judge may be discontinued or suspended only in accordance with the procedure and on the grounds established by federal law.

Article 122

1. Judges shall be inviolable.
2. No judge shall be prosecuted otherwise than in accordance with the procedure established by federal law.

Article 123

1. Proceedings in all courts shall be open. Hearings in camera shall only be allowed in cases provided for by federal law.
2. No criminal charge shall be considered in a court in the absence of the defendant, except for the cases provided for by federal law.
3. Judicial proceedings shall be conducted on the basis of adversary procedure and equality of the parties.
4. Judicial proceedings shall be conducted with the participation of a jury in cases provided for by federal law.

Article 124

Courts shall be financed out of the federal budget only, and in such a way that the courts shall be able to administer justice fully and independently in accordance with federal law.

Article 125

1. The Constitutional Court of the Russian Federation shall be comprised of nineteen judges.
2. At the request of the President of the Russian Federation, the Federation Council, the State Duma, one-fifth of the members of the Feder-

ation Council or deputies of the State Duma, the Government of the Russian Federation, the Supreme Court of the Russian Federation, the Supreme Arbitration Court of the Russian Federation, and the bodies of legislative and executive power of the members of the Russian Federation, the Constitutional Court of the Russian Federation shall decide cases about the compliance of the following enactments and deeds with the Constitution of the Russian Federation:

(a) federal laws and enactments of the President of the Russian Federation, the Federation Council, the State Duma, and the Government of the Russian Federation;

(b) constitutions of the republics, statutes, and also laws and other enactments of the members of the Russian Federation, issued on questions within the jurisdiction of the bodies of state authority of the Russian Federation and joint jurisdiction of the bodies of state authority of the Russian Federation and bodies of state authority of the members of the Russian Federation;

(c) treaties between the bodies of state authority of the Russian Federation and bodies of state authority of the members of the Russian Federation and treaties between the bodies of state authority of the members of the Russian Federation;

(d) international treaties of the Russian Federation that have not come into force.

3. The Constitutional Court of the Russian Federation shall settle disputes about competence:

(a) between the federal bodies of state authority;

(b) between the bodies of state authority of the Russian Federation and bodies of state authority of the members of the Russian Federation;

(c) between the highest bodies of state authority of the members of the Russian Federation.

4. In response to complaints about a violation of the constitutional rights and freedoms of citizens and at the request of the courts, the Constitutional Court of the Russian Federation shall verify the constitutionality of a law that has been used or should be used in a specific case, in accordance with the procedure established by federal law.

5. The Constitutional Court of the Russian Federation shall interpret the Constitution of the Russian Federation at the request of the President of the Russian Federation, the Federation Council, the State Duma, the Government of the Russian Federation, and the bodies of legislative power of the members of the Russian Federation.

6. Enactments or their individual provisions that have been judged unconstitutional shall be invalid; international treaties of the Russian Federation that contravene the Constitution of the Russian Federation shall not be brought into force and shall not be used.

7. At the request of the Federation Council, the Constitutional Court of the Russian Federation shall pronounce its judgment about the observance of the established procedure in bringing against the President of the Russian Federation the accusation of high treason or other grave crimes.

Article 126

The Supreme Court of the Russian Federation shall be the highest judicial authority on civil, criminal, administrative and other cases within the jurisdiction of the common pleas courts, shall effect the judicial oversight of their activities in accordance with the procedure established by federal law, and shall give explanations on questions pertaining to legal practice.

Article 127

The Supreme Arbitration Court of the Russian Federation shall be the highest judicial authority in settling economic and other disputes within the jurisdiction of the courts of arbitration, shall oversee the latter's activities in accordance with the procedure established by federal law, and shall give explanations on questions pertaining to legal practice.

Article 128

1. The judges of the Constitutional Court of the Russian Federation, the Supreme Court of the Russian Federation, and the Supreme Arbitration Court of the Russian Federation shall be appointed by the Federation Council upon nomination by the President of the Russian Federation.

2. Judges of the other federal courts shall be appointed by the President of the Russian Federation in accordance with the procedure established by federal law.

3. The powers and the procedure for the creation and activity of the Constitutional Court of the Russian Federation, the Supreme Court of the Russian Federation, the Supreme Arbitration Court of the Russian

Federation, and other federal courts, shall be established by federal constitutional law.

Article 129

1. The Prosecutor's Office of the Russian Federation shall constitute a single centralized system, in which the lower-level prosecutors shall be accountable to the higher-level prosecutors and the Prosecutor-General of the Russian Federation.
2. The Prosecutor-General of the Russian Federation shall be appointed and dismissed by the Federation Council on the recommendation of the President of the Russian Federation.
3. The prosecutor of the members of the Russian Federation shall be appointed by the Prosecutor-General of the Russian Federation with the consent of its members.
4. Other prosecutors shall be appointed by the Prosecutor-General of the Russian Federation.
5. The power, organization of work, and the procedure regulating the activities of the Prosecutor's Office of the Russian Federation shall be established by federal law.

Chapter 8. Local self-government

Article 130

1. Local self-government within the Russian Federation shall guarantee the population the possibility of independently solving questions of local importance and owning, using, and managing municipal property.
2. Local self-government shall be effected by citizens through referendums, elections, and other means of direct exercise of their will, and through the elected and other bodies of local self-government.

Article 131

1. Local self-government shall be instituted in urban and rural settlements and in other territories with consideration for historical and other local traditions. The structure of the bodies of local self-government shall be determined by the population independently.
2. The borders of territories in which local self-government is instituted may be changed should the population of such territories so desire.

Article 132

1. The bodies of local self-government shall independently manage municipal property; prepare, approve, and execute the local budget; establish local taxes and levies; maintain public order; and decide other questions of local importance.
2. The bodies of local self-government may be vested by law with some state powers and shall receive the required material and financial means for the implementation of these powers. The state shall oversee the implementation of these powers.

Article 133

Local self-government within the Russian Federation shall be guaranteed by the right to legal protection, compensation for the additional expenses resulting from the decisions taken by the bodies of state authority, and a ban on restrictions of the rights of local self-government as established by the Constitution of the Russian Federation and other federal laws.

Chapter 9. Constitutional amendments and revision of the Constitution

Article 134

Proposals for amending and reviewing any provisions of the Constitution of the Russian Federation may be submitted by the President of the Russian Federation, the Federation Council, the State Duma, the Government of the Russian Federation, the legislative (representative) bodies of the members of the Russian Federation, and a group of at least one-fifth of the members of the Federation Council or deputies of the State Duma.

Article 135

1. No provision contained in Chapters 1, 2, and 9 of the Constitution of the Russian Federation shall be reviewed by the Federal Assembly.
2. Should a proposal for a review of the provision of Chapters 1, 2, and 9 of the Constitution of the Russian Federation receive the support of three-fifths of the total number of members of the Federation Council and deputies of the State Duma, a Constitutional Assembly shall be convened in accordance with the federal constitutional law.

3. The Constitutional Assembly shall either confirm the immutability of the Constitution of the Russian Federation or draft a new Constitution of the Russian Federation, which shall be considered passed if it receives two-thirds of the votes of all members of the Constitutional Assembly, or shall be put to nationwide vote. Should the draft of a new Constitution of the Russian Federation be put to nationwide vote, it shall be considered passed if more than half of the voters who have taken part in the vote have voted for it, provided that more than half of the eligible voters have taken part in the vote.

Article 136

Any amendments to Chapters 3 through 8 of the Constitution of the Russian Federation shall be passed in accordance with the procedure established for the adoption of a federal constitutional law and shall come into force after their approval by the legislative bodies of power of at least two-thirds of the members of the Russian Federation.

Article 137

1. Any change in Article 65 of the Constitution of the Russian Federation, establishing the make-up of the Russian Federation, shall be made on the basis of the federal constitutional law on the Admission to the Russian Federation and creation within it of a new member to the Russian Federation and on the change of the constitutional and legal status of a member of the Russian Federation.
2. Should the name of a republic, territory, region, federal-status city, autonomous region or autonomous area be changed, the new name of the member of the Russian Federation shall be included in Article 65 of the Constitution of the Russian Federation.

PART 2

Concluding and transnational provisions

1. The Constitution of the Russian Federation shall come into force on the day it is officially made public in accordance with the results of the nationwide vote.

December 12, 1993, the day of the nationwide vote, shall be considered the day of the adoption of the Constitution of the Russian Federation.

The Constitution (Fundamental Law) of the Russian Federation – Russia, passed on April 12, 1978, with all its subsequent amendments, shall become null and void simultaneously.

Should the provisions of the Federation Treaty – the Treaty on the Delimitation of Jurisdiction and Powers between the Federal Bodies of State Authority of the Russian Federation and the Bodies of State Authority of the Sovereign Republics within the Russian Federation, the Treaty on the Delimitation of Jurisdiction and Powers between the Federal Bodies of State Authority of the Russian Federation and the Bodies of State Authority of the Territories, Regions and the Cities of Moscow and St. Petersburg, the Treaty on the Delimitation of Jurisdiction and Powers between the Federal Bodies of State Authority of the Russian Federation and the Bodies of State Authority of the Autonomous Region and Autonomous Areas within the Russian Federation and other treaties between the federal bodies of state authority of the Russian Federation and the bodies of state authority of the members of the Russian Federation and treaties between the bodies of state authority of the members of the Russian Federation – contravene those of the Constitution of the Russian Federation, the provisions of the Constitution of the Russian Federation shall apply.

2. All laws and other legal acts enforced throughout the territory of the Russian Federation before this Constitution became effective shall remain valid as long as they do not contravene the Constitution of the Russian Federation.

3. The President of the Russian Federation, elected in accordance with the Constitution (Fundamental Law) of the Russian Federation – Russia, since the day on which this Constitution became effective, shall carry out his duties established by it until the expiration of the term for which he was elected.

4. The Council of Ministers – Government of the Russian Federation, as of the day on which this Constitution shall come into force, shall acquire the rights, duties and responsibility of the Government of the Russian Federation, and shall be named henceforth the Government of the Russian Federation.

5. The courts in the Russian Federation shall administer justice in accordance with their powers established by this Constitution. When this Constitution becomes effective, the judges of all courts of the Russian Federation shall retain their powers until the expiration of the

term for which they were elected. Vacancies shall be filled in accordance with the procedure established by this Constitution.

6. Until the enforcement of the federal law establishing the procedure for the court hearing of cases with the participation of a jury, the former procedure for hearing the corresponding cases in court shall be preserved.

Until the law of criminal procedure of the Russian Federation is brought into conformity with the provision of this Constitution, the former procedure for arresting, holding in custody and detaining persons suspected of having committed a crime shall be preserved.

7. The Federation Council of first convocation and the State Duma of first convocation shall be elected for a term of two years.

8. The Federation Council shall meet for its first session on the thirtieth day after its election. The first session of the Federation Council shall be opened by the President of the Russian Federation.

9. A deputy to the State Duma of first convocation may be concurrently a member of the Government of the Russian Federation. The members of the Government of the Russian Federation, who are concurrently deputies to the State Duma, shall not be covered by the provisions of this Constitution concerning the immunity of deputies in the sense of accountability for actions (or inaction) connected with the performance of their official duties.

Deputies to the Federation Council of first convocation shall carry out their duties on a part-time basis.

Notes

1 Pre-revolutionary Russian law

1 Quoted in John L. Stoddard, *Lectures*, vol. VI (Boston: Balch Brothers, 1898), p. 227.
2 Darrell P. Hammer, "The Character of the *Russkaya Pravda*," *Slavic Review*, 31:2 (June 1972), 291–295.
3 Cited in Harold J. Berman, *Justice in the USSR* (Cambridge: Harvard University Press, 1966), p. 191.
4 Cited in Harold J. Berman, *Law and Revolution: The Formation of the Western Legal Tradition* (Cambridge: Harvard University Press, 1983), p. 297.
5 Richard Pipes, *Russia under the Old Regime* (Cambridge: Harvard University Press, 1974), pp. 50–51.
6 Cited in Berman, *Justice in the USSR*, p. 196.
7 B. H. Summer, *Peter the Great and the Emergence of Russia* (New York: Collier, 1962).
8 Richard S. Wortman, *The Development of a Russian Legal Consciousness* (Chicago: University of Chicago Press, 1976), p. 15.
9 Cited in Berman, *Justice in the USSR*, p. 211.
10 Ibid., p. 22.
11 Darrell P. Hammer, "Russia and the Roman Law," *The American Slavic and East European Review*, 26:1 (1957), 7.
12 Berman, *Justice in the USSR*, p. 210.
13 The figures are those of Vasily Ivanovich Senaevsky, cited in Nicholas V. Riasanovsky, *A History of Russia*, 2nd ed. (New York: Oxford University Press, 1969), p. 410.
14 Jerome Blum, *Lord and Peasant in Russia* (Princeton: Princeton University Press, 1961), p. 420. This figure is based on Blum's estimate of the percentage of male serfs among the total male population. At the time of emancipation, the total peasant population in Russia is estimated to constitute 80 to 90 percent of the population.
15 Wortman, *Russian Legal Consciousness*, p. 198.
16 Cited in ibid., p. 216.
17 Ibid., p. 254.
18 Ibid., p. 281.
19 Based on figures cited in Pipes, *Russia under the Old Regime*, p. 310.
20 V. O. Kliuchevsky, *A Course of Russian History*, trans. C. J. Hogarth (London: J. M. Dent, 1911).
21 Ibid., p. 257.
22 Cited in Pipes, *Russia under the Old Regime*, p. 290.

2 The Bolshevik experience

1 Andrei Ya. Vyshinsky, *Sudoustroistvo v SSSR*, 2nd ed. (Moscow: Yuridicheskaya literatura, 1935), p. 32.

2 Karl Marx and Friedrich Engels, *Selected Works*, vol. III (Moscow: Politizdat, 1966), pp. 492–493.

3 Ibid.

4 In 1905 public disaffection with the tsarist regime culminated in mass strikes and protests. On October 30, 1905 Count Witte issued a manifesto that recognized civil liberties, legalized the formation of political parties and created a duma or Constituent Assembly. The Revolution of 1905 was a tentative step toward transforming the tsarist regime into a constitutional monarchy. In practice, however, these reforms did not significantly impinge on the powers of the tsar.

5 John Hazard, *Settling Disputes in Soviet Society* (New York: Columbia University Press, 1960), p. vi.

6 Cited in Peter Juviler, *Revolutionary Law and Order* (New York: Free Press, 1976), pp. 18–19.

7 V. I. Lenin, "O dvoinom podchinenii i zakonnosti," reprinted in *Sovetskaya prokuratura: sbornik vazhneishikh documentov* (Moscow: Yuridicheskaya literatura, 1972), pp. 100–102.

8 Ibid.

9 V. I. Lenin, *Polnoe sobranie sochinenii*, 4th ed., vol. XXXVI (Moscow: Politizdat, 1958–1965), p. 195.

10 See Darrell P. Hammer, "Bureaucracy and the Rule of Law in Soviet Society," in Clifford M. Foust and Warren Lerner, eds., *The Soviet World in Flux: Six Essays* (Atlanta: Southern Regional Education Board, 1966), pp. 87–110.

11 John N. Hazard, "Foreword," in Piers Beirne and Robert Sharlet, eds., *Pashukanis: Selected Writings on Marxism and Law* (London: Academic Press, 1980), pp. xi–xii.

12 The New Economic Policy (NEP) was a program introduced by Lenin in 1921 in order to consolidate the gains of the revolution and win support of the peasants. Under NEP the peasants were allowed to farm as they wished and sell their produce on a relatively free market. Small-scale private enterprise was legalized, while large-scale industries, banking, and foreign trade remained in the hands of the state. The early NEP years were also characterized by innovation and experimentation in legal administration, family policies, education, and the arts. NEP ended under Stalin with the introduction of the First Five-Year Plan in 1928.

13 Cited in Beirne and Sharlet, *Pashukanis*, p. 13.

14 Ibid., p. 19.

15 Quoted in E. B. Pashukanis, "The Situation on the Legal Theory Front," translated in John N. Hazard, ed., *Soviet Legal Philosophy* (Cambridge, MA: Harvard University Press, 1951), pp. 250, 253.

16 Joseph Stalin, cited in Beirne and Sharlet, *Pashukanis*, p. 26.

17 Joseph Stalin, "Political Report of the Central Committee to the XVIth Congress, 1930)," in John N. Hazard, ed., *Soviet Legal Philosophy* (Cambridge, MA: Harvard University Press, 1951), p. 234.

18 Beirne and Sharlet, *Pashukanis*, p. 293.

19 Ibid., p. 278.
20 See Robert Sharlet, "Stalinism and Soviet Legal Culture," in Robert C. Tucker, ed., *Stalinism* (New York: W. W. Norton, 1977), pp. 172–173.
21 Ibid., p. 169.
22 Ernst Frankel, *The Dual State* (London: E. A. Shils, 1941).
23 A. F. Kleinman, *Grazhdanskii protsess*, 4th ed. (Moscow: Yuridicheskaya literatura, 1938) and M. S. Strogovich, *Ugolovny protsess*, 4th ed. (Moscow: Yuridicheskaya literatura, 1938).
24 A. Ya. Vyshinsky, *Sudoustroistvo v. SSSR (Moscow: 1936)* translated in Zigurds Zile, *Ideas and Forces in Soviet Legal History* (Oxford: Oxford University Press, 1992), pp. 266–268.
25 Andrei Vyshinsky, "Raise Higher the Banner of Socialist Legality," *Sotsialisticheskaya zakonnost'*, 11 (1936).
26 Naum Jasny, "Labor and Output in Soviet Concentration Camps," *Journal of Political Economy*, 59 (October 1951), 405.
27 The Russian Soviet Federated Socialist Republics (RSFSR) or Russian Republic was the largest of the fifteen union-republics that made up the former USSR.
28 See M. Lewin, *Russian Peasants and Soviet Power* (London: 1968), pp. 504–505.
29 Ronald Hingley, *The Russian Secret Police* (London: Hutchinson, 1970), p. 161.
30 Ibid., pp. 166–167.
31 *Argumenty i fakty*, February 4, 1989. Robert Conquest suggest that 20 million died during the Stalin era. See Robert Conquest, *The Great Terror* (London: Macmillan, 1969), p. 533. More recent estimates by Conquest place the death toll due to collectivization and famine at 14.5 million; see Robert Conquest, *The Harvest of Sorrow* (New York: Oxford University Press, 1986), p. 306. These estimates, along with his previous figure of 13 million killed during the period 1936–1950, indicate that as many as 27.5 million people may have perished as a result of Stalin's policies.
32 See the Constitution of the USSR (1977), Articles 2 and 108.
33 See "Zakon SSSR o vseobshei voinskoi obyazannosti," enacted at the third session of the USSR Supreme Soviet, October 12, 1967; "Zakon SSSR ob okhrane i ispol'zovanii pamyatnikov istorii i kul'tury," enacted by the USSR Supreme Soviet, October 29, 1976; and "Polozheniie o prokurorskom nadzore v SSSR," enacted by the Presidium of the USSR Supreme Soviet, May 24, 1955.
34 Constitution of the USSR (1977), Article 6.
35 W. E. Butler, "Necessary Defense, Judge-made Law, and Soviet Man," in Butler, O. Maggs, and O. Quigley, *Law After Revolution* (1988), pp. 99–130.
36 Today both the Russian Federation Supreme Court and the Higher Commercial Court also issue instructions and interpretations that influence lower courts' determinations. For a discussion of recent developments in using judicial precedent as a source of law, see John N. Hazard, "Is Russian Case Law Becoming Significant as a Source of Law?" *The Parker School*

Journal of East European Law, 1:1 (1994), 23–46 and John N. Hazard, "Russian Judicial Precedent Revisited," *The Parker School Journal of East European Law*, 1:4 (1994), 471–477.

37 Cited in W. E. Butler, *Soviet Law*, 2nd ed. (London: Butterworth, 1988), p. 102. Another source indicates that people's courts handle 98 percent of all criminal cases and 99 percent of all civil cases. "Nardom izbrannye," *Byulleten' Verkhovnogo suda SSSR*, 1 (1970), 3.

38 M. A. Kopylovskaya, *Nauchno-prakticheskii kommentarii k osnovam zakonodatel'stva o sudoustroistve soyuznikh avtonomnikh respublik* (Moscow: Yuridicheskaya literatura, 1961), p. 67.

39 T. H. Rigby, *Communist Party Membership in the USSR, 1917–1967* (Princeton: Princeton University Press, 1968), p. 425.

40 Protests also occurred in the case of convictions, where the prosecutor or the president of the people's courts felt that the sentence was inappropriate or that the court's ruling was contrary to the evidence. It was also possible for a person acquitted in a criminal case to appeal the court's decision, when for example, the person was acquitted for the wrong reason, leaving him vulnerable to civil liability.

41 In fact, there was little turnover on the court, especially during the post-Stalin period.

42 Program of the CPSU, *Pravda*, March 7, 1986, pp. 3–10.

43 "Partiinye organizatsii sudov i ukreplenie sotsialisticheskoi zakonnosti," *Sovetskaya Yustitsiya*, 6 (1971), 3.

44 M. S. Strogovich, ed., *Pravovye garantii zakonnosti v SSSR* (Moscow: Yuridicheskaya literatura, 1962), p. 179.

45 Geroge Feifer, *Justice in Moscow* (New York: Simon and Schuster, 1964), pp. 248–249.

46 Ibid.

47 Ibid.

48 See Jerry Hough, *The Soviet Prefects* (Cambridge: Harvard University Press, 1969).

49 *New York Times*, December 28, 1975, p. 7.

50 *Rules of the Communist Party of the Soviet Union*, approved by the 27th Congress of the CPSU, March 1, 1986 (Moscow: Novosti Press, 1986), p. 10.

51 See Butler, *Soviet Law*, p. 170.

52 Cited in David Shipler, *Russia: Broken Idols, Solemn Dreams* (London: Macdonald, 1983), p. 237.

53 *Molodoi kommunist*, 9 (September 1975), 102.

54 See comments by S. Gusev, first vice-chairman of the USSR Supreme Courts, *Izvestiya*, April 19, 1984, p. 2.

55 These figures were compiled by Il'ya Zemtsov in "Problems of the Soviet Youth," *Radio Liberty Research Paper*, 125 (March 1975), 10.

56 *Sotsiologicheskie issledovanniya*, 3 (1977).

57 Ibid.

58 Criminal Code of the RSFSR, Articles 89 and 144.

59 Ibid., Articles 99 and 150.

60 Ibid., Article 154. This definition of speculation was changed by a law of October 31, 1990 to specify only goods subject to state pricing. The new law defined speculation as "the buying up of goods for which state retail prices have been established ... and their resale for the purposes of profit." "Law of the USSR on Increased Liability for Speculation and Illegal Trade Activity and for Abuses in Trade," *Pravda*, November 4, 1990, pp. 1–2.

61 Twenty years for a commuted death penalty.

62 For an analysis of the death penalty in the former USSR, see Ger P. van den Berg, "The Soviet Union and the Death Penalty," *Soviet Studies*, 35:2 (April 1983), 154–174.

63 *Sel'skaya zhizn'*, March 24, 1985, p. 4.

64 M. S. Studenikina, *Zakonodatel'stvo ob administrativnoi otvestvennosti kodifikatsiya* (Candidate dissertation, All-Union Scientific Research Institute on Soviet Legislation, Moscow, 1968), pp. 250–251.

65 Cited in Walter Connor, *Deviance in Soviet Society* (New York: Columbia University Press, 1972).

66 Harold J. Berman, *Justice in the USSR* (Cambridge: Harvard University press, 1966), pp. 283–284.

67 D. I. Kursky, cited in Eugene Kamenka, "The Soviet View of Law," in Richard Cornell, eds., *The Soviet Political System* (Englewood Cliffs, NJ: Prentice-Hall, 1970), p. 315.

68 See *RSFSR Criminal Code* (1960), Article 20.

69 Cited in Leon Lipson, "Hosts and Pests: The Fight against Parasites," *Problems of Communism*, 9 (March–April 1965), 78–79.

70 Ibid., p. 80.

71 Ibid., pp. 78–79.

3 The history of legal reform

1 Anatoly Sobchak, *For a New Russia* (New York: Free Press, 1992), p. 87.

2 The name of the security police was changed from NKVD to the People's Commissariat of State Security (NKGB) in 1941 and again in 1946 when people's commissariats became ministries, thus MGB. The Committee of State Security (KGB) was formed in March 1954.

3 For example, see A. A. Piontkovsky, "Osnovye voprosy proekta ugolovnogo kodeksa SSSR," *Sotsialisticheskaya zakonnost'*, 1 (1954), 25–38; and V. M. Chikhvadze, "Nekotorye voprosy sovetskogo ugolognogo prava v svyazi s razrabotkoe proekta Ugolovnogo Kodeksa SSSR," *Sovetskoe gosudarstvo i pravo*, 4 (1953), 59–71.

4 For example, see P. S. Romashkin, "Osnovnye problemy kodifikatsii sovetskogo ugolognogo zakonodatelstva," *Sovetskoe gosudarstvo i pravo*, 5 (1957), 73–74.

5 For an interesting analysis of the presumption of innocence in Soviet law, see Harold J. Berman and James W. Spindler, *Soviet Criminal Law and Procedure: The RSFSR Codes*, 2nd ed. (Cambridge: Harvard University Press, 1972), p. 62.

6 V. I. Terebilov, *Pravda*, December 5, 1987, p. 3.
7 "Ukrepleniye sotsialisticheskoi zakonnosti i yuridicheskaya nauka," *Kommunist*, 11 (November 1956), p. 20.
8 S. Kechekian, *Pravootnosheniya v sotsialisticheskoi obshchestve* (Moscow: Yuridicheskaya literatura, 1958), p. 68.
9 For example, see *Izvestiya*, December 19, 1961, p. 2.
10 For example, see A. E. Lunev, "Voprosy administrativnogo protessa," *Pravovedeniye*, 2 (1962), 44.
11 Among the advocates for this position were M. I. Piskotin, P. S. Dagel', V. A. Kuklin, A. I. Nesterov, P. F. Eliseikin, I. F. Bartykov, D. M. Chechot, and V. D. Sorokin. For example, see P. F. Eliseikin, "Sudebnyi nadzor za deyatel'nostyu administrativnykh organov," *Problemy gosudarstva i prava na sovremennom etape* (Vladivostok: Dal'nevostochny universitet, 1963), pp. 35–36.
12 See Gordon B. Smith, *The Soviet Procuracy and the Supervision of Administration* (Alphen aan den Rijn, The Netherlands: Sijthoff & Nordhoff, 1978), pp. 49–50.
13 Address of Nikita Khrushchev, 21st Congress of the Communist Party of the Soviet Union, January 27, 1959, *Pravda*, January 28, 1959, p. 1.
14 N. S. Khrushchev, "Nasha rabota po preduprezhdenyu prestuplenii," *Sovetskaya Yustitsiya*, 22 (1963), 10–11.
15 Order No. 3 of a Plenary Session of the Soviet Supreme Court, June 19, 1959; Order No. 43 of the procurator-general, July 20, 1959.
16 Amendment to Article 51 the RSFSR Criminal Code of July 3, 1961.
17 V. Kazin, "Sud tovarishchei," *Pravda*, November 13, 1963, p. 4.
18 Ioffe and Shargorodsky, "Oznachenii obshchikh opredelenii v issledovanii voprosov prava i sotsialisticheskoi zakonnosti," *Sovetskoe gosudarstvo i pravo*, 5 (1963), 54.
19 G. Z. Anashkin, "Rol' pravosoznaniya i obshchestvennogo mneniya pri naznachenii nakazaniya," *Sovetskoe gosudarstvo i pravo* 1 (1967), 42–48.
20 R. Rakhunov, "Zakonnost' i pravosudiye," *Pravda*, September 22, 1965, p. 3.
21 *Izvestiya*, September 11, 1968, p. 3.
22 *Izvestiya*, August 1, 1970, p. 5.
23 For example, in 1977 a new RSFSR Statute on Comrades' Courts allowed for appeals of comrades' courts decisions and required the tribunals to provide justifications for their actions. See W. E. Butler, "Comradely Justice Revised," *Review of Socialist Law*, 3 (1977), 325–343.
24 R. A. Rudenko, "Leninskie idei sotsialisticheskoi zakonnosti, printsipy organizatsii i deyatel'nosti sovetskoi prokuratury," in *Sovetskaya prokuratura* (Moscow: Yuridicheskaya literatura, 1977), pp. 25–26.
25 Despite the fact that the 1977 Constitution followed the USSR's ratification of the UN Covenants on Human Right of 1966 and 1973 and the 1975 Helsinki Final Act.
26 USSR Constitution, Article 50.
27 USSR Constitution, Article 59.

28 USSR Constitution, Article 60.

29 USSR Constitution, Article 61.

30 Statute on the Procuracy of the USSR (1979), Article 3.

31 The Sinyavsky and Daniel case raised several important legal issues, such as the necessity of direct intent and application of Article 70 in artistic works. See Berman and Spindler, *Soviet Criminal Law*, pp. 81–82.

32 Cited in Joshua Rubenstein, "Dissent," in James Cracraft, ed., *The Soviet Union Today* (Chicago: Bulletin of the Atomic Scientists, 1983), p. 66.

33 It is unclear what the legal authority was for Sakharov's house arrest.

34 Ibid.

35 *Chronicle of Current Events*, 27, October 15, 1972, pp. 337–338.

36 See ibid., 34 (1974), pp. 92–93.

37 See George Ginsburgs, "The New Soviet Citizenship Law and the Universal Declaration of Human Rights," in *A Chronicle of Human Rights in the USSR*, 33 (1979), 47–54.

38 Cited in Joshua Rubenstein, "Dissent," in James Cracraft, ed., *The Soviet Union Today* (Chicago: Bulletin of the Atomic Scientists, 1983), p. 70.

39 Some 150 political prisoners were amnestied in February 1987 under an extraordinary decree of the Presidium of the USSR Supreme Soviet. The majority of those released had been convicted under Article 70 of the RSFSR Criminal Code. *New York Times*, February 18, 1987, pp. A1, A12.

40 *Vedomosti Verkhovnovo Soveta SSSR*, 3, item 58 (January 18, 1985), 91–93.

41 See Peter H. Juviler, "Diversion from Criminal to Administrative Justice: Soviet Law, Practice, and Conflicts of Policy," in F. J. M. Feldbrugge and William B. Simons, eds., *Perspectives on Soviet Law in the 1980s* (The Hague: Martinus Nijhoff, 1982), pp. 153–170.

42 See Konstantin Simis, *USSR, The Corrupt Society* (New York: Simon and Schuster, 1982).

43 For a detailed account of official corruption, see William Clark, *Crime and Punishment in Soviet Officialdom: Combatting Corruption in the Political Elite, 1965–1990* (Armonk, NY: M. E. Sharpe, 1993).

44 *Izvestiya*, November 3, 1987, p. 1.

45 *Pravda*, December 31, 1988, p. 1.

46 *Pravda*, March 7, 1986, p. 1.

47 John Quigley, "Law Reform in the Soviet Courts," *Columbia Journal of Transnational Law*, 28:1 (1990), 66.

48 George P. Fletcher, "In Gorbachev's Courts," *New York Review of Books*, 36:8 (May 18, 1989), 13.

49 *Volksstimme*, March 5, 1986, p. 12.

50 *Pravda*, January 18, 1986, p. 1.

51 *Izvestiya*, January 22, 1986, p. 1.

52 Ibid.

53 *Literaturnaya gazeta*, 19 (1986), 12.

54 Ibid.

55 *Sovetskaya Belorussiya*, June 3, 1987; *Sovetskaya Belorussiya*, October 5, 1986, p. 3; and *Sovetskaya Rossiya*, June 14, 1987.

56 See *Literaturnaya gazeta*, 52 (1986), 13.

57 Cited in *Pravda*, June 14, 1986, p. 1.

58 Ibid.; *Pravda*, January 28, 1987, p. 1; and Dmitri Likhanov, "Klan: Ocherk-preduprezhdeniye," *Strana i mir*, 4:40 (July–August 1987), 45–53.

59 Likhanov, "Klan."

60 *Pravda*, February 8, 1987, pp. 1–2.

61 *Pravda*, September 12, 1985, p. 1.

62 *Vedomosti Verkhovnogo Soveta SSSR*, 22 (1986), 367–368.

63 Ibid.; and *Pravda*, May 28, 1986, p. 2.

64 Ibid.

65 *Pravda*, September 25, 1987, p. 1.

66 See Karl-Eugen Waedekin, "The New Kolkhoz Statute: A Codification of Restructuring on the Farm," *Radio Liberty Research Bulletin*, 32:5 (January 28, 1988), 1–4.

67 M. Mozyr' and F. Rayznov, *Sel'skaya zhizn'*, January 14, 1988, p. 1.

68 *Izvestiya*, June 29, 1988, p. 1.

69 *XIX vsesoyuznaya konferentsiya kommunisticheskoi partii sovetskogo soyuza*, vol. II (Moscow: Politicheskaya literatura, 1988), p. 173.

70 Vladimir Kudryavtsev, "Toward a Socialist Rule-of-Law State," in A. G. Aganbegyan, ed., *Perestroika* (New York: Charles Scribner & Sons, 1988), pp. 109–125.

71 Deputies ran unopposed in slightly more than one-quarter of the races for the 2,250 seats in the Congress.

72 *Vedomosti Verkhovnogo Soveta SSSR*, 49, item 727, translated in "Comparative Text of the 1977 USSR Constitution with Draft and Final Amendments," *Review of Socialist Law*, 15:75 (1989).

73 Constitution of the USSR, Article 124, as amended by 1988 Constitutional Amendments.

74 Constitution of the USSR, Article 155.

75 *Law on Responsibility for Disrespect to a Court* made attempts to interfere in the work of the courts punishable by up to three years incarceration, in cases where the interference had "serious consequences." The law was reprinted in *Izvestiya*, November 16, 1989, p. 1.

76 *Law on the Status of Judges*, reprinted in *Izvestiya*, August 12, 1989, p. 1.

77 See *Pravda*, July 16, 1989, p. 2.

78 Initially, it was not referred to as jury, but a "collegium of people's assessors." See *1989 Fundamental Principles on Court Structure*, reprinted in *Izvestiya*, November 16, 1989, p. 1.

79 Eugene Huskey, "Between Citizen and State: The Soviet Bar under Gorbachev," *Columbia Journal of Transnational Law*, 28:1 (1990), 111.

80 Vladimir N. Kudryavtsev, "Towards a Socialist Rule-of-Law State," in Abel Aganbegyan, ed., *Perestroika 1989* (New York: Scribner, 1988), p. 117.

81 Account of Jane Henderson of a conversation with Professor Savitsky during a symposium on "Criminal Law Reform: Anglo-Soviet Perspectives," University College London, March 26–28, 1990.

82 For a discussion of leadership receptivity and reform, see Thane Gustafson, *Reform in Soviet Politics* (Cambridge: Cambridge University Press, 1981).

83 Interview with Aleksandr I. Bastrykin, director of the Institution for Training Procuratorial Investigators, Leningrad, June 11, 1991.

4 Forging a new constitution

1 Louis Fisher is Senior Researcher with the Congressional Research Service of the US Library of Congress. See Louis Fisher, "Social Influences on Constitutional Law," *Journal of Political Science*, 15:1&2 (Spring 1987), 7.

2 Related to the author by a friend who was at the White House in Moscow on October 4, 1993.

3 For an analysis of the 1977 Constitution and Brezhnev's motivations in enacting it, see Robert Sharlet, *The New Soviet Constitution of 1977: Analysis and Text* (Brunswick, OH: King's Court Communications, 1978) and Robert Sharlet, *Soviet Constitutional Crisis: From De-Stalinization to Distintegration* (Armonk, NY: M. E. Sharpe, 1992).

4 Constitution of the USSR (1977), Article 1.

5 Constitution of the USSR (1977), Article 58.

6 For an analysis of the 1987 USSR Law on Procedures for Appealing to the Courts Unlawful Actions by Officials that Infringe the Rights of Citizens, see Gordon B. Smith, "The Procuracy, Citizens' Rights and Legal Reform," *Columbia Journal of Transnational Law*, 28:1 (1990), 77–93.

7 Constitution of the USSR (1977), Article 39.

8 Ibid., Article 59.

9 Ibid., Article 50.

10 Ibid., Article 160.

11 "Demokratizatsiya i zakonodatel'stvo," *Sovetskaya Yustitsiya*, 18 (1988), 2–4.

12 Cited in David Remnick, *Lenin's Tomb: The Last Days of the Soviet Empire* (New York: Vintage, 1994), pp. 461–462.

13 Ibid., p. 466.

14 See Article 11 of the Agreement on the Creation of a Commonwealth of Independent States, *Rossiiskaya gazeta*, December 10, 1991, pp. 1–2. However, parliaments of the successor states of the USSR, including the Russian Federation, voted to continue to observe former USSR laws unless they conflicted with republic constitutions and laws.

15 Consultation with prosecutors in the Procuracy of the Russian Federation, Moscow, November 1993.

16 Anatoly Kostyukov in *Megapolis-Express*, April 22, 1992, p. 3.

17 Article 104 (as amended on October 27, 1989) and Article 121-1 of the RSFSR Constitution of 1978. For a discussion of these provisions, see F. J.

M. Feldbrugge, *Russian Law: The End of the Soviet System and the Role of Law* (Dordrecht, The Netherlands: Martinus Nijhoff, 1993), pp. 172–173 and 177.

18 *Moskovskiye novosti*, April 5, 1992, pp. 6–7.

19 At the time of the March 1990 elections to the Russian Federation Congress of People's Deputies, the CPSU was the only political party allowed to exist in the country, although alternative "movements" were rapidly springing up. Article 6 was amended after the Congress. Communist Party candidates captured 49.1 percent of the seats overall, and 88 percent of the seats from the ethnically designated autonomous republics. *Sovetskaya Rossiya*, March 28, 1990, p. 1.

20 Constitution of the RSFSR (1978), Article 121-1.

21 *Rossiiskaya gazeta*, July 30, 1992, pp. 1–2.

22 *Nezavisimaya gazeta*, March 18, 1992, p. 1.

23 *Izvestiya*, March 19, 1992, p. 2.

24 *Izvestiya*, July 30, 1992, p. 2.

25 The Constitutional Court of the Russian Federation ruled that for the results of the referendum to be binding, thus forcing early elections for either president or parliament, a majority of all eligible voters must vote "yes." The questions on voter confidence in President Yeltsin's leadership and policies were considered to be non-binding and would be decided by a simple majority of those voting. See a report on the Constitutional Court's decision in *Sevodnya*, April 23, 1993, p. 2.

26 See *Moscow News*, June 11, 1993, pp. 1–2.

27 *Rossiiskiye vesti*, February 20, 1993, p. 1.

28 Ibid.

29 *Izvestiya*, March 10, 1993, p. 1.

30 *Nezavisimaya gazeta*, February 18, 1993, p. 1; and *Izvestiya*, February 24, 1993, p. 1.

31 "Itogi," Ostankino Television, March 14, 1993.

32 *Izvestiya*, March 24, 1993, p. 2.

33 "Novosti," Ostankino Television, March 24, 1993.

34 Reported by ITAR-TASS, March 17, 1993.

35 *Izvestiya*, April 28, 1993, p. 2.

36 The Russian Federation consists of twenty-one republics, six territories, forty-nine regions, two cities, one autonomous region, and ten autonomous areas. However, this includes the Chechen Republic, which never recognized its inclusion in the Russian Federation.

37 The drafts incorporated provisions of the Russian Federation Declaration of Human Rights and Freedoms of the Individual and Citizen which was adopted in November 1991. The Declaration generally complies with internationally recognized principles of human rights. However, the Lawyers Committee for Human Rights task force examining the status of human rights in Russia found several inadequacies in Russian human rights laws and their enforcement. The task force recommended the adoption of new laws on security organs and law enforcement agencies. Russian law con-

tinues to maintain that state security interests supersede human rights. The panel recommended providing judicial review for search warrants and other invasions of privacy, guarantees of freedom of movement and residence, and rights to conscientious objectors. Finally, they urged Russian jurists to devise laws on conflicts of interests for members of various governmental and legislative bodies. See *Human Rights and Legal Reform in the Russian Federation* (New York: Lawyers Committee for Human Rights, 1993).

38 In reality, only 176 deputies were elected to the Council of the Federation because the Chechen Republic refused to acknowledge its membership in the Russian Federation. For the same reason, the State Duma initially had fewer than its full complement of 450 members.

39 Articles 87 and 88.

40 Article 93 states that the Supreme Court of the Russian Federation must confirm that the actions of the president contain the elements of a crime and the Constitutional Court must verify that the established procedure for filing the charge has been observed. See Constitution of the Russian Federation, Article 93-1.

41 Article 155 does provide that decrees and directives of the government of the Russian Federation that are at variance with the constitution, federal laws or edicts of the president may be rescinded by the president. However, this right rests solely with the president, not with other organs or injured parties, and is exercised at his discretion.

42 Article 85 stipulates that should the president's conciliation efforts fail, he may refer the matter to "the appropriate court" for resolution.

43 See note 37 above. One major improvement over previous constitutions was Article 18 which declares "Human and civil rights and freedoms are direct-acting." In other words, the Russian Federation recognizes international covenants on human rights and these norms can be applied by courts of the Russian Federation; no enabling legislation is required for such norms to have legal effect.

44 Article 88 qualifies the power of the president to declare a state of emergency by asserting that such an action must be undertaken in circumstances and according to a procedure established in federal constitutional law. To date, no such law has been enacted.

45 *Sevodnya*, November 13, 1993, p. 2.

46 *Nezavisimaya gazeta*, November 11, 1993, p. 1.

47 *Rossiiskiye vesti*, December 25, 1994 reported that only 56.6 percent of the voters supported the draft constitution.

48 For an analysis of the elections in detail, see Aleksandr Rahr, "The Implications of Russia's Parliamentary Elections," *RFE/RL Research Report*, 3:1 (January 7, 1994), pp. 32–37.

49 For example, see Vladimir Lysenko in *Nezavisimaya gazeta*, November 11, 1993, p. 1; Oleg Rumyantsev cited in *Sevodnya*, November 13, 1993, p. 2; and Konstantin Lubenchenko in *Moskovskiye novosti*, 47, November 21,

1993, p. A13, who claims that the draft constitution codifies a "totalitarian state."

50 See, *Moskovskiye novosti*, November 21, 1993, p. 13.

5 Citizens and the state: the debate over the procuracy

1 Attributed to Joseph Stalin, see John Bartlett, ed., *Bartlett's Familiar Quotations* (Boston: Little, Brown, 1982), p. 766.

2 Cited in Robert Conquest, *The Harvest of Sorrow: Soviet Collectivization and the Terror-Famine* (New York: Oxford University Press, 1986), p. 306; and Robert Conquest, *The Great Terror* (London: Macmillan, 1969), p. 533. This figure includes all deaths attributed to Stalin and his policies. The number who died as a direct result of procuratorial activity has never been published.

3 Cited in S. G. Berezovskaya, "Proshloe i nastoyashchee obshchego nadzora," *Sotsialisticheskaya zakonnost'* (June 1937), 24–27.

4 M. Braginsky and N. Lagovier, *Revolyutsionnaya zakonnost' i prokurorskii nadzor v selskokhozyaistvennykh politicheskikh kampaniyakh* (Moscow: Sovetskoe zakonodatel'stvo, 1933).

5 *Pravda*, April 12, 1955, p. 1.

6 See Gordon B. Smith, *The Soviet Procuracy and the Supervision of Administration* (Alphen aan den Rijn, The Netherlands: Sijthoff & Noordhoff, 1978).

7 This figure is based on an analysis of protests during the period 1955–1974, ibid., p. 88.

8 Ibid., pp. 88–104.

9 See Gordon B. Smith, *Soviet Policies: Continuity and Contradiction* (New York: St. Martin's Press, 1988), pp. 294–304.

10 Smith, *The Soviet Procuracy*, p. 23.

11 Consultation with N. S. Aleksandrov, the dean of the Juridical Faculty, Leningrad State University, November 6, 1975.

12 *Literaturnaya gazeta*, 38 (1985), 13; *Literaturnaya gazeta*, 19 (1986), 12; and *Literaturnaya gazeta* (January 5, 1986), 14.

13 *Literaturnaya gazeta*, 19 (1986), 12.

14 See *Zhurnalist*, May 1986, cited in Tolz, "Procurator-General Rekunkov Attacks Journalists Who Criticize Soviet Justice Apparatus," *Radio Liberty Research Bulletin* (RL 265), July 11, 1986, p. 1.

15 Julia Wishnevsky, "Politburo Calls for Restructuring of Legal Bodies," *Radio Liberty Research Bulletin* (RL 386), October 9, 1986, p. 1.

16 Ibid.

17 *Pravda*, June 19, 1987, p. 1.

18 Ibid.

19 Ibid.

20 Consultation with Aleksandr Bastrykhin, director, Institute for the Improvement of Investigators of the USSR Procuracy, June 11, 1991, Leningrad.

21 Consultation with Professor Vladimir Daev, Leningrad State University, June 11, 1991.
22 *Izvestiya*, June 29, 1988, pp. 3–4.
23 Ibid.
24 Consultation with the procurator of Leningrad, Dmitri Verovkin, June 19, 1991.
25 *Pravda*, July 22, 1990, p. 2.
26 Cited in Conrad B. Hohenlohe, "Procedural Reform and Legal Guarantees of Civil Rights," *New Outlook*, 2:2 (Spring 1991), 20.
27 Ibid., pp. 20–21.
28 Ibid., p. 21.
29 Consultation with Valentin Stepankov, then procurator-general of the Russian Federation, Moscow, June 24, 1991.
30 Draft Law on the Procuracy of the Russian Republic (1991), pp. 2–3.
31 Consultation with Valentin Stepankov, June 24, 1991.
32 As we noted in Chapter 4, speculation was redefined on October 31, 1991. Nevertheless it remained a criminal offense to sell goods for a profit for which state prices had been established.
33 Consultation with Dmitri Verovkin, procurator of Leningrad, June 19, 1991.
34 *Izvestiya*, August 24, 1991, p. 1.
35 See regional accounts of coup-related activities in various regions and cities in *Three Days in August* (Moscow: PostFactum News Agency, 1991), pp. 11–13, 28, and 38.
36 *Izvestiya*, August 24, 1991, p. 1.
37 *Izvestiya*, September 3, 1991, p. 2.
38 *Izvestiya*, August 23, 1991, p. 1.
39 Cited in Radio Liberty, *Report on the USSR*, 3:43 (October 25, 1991), 33.
40 *Izvestiya*, August 24, 1991, p. 1.
41 Reported in Radio Liberty, *Report on the USSR*, 3:44 (November 1, 1991), 31.
42 Ibid.
43 Reported in Radio Liberty, *Report on the USSR*, 3:47 (November 22, 1991), 42.
44 Consultation with Saifkhan Nafeev, procurator of Tatarstan, Kazan, April 6, 1993.
45 Reported in Larry Ryckman, "Crime's Spillover Worries Muscovites," *Charlotte Observer*, July 22, 1993, p. 10A.
46 *Izvestiya*, February 20, 1993, p. 4.
47 *Pravda*, October 16, 1991, p. 3.
48 Cited in *Rossiiskaya gazeta*, October 11, 1992, p. 3.
49 "Law on the Procuracy of the Russian Federation," Article 1.
50 The right to be present at sessions of legislative bodies has now been extended to the Council of the Federation and the State Duma.
51 As of late 1994, no such investigatory agency has been formed, nor have appropriations been made to establish it. In the interim, the powers of the Procuracy to conduct criminal investigations have not changed.

52 ITAR-TASS, April 29, 1993.
53 Consultation with N. A. Karavaev, deputy procurator-general of Russia, Moscow, April 9, 1993.
54 Ibid.
55 Ibid.
56 Consultation with V. K. Goncharov, senior assistant procurator of Moscow, April 8, 1993.
57 Ibid.
58 Consultation with Aleksandr Fedotov, Procurator of Nizhny Novgorod, April 7, 1993.
59 Reported on ITAR-TASS, July 26, 1993.
60 Consultation with N. A. Karavaev, deputy procurator-general, April 4, 1993, Moscow.
61 Cited in *Izvestiya*, November 25, 1992, p. 2.
62 Ibid.
63 ITAR-TASS, April 22, 1993.
64 Reported in *Izvestiya*, April 29, 1993, p. 2.
65 *Izvestiya*, April 30, 1993, pp. 3–5.
66 *Izvestiya*, May 20, 1993, p. 5.
67 Igor Achildiyev, "Three Against All the Prosecutor's Men," *Megapolis-Express*, May 26, 1993, p. 5; and Fedor Burlatsky in *Nezavisimaya gazeta*, June 30, 1993, p. 5.
68 *Izvestiya*, May 20, 1993, p. 5.
69 Consultation with Marat M. Orlov, deputy procurator-general, Moscow, November 24, 1993.
70 Ibid.
71 Ibid.
72 This account came from a consultation with Professor Aleksandr M. Larin, Institute of State and Law, Moscow, November 25, 1993.
73 For example, consultation with Deputy Procurator-General Marat M. Orlov, Procurator of the Russian Federation, Moscow, November 23, 1993.
74 For an analysis of the decree, see Donald D. Barry, "Amnesty under the Russian Constitution: Evolution of the Provision and its Use in February 1994," *Parker School Journal of East European Law*, 1:4 (1994), 437–461.
75 *Izvestiya*, March 1, 1994, p. 2.

6 In search of a just system: the courts and judicial reform

1 Quoted in *The Christian Science Monitor*, April 7, 1992, p. 13.
2 *Izvestiya*, January 29, 1992, p. 2.
3 Ibid.
4 *Argumenty i fakty*, 21 (1992), p. 2.
5 Ibid.
6 If a person commits several crimes, one of which would normally be heard by a military tribunal, then all of the criminal acts will be heard before a military tribunal. Similarly, if a group of people commit a crime or crimes

which would normally be heard by a military tribunal, then all members of the group of defendants fall under the jurisdiction of the military tribunal. For example, the criminal case of the leaders of the August 1991 attempted *coup d'état* was tried by the Military Collegium of the Russian Federation Supreme Court since Dmitri Yazov, former minister of defense, Vladimir Kryuchkov, former head of the KGB, and several of the other defendants cases would require hearing before a military panel. For a discussion of the military tribunals and other special courts, see Ger von den Berg, "Special Courts in the USSR," *Review of Socialist Law*, 8:3 (1982), 237–250.

7 V. Kazin, "Sud tovarishchei," *Pravda*, November 13, 1963, p. 4.

8 For example, in Ukraine justices of the peace have replaced the comrades' courts. See Lisa Halustick, "Judicial Reform in Ukraine: Legislative Efforts to Promote an Independent Judiciary," *Parker School Journal of East European Law*, 1 (1994), 683.

9 For a detailed analysis of the Constitutional Court and its first year of operations, see Robert Sharlet, "The Russian Constitutional Court: The First Term," *Post-Soviet Affairs*, 9:1 (January–March 1993), 1–39.

10 Cited in ibid., p. 8.

11 Ibid.

12 Ibid.

13 *Moscow News*, no. 46, November 17, 1991, p. 4. Zorkin's prejudicial remarks raised serious questions as to his impartiality in considering the case.

14 The recovery of confiscated property fell within the jurisdiction of ordinary courts, not the Constitutional Court.

15 Cited in Sharlet, "Russian Constitutional Court," 30.

16 See *Megapolis-Express*, no. 23, June 16, 1993, p. 2; and *Moskovskiye novosti*, no. 25, June 20, 1993, p. A9.

17 The decree was printed in *Rossiiskaya gazeta*, October 9, 1993, p. 1.

18 Law on the Constitutional Court of the Russian Federation, July 21, 1994.

19 For a discussion of the Federation Council's debate over Yelstin's nominees to the Constitutional Court, see *Sevodnya*, October 25, 1994, p. 1.

20 From a criminal case observed by the author in the Kalinin raion criminal court in Leningrad, March 1976.

21 Cited in Dorothy Atkinson, Aleksandr Dallin and Gail Lapidus, *Women in Russia* (Stanford: Stanford University Press, 1977), p. 262. The predominance of women on the bench may also have been a sign of the low status of judicial personnel in the Soviet legal system.

22 Cited in Peter H. Solomon, *Soviet Criminologists and Criminal Policy* (New York: Columbia University Press, 1973), p. 25.

23 Criminal Code of the RSFSR (1960), Article 3.

24 M. A. Kopylovskaya, *Nauchno-prakticheskii kommentarii k osnovam zakonodatel'stva o sudoustroistve soyuza SSR, soyuznikh avtonomnikh respublik* (Moscow: Yuridicheskaya literatura, 1961), p. 425.

25 *Pravda*, January 10, 1968, pp. 2–3.

26 R. A. Rudenko, "Leninskye idei sotsialisticheskoi zakonnosti, printsipy organizatsii i deyatel'nosti sovetskoi prokuratury," in *Sovetskaya prokuratura* (Moscow: Yuridicheskaya literatura, 1977), pp. 25–26.

27 Statute on the Procuracy of the USSR (1979), Article 3.

28 Stanislaw Pomorski, "Criminal Law Protection of Socialist Property in the USSR," in D. Barry, G. Ginsburgs, and P. Maggs, eds, *Soviet Law After Stalin: Part I: The Citizen and the State in Contemporary Soviet Law* (Leiden: Sijthoff & Noordhoff, 1977), p. 235.

29 Cited in George Feifer, *Justice in Moscow* (New York: Simon and Schuster, 1964), pp. 248–249.

30 Cited in *Literaturnaya gazeta*, 19 (1986), 12.

31 *Kazakhstanskaya pravda*, May 14, 1986.

32 *Literaturnaya gazeta*, 38 (1985), 13.

33 See "The Death Penalty in the USSR," *Radio Liberty Research Bulletin* (January 25, 1988), 1.

34 See *Moskovskiye novosti*, nos. 16, 25, 41 and 50 (1987); *Nedelya*, nos. 42 and 51 (1987); and *Ogonek*, nos. 33 and 49 (1987).

35 *Sovetskaya Belorussya*, June 3, 1987.

36 *Sovetskaya Belorussya*, October 5, 1986, p. 3.

37 See *Literaturnaya gazeta*, 52 (1986), 13; and *Sovetskaya Rossiya*, June 14, 1987.

38 *Law on Responsibility for Disrespect of a Court*, reprinted in *Izvestiya*, November 16, 1989, p. 1.

39 *Izvestiya*, August 23, 1988, p. 6.

40 *Law on the Status of Judges*, Article 18, para. 3.

41 Cited in *Izvestiya*, November 18, 1993, p. 1.

42 Exceptions are now possible in jury trials and some minor offenses where cases are heard by a single judge.

43 The draft Fundamental Principles on Court Structure proposed either a court of two judges and three assessors or one judge and four lay assessors. *Pravda*, July 16, 1989, p. 2.

44 *New York Times*, December 19, 1993, p. A10.

45 Ibid.

46 *Izvestiya*, October 27, 1993, p. 4.

47 Consultation with N. A. Karavaev, Head of the Office for Legal Security, Russian Federation Procuracy, Moscow, April 9, 1993.

48 *Izvestiya*, October 27, 1993, p. 4.

49 Ibid.

50 Consultation with N. A. Karavaev, head of the Office of Legal Security, Russian Federation Procuracy, April 9, 1993.

51 Cited in *Christian Science Monitor*, April 7, 1992, p. 12.

52 Ibid.

53 Ibid.

54 Cited in Michael Burrage, "Russian Advocates: Before, During, and After Perestroika," *Law and Social Inquiry*, 15:3 (Summer 1990), 586.

55 In April 1990 the right to counsel was extended to all people from the moment of presentation of accusation. However, the 1992 draft takes the

right of counsel further, in that a suspect has the rights to an attorney even before a formal charge has been made.

56 *Selskaya zhizn'*, March 24, 1985, p. 4.
57 For example, see *Moscow News*, nos 16, 25, 41 and 50, 1987; *Nedelya*, nos. 42 and 51, 1987; and *Ogonek*, nos. 33 and 49, 1987.
58 Cited in *Izvestiya*, October 2, 1992, p. 8.
59 Marshall MacDuffie, *The Red Carpet: 10,000 Miles through Russia on a Visa from Khrushchev* (New York: W. W. Norton, 1955), pp. 51–63.
60 Criminal Code of the RSFSR, Article 154.
61 Cited in Burrage, "Russian Advocates," 580.
62 For a discussion of the draft criminal code, see *Moscow News*, no. 28, July 15–21, 1994, p. 13.
63 *Izvestiya*, October 2, 1992, p. 8 and *New York Times*, January 30, 1994, p. 6.
64 *Izvestiya*, December 7, 1993, p. 6; and *Izvestiya*, August 12, 1993, p. 8.
65 *Izvestiya*, October 2, 1992, p. 8.
66 *New York Times*, January 30, 1994, p. 6.
67 Ibid.
68 Ibid.
69 Cited in David Remnick, "The Hangover," *The New Yorker*, November 22, 1993, p. 55.
70 *Izvestiya*, August 11, 1993, p. 8.
71 Cited in *Izvestiya*, August 11, 1993, p. 8.
72 Ibid.
73 *Izvestiya*, December 7, 1993, p. 6.
74 Cited in Remnick, "The Hangover," 57.
75 *Izvestiya*, October 14, 1993, p. 5.
76 *Sevodnya*, October 21, 1993, p. 7.
77 Although the deportations were probably illegal, a poll published in *Izvestiya* reported that three-quarters of all Muscovites welcomed the state of emergency. See Remnick, "The Hangover," 54.
78 *New York Times*, December 3, 1993, p. B9.
79 Ibid.

7 Law and the transition to a market economy

1 Samuel P. Huntington, *Political Order in Changing Society* (New Haven: Yale University Press, 1968), p. 69.
2 Many of the codes and laws governing economic activity were enacted at the union-republic level and, thus, remained in force after the break-up of the USSR.
3 See *Izvestiya*, August 12, 1983, p. 1.
4 *Pravda*, February 8, 1987, pp. 1–2.
5 *Pravda*, September 12, 1985, p. 1.
6 Central Intelligence Agency, *The Russian Economy in 1993* (Washington: CIA, March 1994), p. 9.
7 ITAR-TASS report of August 7, 1995 from *OMRI Daily Digest*, part 1, August 8, 1995.

8 *Vedomosti Verkhovnogo Soveta SSSR*, 22 (1986), 367–368.

9 *Vedomosti Verkhovnogo Soveta SSSR*, 22 (1986), 369–373; and *Pravda*, May 28, 1986, p. 2.

10 Cited in Central Intelligence Agency, *Russian Economy*, p. 13.

11 Ibid.

12 *OMRI Daily Digest*, part 1, August 15, 1995.

13 For an expanded discussion of various forms of business organization in Russia, see Roman Frydman, Andrezej Rapaczynski and John S. Earle, *The Privatization Process in Russia, Ukraine, and the Baltic States* (Budapest: Central European University Press, 1993), pp. 18–32.

14 Cited in ibid, p. 22.

15 Ibid.

16 Cited in ibid., p. 25.

17 Ibid., p. 25.

18 Central Intelligence Agency, *Russian Economy*, p. 13.

19 Ibid.

20 Ibid., and Central Intelligence Agency, *Measuring Russia's Emerging Private Sector* (Washington: CIA, November 1992), p. 15.

21 The Law on Enterprises and Entrepreneurial Activity, Article 9.

22 Ibid., Article 9.

23 Price Waterhouse, *Doing Business in the Russian Federation* (April 1994), p. 63.

24 Ibid., pp. 63–64.

25 As of July 1, 1994, 70 percent of all state-owned enterprises had been reorganized as joint-stock companies. "Privatization in Russia after July 1, 1994," *Parker School Journal of East European Law*, 1 (1994), 503.

26 *Izvestiya*, November 27, 1991, p. 1.

27 *Pravda*, January 28, 1990, pp. 1–3.

28 Ibid.

29 CIA, *Measuring*, p. 13.

30 This account was related to the author by officials in the Leningrad City Soviet, March 1992.

31 Decree No. 66 "On Accelerating Privatization of State-Owned and Municipal Enterprises" of January 29, 1992 and "Basic Provision of the State Program for Privatization of State and Municipal Enterprises in the Russian Federation in 1992" issued in December 1991.

32 Presidential decree No. 721 "On Organizational Measures for Transforming State Enterprises and Voluntary Associations of State Enterprises into Joint-Stock Companies."

33 Ibid., p. 48.

34 Andrew Freris, *The Soviet Industrial Enterprise* (London: Croom Helm, 1984), p. 8.

35 Frydman, Rapaczynski, and Earle, *Privatization Process*, p. 64.

36 CIA, *The Russian Economy in 1993*, p. 13.

37 Frydman, Rapaczynski, and Earle, *Privatization Process*, p. 65.

38 Ibid.

39 *Izvestiya*, September 25, 1987, p. 1.
40 Decree "On Urgent Measures to Implement Land Reform in the RSFSR," December 27, 1991.
41 Cited in Don Van Atta, "Yelstin Decree Finally Ends Second Serfdom in Russia," *Radio Liberty Research Report*, 2:46 (November 19, 1993), 36.
42 Central Intelligence Agency, *The Russian Economy in 1993*, p. 13.
43 Ibid.
44 Van Atta, "Yeltsin Decree," 36.
45 "Decree of the President of the Russian Federation on the Regulation of Land Relations and the Development of Agrarian Reform in Russia," *Rossiiskiye vesti*, October 29, 1993, p. 2. See also Don Van Atta, "Yeltsin Decree," *RFE/RL Research Report*, 2:46 (November 19, 1993), 33–38.
46 Ibid.
47 Vera Tolz, "Russia's Parliamentary Elections," *RFE/RL Research Report*, 3:2 (January 14,1994), 3.
48 Cited in Frydman, Rapaczynski and Earle, *Privatization Process*, p. 74.
49 Calculated from information in ibid., p. 74.
50 Ibid., p. 32
51 Ibid., p. 33.
52 Central Intelligence Agency, *The Russian Economy in 1993*, p. 6.
53 Cited in a report by the Associated Press, "Avalanche of Taxes Burying Russians," *The State* (Columbia, SC), April 3, 1994, p. A6.
54 Ibid.
55 Reported in *Sevodnya*, June 17, 1995, p. 1.
56 Cited in *New York Times*, May 25, 1990, p. A6.
57 Marie Lavigne, "Financing the Transition in the USSR," Public Policy Paper no. 2 (New York: Institute for East–West Security Studies, 1990), p. 29.
58 Reported in Central Intelligence Agency, *The Russian Economy in 1993*, p. 4.
59 Cited in a letter to the editor by Padma Desai, *New York Times*, April 19, 1994, p. A12.
60 Central Intelligence Agency, *The Russian Economy in 1993*, p. 7.
61 Ibid., pp. 7, 11.
62 Ibid.
63 Ibid.
64 Ibid., p. 9.
65 See Frydman, Rapaczynski and Earle, *Privatization Process*, p. 75. See also, Philip Hanson, "The Center versus the Periphery in Russian Economic Policy," *RFE/RL Research Report*, 3:17 (April 29, 1994), 25–28.

8 Legal reform in the republics

1 Quoted in Malachi Martin, *The Keys of this Blood* (1990).
2 F. J. M. Feldbrugge, ed., *Encyclopedia of Soviet Law*, vol. I (Leiden: A. W. Sijthoff, 1973), p. 398.

3 For a discussion of the 1922 Constitution, see Albertas Gerutis, ed., *Lithuania: 700 Years* (New York: Maryland Books, 1969), p. 198.

4 Saulius Girnius, "The Lithuanian Economy in 1992," *RL/RFE Research Report*, 2:16 (April 16, 1993), 29.

5 Ibid., p. 102.

6 Saulius Girnius, "Lithuania: Former Communists Return to Power," *RL/RFE Research Report*, 2:1 (January 1, 1993), 100.

7 Saulius Girnius, "Lithuania," 99.

8 Cited in Saulius Girnius, "Political Turmoil in Lithuania," *RL/RFE Research Report*, 3:27 (July 8, 1994), 19.

9 See, Alfred Bilmanis, *Latvia As an Independent State* (Washington: Latvian Legation, 1947), pp. 75–76 and 379–385.

10 The Latvian declaration of independence was recognized by the USSR on September 6, 1991.

11 Dzintra Bungs, "Latvia," *RL/RFE Research Report*, 1:27 (July 3, 1992), 63–64.

12 Ibid., p. 63.

13 Cited in ibid., p. 65.

14 Yeltsin declared: "Latvia has chosen to divide the country's residents into first- and second-class people and has legitimized discrimination on ethnic grounds." See *Izvestiya*, August 6, 1994, p. 1.

15 Dzintra Bungs, "Latvia: Toward Full Independence," *RL/RFE Research Report*, 2:1 (January 1, 1993), 98.

16 Riina Kionka, "Estonia: A Difficult Transition," *RL/RFE Research Report*, 2:1 (January 1, 1993), 89.

17 Reported in *RL/RFE Research Report*, 1:27 (July 3, 1992), 61.

18 Villu Kand, "Estonia: A Year of Challenges," *RL/RFE Research Report*, 3:1 (January 7, 1994), 93.

19 Ibid., p. 92.

20 Ibid., p. 94.

21 *Izvestiya*, September 28, 1994, p. 3.

22 *OMRI Daily Digest*, no. 123, part 2, 26 June 1995.

23 Cited in George Saunders, ed., *Samizdat: Voices of the Soviet Opposition* (New York: Monad Press, 1974), pp. 421–422.

24 Ibid., pp. 441–442.

25 *Pravda*, July 5, 1988.

26 *Izvestiya*, July 16, 1988.

27 See, Bohdan Nahaylo, "Ukraine," *RL/RFE Research Report*, 1:27 (July 3, 1992), 52.

28 For a copy of Rukh's manifesto, see *Literaturnaya Ukraina*, February 16, 1989, p. 1.

29 *Literaturnaya Ukraina*, October 19, 1989 and Nahaylo, "Ukraine," 51–52. These principles parallel those incorporated in the resolutions of the 19th Party Conference in Moscow in 1988.

30 Zakon Ukrainy, Pro Konstytutsiinyi Sud Ukrainy, June 3, 1992, in *Pravo Ukrainy*, no. 10, 1992, pp. 59–65.

31 Cited in Bohdan Nahaylo, "Ukraine," *RFE/RL Research Report*, 1:27 (July 3, 1992), 53.

32 Ibid., p. 54.
33 Ibid.
34 Cited in Roman Solchanyk, "Ukraine: A Year of Crisis," *RFE/RE Research Report*, 3:1 (January 7, 1994), 38.
35 Cited in Erik Whitlock, "The CIS Economies: Divergent and Troubled Paths," p. 14.
36 For an analysis of the draft Ukrainian constitution, see David Lempert, "The Proposed Constitution of Ukraine: Continuity under the Banner of Change," *Demokratizatsiya*, 2:2 (Spring 1994), 268–296.
37 In this respect, the draft Ukrainian constitution is similar to that in France.
38 Reported in D. N. Prityka, "Ukraine's Commercial Courts: Achievements and Prospects," *Rule of Law Consortium Newsletter*, 2–3 (July–August 1995), 5.
39 Judges serving for the first time are selected for a five-year term.
40 Zakon Ukrainy, Pro status suddiv, December 15, 1992, Article 14, available in *Holos Ukrainy*, February 10, 1993, p. 3.
41 Ibid. See also Lisa Halustick, "Judicial Reform in Ukraine: Legislative Efforts to Promote an Independent Judiciary," *Parker School Journal of East European Law*, 1 (1994), 663–686.
42 *Holos Ukrainy*, October 5, 1991, p. 7.
43 See, Dominique Arel and Andrew Wilson, "The Ukrainian Parliamentary Elections," *RL/RFE Research Report*, 3:26 (July 1, 1994), 6.
44 Cited in Aleksandr Lukashuk, "Belarus: A Year on a Treadmill," *RL/RFE Research Report*, 2:1 (January 1, 1993), 66–67.
45 Cited in Ustina Markus, "Belarus: Slowly Awakening to New Realities," *RFE/RL Research Report*, 3:1 (January 7, 1994), 45.
46 *Sevodnya*, March 16, 1994, p. 1.
47 *Nezavisimaya gazeta*, March 3, 1994, p. 3.
48 Ustina Markus, "Belarus Elects its First President," *RL/RFE Research Report*, 3:30 (July 29, 1994), 1–7.
49 *Sevodnya*, October 1, 1994, p. 5.
50 *Sevodnya*, October 12, 1994, p. 4.
51 *Sevodnya*, December 24, 1994, p. 4.
52 Cited in Elizabeth Fuller, "Transcaucasia: Ethnic Strife Threatens Democratization," *RL/RFE Research Report*, 2:1 (January 1, 1993), 20.
53 See Commission on Security and Cooperation in Europe, "Report on Armenia's Parliamentary Election and Constitutional Referendum" (Washington: CSCE, August 1995), p. 8.
54 Ibid.
55 Ibid., p. 21.
56 *Bakinsky rabochii*, October 20, 1992, cited in ibid., p. 21.
57 Elizabeth Fuller, "The Transcaucasus: War, Turmoil, Economic Collapse," *RFE/RL Research Report*, 3:1 (January 7, 1994), 54.
58 Ibid.
59 *Izvestiya*, October 11, 1994, p. 2.
60 Fuller, "Transcaucasus," 23.
61 Ibid., 58.

62 Cited in Vladimir Socor, "Moldova's 'Dniester' Ulcer," *RL/RFE Research Report*, 2:1 (January 1, 1993), 15.
63 *Sevodnya*, March 2, 1994, p. 5.
64 *Sevodnya*, July 30, 1994, p. 4.
65 Cited in Bess Brown, "Central Asia: The Economic Crisis Deepens," *RL/RFE Research Report*, 3:1 (January 7, 1994), 61.
66 *Nezavisimaya gazeta*, March 15, 1994, p. 3.
67 Ibid.
68 Commission on Security and Cooperation in Europe, *Human Rights and Democratization in the Newly Independent States of the Former Soviet Union* (Washington: CSCE, January 1993), p. 193.
69 See *CEELI Update*, 5:2 (Summer 1995), 20.
70 CSCE, *HUman Rights*, p. 208.
71 Ibid., p. 68.
72 Erik Whitlock, "The CIS Economies: Divergent and Troubled Paths," *RFE/RL Research Report*, 3:1 (January 7, 1994), 14.
73 *Los Angeles Times*, October 23, 1994, p. A6.
74 Ibid.
75 Cited in Bess Brown, "Central Asia: The First Year of Unexpected Statehood," *RL/RFE Research Report*, 2:1 (January 1, 1993), 35.
76 For example, see *Sevodnya*, November 10, 1994, p. 10.
77 Ibid.
78 Whitlock, "The CIS Economies," 14.

9 Legal reform and the transition to democracy in Russia

1 Aleksandr Zinoviev, *The Yawning Heights* (New York: Random House, 1978), pp. 306–307.
2 Central Intelligence Agency, *The Russian Economy in 1993* (Washington: CIA, March 1994), pp. 7–8.
3 Reported in *Open Media Research Institute Daily Digest* (OMRI), March 17, 1995.
4 See Wayne DiFranceisco and Zvi Gitelman, "Soviet Political Culture and Covert Participation in Policy Implementation," *American Political Science Review*, 78 (1984), 603–621.
5 *Sevodnya*, May 26, 1994, p. 3. It is likely, however, that these concepts had radically different meanings to different respondents.
6 Ibid.
7 William Mishler and Richard Rose, "Trust, Distrust and Skepticism," in *Studies in Public Policy* (Glasgow: Centre for the Study of Public Policy, University of Strathclyde, 1995).
8 Richard Rose, "Distrust as an Obstacle to Civil Society," in *Studies in Public Policy* (Glasgow: Centre for the Study of Public Policy, University of Strathclyde, 1994), p. 12.
9 Dmitri Chubukov, "Democracy Tested in Battle," *Moscow News*, no. 8, February 24–March 2, 1995, p. 3 and Rose, "Distrust," 12.

10 It is not clear under what authority the president had the right to impose such a curfew.

11 Sir Henry Maine, *Ancient Law* (New York: Dutton, 1972), pp. 179–215.

12 Russia has tort law derived from the 1991 USSR Fundamental Principles of Civil Law, however, most citizens are not aware of its protections. See Donald Barry, "Soviet Tort Law and Development of Public Policy," *Review of Socialist Law*, 5:3 (1979), 229–249.

13 Aleksei Kakotkin, "One Example Shows How to Beat Crime," *Moscow News*, no. 4, January 27–February 2, 1995, p. 12.

14 Ibid.

15 *OMRI Daily Digest*, March 16, 1995.

Index